Atlantic Empires of France and Spain

Atlantic Empires of France and Spain

Louisbourg and Havana, 1700–1763

John Robert McNeill

The University of North Carolina Press

Chapel Hill and London

Library of Congress Cataloging in Publication Data

McNeill, John Robert.
   Atlantic empires of France and Spain.

   Bibliography: p.
   Includes index.
   1. Havana (Cuba)—History.   2. Louisbourg (N.S.)—
History.   3. Havana (Cuba)—Commerce—History—18th
century.   4. Louisbourg (N.S.)—Commerce—History—18th
century.   I. Title.
F1799.H357M36   1985   971.6'95   85-1105
ISBN 0-8078-1669-8

This book is dedicated
to the memory of
John Elliott Hawthorne
1955–1977

Contents

Tables

Maps and Graphs

Preface

The work that follows arises from three convictions. The first concerns the merits of comparative history, the second involves my conception of imperial history, and the third stems from my view of preindustrial history in general. None of these convictions is especially new or unusual, but I think it is best to spell them out nevertheless.

Comparative history has simple advantages of which historians have long been aware. In my case, learning about Havana suggested new ideas and questions about Louisbourg, and vice versa. Matters that at first glance seemed perfectly natural suddenly demanded explanation when compared to another case. Merely using another colonial seaport as a point of reference enriched my understanding of both Havana and Louisbourg; and my understanding of both ports has, in turn, enriched my understanding of the colonial systems in which they participated, indeed of the whole Atlantic world of the eighteenth century. In this process lies much of the value of comparative history. One of the pitfalls of comparative history is that in dividing one's attention between two or more cases one risks never delving adequately into any particular case. In my choice of Havana and Louisbourg I have tried to take full advantage of the comparative method and sidestep the pitfalls by confining my attention to certain selected aspects of the experience of these two ports.

Havana and Louisbourg are two colonial seaports which appear to have no more in common than that they are colonial seaports. I chose them for comparison not because their internal histories are especially similar—they are not—but because their assigned roles within their respective imperial systems were nearly identical, as were the problems of economic and defense policy. Much of this derives from a similarity in their geographic positions, which I shall address in the first chapter. Both ports overlooked important communication routes. Both faced numerous, energetic, and generally hostile British neighbors. Both were well-situated for a lively entrepôt trade within their imperial systems, and an equally lively smuggling trade without. Both served as the military, commercial, demographic, and administrative center of a strategic island. Both fulfilled administrative responsibilities in adjacent settlements. Each was nominally subject to a higher authority (the Viceroy of New Spain and the Governor of New France, respectively), but both found themselves largely autonomous in practice. Both were heavily and expensively fortified and thus became symbols of the might of their colonial empires. And last, but far from least, both channeled the production of highly valuable hinterlands to Europe. Of course, important differences existed. Europeans found Cuba a most unhealthy place and Louisbourg comparatively salubrious. Louisbourg's population never exceeded 5,000, while Havana's approached 35,000 by 1760. But despite these and many other differences, imperial dilemmas and responsibilities in Havana and Louisbourg were very much the same. In comparing the two port cities I compare the ways in which different imperial systems responded to the same sorts of problems.

My conception of imperial history is that it is the product of metropolitan logic and decisions imperfectly inflicted on people and places poorly understood by the metropolitans. Early generations of imperial historians, I think, concentrated on metropolitan policy in the belief that colonial history was but an extension of the mother country's, minimizing the importance of colonial people and places. Subsequent generations have stressed colonial people and places, underestimating, it seems to me, the impact of metropolitan policy and thus making a mistake as large as their forebears'.

I have tried to keep in view both European and colonial concerns in this study. Persistent readers will note that the text meanders (some will say jumps) from one side of the Atlantic to the other. This bifocal approach helps to identify the gap between theory and practice in the running of overseas empires, one of the central themes of this book. A second theme highlighted by the bifocal approach involves the role of colonial seaports as links between colonial production and markets and European markets and production. The cities of Havana and Louisbourg (or Calcutta, Djakarta, or Capetown) served as filters, valves, bottle-necks, defining relations between Europe and the fields and fisheries of colonial domains.

My view of preindustrial history boils down to the fact that the natural environment, until quite recently, exercised a tyranny over what human beings could and could not do unmatched by any mortal tyrant from Peisistratus to Stalin. Since the eighteenth century we have almost anni-hilated distance and accelerated the pace of so many human activities that a feat of imagination, at least for those of us in the Western world, is required to understand the preindustrial human relationship to space and time in the past. Accordingly I have paid great attention to matters of geography and communication in this book. Other facets of this tyranny are equally important: in large part Havana and Louisbourg derived their imperial roles, their characters, and to some extent their historical experi-ence from their location (in relation to winds and currents as well as to Europe and America), climate, soils, disease environment, and the com-position of the biota of their hinterlands. In a world where one can travel from New York to New Zealand in less time than it took in the eighteenth century to go from Havana to Santiago de Cuba; where crops prosper in former deserts; where prophylactic medicine can safeguard us from deadly diseases; it is easy to forget how domineering the natural environ-ment once was. I have tried to remind the reader.

In the course of this project I have incurred many debts. Most must go unmentioned, but I am happy to thank the staffs of the various archives and libraries in Europe and America where this work took shape. Espe-cially helpful were people at the Archivo General de Indias and the Fortress of Louisbourg. I must also single out those who have taken the trouble to read this manuscript and offer their opinions: John W. Cell, G. Douglas Inglis, Ruth McNeill, William McNeill, Richard A. Preston, Theodore Ropp, Julius Scott, John TePaske, and Peter Wood. Heartfelt thanks also go to Gwen Duffey of the University of North Carolina Press and to Donna Grebe for her timely help with the prepara-tion of the index. Equally deserving is the one person, Dorothy Sapp, who has read this work more often than any other, for she typed it several times with high accuracy, great speed, and good humor.

Atlantic Empires of France and Spain

1 Havana and Louisbourg in the Geopolitics of the Eighteenth-Century Atlantic World

By the eighteenth century, the nations of Europe's Atlantic shore had accumulated lengthy experience in the management of overseas empires. The Portuguese, Spanish, French, Dutch, and British had all developed a set of ideas about how and to what end to conduct such empires. On the details of execution there was much disagreement, but on the question of purpose there was very little. The principal purpose of overseas empires was to increase the power and wealth of the mother country.[1]

Armed with this general idea about the purpose of overseas empires, European states developed various strategies for achieving wealth and power. These strategies differed considerably, but all contained certain core elements. First among these was the importance of a large and vigorous commerce between colonies and mother country. Europeans believed that the wealth of the world was a fixed quantity, and thus whatever economic gains one polity might make must inevitably come at the expense of another. The competition for shares of this fixed quantity assumed the form of commercial rivalry, for commerce, they believed, offered the surest route to national wealth. This commerce ideally provided raw materials for domestic manufacturing, markets for domestic manufactures, independence from unreliable foreign markets and sources of supply, revenue for state coffers, and a supply of ships and seamen for the nation in time of need. Second was the belief in the value of secure land bases and strong seaborne forces to protect commerce and colonies against foreign depredation and to harass foreign competitors. These forces might consist solely of a regular navy, or might include corsairs and privateers. Tactics might be offensive or defensive, but strong seaborne forces must exist.

With empires stretching around the globe, eighteenth-century metropolitan states had to cope with a broad range of local conditions in their overseas holdings. Europeans could settle in some habitats but not in others; indigenous populations withstood imported diseases well in some regions but not in others; precious metals were there for the taking in some areas but not others.

North America included three representatives of European empire: the French, the Spanish, and the British. The French empire in America in 1713 consisted of two parts, one Caribbean and one North American.[2] In the Caribbean the French possessed roughly one-third of the island of Española (which they called St.-Domingue), St. Vincent, and the sugar islands of Martinique, Guadeloupe, Dominica, Marie Galante, and St. Lucia. In South America the French held an unhealthy strip of coast known as French Guiana. In French eyes the principal value of these Caribbean possessions lay in their capacity to produce sugar. They were all slave colonies.

Further north, the French possessed the vast reaches of New France, which on maps spread from the valley of the St. Lawrence river through the Great Lakes region to the Mississippi basin. Settlement, however, covered only the banks of the St. Lawrence and, on a very small scale, the Mississippi delta. The islands in the Gulf of St. Lawrence, Ile St. Jean and Ile Royale (now Prince Edward Island and Cape Breton Island respectively), were virtually empty. The value of New France hinged on the fur trade. European fashions created a steady market for beaver fur, and the more northerly reaches of the rodent's habitat provided the best pelts.[3] French authorities would have preferred a colony of settlement, but the few willing migrants to Canada generally found trading and trapping more attractive than tilling the soil. The French establishments around the Gulf of St. Lawrence remained small fishing communities until after 1713.

The Spanish empire in America also consisted of Caribbean and mainland colonies.[4] Those in the Caribbean included Cuba, Puerto Rico, the remaining two-thirds of Española, Trinidad, Tobago, and a few smaller islands. Sugar had not emerged as the mainstay of these colonies by 1713, so their population included fewer Africans and more Europeans than that of the French (or British) Caribbean islands.

On the mainlands of North and South America, the Spanish empire stretched from Texas to Tierra del Fuego, incorporating mines, planta-tions, subsistence farms, cosmopolitan cities and backward villages, vast deserts, and some of the world's richest soil. The empire consisted of two viceroyalties, corresponding to the two main economic and de-mographic centers: Mexico and Peru. Their chief value lay in their production of precious metals. Output had declined from levels achieved in the era of Philip II (1556–98), but mining nonetheless remained the most profitable enterprise in the Indies, and the heart of the empire from the imperial point of view.

Both the French and Spanish empires organized imperial export economies through more or less sharply defined commercial systems. The French encouraged a triangular trade between France, New France, and the French West Indies. They hoped to market French manufac-tures in both colonial areas, to sell sugar and rum from the Caribbean to both France and New France, to sell northern furs to France, and to provide enough grain from New France to feed the French West Indies. This program for French imperial commerce dates from the ministry of Jean-Baptiste Colbert in the late seventeenth century. Legislation dis-couraged trade with foreigners. The French never required the tri-angular trade by law, but encouraged it through tax incentives and exhortation.

The Spanish commercial system was older and more rigid, although beginning to loosen up in the eighteenth century. Strict legislation car-ried stern penalties for miscreants. Spanish authorities hoped to mini-mize intercolonial trade and to maximize the role of Spain itself as a market and supplier. The Crown, for instance, had outlawed trade be-tween Mexico and Peru. The Casa de Contratación (Board of Trade) tightly regulated commerce between Spain and its American colonies, as well as the Pacific trade.[5] The Crown aimed to prevent foreign inter-loping, to foster Spanish industries, and to secure the treasure of the Indies as it crossed the Atlantic. Accordingly, large fleets carried care-fully enumerated goods to prescribed ports. This commercial system, revived after the interruption of the War of the Spanish Succession (1701–15), suffered from many weaknesses, which prompted its modi-fication, beginning perhaps in the 1740s, that was well underway by the 1760s and 1770s. Like the French, the Spanish could not prevent merchants, peninsular and colonial, from following the dictates of the

marketplace, and so both venality and contraband flourished throughout the empire. The problems of enforcement at transoceanic distances
overmatched the resources of the Spanish Crown, contributing to the
impetus for reform of the commercial system.

Both the French and the Spanish failed to stop their colonies from
trading with foreigners. In addition, the French failed to stimulate a
large trade among their overseas colonies, while the Spanish failed to
prevent one. Both the Bourbon empires faced the problem of defending
their territories and trade from foreign attack. Since the days of Drake and
Hawkins, the preferred method of profiting from a rival's empire was to
seize commerce at choke points on the high seas. Annexing territory
involved problems of administration, production costs, and, in turn,
defense. Thus protection of trade formed the crux of the dilemma of
imperial defense. Since French trade was less alluring than the Spanish, it
required less protection. The French could rely on dispersal. French
commerce filled a sufficient number of hulls that the French could afford
to absorb some losses. Although shipping routes were well known to all,
the vast majority of French shipping usually reached its destination
unharmed. In wartime, the French occasionally resorted to a convoy
system, but never in time of peace.[6] Spanish treasure, however, attracted
many predators, prompting the Spanish to rely on a convoy system in
peace and war. They tried to put most of their eggs in a single basket, the
flota, and used the navy to protect it. Increasingly, in the eighteenth
century, individual ships plied the seas between Spain and the Indies, but
the majority of goods still traveled with the *flota*. This annual (in theory)
procession of ships to and from the New World served Spanish purposes
well in the sixteenth and seventeenth centuries. The outbound fleets
laden with European goods and the returning treasure fleets were lost
only rarely. Furthermore, the *flota* system helped to minimize the costs of
combating contraband. But by 1715 gradual economic, demographic,
and commercial expansion in the Indies would soon make the *flota* system
an unwieldy anchor, limiting the growth of the trade which this system
was supposed to encourage.

The French and Spanish both maintained a naval presence in American
waters. The French preferred to send out a fleet each spring from bases in
France—they had no year-round naval bases in the Americas. The Spanish on the other hand maintained a small squadron in the Caribbean, the

Armada de Barlovento. One common characteristic greatly outweighed the differences between the two Bourbon fleets: neither cared to do battle with the British, an indisposition developed in the wars of Louis XIV (1678–1713). Their strategy and tactics hinged on the belief that to engage the British navy was to court disaster. Maintaining a navy meant refusing to fight whenever possible. Thus, by 1700, the French and Spanish had conceded what naval thinkers have since come to call "command of the sea."[7] Fortified bases had been the mainstay of earlier maritime empires, such as the Venetian and Portuguese, which had never developed standing navies. Only in the eighteenth century did a large imperial navy emerge as a standing instrument of colonial policy and defense. The British pioneered this use of the navy and thereby revolutionized maritime strategy. In the absence of naval forces which could defeat the British, the French and Spanish relied on a traditional policy of colonial fortification to defend their New World territories and trade.

Neither the Bourbon nor the British empires encompassed the heartland of North America. The forests and plains between the Appalachians and the Rockies had little to offer those who hoped to get rich quickly, and so had been largely left to the indigenous population. This does not mean, however, that the French, Spanish, and British did not covet this heartland; they did, and their imperial strategies reflected their ambitions.

Two rivers allowed access to the interior of the continent, the St. Lawrence and the Mississippi, so control of each held tremendous potential strategic value. From a maritime perspective, the choke points of these rivers lay not at their mouths, but at the mouths of their gulfs: the open water between Newfoundland and Cape Breton Island in the case of the St. Lawrence, and the stretch between Yucatán and Florida in the case of the Mississippi. The British, whose colonial population in North America was thirty times that of the French by 1750, controlled neither of these river routes and found the Appalachians an effective barrier to territorial expansion until later in the century. As far as the North American heartland was concerned, French control of the approach to the St. Lawrence and Spanish domination of the access to the Mississippi offset British advantages of greater population and naval strength.

The strategic value of the mouths of the gulfs also hinged on their positions vis-à-vis transatlantic sailing routes. The prevailing westerlies

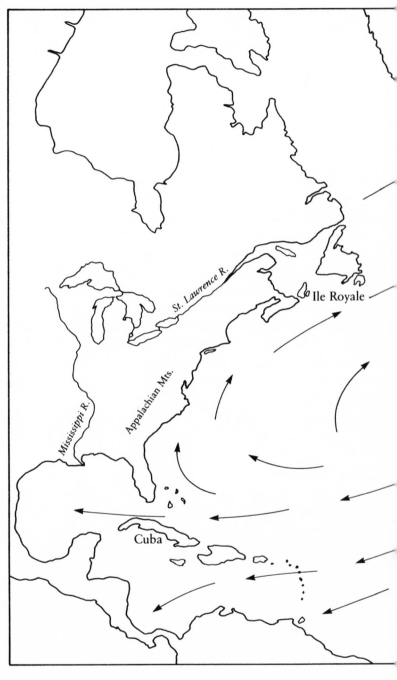

Map 1.1 Winds of the North Atlantic World

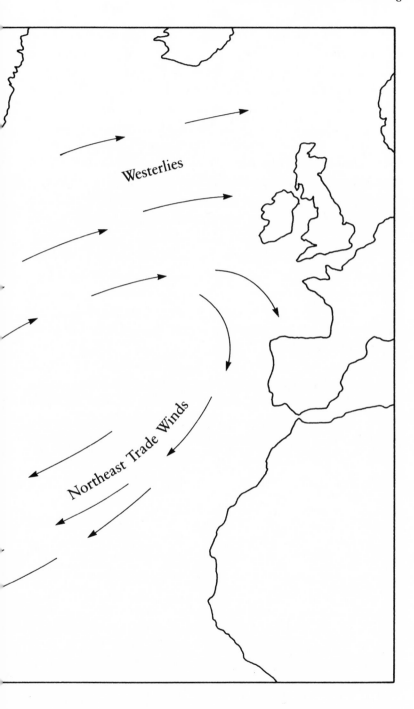

Westerlies

Northeast Trade Winds

of the northern hemisphere encouraged ships to cross the ocean west to east at a latitude above 45° in summer and above 40° in winter (global wind patterns fluctuate with the seasons). Traffic from the Caribbean, or almost anywhere in the American tropics, found it convenient to sail with the Gulf Stream through the Florida Channel until far enough north to take advantage of the westerlies. Most any Caribbean ship west of the Windward Passage sailed through the straits of Yucatán and north of Cuba before entering the Atlantic, rather than buck the northeast trades. The trade winds combined with the North Equatorial Current to prevent an easy crossing to Europe at a latitude south of the westerlies, so the takeoff point for any eastward Atlantic crossing was about the latitude of Cape Breton Island, wherever the voyage originated. Thus the key strategic point in the northern approach to North America was the straits between Newfoundland and Cape Breton Island, and the key to the southern approach was the mouth of the Gulf of Mexico (which might be better understood if it were called the Gulf of the Mississippi). The French and Spanish controlled these strategic points as best they could without dominant navies.

In the eighteenth century two cities presided over these key points: Louisbourg in the north and Havana in the south. Perched astride the routes to and from Europe and the routes into the heartland of the North American continent, these cities often went by almost the same name: Louisbourg was "la clef de l'Amérique," and Havana, "la llave del Nuevo Mundo."[8] Let us turn to these port cities and their environs in the next chapter.

2 Colonial Landscapes and Seascapes

The geographical, ecological, and demographic characteristics of Cape Breton Island and Cuba prescribed limits to what the French and Spanish might extract from and accomplish in these parts of their empires. The islands' natural and human resources largely determined the degree to which they might fulfill the roles into which metropolitan policy cast them. These characteristics loom so importantly in imperial history precisely because Bourbon policymakers so poorly understood them. Their ignorance, while it scarcely distinguished them from their British, Dutch, or Portuguese rivals, encouraged French and Spanish ministers to persist in policies of dubious wisdom in colonial matters.

Cape Breton Island is the northern extremity of the Appalachian Mountains. It consists of 6,403 square kilometers (3,970 square miles) of sedimentary, metamorphic, and igneous rock arranged in a complex mosaic. The rock is aged—ranging from Precambrian (Hadrynian) to Carboniferous—and in its time has undergone a good deal of twisting and folding. Glaciation (as recent as 7,000 years ago in the island's center) scooped out lakes and valleys and erected a few small moraines, but no terminal moraines (presumably these existed in areas now beneath the sea). Glaciation has had little effect on soil distribution: the soil is stony where the bedrock is hard and has undergone much folding; it is fine where the underlying rock is soft and has aged uneventfully. For the most part, Cape Breton's soil is rocky, although several areas have responded well to agriculture. In the vicinity of Louisbourg the bedrock is mostly hard crystalline limestone, and the soils derived from it are poor and stony.[1]

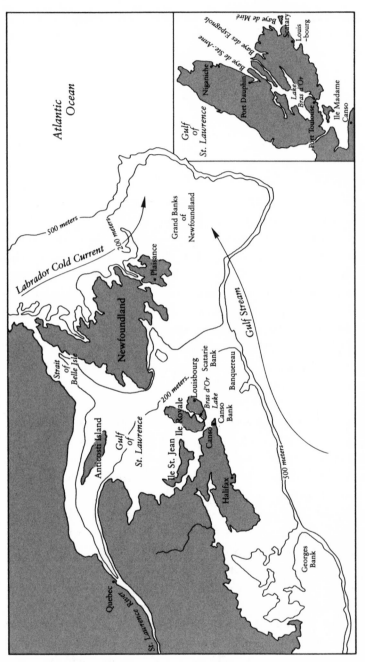

Map 2.1 Cape Breton Island and Environs

Although the island is generally hilly, flat land surrounds Bras d'Or Lake—actually a fjord—and slopes to the sea in the northeast, where most of the population has always lived. The large saltwater inlet in the interior and the channels to its north afford easy communication, from which only the northern highlands are excluded. Small lakes and streams abound, but have no value as avenues of transport. Glaciation and moderate emergence and submergence along the coast has created a proliferation of bays and inlets, some making fine ports, most notably Sydney Harbor and St. Anns Harbor.

The town of Louisbourg lay near the eastern extreme of Cape Breton Island on a small marshy promontory, nowhere higher than twenty meters above sea level. The promontory defines the south side of the harbor's mouth; Lighthouse Point, which defines the north side, is only several hundred meters away. A battery of rocks and shallows makes the entrance to the harbor even narrower, requiring entering ships to steer northeast toward Lighthouse Point before bearing toward the docks of the old port. The wind generally blows from the west and southwest, roughly perpendicular to the harbor's mouth, facilitating both entry and exit. Once inside the harbor mouth, sailing ships confronted a commodious anchorage of perhaps 2 or 3 square kilometers, free from the turbulence of the open sea and reasonably free from strong winds.[2] Although thousands of ships used the harbor in the French period, only twelve shipwrecks occurred inside the harbor.[3]

The old town of Louisbourg was laid out on an east-west grid. Warehouses dominated the waterfront; further inland, dwellings were interspersed with inns, shops, bakeries, and the like. Wooden houses built on stone foundations lined comparatively broad streets. Many homes had gardens of considerable proportions, since land was not especially scarce. The military installations of the Bastion du Roi and the Demi-bastion Dauphin guarded the southern and western ends of the town respectively. Both had guardhouses and barracks. Between them the Demi-bastion and the larger Bastion du Roi protected the landward approaches to Louisbourg.

The climate of Louisbourg is an unprepossessing one, with brief summers and long winters, and it could not have differed much in the eighteenth century.[4] One resident in the 1750s wrote that there were only two seasons—autumn and winter.[5] The presence of the sea serves to moderate temperatures, but nonetheless they range from −25° to 35° C (−13° to 95° F). These are recorded extremes; the average January temperature is −4° C (24° F), and that of July is 18° C (64° F). In representative years, frost appears in the middle of October and disappears toward the end of May. Louisbourg enjoys only 100 to 140 frost-free days, making for a brief growing season. Precipitation averages about 134 centimeters (53 inches) annually, of which 29 (12 inches) fall as snow. It is fairly evenly distributed around the year with some sort of precipitation falling on 160 to 200 days of the year. The July monthly average is 7.9 centimeters (3 inches), and that of December is 14 centimeters (6 inches). Drift ice imperils or prohibits the use of Louisbourg harbor for a few months each winter and spring, with great fluctuations from year to year. Strong winds buffet Louisbourg constantly (19 kilometers per hour is the average at nearby Sydney) with shore winds complicating the comparatively steady westerlies. The juncture of the Labrador Cold Current and the warm Gulf Stream creates plentiful fogs that add to the hazards of navigation and the general unpleasantness of the climate. Sydney enjoys an average of four to five hours of sunshine per day, and Louisbourg probably less. "Clouds of thick fog which come from the southwest cover it [Louisbourg] generally, from the month of April until the end of July to such a degree that sometimes for a month together they never see the sun, at the same time that there is bright clear weather at the distance of two or three leagues from it."[6]

Cape Breton temperatures range lower than French temperatures by about 10° C in January and by next to nothing in July. On the whole Cape Breton is cloudier, wetter, windier, and more snowy than coastal or central France. To any Frenchman the climate of Cape Breton appeared more difficult than that left behind.[7] The Cape Breton climate also compares unfavorably with that of the St. Lawrence valley, particularly in the summer months.

Louisbourg lies on the same latitude as La Rochelle in France, just south of 46° north, well within the zone of the prevailing westerlies. At 60° west longitude, Louisbourg is perched almost on the edge of the Gulf Stream as it veers away from North America toward Europe. The voyage by sail to France took perhaps thirty days in good weather, a comparatively quick and easy trip.[8] The current and wind which made the eastbound voyage simple, however, complicated the return trip. Nonetheless, by virtue of its latitude, French ships bound for America found Louisbourg a convenient destination for which to aim: in the eighteenth century the art of fixing longitude was just emerging, so that sailors crossing the ocean frequently seized upon a chosen parallel and followed it across, so as to know their whereabouts upon sighting land.[9] For the French it was important not to land at Newfoundland, Nova Scotia, or New England, where they were unwelcome, so following the forty-sixth parallel to Louisbourg was the safest course.

Other routes to and from Louisbourg involved less dramatic variations between inbound and outbound voyages. A trip from Louisbourg to New England or the Caribbean generally went much more slowly than the return because the winds and currents favor westerly and northwesterly sailing. The belt of prevailing westerlies, although it fluctuates with the season, invariably includes Louisbourg within it. Although the westerlies are neither as powerful nor as steady as the trade winds of the tropics, and thus exercise a lesser tyranny over sailors' freedom of direction, their influence is buttressed by the Gulf Stream, which flows east-northeast at the latitude of Louisbourg.

Winds and currents exerted strong local influences too. The Labrador Current, which flows from northeast to southwest, usually grazes the eastern shore of Cape Breton Island; the Gulf Stream passes a few kilometers offshore. The constancy of these two currents created in effect a two-lane highway for coastal navigation. Close-in shore winds mitigated the effect of the westerlies, permitting eastward and southeastward sailing along the coast. This blessing does not extend any farther south than Cape Breton Island, however, since the Labrador Current disappears around 45° north latitude. So while coastal navigation around Cape Breton benefited from the elements, long-distance sailing, except in a westerly and northwesterly direction, did not.

The sea lanes connecting Louisbourg to the rest of the Atlantic world passed through the port's great natural resource: the offshore fishing banks. By virtue of its position, Louisbourg commanded natural resources as valuable as any in North America, excepting the silver veins of Mexico (with which the fishing banks were occasionally compared). While the bounty of nature was scant indeed on the landward side of Louisbourg, offshore the sea teemed with marketable fish. Cod, highly nutritional and easier to preserve than any other fish, made Louisbourg important to Europe. The continental shelf extends several hundred kilometers to the east of Cape Breton, forming an undersea plateau seldom more than one hundred meters beneath the surface.[10] An abundance of plankton in these comparatively warm waters attracts fish from all over the North Atlantic, especially during the mating season (newborn cod feed almost exclusively on plankton). This creates a dense population of large edible fish unequalled anywhere in the world. Cod predominate in these waters, but other species flock there too, some to lay eggs, others to prey upon smaller fish.

Louisbourg's underwater hinterland required neither roads nor property boundaries, minimizing the overhead costs of exploitation. Cheap seaborne transport further lowered costs: cod caught offshore floated to Louisbourg for export. In contrast, Pennsylvania wheat, Maryland tobacco, Caribbean sugar, or any other colonial product, had to be carried or rolled to the point of export, consuming a larger share of the sale price in transport costs. In this way an offshore hinterland like Louisbourg's offered significant advantages over an inland one. On the other hand a city, a government, or a merchant elite could more easily establish ownership and control over land than over the sea. At Louisbourg, the French found it impossible to exclude New England competition from the fishing banks. Before 1713, Breton, Norman, Basque, and West Country English fishermen struggled for access to cod and suitable places to dry them. None could drive out the others because of the difficulty of asserting dominion over the sea. Fishing rights and marine rights remain hazily defined and hard to enforce to this day.

The resources of Cape Breton Island paled beside Louisbourg's offshore hinterland. The rocky landscape around Louisbourg could not support significant agriculture. When the French first arrived, forests covered the island,[11] but the timber proved poor, except in the interior. The coastal regions featured bogs, barrens, and forests of fir and spruce, often stunted and entirely useless except as firewood. The eastern shore, where Louisbourg stood, had the poorest forest of the island: few full-grown trees exceeded 10 meters in height. The best forest lay around Bras d'Or Lake, at St. Anns, and on Boularderie Island. Here travelers found stands of hardwoods, including oak and ash (which are rare today), mixed with spruce and pine. The lack of undergrowth and the large size of these trees (up to 75 centimeters or 30 inches in diameter) indicates that this formed the climax vegetation in these regions. The tall, straight, majestic white pine, the ideal mast timber, did not decorate the Cape Breton landscape.[12] In the last 150 years, mineral resources have served as the mainstay of Cape Breton Island's economy. Easily accessible coal deposits in the northeast have been worked to exhaustion. The largest seam, of which the French were well aware, ran from Cow Bay to Sydney Harbor, conveniently close to the sea. Coal and timber resources, however, while not perhaps negligible, amounted to very little in comparison to the bounty of the sea. The true hinterland of Louisbourg, and the source of its wealth, lay offshore.

In 1713 the human resources of Cape Breton Island were almost negligible from the imperial point of view. The indigenous population of Micmac Indians numbered only in the hundreds. The Micmacs, Algonquin speakers, lived by hunting and gathering. They planted no crops, domesticated no animals other than the dog, and confined their fishing almost exclusively to fresh water. They migrated continually, on foot and by canoe (outfitted with a moosehide sail for sea voyages), and so the French could never accurately know their numbers. They did not have to know, however, since the Micmacs could never effectively contest the sovereignty of their island with Europeans and normally found it preferable to cooperate with white men rather than to resist them. By 1713 the Micmacs had already had some experience with Europeans in the context of a small fur trade with visiting fishermen.[13] After 1713 this trade diversified, assuming the character so common in relations between whites and Indians in North America: the Micmacs exchanged scouting and fighting services as well as furs, for blankets, muskets, ammunition, hatchets, and sundry other items. The French made no effort to exterminate the Micmacs but inadvertently must have reduced their numbers through exposure to European diseases. By 1750 the Micmac population on Cape Breton Island had, however, recovered to perhaps two thousand in all, a density of about .3 persons per square kilometer.[14]

Throughout the French period, the Micmacs remained primarily interested in the interior of Cape Breton Island, while the activities of Europeans focused on the sea. Not that the Micmacs did not occasionally fish and the French occasionally farm—they did—but on the whole they had little occasion to interact. The Micmac influence on the French settlement at Louisbourg was remarkably slight.

The first European immigration to Ile Royale (as Cape Breton Island was known from the time of its settlement)[15] came from Newfoundland in 1713. The terms of the Treaty of Utrecht turned Newfoundland over to the British, and with the exception of fewer than ten persons who chose to remain and take an oath of allegiance to the British Crown, the French community resolved to depart. The original founders of Louisbourg numbered 110 men, 10 women, and 23 children.[16] From these modest beginnings, the colony of Ile Royale grew to number several thousand within the span of two generations. Natural increase accounted for some, but immigration provided the largest part of the population growth.

Immigrants came from three sources. The first of these was Acadia, an agricultural community of perhaps 10,000 people of French origin, officially British subjects since 1713 but in practice quite independent.[17] With the birth of the colony at Ile Royale, the French conceived the policy of recruiting Acadians, first to Ile Royale and then to Ile St. Jean as well, a policy they never abandoned.[18] The second source of immigrants to Ile Royale was the French army. Officials encouraged discharged soldiers to stay in the colony. Since most French soldiers were peasants, French authorities hoped to use them to create a viable agricultural community at Ile Royale.[19] The French encouraged soldiers at Ile Royale to marry, a most unusual policy which reflected an emphasis on population growth.[20] Sailors, traders, and fishermen from Brittany, Normandy, and the Basque country formed the third source of immigration. Normally hundreds of French fishermen flocked to the shores of Ile Royale early each summer, and others followed to supply the fishermen with food and supplies. Whenever opportunity beckoned, a proportion of these remained behind in Louisbourg to establish themselves as fishermen, traders, or laborers, a practice countenanced by French policy.[21] Although French officials instructed Quebec authorities to permit any emigrants who wished to go to Ile Royale, few Canadians obliged.[22]

Western France provided the largest share of Ile Royale immigrants. The 1752 census taken by Sieur de la Roque reveals the geographic origin of 828 people above the age of fifteen. Of the 372 from France, the preponderance hailed from Normandy, Brittany, and the Basque country.

Table 2.1

Origins of the Ile Royale Population, 1752

Acadia	251	30.3%
Ile Royale	157	18.9%
Canada	8	0.9%
Newfoundland	30	3.6%
Unspecified Quebec	1	0.1%
France	372	44.9%
Other countries	9	1.1%

Source: Pouyez, "La population de l'Isle Royale en 1752,"
p. 172.

Bayonne alone contributed 108 settlers; St.-Mâlo, 63; Coutances, 47; and Avranches, 38. Paris provided only eight.[23] As a common practice, immigrants tended to congregate where they could find their fellows. Almost all of those who came from Bayonne lived at Petit Degrat on the east coast; the Malouins clustered in the settlements north of Louisbourg; the Acadians lived almost exclusively at Port Toulouse and the bays of the northern part of the island.[24]

The population of Ile Royale was highly mobile. Fishermen migrated from year to year according to the abundance of cod, erecting temporary dwellings as they went. The erratic population totals of the Ile Royale outports (Niganiche, for example) reflect this nomadic character of the population.[25] Acadians as well as fishermen (the two categories were largely, though not entirely, mutually exclusive) moved about freely. They routinely came to Ile Royale to enjoy the largesse of the Crown for three years and then returned to their homes along the Bay of Fundy. While the population of Ile Royale as a whole grew fairly steadily, the pattern of distribution within the island showed a skittish sensitivity to the performance of the twin pillars of the colony's economy: the fishery and seaborne commerce. When the fishery peaked around 1730, the population of the outports approached maximum levels. By the 1750s, when the cod catch had shrunk but Louisbourg's entrepôt trade expanded, the outports' population dwindled, while the largest port burgeoned.

Several censuses recorded the French population of Ile Royale between

Table 2.2

The Growth of the Ile Royale Population, 1716–1753

Year	Outports	Louisbourg[a]	Ile Royale[b]	Ile Royale and Ile St. Jean
1716	1,042	885	2,346	2,446
1720	1,077	950	2,446	2,696
1723	1,777	1,130	3,326	3,641
1724	1,361	1,235	3,015	3,396
1726	2,127	1,307	3,853	4,234
1734	2,263	1,584	4,318	4,891
1737	2,575	1,975	4,969	5,547
1752–53	1,687	4,853	6,959	9,600

Source: Durand, "Etude sur la population de Louisbourg, 1713–1745"; Clark, *Acadia*, 274–96. Surlaville, *Les derniers jours*, p. 14. McLennan, *Louisbourg, Foundation to Fall*, Appendix 3. *Report of the Canadian Archives 1905*, 2:4–76. AN, Outre-Mer G¹, vol. 466, pièces 67, 69. AC, C¹¹B, 1:495; AC, C¹¹B, 3:25, 479–80; AC, C¹¹B, 4:21. See also the sources listed in Tables 2.3 and 2.4.

[a] Includes both civilian and military population.
[b] Includes Indians.

1713 and 1758.[26] The seasonal migrations of the population created problems beyond the capacity of census takers to solve, so the student of the Ile Royale population must accept inexact figures. Various subsequent efforts have been made to determine the size of the Louisbourg population, that of the outports, and that of Ile St. Jean.[27] No systematic effort has been made to estimate the entire population subject to the authority of the colonial government: the civil populations of Louisbourg, the Ile Royale outports, Ile St. Jean, the garrison population, and the Indians. (Many of these people of course escaped the effective control of the government, especially those at Ile St. Jean or in the interior of Ile Royale). Table 2.2 shows the growth of the colony's population from 1716 to 1752.[28]

The inhabitants of Ile St. Jean remained very few until the turmoil of the 1750s brought large numbers of Acadian refugees (see Table 2.3). French policy discouraged fishing at Ile St. Jean in the hope of developing the island as a breadbasket for Louisbourg, a most reasonable expectation in light of the fertility of the island's soil. Nonetheless, until late in the

Table 2.3

The Population of Ile St. Jean, 1720–1758

Year	Habitants (settlers)	Fishermen	Total
1720	250[a]	—	250[a]
1728	297	127	424
1730	325	131	456
1731	347	125	472
1734	396	176	573
1735	432	131	563
1747	—	—	653
1748	—	—	735
1752	—	—	2,223
1753	—	—	2,641
1755	—	—	2,969
1756	—	—	4,400–4,500[a]
1758	—	—	4,600–4,700[a]

Source: Harvey, *French Regime*, appendix C.

[a] Estimates.

French period the scant population at Ile St. Jean included many fishermen and far fewer farmers than the French wished.[29]

The French soldiery at Ile Royale grew along with the civilian population, amounting to somewhere between one-fourth and one-third of the Louisbourg population throughout the French regime. Port Toulouse and Port Dauphin supported small detachments, but normally well over 70 percent of the troops were quartered in Louisbourg.[30] Officers might live in the town, marry, and engage in the fishery or even commerce; the enlisted men lived in barracks. Death and desertion took a toll reflected in an annual turnover rate of 10 to 15 percent in the 1730s.[31] Desertion accounted for more than death: a soldier's life at Louisbourg was not only tedious but very uncomfortable, and passing ships or the wilderness looked tempting by comparison.[32]

The population of the Louisbourg barracks appears in none of the several censuses taken by the French authorities. Thus Table 2.4 is drawn

Table 2.4

The Garrison Population of Ile Royale, 1717–1758

Year	Companies	Soldiers	Source
1718	7	149[a]	AC, C^{11}B, 3:109–12
1720	7	317	AC, C^{11}B, 5:267
1722	7	330	AC, C^{11}B, 6:68
1731	8	389	AC, C^{11}B, 12:32–35
1734	8	560[b]	MP, OSU, Lot 2–2
1740	—	556	AC, C^{11}B, 22:114–15
1741	—	710	AC, C^{11}B, 23:71
1749	24	1,200[b]	AC, C^{11}C, 15:272
1750	24	1,200[b]	AC, B, 91:348
1755	—	2,300	AC, C^{11}C, 15:272
1757	—	2,300	AC, C^{11}C, 15:280
1758	—	3,740[c]	*Collection de manuscrits*, 3:489

[a] Another 150 soldiers passed the winter in Quebec to avoid starvation.

[b] This figure represents the full strength of the given number of companies. The actual population of soldiers must have been somewhat lower.

[c] Only 2,455 remained when Louisbourg fell to the British on 30 July.

from a variety of disparate sources. Clearly the French held the number of troops to a minimum (only in the West Indies could it have been more expensive to feed a soldier in the French empire), providing additional troops only when war threatened.

The steady growth of the Ile Royale population has been demonstrated in Table 2.2. No demographic catastrophes occurred, suggesting that Louisbourg was a fairly healthy place. The documents show only two epidemics in the entire French period, both of smallpox.[33] Scurvy, however, visited the residents almost every winter, a result of vitamin deficiencies in the diet, which in the winter months featured biscuit and fish very prominently. Many of the homes at Louisbourg had vegetable gardens, which helped reduce the monotony of the diet during the summer months, as did a little hunting; but generally Louisbourg had to rely on accumulated food stocks for the long winter. Residents could eat only foods that would not spoil quickly, such as salt fish and flour.

This unbalanced diet supported an unusually healthy population. The rate of child mortality, often a good index to the general health of a community, has been calculated at 19 percent for the years 1723–24 in Louisbourg. This is lower by 4 to 10 percent than the comparable rate in Anjou, a region of western France typical of those which supplied immigrants.[34] Considering that Louisbourg's port handled hundreds of ships a year from the entire Atlantic world, including the unhealthy Caribbean, its general good health is remarkable. Although this was one of the cheerier facts of life at Louisbourg, it must be remembered that good health by eighteenth-century standards allowed for strong possibilities of catching very nasty diseases.

Hospital records reveal patterns in the incidence of disease among the garrison at Louisbourg.[35] Civilian experience may have differed, but probably only slightly. Smallpox and tuberculosis visited the barracks most commonly. In a given twelve-month period, the garrison stood to lose anywhere between 5,800 and 8,700 man-days, the mean being 7,742. This meant each man might expect to spend two or three weeks of the year in the hospital. This record does not sound healthy by today's standards, but in an era before preventive medicine and with cures as dangerous as diseases, this qualified as a comparatively salubrious environment. French health measures, such as the quarantine system for incoming vessels instituted in 1734, had less to do with this good health than the climate.[36] Table 2.5 shows the variations in the incidence of hospitalization among the garrison at Louisbourg, 1732–52.

Perhaps the age structure of the Ile Royale population helps to explain its comparative good health. Young males composed a disproportionately large share of the population, as Tables 2.6 and 2.7 reveal. Table 2.6 consists of data drawn from the various censuses and refers to Louisbourg only. Table 2.7 presents data for the outports and the interior of the island in 1752. At Louisbourg, if one excludes fishermen, the numbers of men and women were roughly equal after the colony's first generation. In the outports men outnumbered women significantly (by 50 percent overall) even in 1752, especially among the twenty to forty-five-year-olds. This of course represents the large numbers of fishermen, for the most part young and unmarried men; without them the character of the population would probably resemble that of Louisbourg in the early years of settlement. Children accounted for 40 percent of the population in the out-

Table 2.5

Losses to the Garrison at Louisbourg through Hospitalization, 1732–1752

		Man-days lost		Sick days per soldier
Year	Garrison	Soldiers	Sailors	
1732	—	5,811	1,098	—
1733	—	8,333	421	—
1734	560	8,746	1,375	15.5
1735	—	7,502	1,023	—
1736	—	8,540	1,506	
1737	—	8,268	777	
1741	710	6,985	55[a]	9.8
1751–52[b]	—	10,640	—	—

Source: See note 35 and Table 2.4.
[a] Includes only January through September.
[b] Includes October 1751 through September 1752.

Table 2.6

The Civilian Population of the Town of Louisbourg, 1713–1737

	1713	1715	1716	1717	1720	1723	1724	1726	1734	1737
Habitants	116	125	56	58	69	68	113	144	141	163
Femmes	10	89	44	37	50	50	84	97	134	157
Enfants	23	179	119	115	142	160	239	298	394	664
Valets	11	62	—	—	—	—	77	94	157	229
Pêcheurs	—	291	366	358	372	515	377	314	296	250
TOTAL	160	746	585	568	633	793	890	947	1,122	1,463

Source: AN, Outre-Mer, Série G¹, vol. 466, pièces 50, 51, 52, 55, 62, 65, 67, 68, 69, 73.
Cited in Durand, "Etude de la population de Louisbourg, 1713–45."

ports and interior; fertility was high and infant mortality low. In Louisbourg in 1737, children were even more prominent: 45 percent of the total civil population.[37] Detailed census data for Louisbourg after 1737 are lacking, but one might expect a larger proportion of females to males there than either in the outports or in Louisbourg in the early years,

Table 2.7

Males per Hundred Females in the Ile Royale Population in 1752 by Age Group

0–1 years	106.7		
1–4 years	95.9		
5–9	90.0		
10–14	114.3	0–14 years	100.3
15–19	128.2		
20–24	202.6		
25–29	181.3	15–29 years	167.6
30–34	165.9		
35–39	200.0		
40–44	231.6	30–44 years	190.0
45–49	148.0		
50–54	206.2		
55–59	190.0	45–59 years	174.5
60–64	120.0		
65 and over	180.0	60 and over	160
All ages	145.0		

Source: Pouyez, "La population de l'Isle Royale en 1752," p. 161.

and perhaps even more children.[38] It cannot be verified, but apparently the population of the interior was evenly balanced in sex ratio, and very young on average, because the settlers were for the most part Acadians who had immigrated *en famille*. On the coast, where the fishermen lived—generally French, young, and unmarried—the sex ratio was extremely unbalanced and children were few. The youth of the colony's population, especially in the early years, no doubt reduced mortality and morbidity rates.

The diversity of social rank in French society did not exist in the colony of Ile Royale.[39] The nobility had few representatives, mostly army officers and decidedly lesser nobles. A handful of missionaries to the Micmacs and a very few clerics in the town of Louisbourg represented the second estate.[40] Only those who worked the soil in the interior qualified as peasants, and most of these arrived only after 1749.[41] Fishermen always made up the bulk of the laboring class, especially in the outports where many communities devoted themselves entirely to the pursuit of cod. Pilots accounted for 14 percent of the outports' population in 1752, many of them residents of Port Toulouse. No other occupational groups accounted for more than a tiny fraction of the outports' population.

Merchants centered in Louisbourg, where they constituted 1 percent of the town population from 1719 to 1752.[42] Together with the *habitant-pescheurs* (fishing fleet owners), they constituted a local bourgeoisie that clearly dominated Louisbourg civil society. Society outside Louisbourg had no clear masters; no one of social rank chose to live outside the town. The bourgeois families often intermarried with officers' families, blurring the distinction between noble and bourgeois. This had the effect of increasing the social and political prominence of the Louisbourg bourgeoisie.

The setting, population, and resources of Cuba were different from Cape Breton's in quantity and in detail. The overall patterns created by the setting and resources, however, bore strong resemblances in the two island outposts. The island of Cuba, including the Isla de Pinos (now called the Isle of Youth) and more than 1,600 keys, encompasses 114,524 square kilometers (44,028 square miles), roughly the size of Tennessee or Newfoundland. Its coastline covers 5,746 kilometers or 3,563 miles. It is long (1,203 kilometers or 746 miles) and narrow (average width 100 kilometers or 62 miles) in shape, extending from 74° to 85° W longitude, and from 20° to 23° N latitude. It accounts for more than half of the total area of the Antilles and is the largest tropical island in the western hemisphere. It consists of comparatively young metamorphic and igneous rock, arranged in kaleidoscopic disarray as a result of much folding and twisting in the Eocene. Later erosion has produced broad plains, though low mountains still remain in three clusters, most notably in the east. Littoral submergence and emergence during the Pleistocene has created many fine harbors and bays. Large bottleneck harbors exist at Honda, Cabañas, Mariel, Havana, Nuevitas, Puerto Padre, Nipe, and Tamano on the north coast, and at Guantánamo, Santiago de Cuba, and

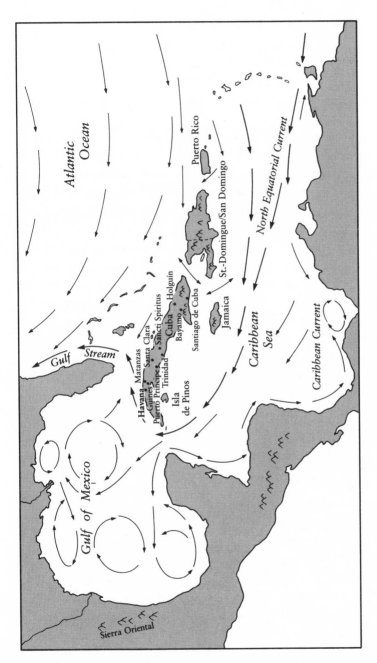

Map 2.2 Cuba and Environs

Cienfuegos (Jagua) on the south coast. Over 200 rivers drain the island, none very long, but some with wide estuaries (again the product of coastal submergence) permitting some inland navigation.

The harbor at Havana is one of the finest in the world. The anchorage is very spacious, 4 kilometers across and equally long, and deep enough to accommodate the largest vessels.[43] The prevailing winds cross the entrance channel perpendicularly, facilitating both entry and exit. In the winter and spring, the winds blow from a more northerly direction, driving ships onto offshore reefs, which, combined with a lack of fresh water in the vicinity, made blockade difficult. The strongest ocean current in the world, the Gulf Stream, passes by at up to 10 kilometers per hour, further complicating blockade.

The old city of Havana perched on a promontory forming the western shore of the harbor mouth.[44] The bastioned walls, pierced by two main gates, enclosed an area of about 2 square kilometers, including 179 blocks, three plazas, six wharfs, and fourteen churches. Two castles, the Morro and the Punta, guarded the harbor mouth. Narrow and unpaved streets, dusty for much of the year and muddy for the remainder, formed an irregular grid. Baron Alexander von Humboldt wrote that he had never seen a city dirtier than Havana, and his visit came half a century after the first organized street cleaning.[45] Children and livestock roamed the streets during the day; at night the unlit town belonged to adult males, many of them sailors. Havana had no police force, and it could be perilous in the vicinity of the docks. It was larger than Louisbourg, more anonymous, more boisterous, and more dangerous.

Internal communication in Cuba was much more difficult than in Cape Breton. Coastal transport posed comparatively few problems, but no waterways served the interior. Mountains impeded overland communication, less convenient than waterways under the best of circumstances.[46] Large sections of the interior were isolated, which has inspired some to conjure up two Cubas: the Havana sector and the rest of the island.[47] A more appropriate division of the island distinguishes between the regions accessible to water transport and those not. Any community connected by sea to Havana enjoyed cheap and easy contact with the wider world.

In general, the climate of Cuba is very agreeable. The trade winds, the influence of the sea, and the proximity of the North American land mass combine to provide fairly equable temperatures year round. No point in Cuba is very far from the sea, which moderates temperatures considerably. North American air in the winter months helps to cool Cuba further, particularly in the western end of the island. The result is a narrow range of average temperatures that are low for the tropics. Mean winter temperature in the interior is 21° C (70° F), and the summer mean is 27° C (79° F). Freezing temperatures, even in the mountains, are virtually unknown, and in the most torrid spells the Havana temperature almost never exceeds 36° C (97° F). Extremes are caused by the southward expansion of polar fronts over North America in winter, and in summer by very low pressures in the center of North America that bring hot dry winds north from the Caribbean across Cuba.[48]

The regularity of temperatures makes rainfall the important variable in the climate of Cuba. Precipitation varies markedly during the course of the year, although the general pattern is highly predictable. In effect there are but two seasons—the wet season from May to November and the dry season from December to April. More than three-fourths of the annual precipitation (137 centimeters or 55 inches average) falls in the rainy season, although even in the dry season it is a rare month that has no rain. Patterns vary somewhat from place to place on the island, but in general there are two maxima: one in June, a result of the evaporation and convection that are at their height when the sun is most direct, bringing daily thunderstorms; and a second in September, a product of the hurricane season. The west receives more rain than the east, principally because it is in the path of more hurricanes.

The general regime of the winds is as regular as that of rainfall. Cuba's winds are dominated by the northeast trades and directed by the Atlantic anticyclone, a center of high pressure which migrates between 20° and 40° north latitude, depending on the season. The wind is always from the east, but in winter, the high pressure being further north, the trade winds blow from the northeast more than east. In the summer the wind comes more directly from the east, although sometimes, especially along the south coast, from the east-southeast. The wind velocity generally exceeds 5 meters per second (about 9 miles per hour), and frequently surpasses 10 meters per second. The influence of the wind upon Cuban life in the eighteenth century is difficult to exaggerate. Cubans said "upwind" and "downwind" for "east" and "west."

The power and regularity of the trade wind meant that a journey from Havana to the Mexican mainland generally took less than a week, while the return trip invariably consumed several weeks.[49] A voyage from Barbados to Jamaica, about 1,500 kilometers (930 miles), took about a week, while the reverse route could take up to three months.[50] The shortest distance between two points in the age of sail depended on the direction of the wind.

The effect of the trade winds on the Cuban coasts is complicated by shore breezes, especially prominent in the summer when differential heating between land and sea is most pronounced. Small-scale shore winds oscillate daily; a larger one, the North American monsoon, can bring north winds in winter and south winds in summer. Although generally the winds of Cuba are quite reliable for sailing purposes, the hurricane season of late summer and early autumn renders the winds temporarily unpredictable and dangerous.[51]

The coral reefs and littoral currents which surround Cuba compound sailing difficulties.[52] In addition to the Gulf Stream, which carries past Cuba sixty-five times the volume of water of the sum of the world's rivers,[53] several smaller currents skirt Cuba. The sea flows westerly across the northern shore through the Old Bahama Channel as far as San Juan de los Remedios, where it veers north to join the Gulf Stream; this is the tail end of the North Equatorial Current. Farther west, the Gulf Stream flows east across Cuba's north shore, but at the western end of the island, an eddy in the stream produces the Cuban Countercurrent, flowing west and south toward Cape San Antonio. This intermingling of currents, all of which meander to some extent with the season, makes the navigation of the western end of Cuba somewhat tricky.

The southern shore of Cuba is caressed by the westward flow of the North Equatorial Current. Between the Isla de Pinos and Cape San Antonio, however, another eddy veers north and then eastward along the shore through the Gulf of Batabano as far east as the southern keys. This countercurrent is larger in the summer than the winter; its fluctuations, as well as the innumerable reefs, keys, and shallows, make for additional hazards and complexities in the navigation of Cuba's coasts.

The same forces influencing Cuba's climate and currents define the island's position with respect to the sailing routes of the Atlantic. The northeast trades, the wind that helps to power the North Equatorial

Current,[54] formed the highway between Europe and the Caribbean. It was of course a one-way street; ships made the return trip further north, above the thirty-fifth parallel, in the zone of prevailing westerlies (the countertrades). Cuba lies near the northern limit of the northeast trades, and at the head of the Gulf Stream, which bridged the gap between the Caribbean latitudes and the westerlies. Thus, given the constraints imposed by the necessity of sailing before the wind, Cuba lay at a crossroads in both Atlantic and Caribbean communication routes.[55]

Centuries of poverty belie Cuba's wealth of natural resources. By eighteenth-century standards Cuban resources appeared meager, since the island offered no silver and very little gold. To an age less entranced by bullion, Cuba's natural resources would have appeared considerable. First among these is the soil. Almost two-thirds of the island is flat or gently undulating and covered with deep soil, the product of geological calm since the Pliocene. The fertility of Cuban soils, although uneven, is sometimes exceptional. Most of the good agricultural land derives from clay and limestone deposits, 6 meters deep around Matanzas, but only 25 centimeters deep around Havana. The most fertile soils occur beside the few river beds. Cuba's sandy alluvial soils, for example, have yielded the world's finest tobacco: Humboldt found the soil at the fabled tobacco land Vuelta Abajo, to be 86 to 91 percent silica.[56] Tobacco soil, unlike good sugar cane soil, contains no lime.

The fertile soils of Cuba include large expanses that are either too dry or too wet for cultivation. One-fourth of Cuban soil cannot retain enough water to support anything besides shrubs and palms; mangrove swamps cover much of the south coast. Cuban soils are highly variegated, in contrast to the general uniformity of climatic conditions, so the island could provide a wide spectrum of crops. At one time it did so: Ponce de Leon thought the flora of Cuba among the most extraordinary of the world.[57]

The original vegetation of Cuba resembled that of northern South America more than that of Central or North America. The uniformity of climate meant that soils determined patterns of vegetation. In general terms, Cuba has three categories of vegetation: forest, savanna, and coastal. Before the arrival of the Spaniards, forest covered about 60 percent of the island. Cedar, mahogany, oak, ebony, pine, and palm abounded, arranged in zones depending for the most part upon altitude.[58] Today the forest is confined to the mountains, but in the eighteenth century it stretched down to the coastal plains wherever soils could support it. Pines grew in poorer soils and comprised a majority of the Cuban forest. In less acid soils oak predominated.

The savanna accounted for roughly one-fourth of the island and remains today much as in the eighteenth century. In Cuba the presence of soil that cannot retain moisture, rather than the level of rainfall, defines the savanna. The vegetation of these areas consists chiefly of grasses and various sorts of palm trees. The Cuban savanna has always been sparsely inhabited and used for little more than pasture land, though in the Pinar del Río area savanna land supports fine tobacco. Very often savanna areas and forest areas combine in a checkerboard pattern creating semisavannas.[59]

The vegetation of the shore areas of Cuba is of two sorts, halophilous and xerophilous—meaning life adapted to swamps and life adapted to desert. In Cuba halophilous vegetation consists principally of five varieties of mangrove trees, which form almost impenetrable thickets guarding much of the coastline. The mangroves flourish wherever the coast has submerged. Wherever the coastline has emerged, xerophilous vegetation predominates. Here the soil is highly permeable and retains very little moisture. Cacti and small-leaved shrubs and bushes are common. Leafy plants lose too much moisture through transpiration to survive on these coasts. In general, halophilous vegetation covers the southern littoral and the keys of both coasts and xerophilous vegetation is more common along the northern coast, especially in the northeast. One large area of the south coast, the Cienega de Zapata, is given over almost entirely to mangroves, even at some distance inland.

This swampland and desert vegetation has been of little use to human beings in Cuba, even less than the savanna. The forest, however, particularly the tall hardwoods, has proved useful, which explains why so little remains. The destruction of the forest since 1740 has been the most salient change in the structure of Cuban vegetation, indeed of all Cuban natural resources.

Cuba's mineral resources have always been meager. Since the nineteenth century exploitation has intensified, but before 1762 only gold and copper attracted any attention.[60] Holguín produced small amounts of gold in the sixteenth century, as did Jagua and Trinidad in the eighteenth,[61] but Cuba proved disappointing to Spaniards who sought quick fortunes. El Cobre, near Santiago de Cuba, provided copper from 1530 to 1918, with a seventy-year intermission in the late eighteenth and early nineteenth centuries because of earthquake damage. The Spanish found and exploited smaller copper deposits elsewhere on the island, notably on the northern slope of the western mountains, but copper production always centered at El Cobre. The depletion of the copper mines in the eighteenth century, like the destruction of the forest and the exhaustion of the best soils, resulted from the growth of the sugar industry. The demands made by sugar had a powerful effect on the character and extent of Cuba's human resources as well.

The first census of Cuba appeared in 1774, by which time sugar had already begun to transform Cuban society. What passes for knowledge of the Cuban population prior to 1774 is a mixture of hypothesis, conjecture, and extrapolation. Only one document reveals any effort by Spanish authorities to measure Cuba's population, an incomplete *visita* made by a bishop in 1755–57. Thus any remarks on the population of Cuba prior to 1774 deserve a measure of skepticism.[62]

Cuba's indigenous population consisted of two groups of Arawak-speaking Indians, the Taino and the Ciboney. They virtually disappeared within two generations of Columbus's visit in 1492. Archeological evidence suggests that their numbers did not approach the maximum that Cuba's resources and their paleolithic technology would have permitted. The Ciboneys apparently arrived in Cuba first and were subjugated by the Taino who came via the Antilles from South America. The Ciboneys (the word means people of the rock in the Taino language) lived in caves and knew neither agriculture nor towns. Bartolomé de las Casas thought the Taino had arrived in Cuba only fifty years before the Spanish, but archeological evidence indicates a much earlier presence. Taino culture corresponds roughly to the classification of late neolithic; their tools were of stone rather than wood or conch like the Ciboneys. They did not use metals. The Taino lived chiefly by means of extensive and varied agriculture. They raised grains, maize, and fruits. Their staples were cassava bread and maize, the virtues of which Columbus duly noted.[63] The Taino lived in villages for the most part, spent their lives scratching a living out of the soil, and did not practice warfare on any scale. Their food-producing and perhaps military superiority made the reduction of the Ciboneys a simple matter and required no large scale social organization. Since the warlike Caribs—who had made their presence felt in Puerto Rico and Haiti by 1492—had little impact on Cuba, the Taino had no impulse to develop a military tradition. When the Spanish arrived, the Taino could offer only the most feeble and fragmented resistance. The Spaniards found the Taino unable to adapt to the requirements of civilization, meaning regimented labor, and concluded that they were lazy. The effect of new European diseases on a population without any immunities rendered the Indian presence in Cuba negligible by the eighteenth century.

The Indians bequeathed to later Cubans the *bohío*, a mud hut that served for centuries as the typical rural dwelling; the cultivation of cassava, Cuba's principal food source for centuries; and tobacco, Cuba's largest export for centuries. Although exterminated more rapidly and more thoroughly than the Micmacs of Cape Breton Island, the Cuban Indian population left a greater cultural legacy to the immigrant population.[64]

Although Columbus visited Cuba in October 1492, Spanish settlement began only after 1511 under Governor Diego de Velázquez. A population of adventurers, traders, soldiers, sailors, and clergymen soon grew up, but with the development of more spectacular opportunities in Mexico and Peru, Cuba attracted very little European population and lost much of what it formerly had. For centuries thereafter, immigration to Cuba languished on account of the absence of a surplus Spanish population, imperial regulations, and the comparative unattractiveness of Cuba. With the demise of the Indian population, Cuba offered no supply of labor with which a Spaniard could hope to achieve wealth and status; thus Spaniards much preferred to go elsewhere in the Spanish Empire.

Cubans who wished to live off the exertions of others had to import labor, producing a multiracial society. The first African immigrant arrived in 1513; Indians from the Yucatán were also recruited.[65] According to one authority, in 1532 there were 300 whites and 500 blacks on the island. By 1620 this proportion had radically changed: 460 blacks to 6,976 whites.[66] Immigration remained small throughout the sixteenth and seventeenth centuries, although influxes of white population occurred in 1655 when the English seized Jamaica and in 1697 when the

Spanish ceded a third of the island of Hispaniola to the French. What few European immigrants came to Cuba in the sixteenth and seventeenth centuries hailed chiefly from the Canary Islands or the Basque country, especially Navarre. The Canary Islanders found Cuba attractive because of their familiarity with the techniques of tobacco and sugar cultivation,[67] and Basques became prominent in the ranks of Havana merchants. Despite these infusions, white population growth proceeded almost exclusively from natural increase.

No systematic estimate of the Cuban population is possible until 1757, but several authors have ventured a guess of 50,000 for 1700.[68] The proportion of whites to blacks within this total is a matter of speculation. The Cuban historian Ramiro Guerra y Sánchez thought the population evenly divided between whites and blacks in 1662, which seems most implausible in light of the failure of the Cuban slave population to reproduce and the modest rate of slave imports in the seventeenth century.[69]

Whatever the truth about the size and racial character of the Cuban population in 1700, it certainly grew very quickly in the next half century, possibly tripling in two generations. Once again an excess of the birth rate over the death rate, rather than immigration, accounted for most of this growth. Figures are unavailable except for one parish, Santa María del Rosario, a village 25 kilometers or so from Havana. According to the parish register, in the years 1733–62 baptisms outstripped deaths by up to ten to one among whites and five to one among blacks.[70] This differential implied tremendous natural increase, but was not typical of the island. The parish was founded in 1733, and many of its inhabitants were newcomers—probably young adults; it is unlikely to resemble the rest of the island either in birth rate or death rate.[71] Nevertheless, substantially higher birth than death rates must have been the rule in most of the island. By 1757 the island's total population had grown to about 160,000, roughly the size of Maryland at that time.[72] Almost a quarter of those were slaves.

In 1754, the new bishop of Havana, Pedro Agustín Morel de Santa Cruz, undertook to visit every community in Cuba, inaugurating an era of greater reliability in population data.[73] The bishop did a thorough job, visiting almost every settlement mentioned in his *visita*, and rarely neglecting to record the population. Where he failed to include a popula-

Table 2.8

Reported Population of Cuba by Community, 1755–1757

District	Community	House-holds	Population
Havana		6,896	22,828[a]
Havana suburbs		600	3,671
Havana hinterland	Jesus del Monte	262	1,318
	Santiago de las Vegas	328	1,954
	San Felipe y Santiago[a]	190	1,658
	Managuana	135	3,154
	Calvario	331	1,879
	San Miguel	199	965
	Potosí	66	642
	Regla	20	[164][b]
	Guanabacoa	637	6,309
	Santa Maria del Rosario	—	1,598
	Batabano	43	315
Western Cuba	Isla de Pinos	—	40
	Quemados	183	1,462
	Cano	310	2,732
	Guanajay	33	268
	Santa Cruz de los Pinos	65	400
	Consolación	142	753
	Pinar del Río	76	640
	Guane	98	700
	Cacaraxicaras	33	238
Central Cuba	Río Blanco	71	670
	Matanzas (town)	121	[740][b]
	Matanzas (partido)	—	1,370
	Macuriges	—	[400][c]
	Guamacaro	7	96
	Alvarez	75	163
	Hanabana	95	466
	Guamutas	47	186
	Camarones	—	[500][c]
	Santa Clara	669	4,293
	Los Remedios	398	2,527
	Sancti Spiritus	909	5,492
	Trinidad	792	5,840
	Palmarijo	108	422
	Ciego de Avila	—	[350][c]

Table 2.8 (continued)

District	Community	House- holds	Population
Puerto Príncipe	Puerto Príncipe	1,506	12,000[d]
Santiago	Holguín	345	1,751
	Bayamo	2,530	12,653
	Jiguani	102	588
	El Cobre	—	1,183
	Caney	83	500
	Iguabos	—	419
	Baracoa	217	1,169[e]
	Mayarí	—	300[e]
	Santiago de Cuba	1,419	15,471

Sources: *Visita* compiled by the Bishop Morell y Santa Cruz, AGI SD 2227; AGI SD 534.

[a] Includes only *personas de comun*.

[b] Projection based on household number and average household size in appropriate district.

[c] Estimate.

[d] "More than 12,000" reads the *visita*.

[e] "More than 300 *vegueros*" reads the *visita*.

tion figure he generally offered a number of households, allowing a fairly confident projection (see Tables 2.8 and 2.9). His only major lapse was the city of Havana, for which the bishop reported only *personas de comun* (persons having received communion)—22,828, and the number of households in Havana—6,896. What was the population of Havana? Multiplying the number of households by the average ratio of persons per household in the Havana suburbs and hinterland (7.78) one gets about 54,000—more than the city's population thirty-seven years later.[74] Using the Havana suburbs as the source for a multiplier (6.12), one gets about 42,000. This means that there were about 20,000 people too young to receive communion, which still seems a trifle high; very likely the average household size in Havana was smaller than in the countryside or the towns immediately around the city. A 1728 count showed only 21,310 for the total population of Havana, including 3,596 children (*parbulos*).[75] If this proportion between adults and children equalled the ratio between *personas de comun* and those too young for communion in 1755, the total Havana population in that year comes to only 26,632.

Table 2.9

Estimated Population of Cuba by District, 1755–1757

District	Households[a]	Reported Population	Adjusted Population (I)[b]	Adjusted Population (II)[c]	Avg. House-hold Size[d]
Havana	6,896	22,828	35,000	35,000	3.31
Havana Suburbs	600	3,671	3,671	4,589	6.12
Havana Hinterland	2,211	19,792	19,956	24,945	8.23
Western Cuba	940	7,233	7,233	9,041	7.65
Central Cuba	3,292	21,525	23,515	29,394	6.12
Puerto Príncipe	1,506	12,000	12,000	15,000	7.97
Santiago	4,696	34,034	34,034	42,543	6.84
	20,141	121,083	135,409	160,512	

Sources: Visita of Bishop Morell y Santa Cruz, AGI SD 534; AGI SD 2227.

[a]Excludes the nine communities (see Table 2.8) for which Bishop Morell included no data on number of households.

[b]Includes estimates for five communities for which Morell included no population data.

[c]Includes 20 percent for ecclesiastical underreporting (see note 77), except for Havana where the table's figure is not based on the bishop's count.

[d]Derived from raw data in 2.8; only communities for which Bishop Morell includes both population and households.

However, the 1728 figure for children probably excluded slave children, and it may also refer to a group younger than that excluded by the bishop in 1755. Admittedly Havana had a disproportionately large share of adults—people involved in servicing ships and migrants just in from the countryside—but a city with only 17 percent children seems implausible. Certainly the Havana population exceeded 26,632 in 1755–57, but it probably did not reach 42,000, a total which requires that Havana households include as many children as those in rural Cuba. A figure of 35,000 for the 1755–57 Havana population seems nearer the mark.[76]

Forty-five locales besides Havana are entered in the bishop's *visita*, and their population totals appear in Tables 2.8 and 2.9.[77] Close to a quarter of the island's population lived in Havana and its environs. More general attempts at urban-rural breakdown involve guesswork. It is unclear in the cases of Santiago de Cuba, Puerto Príncipe, and other towns just what proportion of the bishop's total lived in town or in the surrounding *partido*. Maps of Santiago de Cuba show a small town, suggesting that most of the 15,471 reported in the *visita* lived in the countryside. Levi Marrero writes that the population of Cuba in 1755–57 was predominantly urban, but he arrives at this conclusion by considering urban anyone who resided in a community of more than twenty households.[78]

Although the documents do not permit precise statements, clearly well under half of the Cuban population lived in cities. Centers such as Puerto Príncipe and Bayamo could probably be more accurately described as market towns than cities in 1755, but even if one counts them with Havana and Santiago de Cuba as cities, the proportion of urban dwellers remains lower than 47 percent. A more appropriate figure is 30 to 35 percent, considering Puerto Príncipe and Bayamo as agricultural centers and much of their reported population as rural.[79]

While the population of Cuba lived predominantly on the land, it was nonetheless arranged geographically around two major urban centers, Havana and Santiago de Cuba. Each of these ports had agricultural hinterlands, which supported ranching, sugar, tobacco, and food crops, and also contained much of the Cuban populace. Most of the western end of the island served as Havana's hinterland: its cash crops went to Havana, some of the food produced there went to Havana, and most of what the outside world provided came through Havana. Santiago de Cuba had a parallel but lesser role in the eastern end of the island. Bayamo and especially Puerto Príncipe, market towns of some size, provided for the east and center much of what Havana provided for the west. In Bayamo and Puerto Príncipe the link with the wider world was less regular even than in Santiago de Cuba. Santiago de Cuba in turn was less cosmopolitan than Havana, despite regular ties with the north coast of South America. In the eastern end of Cuba, presumably, the amenities of Europe were scarcer than in the west, and the reliance on local products, such as food, clothing, furniture, and tools more complete. Isolation was greater still in the center of the island.

Disease was the single most important factor governing both the size and distribution of population in eighteenth-century Cuba. Emigration and white immigration were almost negligible, so natural increase, strongly influenced by disease, assumed great importance. Yellow fever, which the Spaniards generally called the black vomit, probably came to the Caribbean from West Africa, where it afflicts monkeys more than human beings. It is a virus carried by the Aedes aegypti (or stegomya) mosquito. The virus requires temperatures above 16° C (60° F) to survive, and the mosquito needs temperatures above 27° C (80° F) to prosper. At 10° C (50° F) the mosquito lapses into a coma, and at freezing it dies. Thus the fever is chiefly tropical and has sharp geographical limits, though these vary with the season: yellow fever made occasional summer appearances in Philadelphia, New York, and New England in the eighteenth century. The Aedes aegypti is an eccentric: it breeds only in stagnant water and much prefers waters kept in containers with solid sides and flat bottoms, like cisterns or water casks. Thus it generally flourishes only where it can keep human company. The virus produces a violent reaction in susceptible human beings, resulting either in death, usually within five days, or in lifelong immunity. Case mortality ranges up to 80 percent.[80]

Yellow fever first appeared in Havana in 1648 and, in conjunction with a myriad of less lethal diseases, made the West Indies a most unhealthy place.[81] The British Royal Navy, which in the eighteenth century had worldwide experience, considered the West Indies the unhealthiest region of all. Yellow fever epidemics broke out in Cuba six times between 1731 and 1762.[82] The continual presence of yellow fever in Cuba meant that virtually every adult had encountered the disease as a child, and the survivors developed immunity. Those who had spent childhoods in Europe, however, had no defense against yellow fever and remained highly susceptible as adults. Yellow fever is more lethal to adults than to children, and so newcomers to places like Cuba took their lives in their hands. New arrivals to the West Indies faced roughly a 20 percent chance of dying within a year; a British garrison at Barbados reported an annual death rate of 18 percent.[83] The medical profession could do little to help. No one knew whether or not yellow fever was contagious, and no agreement existed as to treatment beyond the necessity of bleeding the patient. Thousands of Europeans, less willful and perspicacious than Smollett's Roderick Random, died from attempted cures.[84]

Yellow fever is in fact not contagious and does not depend on a large assembly of hosts for its survival. Nonetheless it plagued the town more than the country, because the Aedes aegypti was a domesticated mosquito, dependent upon water casks and cisterns, and it congregated wherever human beings gathered. Foreigners without immunities tended to go no further than the cities, which helped make yellow fever more noticeable in Havana than elsewhere.

Contagious diseases flourished in Havana, too, precisely because of the city's size. In order to survive, a contagion must find new hosts continually, and this requires large concentrations of population. From the epidemiological point of view, Havana was an extended city: in addition to the residents, pathogens might attack the contingents of sailors, soldiers, and travelers who passed through. Havana offered contagious diseases a larger number of potential hosts and more constant infusions of nonimmunized blood than did the countryside. Thus all varieties of contagion, from smallpox to typhus, ravaged Havana more often than the rural communities. Indeed the human traffic in the port of Havana ensured that the city accommodated a correspondingly large microbiotic traffic. Astride the major sea routes of the Atlantic world, Havana functioned as a clearinghouse of contagion, uniting the disease pools of Europe, Africa, and the Americas.[85] Travelers to Havana met a wide variety of contagious diseases, and if they lacked a complete portfolio of immunities they stood an excellent chance of falling ill and a good chance of dying.

Despite the high level of contact between Havana and its rural hinterland, rural communities were sufficiently isolated from one another and human concentrations sufficiently low that contagious disease could not flourish for long outside the city. The pathogen would normally kill an uninitiated host before it could be communicated to another; an infection could not sustain itself without larger numbers of susceptible hosts than the countryside could provide. So, like yellow fever, contagious diseases affected country less than town.

The differential incidence of lethal diseases between town and country created population flows in Cuba. The death rate in Havana must certainly have been significantly higher than in the countryside and probably significantly higher than the birth rate in Havana as well; left to its own devices the city would have lost population and ceased to exist. That it continued to exist, and even to grow, testifies to the size of the influx from the countryside. Havana was in effect a sinkhole for humanity. It survived only because it continually attracted newcomers, not so much from abroad, but from the *partidos* of Cuba. Since urbanites died more rapidly than they were born, Havana almost invariably needed labor, which meant Havana offered opportunity. At the same time, the countryside produced too many adults because of its comparative freedom from contagious disease. Excess rural population required out-migration of some sort to avoid a constant lowering of living standards. Some sons surviving to adulthood inherited no land; in order to make a living and to merit a bride, they had to leave their place of birth. Up to a point they could clear new land in the Cuban forest, but this was usually less attractive than going to the city. Thus a homeostasis of sorts between urban and rural Cuba had emerged by the eighteenth century. Static it was not: the populace grew, cleared new land, and founded new towns and villages. A movement toward the frontier of the forest coincided with a movement to the city. Havana survived and grew, while the forest shrank.[86]

Unlike Ile Royale, Cuba to some extent supported a peasant society: large numbers of Cubans produced their own food and met a majority of their other needs by themselves, living on the land they worked (though not necessarily owning it). In this respect, as in several others, Cuba resembled Spain more than Ile Royale resembled France. Indeed, Cuban society reflected Spanish society a good deal more than did most parts of Spanish America.

Of the social classes present in Spain, Cuba lacked only a powerful landed nobility. Titled landowners were very rare in the eighteenth century, and the only other nobles, officers in the army, represented only .0006 of the Cuban population. A landed aristocracy of sorts decorated Cuban society, ranch owners and sugarmill owners for the most part; but few of these owned large tracts, and few lived handsomely off their holdings. Since sugarmills remained fairly small-scale operations until later in the century, these persons are perhaps better described as a rural bourgeoisie (if one can overlook the paradox): they were as concerned with transport and marketing as they were with rents. In order to live well off of rents one must have, one way or another, a captive tenantry. With good land uncleared and the city beckoning, landowners without slaves faced stiff competition for population, and consequently did not flourish in eighteenth-century Cuba. Each rural landowner employed overseers, perhaps slave drivers, and sugarmasters, too. But the mass of white rural population worked as landless laborers or was self-employed. The self-employed might raise tobacco or food crops and probably very often both, because neither tobacco nor food was raised on the plantation system but on small holdings or family farms. Country towns had a laboring class, employed in building, hauling, etc., and a small class of marketeers, warehousers, retailers, and, occasionally, bureaucrats.

In Havana and Santiago de Cuba, the social scene varied more widely. Joining the laborers and the small bourgeoisie of the towns were the international merchants—people with partners in Spain or Vera Cruz or Cartagena, regular access to the wider world, a certain amount of wealth, and perhaps learning. Several of these merchants owned land as well but rarely visited it, preferring the sophistication and excitement of the city. Havana had a small professional class: army officers and bureaucrats employed by the state; lawyers, doctors, and chemists, often self-employed; ship captains, priests, and even university professors after 1728. As port towns, Havana and Santiago de Cuba supplied ships with provisions and crews with entertainment. Thus the cities included large numbers of shopkeepers, butchers, salters, tavernkeepers, wine merchants, and prostitutes. The urban laboring class naturally pursued different employments than rural workers; in Havana and Santiago de Cuba they toiled as stevedores, ditch diggers, construction workers (often employed by the state for public buildings or fortifications), carpenters, masons, fishermen, and, of course, soldiers and sailors. Cubans showed keen awareness of social rank and gradations. Social mobility was the exception to the rule; occasionally a newcomer to Havana might parlay a decade's savings into ships, warehouses, and a small fortune, or a *Habañero* (Havana native) might gain title to enough land to become a prosperous rancher or sugar planter. But for the vast majority, their station in life when born remained theirs until they died, whether or not they moved around the island.

In addition to the white society sketched above, a small but growing society of slaves existed in Cuba. By the standards of the Antilles their numbers were small. While Jamaica and Haiti counted their slaves in the hundreds of thousands, Cuba had about 5,000 in 1700 and 35,000 in 1762.[87] State slaves worked the copper mines at El Cobre and labored on the fortifications at Havana; other slaves toiled in the fields. In the mid-eighteenth century *ingenios* (sugar plantations) around Havana averaged forty-five slaves each. These slaves fed themselves from plots called *conucos*, using free time when the cane needed little attention. Some slaves worked in the tobacco *vegas*, not in gangs as with sugar, but individually or in pairs beside the *veguero* (tobacco grower) and his family. A large contingent of slaves worked as domestics in the wealthier homes of Havana and the countryside. Before 1762, Cuban slaves had little chance to develop any community because they remained too few and too isolated from one another. Some worked underground, some in the fields, others in the finest houses; all they had in common was their slavery and African descent.

Most Cuban slaves came from Jamaica, but had been born in Africa.[88] By the eighteenth century, Jamaica had emerged as the center of the Caribbean slave trade, and because the Spanish had no African stations of their own they bought from Jamaican slavers. Initially the Portuguese and then the French sold slaves to the Spanish Caribbean, but in 1713 the British won a monopoly that the South Sea Company exercised for twenty-six years. The official price was high, 300 *pesos*, the equivalent in Havana prices of 12 teams of oxen, 100 cowhides, 1,500 pounds of low-grade tobacco, or a year's wages for a common laborer.[89] A duty of 11 percent helped to encourage large-scale smuggling of slaves into Cuba, at prices between one-third and one-half the official one.[90] A system of registration and branding for legally entered slaves, designed to discourage smuggling, probably produced the reverse effect because of the fee involved. Cuba's south coast was only two days' sail from Jamaica, whereas Havana was five times as far away. For the Jamaican slaver the temptation to trade illegally on the south coast was as strong as for the Cuban to avoid paying the duty and the *indulto de negro*.

The slave trade continued because slave society in Cuba, like the city of Havana, proved a net consumer of human beings (see Chapter 6, pp. 167–70). Above and beyond the rigors of the labor they performed and the disinclination to bring children into a world such as theirs, three reasons explain the failure of the slaves to maintain their numbers. First, the majority of the Africans entered a new disease climate when they reached the Caribbean; mortality on the transatlantic voyage was severe enough, but from the microbiotic point of view the slaves' condition only worsened when they arrived in the Antilles.[91] Secondly, slave owners actively discouraged procreation among slaves; it cost less to buy a new slave than to pay for the food and clothing, however meager, of a child until it grew strong enough to work. Slave owners preferred that children be raised in West Africa at no cost to themselves, leaving them only the cost of the finished product, as they viewed it.[92] Lastly, a gross imbalance between the sexes inhibited reproduction; in the canefields, at least, 89 percent of Cuban slaves were male.[93]

On the whole, the island of Cuba in the eighteenth century possessed resources far superior to those of Cape Breton. While both islands enjoyed an advantageous location for trade, Cuba had good soil and a large population, which Cape Breton did not. Cape Breton had the fishery, which produced an export crop just as reliably as did the Cuban soil; Cape Breton, however, could not feed a large population in addition to producing a cash crop, which Cuba could. The climate of Cuba was gentle, but not its disease climate; Cape Breton's climate was harsh, but it was a far healthier place.[94] Mineral resources were nearly negligible in both places, but Cuba offered a magnificent forest in comparison to Cape Breton's. Cuba's harbors were better and more numerous, its winds more reliable, and its coastal (but not interior) communications easier, if only because Cuba's hurricane season was shorter than the ice season in Cape Breton. Cuba had a larger population with more variegated skills and experience than Cape Breton, although by midcentury, population densities in the two islands were roughly equal.[95] Economic opportunities in Cuba were greater than those in Cape Breton, but the strategic advantages of each were roughly similar.

Local conditions form colonial history only in partnership with imperial policy, so before examining the economic and military records of Cape Breton and Cuba we must consider the contexts of metropolitan policy. Thus we turn to the economic ideas and the oceanic navies of Bourbon imperialism in the next chapter.

3 European Navies and Seaborne Empires

The limited resources of the Cape Breton and Cuban hinterlands constrained the imperial roles of Louisbourg and Havana somewhat, but the weakness of the French and Spanish navies proved even more restrictive. Given their locations, both ports might have played critical roles in the contest for Atlantic empire, which climaxed in the eighteenth century. In fact they played local defensive roles, helping to minimize British seizures of imperial trade. The failure of the French and Spanish to profit from the strategic positions of Louisbourg and Havana proceeded directly from the traditional—rather than imperial—approaches of their navies. The failure to challenge the British at sea hinged on the size of the Bourbon navies, which in turn rested on their inability to recruit adequate amounts of money, men, and mast timber. Commercial inferiority (to the Dutch) produced in France and Spain a defensive strategy designed to preserve and expand the profits of empire: mercantilism. Naval inferiority (to the British) in the eighteenth century produced a stubborn reliance on traditional wisdom, appropriate to their resources but inadequate for the extensive tasks which mercantilist strategy required of navies.

Rather like barbarians, mercantilism has had the misfortune to be historicized by its avowed enemies. As a result it has been maligned and misunderstood, and subsequent efforts to redeem its reputation have only added to the confusion. Mercantilism has become a small quagmire for economic historians.

What precisely was mercantilism? It was neither theory nor policy, but rather an agglomeration of ideas concerning the means and ends of state policy. First among them was the notion that trade and production were proper concerns of the state: a belief in the justice and efficacy of interventionist policies underlay all mercantilist thought. Further, the state ought to regulate trade (and perhaps production) so as to create an excess of exports over imports, producing a net influx of specie. The amount of bullion in a state corresponded to its wealth, and the net flow of bullion indicated the state's economic health. Since a positive trade balance led to national wealth, the competition for export markets grew fierce. Trade, according to Colbert, was perpetual combat. This approach to economic policy hinged on the belief—undisputed until the late eighteenth century—that the world's trade amounted to a fixed quantity, so that enlarging one's own share necessarily meant diminishing someone else's. In this context, enterprises such as the cod fishery of the north Atlantic acquired the utmost importance because they ensured a regular bullion influx. To avoid substantial bullion exodus through a negative balance of trade, European states maintained colonial empires to provide products which the mother country could not produce. Thus, for instance, each European state wanted its own Caribbean sugar islands in order to avoid large sugar imports. From this evolved the prevailing mercantilist conception of the relationship between colonies and metropoles. Colonies had but one major purpose: to satisfy demand for articles that would otherwise endanger the balance of trade. Secondly, colonies served as markets for metropolitan manufactures. The relationship was one of master and servant, and the metropole expected to direct the economic life of its colonies to the fullest extent possible, with the aim of improving its trade balance (and in some cases its strategic security). Thus colonies must not import goods from foreigners, but only from the mother country.

These ideas constitute the core of mercantilist thought. Certain countries emphasized different aspects of this corpus of ideas, so that mercantilism varied from one country to the next. The French and British, for instance, stressed the production of manufactures as a means to higher exports, whereas the Portuguese preferred to concentrate on trade alone. National differences, however, did not overshadow a basic consensus in the economic thought of Western Europe in the seventeenth century.[1]

Generally speaking, modern liberal writers have seen mercantilism as a set of misguided principles which inhibit trade and prosperity. So thought Adam Smith, who coined the phrase "mercantile system," and so thought Eli Heckscher whose ponderous treatise remains the most thorough study of the subject.[2] When judged by liberal standards, mercantilism is invariably found wanting; mercantilist concern with trade balances, for instance, struck liberals as a "puerile obsession."[3] It is no surprise, therefore, that the first attempt to vindicate mercantilism came from thinkers who rejected the premises of liberal economics.

Prussian economic nationalists of the nineteenth century admired mercantilism not as a commercial system but rather as a system of power or state building. Indeed they considered the mercantilism of maritime nations corrupt insofar as it emphasized the use of power to achieve wealth, for they felt the proper formula—proper to Germany of their day—emphasized the use of wealth to achieve national power. Their ideas, which were very shortly translated to the English context, have greatly complicated the meaning of the word mercantilism, attaching to it much more than Adam Smith had ever meant by his phrase "mercantile system."[4]

Ignoring the state-building aspects of Prussian *merkantilismus*, the problem of mercantilism in European history becomes less intractable. In some form it had informed the policy of the Venetian, Genoese, and Portuguese empires. Mercantilist ideas found their fullest expression in Spanish policy designed to monopolize the wealth of the Indies, and mercantilism dominated economic thought throughout the maritime states of Western Europe from the seventeenth century. There was one partial exception: the Dutch generally abandoned mercantilist precepts, because, except in the East Indies, exclusionary practices did not benefit them. Their imperial holdings were few and much of their prosperity came from organizing and carrying the colonial trade of other states: in the late seventeenth century Dutch shipping amounted to 568,000 tons, well over the combined total of the rest of western Europe.[5] Indeed, mercantilist legislation in the rest of maritime Europe had among its intentions the elimination of Dutch competition. The English Navigation Acts of the seventeenth century and much of Colbert's legislation in France (1665–83) explicitly aimed to appropriate trade which the Dutch were carrying.[6]

Aside from the exclusion of the Dutch, mercantilism arose from two other motives. The first was a desire to avoid the fate of imperial Spain, whose manifest decline Europeans attributed to the failure to retain the treasure of the Indies. The second motive, probably the more compelling of the two, concerns one of the most controversial aspects of mercantilism: the relationship between power and wealth as objectives of mercantilism. By the seventeenth century warfare in Europe had become the specialty of expensive professionals.[7] Success in war required professionalization and professionalization required a steady source of money with which to supply and pay an army. Warriors became uncontrollable when not paid: they forcibly extracted what they wanted from the local citizenry. Rulers much preferred to routinize this process by paying for professionals in both peace and war, but this required ready money. So rulers had to expand state revenues; they found it desirable to foment taxable trade and industry. Among the approved methods of fomenting trade was the accumulation of bullion, which encouraged exchange in an era when credit facilities, especially outside of England and Holland, remained modest. Although by 1700 bills of exchange had found wide acceptance in most parts of western Europe, merchants still complained of a dearth of coin well into the eighteenth century. Some markets, such as the Russian and East Indies, still accepted little but bullion. And when war threatened—a routine occurrence in the seventeenth and eighteenth centuries—the bills of exchange, which in peacetime greased the wheels of commerce, became less acceptable. Dutch willingness to expend as well as amass bullion helped to make them masters in the Baltic and East Indies markets, giving other states all the more reason to hoard treasure: by keeping silver from the Dutch they handicapped the trades that nourished the Netherlands. Seen in this light, the puerile obsession of mercantilists made good sense, especially in the seventeenth century.[8] Wealth, at least in the early stages of mercantilism, was a means to power but also a means to freedom from the pestilential ravages of uncontrolled armed men; and the accumulation of bullion genuinely helped the state to expand revenues.

By the eighteenth century, when regular pay, supply, and drill had largely disciplined western European armies, this consideration lost importance, and the question of wealth versus power as means or ends of mercantilism arises once more. No satisfactory answer exists, however, because emphasis differed between nations and over time. The men of the time scarcely distinguished between power and plenty as goals or policy: just as the difference between warships and merchant ships evolved only in the late seventeenth century, so with the goals of state economic policy in the eighteenth. As late as 1750 wealth and power seemed indivisible to European statesmen, and mercantilist ideas supported the identification of one with the other.[9]

To what extent did French and Spanish decision makers of the eighteenth century accept the guiding principles of mercantilism? French and Spanish economic thought offered no systematic alternative until the physiocracy of the 1760s and 1770s. French writers on the whole defended the example of Colbert: their writings were apologia for existing policy, although they might include suggestions for minor revisions on particular points. Sebastien le Prestre, seigneur de Vauban, whose *Projet d'une Dixme royale* appeared in 1707, and Dutôt, whose *Réflexions politiques sur les finances et le commerce* appeared in 1738, exemplified this pattern. Colbertism had its critics—often landowners like Pierre le Pesant de Boisguilbert—but they confined their objections to particular aspects of French practice. Although the first murmurings of physiocracy became audible early in the eighteenth century, mercantilist ideas remained dominant in French economic thought until the 1760s, especially in the work of François Véron de Forbonnais. As the century wore on, mercantilism acquired more and more critics, who added more and more caveats, exceptions, and special cases, but not until late in the century did systematic new ideas, later to crystallize into classical economics, replace mercantilism. The tenacity of mercantilist ideas in eighteenth-century France owed much to the disastrous failure of John Law's schemes (1718–21), which retarded the development of faith in credit, banking, paper money, and encouraged bullionism and mercantilist trade balance theory.[10]

Bullionism was the only consistent feature of Spanish economic thought before the eighteenth century. The Indies were seen as a source of gold and silver more than as a trading partner, and the problem of retaining the bullion of the Indies occupied most Spanish economic thinkers before 1720.[11] The collapse of Spanish trade in the War of the Spanish Succession (1701–13) and the humiliating commercial terms of the subsequent peace, however, provoked a spirit of Spanish economic nationalism: a rather crude bullionism blossomed into a fuller mercantilism based on northern European practice. The theoretical objections to mercantilism voiced in eighteenth-century northern Europe filtered through the Pyrenees only slowly. The first consequential Spanish political economist of the eighteenth century, Gerónimo de Uztáriz, distilled wide reading of foreign authors and years of administrative experience into the first coherent and systematic treatment of the problems of the Spanish economy: his *Theórica y práctica de comercio y de marina* first appeared in 1724; English and French editions came out in the 1750s. Uztáriz explicitly admired the practice of Colbert and counseled attention to industries as well as trade in creating a positive trade balance.[12] The same mercantilist principles inform the work of José de Campillo y Cosio (1693–1743)[13] and other luminaries of Spanish economic thought.[14] Emphases and details varied among writers (particularly concerning the efficacy of chartered companies), but all accepted the basic tenets of mercantilism.

French and Spanish economic thought may have offered no plausible alternative to mercantilist orthodoxy, but did Bourbon decision makers adhere to prevailing ideas in making policy? In France policy largely preceded theoretical justifications: mercantilist practice had existed from the time of Cardinal Richelieu (1624–42). As in England, economic literature bore a close relationship to policy.[15] Colonial and naval affairs were entrusted to the Conseil de la Marine (1715–23) during the minority of Louis XV; from 1723 on a minister of the marine oversaw those areas to which mercantilist precepts principally applied. In the eighteenth century the minister of marine always lacked the decisive power which Colbert had enjoyed; other ministers held greater power in the French government. Thus the latitude within which ministers might make policy was narrower after Colbert; indeed the prestige which accompanied his legacy made departure from tradition (as defined by Colbert's practice) extremely difficult. There is little to suggest, however, that any of Colbert's successors wished to restructure policy.

Jean-Frédéric Phélypaux, comte de Pontchartrain et Maurepas (1701–81), headed the ministry of marine from 1723 to 1749.[16] His father and grandfather had held the same position under Louis XIV. Maurepas proved an able and energetic administrator, and he might well have spent another two decades as minister had he not offended the King's favorite, Madame de Pompadour, with an unflattering rhymed couplet in 1749. His letters, his memoranda, and his *Mémoires* all indicate an undying allegiance to the practice of Colbert and the ideas of contemporary political economists. His faith in bullion was a strong reaction against John Law's projects for French trade and finance, the aftermath of which Maurepas confronted upon accession to office.[17] His thoughts on commerce echoed Colbert's precisely: "Commerce is the source of a state's happiness, power and wealth. . . . Wealth and power are the true interests of a nation, and nothing but commerce can procure them both."[18] In tone and substance Maurepas remained a mercantilist in the seventeenth-century tradition. His thought, even late in life, showed no signs of infiltration by rival schools of political economy.

Maurepas's successors imitated his example as thoroughly as he had followed Colbert's. None of them had much chance to redirect French policy even had they wished to, since six men filled the office between 1749 and 1761.[19]

In the French system of administration, the minister of marine was fully responsible for imperial policy. No other institutions—except for charter companies, which had diminished in importance by the eighteenth century—shared this duty. In wartime higher authorities might call upon the navy to cooperate in some general strategy, but normally the marine was left to itself. Louis XV had no interest at all in maritime matters.[20]

The legacy of Colbert influenced the French naval and colonial administration from top to bottom, but especially at the top. Anyone in a position of power owed his rank in part to the Colbertist orthodoxy of his views. Marcantilism's emphasis on naval power naturally appealed to anyone with a navy career, so for purely selfish reasons the bureaucracy of the French marine enthusiastically espoused traditional mercantilist ideas. Colbert and his apologists guided Maurepas, and Maurepas guided French imperial policy.

No single figure dominated Spanish imperial policy in the early eighteenth century the way Maurepas did French policy. Rather, three men, all of whom rose from the ranks of the naval bureaucracy, left their imprint on Spanish policy. Despite their shorter tenures in office, each had a better opportunity than Maurepas to shape naval and imperial policy, since all three held several ministerial posts at once. José Patiño (1666–1736), a former Jesuit, became Intendant of the navy in 1717 and

Minister in 1726.[21] He was also Minister of War, of Finance, and Minister for the Indies until his death. For ten years Patiño held full responsibility for Spanish imperial policy, and he showed enduring loyalty to traditional mercantilist principles. His ideas about colonies and trade appear to coincide remarkably with those of his contemporary, Uztáriz, Secretary of the Council of the Indies in the 1720s, and occasional employee of the naval, war, and finance ministries—precisely those headed by Patiño. José Campillo y Cosio succeeded Patiño as the guiding spirit behind Spanish imperial policy. Campillo dominated the Admiralty (1736–41), which formally directed the navy after Patiño's death, and became minister in 1741. He additionally held the war and Indies ministries. Campillo believed fervently in the efficacy of mercantilist programs; most of his writings argue that Spanish practice must simply follow established ideas in order for the empire to function smoothly and profitably; he was a fundamentalist reformer. Campillo's death in 1743 allowed the rise of Zenón de Somodevilla, Marqués de Ensenada (1702–81).[22] Ensenada held the naval, war, Indies, and finance ministries until 1754, when he lost favor with the King. For eleven years he directed Spanish policy, showing great talent in administration and no originality whatsoever in his ideas—exactly the combination which allowed a man to rise to the top in the Spanish (or French) administration.

These three men—Patiño, Campillo, and Ensenada—all subscribed entirely to the central principles of mercantilism. They each made their careers in a bureaucracy that endorsed these principles, and their success in rising depended, as in the French navy, on their loyalty to the old ideas to which Uztáriz had recently given new expression. The other ministries involved in making imperial policy—Indies and finance—and the other institutions responsible for the empire and trade (the Council of the Indies and the Casa de Contratación) had less entrenched self-interest in mercantilist ideas. Nonetheless the weight of tradition, bureaucratic inertia, and the power of men like Patiño, Campillo, and Ensenada ensured that these organizations never seriously questioned the ideas of the day. The only major conflict was in the finance ministry, where the short-term need for revenue encouraged high taxation, deleterious to the imperial trade on which the long-term wealth and power of the kingdom partly rested. Mercantilists objected to high taxation, but when charged with responsibility for the royal treasury found they had to bow to expediency.[23]

France and Spain defined imperial success in almost precisely the same way. Those entrusted with making imperial policy scarcely questioned the wisdom of Colbert and his interpreters. Translating general principles into specific legislation and directives to colonial administrators, however, proved a daunting task: the power of special interests often required particularistic legislation; private capital (especially in Spain) often balked at state initiatives; and short-term fiscal needs often vitiated long-term goals. More daunting still was the matter of seeing that mercantilist decisions actually produced the desired effects in the colonies, and here French and Spanish policy diverged significantly.

At times mercantilism seemed more ambition than policy. No problem of colonial administration was more vexing than implementing radical mercantilist change, because colonial bureaucracies proved especially adept at blunting the edge of metropolitan initiative. When, for instance, the Spanish tried to recast Cuban agriculture (a matter taken up more fully in chapters 5 and 6), they created the Havana Company as their agent for vigorous intervention, rather than use the existing imperial bureaucracy.

Certainly they hoped to involve private capital in state projects, but they may have had a more compelling reason for employing a monopoly company. Spanish imperial bureaucrats habitually ignored metropolitan instructions, or more accurately, used their discretion in choosing between contradictory standards and ambiguous goals, the source of the "chasm between law and observance in the Spanish Empire."[24] With two and a half centuries of particularist legislation, imperial bureaucrats could not possibly obey all standards and observe all laws. This system had its advantages, but it jeopardized state projects because the local governor might well choose to ignore difficult instructions and could justify his conduct by pointing to others. By 1740, Campillo felt this independence of local bureaucrats deprived Madrid of adequate control over the Spanish empire, and he proposed a new system of bureaucracy modeled on the French Intendancies to cope with the problem.[25] By creating the Havana Company, the Crown created an alternative bureaucracy and avoided a host of potential delays and disagreements with local officials in Cuba. The instructions to the Havana Company were unambiguous and no accumulation of prior legislation complicated the Company's mission. Furthermore, Havana Company personnel, unaccustomed to the ways of the imperial bureaucracy, were less inclined to behave uncooperatively even when it suited them. The ambiguity and conflicting standards of the bureaucracy may indeed have given "subordinates a voice in decision-making without jeopardizing the control of their superiors over the whole system,"[26] but because local bureaucrats often bowed to local pressures, this system handicapped royal attempts to force radical changes upon a colony.

The French system of administration at Louisbourg also allowed a measure of flexibility for local officials. The respective spheres of the governor and the *commissaire-ordonnateur* never received precise definition, which permitted the French to issue conflicting instructions when they wished to avoid making clear decisions. In effect they could abdicate authority to the men on the spot when it suited them, but without creating inconvenient precedents. In this way the French could, for example, maintain that trade with New England violated the law, yet indirectly encourage the *commissaire-ordonnateur* to overlook useful breaches of mercantilist legislation. Had the French wished to make radical changes in the colony, such as diversifying the economy, they would have found the ossified Old Régime bureaucratic system ill-suited to the task, and they might have resorted to a substitute—a monopoly company—in which subordinates enjoyed much less latitude in executing policy. But the French never wished to recast Ile Royale as the Spanish did Cuba and so remained satisfied with the structural ambiguity and inertia of their bureaucracy.

Although it hamstrung attempts at radical change in the colonies, the structural ambiguity of Bourbon bureaucracies served an important purpose. Delegation of authority to men on the spot was absolutely essential, considering the limited degree to which European ministers understood colonial realities. And any situation which promised to change at faster than a snail's pace required independent action from local officials: recourse to Europe for instructions would take too long.

This ambiguity contributed in turn to the metropolitan ignorance of colonial realities, producing a vicious circle. Ministers relied for information on precisely the same bureaucrats to whom they entrusted their ambiguous instructions. These bureaucrats had to justify their conduct to their superiors, which naturally influenced their reporting on colonial conditions and events. Since men on the spot had to make decisions rather than merely carry out instructions, they had an interest in controlling the information available to metropolitan authorities who would pass judgment on their careers. Paris and Madrid retained the authority to make all the important decisions, but they did so on the basis of information provided by local bureaucrats. This information, precisely because the local bureaucrats enjoyed a measure of responsibility, was often contradictory or simply inaccurate. So metropolitan decisions often arose from ignorance and misinformation about the colonies.

Had French and Spanish patterns of imperial administration delegated less authority to men on the spot, Paris and Madrid would have had more reliable accounts of colonial conditions on which to base policy. In general this system of ambiguity allowed informed small-scale and short-term decisions, since local officials made these. (They might, however, find it preferable and possible to make these decisions in their own interest rather than in that of the metropolitan economy.) More important and far-reaching decisions made in Paris and Madrid rested on lesser understanding. This, perhaps, helps explain the French and Spanish stubborn devotion to impractical forms of mercantilist policy in the American colonies: aware that their grasp of colonial realities left much to be desired, ministers relied on venerated tradition as a guide. All the institutionalized checks upon local bureaucrats—especially common in the Spanish system—could not ensure the provision of reliable information to metropolitan authorities. Indeed, additional informants only added to the confusion of contradictory reporting on colonial conditions.

The character of Bourbon imperial bureaucracies was well suited for management of routine affairs. But their character precluded the option of radical change. Their existence ensured an overriding conservatism, true perhaps of all bureaucracies, but especially so of these. A man in Maurepas's position knew he could do little to narrow the gap between theory and practice in the conduct of colonial affairs, so, rather than waste energy making enemies, he refrained altogether. And if ministers responsible for colonial affairs found it unrewarding to take strong initiatives, it comes as no surprise that monarchs and their advisers should have taken little interest in recasting colonial policy. They, too, felt no compulsion to depart from mercantilist traditions.

No mercantilist doubted that commerce and sea power were "two inseparable companions."[27] The union of the intendancy of the navy and the presidency of the Casa de Contratación in 1717 shows how thoroughly the Spanish recognized the affinity between naval and commercial affairs: in this case at least, administrative practice followed theory.[28] Both Bourbon powers understood the value of a powerful navy, but neither could devote resources to the development of sea power with the single-mindedness of their principal enemy: Great Britain. Britain's insularity made it clear to all that security rested with the navy, but in France and Spain geography and dynastic ambitions complicated matters. French policy always gave high priority to the army and defense by land. Systems of fortification and diplomacy reflected this priority; the eastern and northern frontiers enjoyed first claim on the crown's resources. After 1714, the first claim on Spanish resources belonged to royal projects in Italy. Upon the death of his first wife, Felipe V had married an ambitious Italian, Elizabeth Farnese, who hoped to see her sons ensconced on Italian thrones. After the Wars of the Polish Succession (1733–35) and the Austrian Succession (1740–48), Spanish ambitions triumphed over Austrian claims; the Kingdom of the Two Sicilies was born, and the duchies of Parma and Piacenza became Bourbon heirlooms.[29] The projection of Spanish power in Italy required a navy, as did the commerce with the Indies through which Cardinal Giulio Alberoni expected to raise the needed revenue for Italian wars.[30] No policy that mattered to the French Crown necessitated a navy, and landward defense was so costly that the French could hardly afford one. Social and political structures in both France and Spain assured that representation of maritime interests was haphazard.

European states needed navies to profit fully from their overseas empires through trade, but the general expansion in colonial trade in the eighteenth century made it more difficult to protect the fruits of empire. The British responded to this development by using the navy to guard certain strategic points by which trade necessarily passed—straits, capes—rather than by convoying merchant ships. They aimed to control well-chosen spaces instead of objects. The limited resources of the Bourbon navies prohibited their challenging the British, but by pursuing traditional naval policy and protecting trading ships they could not possibly safeguard more than a small fraction of the growing number of merchant vessels. The French and Spanish dealt with this problem in much the same way, maintaining navies large enough to concern the British but too small to defeat them. Traditional methods served the Bourbons well enough to preserve their imperial holdings until the Seven Years' War (1756–63), but did not allow them to check the British rise to commercial and naval dominance of the Atlantic world.

European navies of the eighteenth century consisted of ships, sailors, and bureaucrats, all supported by the budget of a naval ministry (or intendancy). Naval power depended for the most part on numbers of ships, which in turn depended on the size of budgets. Other variables, such as ship technology and personnel, mattered much less, since after centuries of competition few differences lingered in the relative skill levels of shipwrights, craftsmen, sailors, and gunners.[31] Ordinarily navies divided their ships of the line into five rates, a system of classification based on the numbers and size of cannon each ship carried.

First-rates carried more than 100 cannon, arranged in three tiers, the lowest standing at least 1.5 meters above the waterline. These vessels saw little action in the eighteenth century because the French and Spanish declined to risk first-rates and so the British rarely needed theirs.[32] Second-rates carried upwards of eighty guns and likewise spent most of their careers in port. Third-rates featured only two tiers, with between seventy and eighty guns. These vessels offered greater maneuverability and versatility, accounting for their popularity in most western European navies. An eighteenth-century ship of the line could sail as close as six points from the wind (i.e., within 67.5 degrees of an oncoming wind). Sailing before the wind a French seventy-four-gun ship could attain a speed of 30 percent of the wind velocity up to a maximum of five knots.

In the mid-eighteenth century a French first-rate measured close to 55 meters (170 to 180 feet) in length, almost 16 meters (50 feet) in width, and drew 8 meters (25 feet) of water. The height of the mast equalled two and one-half times a ship's width: about 40 meters (130 feet) in the case of a first-rate. French ships grew in the course of the century; in the late seventeenth century a first-rate measured about 1,500 tons, and by 1750 it might be as large as 3,000 tons. By 1780 a French third-rate seventy-four-gun ship measured 171 feet from stem to stern, the size of a first-rate a generation before.[33]

Spanish ship dimensions betray a general confusion on the part of those in charge of the Spanish navy. No fewer than five systems of proportions were used between 1722 and 1797, and since many warships were built in private yards or purchased abroad the recommended dimensions did not always apply. According to the regulations of 1720, fourth-rates should measure 990 tons; but the *San Fernando*, built in 1727 with sixty-four guns, measured 1,559 tons. The examples of Spanish naval architecture given in Table 3.1 show the inconsistency among ships and the variance between official guidelines and eventual realities. Spanish ships appear to have become longer than French ones of equal armament, at least after 1748. Comparisons are risky, however, because the Spanish generally measured overall length from stem to stern at the level of the first deck (*eslora*), while French lengths might be taken at the waterline, the level of the first deck, or most often, the first battery. Most records do not indicate what is meant by length.[34] Despite official confusion, Spanish and specially recruited English shipwrights regularly built smooth and fast sailers. Their numerous treatises on their craft probably had less to do with this than did astute imitation of foreign examples.[35]

French and Spanish ship dimensions bore strong similarities to one another when compared to the British. Ships of the Royal Navy mounted 50 percent more guns per ton than those in either Bourbon navy, and 18

Table 3.1

Spanish Ship Dimensions, 1727–1755

Ship	Year Launched	Rate	Guns	Prescribed Tonnage in 1720	Tons	Length in feet
San Fernando	1727	4	64	990	1,559	191
Fénix	1749	2	80	1,534	1,889	198
Galicia	1750	3	74	1,095	1,651	185
Oriente	1753	3	74	1,095	1,661	187
Conquistador	1755	4	64	990	1,372	178

Source: Fernández Duro, *Disquiciones náuticas*. 5:206. Uztáriz, *Theory*, p. 240.

to 20 percent more men per gun.[36] Their heavier armament made British ships, especially the larger ones, slow sailers and difficult to maneuver.[37] The French and Spanish could carry larger guns, meaning that British seventy-gun vessels were "little superior to their [Spanish] ships of fifty-two guns."[38] Rough seas often rendered the lowermost tier of cannon useless on British ships, obliging them to fight with fewer and smaller cannon than their enemy. Throughout the eighteenth century, British ships carried fewer and fewer guns per ton: the ships became longer. They remained, however, less seaworthy than their French and Spanish counterparts.[39] British captains always showed great eagerness to command captured vessels rather than those built in England.[40]

The explanation for these differences in ship design lay in the varying power of the bureaucratic regulations governing the navies of Britain, France, and Spain. In France the ministers of marine observed no set rules, but supported the application of mathematics to ship design and encouraged experimentation.[41] The Spanish, despite their multitude of regulations, discarded official guidelines freely, experimenting and imitating French improvements.[42] In Britain, however, the Admiralty instituted the Establishments, ordaining ship dimensions, and while these two were subject to change, they constituted a powerful deterrent to experimentation. The Establishments dated from the Dutch wars of the seventeenth century in which a successful ship did not need to fight in foul weather: British vessels remained ill-suited to the open sea until well into the eighteenth century.[43] British shipwrights working in Cantabrian yards, however, often developed the best Spanish designs. When free from the guidance of the Navy Board, British builders proved the equals of the French and Spanish.[44] The British relied on tradition and experience in shipbuilding although British captains knew this resulted in ships far inferior to the French and Spanish. The most plausible explanation for the bureaucratic conservatism that slowed the improvement of British ship design is financial: by standardizing ship dimensions, requiring adherence to standards, and changing standards only slowly, the British navy lowered the costs of refitting and maintaining its vessels. If ships consisted of virtually interchangeable parts, the task of finding suitably shaped and sized replacements proceeded much more smoothly. In a large navy such as Britain's, economies of scale resulting from standardization held a strong attraction for the Navy Board and Parliament;

in a navy the size of the French or Spanish, the savings proceeding from standardization would have come to much less—indeed perhaps too little to justify inferior ships and the overhead costs of additional bureaucratization.[45]

Like the vessels themselves, shipbuilding costs varied only slightly between nations. In the 1720s, British costs came to about 5 to 10 percent more than French for ships of fifty to seventy guns. The Dutch built more cheaply than the French, and the Genoese more cheaply still, but their ships did not equal the French or British in navigability or armament. Spanish costs ran highest of all, 30 percent above the British.[46]

Besides ships of the line, eighteenth-century navies employed several varieties of lesser vessels. Ships of the fifth-rate and smaller craft served as the eyes and ears of deep-water fleets. These smaller craft included two-masted brigantines, between 70 and 100 tons; and frigates, or fast single-decked ships carrying between twenty-four and thirty-two guns.[47] Frigates displaced about 300 tons. Their suitability for privateering made them common in waters around both Cape Breton Island and Cuba. In addition, both the French and Spanish navies used galleys as coastal craft until midcentury, and a host of still smaller vessels which went by different names in different countries.[48] Such were the ships that made up the navies of western Europe in the eighteenth century. Other things being almost equal, numbers of ships determined the outcome of most battles, and the size of navies determined the outcome of most naval wars.

In the seventeenth century the French had built the most imposing navy Europe had ever seen. At its height it included 105 ships of the line, 358 vessels in all and 23,000 men.[49] Colbert built this navy for Louis XIV, who hoped to invade England with it. Although Colbert's navy successfully secured the West Indies trade for France at Dutch expense, control of the English Channel proved elusive. After the battle of La Hogue (1692), Louis XIV became disenchanted with the battle fleet conception of a navy and reversed French policy. He cut the budget by 70 percent, and the navy, which had cost 301 million livres to build (1662–90), began to wither.[50] It reached its nadir under the regency of Louis XV (1715–23) when administered by the Conseil de la Marine. In

Table 3.2

Estimates of the Average Annual Expenditure of the French Crown
and French Navy, 1690–1759 (in million livres)

Year	Navy			Crown
	I	II	III	IV
1690–94	27.22	25.58	30.08	166.7
1695–99	17.64	14.12	18.88	242.0
1700–04	20.92	18.40	21.96	151.7
1705–09	17.72	16.48	19.56	225.5
1710–14	11.86	7.33	11.40	231.1
1715–19	—	5.98	11.40	—
1720–24	—	8.62	11.40	—
1725–29	—	7.99	11.40	—
1730–34	—	9.90	11.40	183.0 (1730 only)
1735–39	—	9.20	11.40	206.6 (1735 only)
1740–44	—	17.90	14.80	197.6 (1740 only)
1745–49	—	20.90	19.30	275.6 (1745 only)
1750–54	—	16.20	18.76	220.0 (1750 only)
1755–59	—	42.00	41.92	189.7 (1755 only)
				412.9 (1760 only)
				297.9 (1765 only)

Sources: I. MPCU, Lot 38, Item 5.037.
II. BN Nouvelles acquisitions françaises, 5399.
III. Neuville, *Etat sommaire*, pp. 610–11.
IV. Guéry, "Les finances de la monarchie française," pp. 237, 239.

1723, when Maurepas assumed control of the naval ministry, the number
of ships of the line had dwindled to thirty, and the budget stood at
9 million livres (See Tables 3.2 and 3.3).[51] In subsequent decades,
Maurepas expanded the navy slightly by borrowing funds and by con-
vincing the King (and his finance ministers) that the navy needed a larger
appropriation. At the outbreak of the War of the Austrian Succession, the
French navy numbered forty-five ships of the line, less than half its 1692
size. At any given time, a proportion of these ships of the line, perhaps 12
to 25 percent, was unfit for duty. Neglect and old age accounted for more

Table 3.3

Ships of the Line in the French
Navy, 1690–1758

Year	Ships	Year	Ships
1690	105	1744	45
1700	120	1745	46
1715	66	1747	31
1720	30	1751	57
1725	43	1754	63
1729	45	1755	63
1730	45	1756	63
1732	45	1758	77
1739	45		

Sources: Maurepas's 1745 Mémoire. *MPCU*, Lot
38, Item 5.040, 5.036; Lot 42, Item 6.052; Lot
48, Item 9.087; Lot 45, Item 9.022. Tramond,
Manuel d'histoire maritime, p. 378. Mahan, *Sea
Power*, pp. 74–75, 259, 291, 312. Chabaud-
Arnault, "Etudes," p. 53. Nicolas, *Puissance
navale*, pp. 242, 243. Chassériau, *Précis historique*,
1:643. Charnock, *Naval Architecture*, 3:114,
177.

than damage sustained in battle.[52] Others were deemed serviceable but in
need of repair.

Through the period between the Wars of the Spanish and Austrian
Succession, the French naval budget remained fairly stable, and thus so
did the number of ships France could put to sea. The midcentury war
inspired a sharp expansion of naval spending, which allowed France to
build ships slightly more rapidly than they were lost: between 1741 and
1746, twenty-five ships were built or refurbished and two were seized
from the enemy; meanwhile nineteen were rendered out of service and
seven seized by the enemy—thus the first five years of war saw a net gain
of one ship of the line.[53] The French trimmed the naval budget again after
the peace of 1748, but not as sharply as in the 1690s. Expansion continued in these peacetime years so that by 1756 the French had accumulated sixty-three ships of the line, though only forty-five were in good

condition, hardly enough to contest mastery of North Atlantic or Caribbean sea lanes with Britain.[54] The close correlation between the naval budget and the number of ships of the line demonstrates that lack of funds posed the principal problem of the French navy in the eighteenth century.[55]

The French navy competed yearly with other ministries for appropriations because its budget was divided into two parts, a regular allotment called *ordinaire* and a fluctuating one called *extraordinaire*. The latter amounted to zero except when the international situation appeared even more desperate than royal finances. The size of the ordinary budget limited the French navy to no more than fifty ships of the line. Construction could just keep pace with obsolescence. After salaries, wages, and other fixed costs had been met, only about two million livres remained. After maintenance costs—up to 15,000 livres annually on large vessels—only 667,000 livres remained, so less than 7 percent of the budget went to construction.[56] As Maurepas's administration of the navy progressed, this percentage shrank, since outfitting costs doubled between 1726 and 1744, eliminating the possibility of expanding the navy.[57] Under the best of circumstances the French could build three ships annually. Since a good ship lasted twenty years, the French navy could conceivably have grown within its budget to number sixty ships of the line. Louis XV ordained that France should maintain fifty-four, but even this proved beyond the means of his naval ministers.[58]

This slender budget—one-eighth of the French army's budget and less than 9 percent of royal revenues—resulted in part from a British alliance which led French finance ministers to believe that the navy could safely atrophy. The relative sizes of the army and navy budgets reflected French political arrangements. Although merchants from Bayonne to Dunkirk would have gladly welcomed greater expenditure on the navy, the nobility for the most part preferred to see public money spent on the army—protecting land, not trade, and providing more suitable careers. To build a fleet the size of the Royal Navy, France would have had to reduce her army by more than 25 percent, a truncation hard to justify in light of traditional enemies to the east and north. Even had such a realignment of military expenditure proved politically feasible, the imagined advantages would have evaporated: the British would inevitably counter a French naval buildup with one of their own.[59] The landward threat to

France always received higher priority in budgetary decisions; the disaster of La Hogue and the advent of Cardinal Fleury's English policy merely exaggerated the precedence of the army over the navy.

The French crown understood that war with Britain required additional naval expense—thus the *extraordinaire* allotments. Louis XV wanted a navy during wartime without paying for one during peacetime, but this proved hard to achieve. It was difficult to conjure up ships and sailors on short notice and impossible to find the additional funds quickly, obliging the French navy to borrow heavily in the wars of 1740–48 and 1756–63.[60] Even this expedient proved awkward, since the failure of John Law's schemes in 1718–21 had ruined centralized credit in France. Whereas the British Admiralty could rely upon the Bank of England to help equip a fleet rapidly, the French navy depended more upon Crown appropriations because loans were difficult to arrange. Since appropriations came more slowly and more sparsely than loans, the French navy was always at a disadvantage in the wars of the eighteenth century. (Spain had no central bank either, but the Spanish better resisted the temptation to let the navy run down in peacetime, and so they did not face the same emergency upon the outbreak of war.)

With its low budget the French navy could not spend much time at sea. In 1747 six months at sea cost about 175,000 livres per ship,[61] which obliged the French to keep their vessels in port whenever possible. The enemy counted on experience to create proficient seamen, but the French of necessity relied on book learning. Under Maurepas the French systematically educated officers in the arts of shipbuilding, navigation, and seamanship. Maurepas's successor, Antoine-Louis Rouillé, established the Académie de la Marine, where officers studied every science of use to sailors.[62] French officers had far better nautical educations than their British counterparts, but considerably less sailing experience. Ordinary seamen presumably also lacked experience—at least in comparison to the British. For this reason French squadrons usually sailed more slowly than British ones, although individual French ships could move faster.[63] French gunnery suffered from the same lack of practice.

Meager appropriations influenced ambitions as well as skills in the French navy. In the course of their careers, French officers learned to prefer caution to daring in order to preserve ships. They knew that advancement in the service came with seniority rather than from bold strokes. The

British had Admiral Byng shot for "failure to do his utmost" at Minorca; Lieutenant-General Du Bois de la Motte, in contrast, received a pension and eventually the rank of Vice-Admiral after standing by while a storm-shattered enemy squadron limped away from Louisbourg in 1757.[64] Equally revealing was the conduct of the Comte des Gouttes at Louisbourg in 1758. If he had had his way, his five ships would have fled to France rather than assist at the siege: saving ships was his sole interest. (The local Conseil de Guerre overruled Des Gouttes, and he eventually burned four of his ships so the British could not use them.)[65]

Shortages of timber compounded the problems of the French navy. A first-rate consumed more than 4,000 mature oaks—about 25 hectares of oak forest and 11,000 cubic meters (120,000 cubic feet) of timber.[66] Suitably curved timbers for knees (compass timbers) proved especially scarce, since they came from branches of isolated oaks; those in forests invariably lacked the requisite large horizontal branches. Furthermore, compass timbers came from trees more than 120 years old, many of which suffered from rot. In the seventeenth century, France offered vast supplies of good quality oak, but despite the most rational forest policy in Europe, by the eighteenth century the navy had to import oak from Italy and the Balkan provinces of the Ottoman Empire. Cost, in this case a function of difficulty of access rather than availability, caused the supply bottleneck in French naval shipbuilding.[67] Oak comprised nine-tenths of the wood used in French warships; beech and elm, used sparingly, were rarely hard to find; but good mast timber—fir and pine—posed a constant problem.[68] A seventy-four-gun ship generally required about thirty pines for its masts and yards. Colbert had hoped to satisfy the needs of the navy with domestic fir from the Auvergne in the Massif Central and from the slopes of the Pyrenees. He understood the dangers of the Baltic market, which the Dutch or British might interdict in wartime and which always demanded bullion. The quality of French fir and pine, however, disappointed Colbert and his successors; it lacked the durability, suppleness, and resilience of the fir sold at Danzig, Memel, Riga, and later at St. Petersburg. By 1730, Maurepas instructed that no further searching for masts should take place in the Pyrenees. Experiments with mast timber from New France never pleased naval officials; its indifferent quality did not justify the cost. (After 1759, however, the British exploited excellent mast timber in New Brunswick and along the St.

Lawrence.) In 1731 Maurepas decided to stop imports from Quebec. Thereafter, until the 1780s, the French relied on the Baltic market, in which the British enjoyed financial and diplomatic advantages, and on *mâts d' assemblage*, composite masts made of twelve pieces bound by iron hoops.[69] These masts bore up poorly in heavy weather, requiring the French to furl their sails when the British could still use theirs. In this respect alone did French ships not excel the British.

Of course it took much more than timber to build a ship. Hulls, decks, and masts were useless without sails, rope, cables, pitch, tar, and so on. These items amounted to an appreciable share of the total cost of putting a ship in the water. But none of these items was quite as hard to find as good timber, and none of them concerned naval authorities as much as timber—or manpower.[70]

Skilled seamen were as scarce as good timber. The population of France amounted to from 19 to 22 million people in the first half of the eighteenth century, 85 percent of whom were peasants. Only 70,000 Frenchmen were seafarers according to the rolls of the *inscription maritime*, a register of able seamen and the bureaucratic equivalent of the press gang.[71] The French navy at its height (1690) needed about 23,000 sailors, almost half the number then registered. This marked the peak of the manpower shortage since the revocation of the Edict of Nantes in 1685 had driven many Huguenot sailors to Britain and the Netherlands. In subsequent years, as the navy shrank, its manpower needs declined in proportion. Problems persisted into the eighteenth century, however, because the French navy used more men per ship than any other, and because rival employments competed effectively for available sailors.[72] Many Frenchmen preferred the better wages and working conditions in the Spanish or Neapolitan merchant marines, and some served in foreign navies.[73] The tremendous growth of the French merchant marine after 1713 intensified this competition for sailors as did the Compagnie des Indes with its thirty-five ships.[74] And in wartime, privateers lured many sailors into their employ.[75] In order to man its ships in the face of these problems, the navy frequently had to take anyone in port. Boys from eight to ten years old—often bought from orphanages—formed most of the trainees.[76] Throughout the century, the unattractiveness of naval life ensured manpower shortages; those who did serve could not be permitted leave for fear of desertion. Morale remained consistently low. As Dr. Johnson said of the British navy, no man would be a sailor who had contrivance enough to get himself into a jail.[77]

Shortages of good timber and experienced sailors hampered the Spanish navy as well as the French. Indeed they imposed even stricter limitations on the power of the Spanish navy: whereas in France the budget constituted the greatest impediment, in Spain the Crown was more disposed to pay for a navy after 1717 but found it needed more than money.

In the course of the seventeenth century the Spanish navy had almost ceased to exist. What little remained, the British sank at Vigo in 1702. By 1711 the decrepitude of the Spanish navy had reached the point where the traders of St. Mâlo offered their services to keep the British out of Peru and Mexico.[78] At the close of the War of the Spanish Succession, however, Felipe V rebuilt the Spanish navy intending to reduce rebellious Barcelona through blockade.[79] Under the administration of Cardinal Giulio Alberoni (1715–19), Spain nurtured ambitions in Italy which also required a fleet. Alberoni placed Patiño in charge. The Spanish emulated French methods of administration, but in this case without French parsimony. By purchasing ships abroad Patiño rapidly outfitted a large fleet for the Sicilian expedition of 1718, which ended in disaster at Cape Passaro at the hands of the British.[80] Once again Spain built a new navy. Table 3.4 shows the revival of the Spanish navy and its emergence in the 1730s as a genuine naval power in Europe.

Only a firm financial commitment on the part of the Crown allowed the Spanish navy to recover so thoroughly from the effects of war. Despite a great disparity in royal revenues, the Spanish put to sea a fleet almost as large as the French. Greater security by land and greater vulnerability by sea encouraged the Spanish to devote a much higher proportion of military expenditure to the navy than did the French. Whereas the French army received up to eight times the budget of the French navy, in the Spain of Fernando VI (1746–59) the navy budget averaged 57 percent of the army's and by 1760 Spanish naval expenditure amounted to 70 percent of the army's. Whereas French naval expenditure amounted to less than 3 percent of royal expenditure, the navy of Fernando VI accounted for 18 percent of state expenditure and perhaps 2 percent of

Table 3.4
Ships of the Line in the Spanish Navy,
1722–1761

Year	Ships of the Line	Year	Ships of the Line
1722	22	1747	22
1724	11	1751	18
1735	38	1756	46
1737	36[a]	1758	44
1739	41	1760	52[b]
1740	46	1761	49
1746	37		

Sources: 1722: Fernández Duro, *Disquiciones náuticas*,
5:266. 1724: Razon de los navios y fragatas que actual-
mente tiene S.M., AHN, Sección de Estado, 2339.
1735: Observations sur la Marine d'Espagne, MPCU,
Lot 64, Item 5.056. 1737: Fernández Duro, *Armada
española*, 6:224–25. 1739: Richmond, *Navy*,
1:14–15. 1740: Fernández Duro, *Disquiciones náuticas*,
5:266. 1746: Fernández Duro, *Armada española*, 6:382.
1747: Mahan, *Sea Power*, p. 259. 1751: Fernández Duro,
Armada española, 6:378. 1758: Desdevises du Dezert,
"Institutions," p. 442. 1760: Estado actual de las fuerzas
nabales de S.M., 1 agosto 1760, BL, AM 20926,
fol. 19. 1760: Fernández Duro, *Disquiciones náuticas*,
5:266. 1761: Desdevises du Dezert, "Institutions,"
p. 442.
[a]Graham, *Empire*, p. 106, offers 34 for the same year,
as does Rodríguez Villa, *Patiño y Campillo*, p. 187–89.
[b]Clarke, *Letters*, p. 219, has 50.

Spain's national income. Table 3.5 assembles data on Spanish public and
military expenditures, 1705–60.[81]

That Patiño, Campillo, and the Marqués de Ensenada, with their
backgrounds in naval administration, dominated Spanish policy from
about 1726 to 1754 certainly helped. Their influence assured comparatively large naval budgets (although Campillo felt the navy needed
even more);[82] Maurepas, in contrast, never achieved a naval budget to
his liking because Cardinal Fleury and Jean Orry (finance minister,

Table 3.5
Annual Spanish Public and Military Expenditures, 1701–1760
(in millions of pesos)

Year	Total	Navy I	Navy II[a]	Army	Source
1701	31	—	—	—	b
1705–1707	—	0.1	—	11	c
1713–1716	29	2	—	21	c
1717–1718	30	5	—	17	c
1719–1721	32	—	—	—	c
1722	29	—	—	—	d
1722–1727	29	—	1.6	—	c
1728	32	—	1.1	—	c
1729–1734	36	—	1.3	—	c
1735–1736	41	—	2.1	—	c
1737–1738	36	—	2.1	25	c, e
1739–1740	41	—	3.6	—	c
1741	—	6	—	—	f
1741–1744	45	—	—	—	c
1745	37	—	—	—	b
1700–1746	42	—	—	—	c
1751	34	—	13.8	—	h
1755	47	'*9	9.4	17	b, i
1758	—	8	7.3	—	f
1746–1759	42	9	9.1	16	g, h
1760	38	8	6.6	12	j, k

Sources: a) Merino Navarro, *Armada española*, pp. 155–56. b) Plaza Prieto, *Estructura económica en españa*, pp. 824–26. c) Kamen, *War of Succession*, pp. 229–30. d) Uztáriz, *Theory*, p. 61. e) Canga Argüelles, *Diccionario de hacienda* 3:39. f) Ibid., 1:227. g) Canga Argüelles, *Memoria presentada a las Cortes generales*, p. 77. h) Informe al Rey Fernando VI, por Ensenada, in Coxe, *España bajo el reinado de la casa de Borbon*, 4:575. i) *Enciclopedia universal ilustrada* (Madrid, 1948), 21:653, s.v. "España." j) Coxe, *España*, 4:21. k) Clarke, *Letters*, 218–19.

1730–45) made French financial decisions. Furthermore, major Spanish territorial cessions in the Treaty of Utrecht obviated the need for troops in the Netherlands or Italy. After 1700, Spain no longer fought for hegemony in Europe, but Europe fought for hegemony in Spain; and so Spanish ministers saw fit to reduce the army's budget and build up the navy's.

Timber and manpower shortages largely offset the value of comparatively generous appropriations. The Spanish timber problem, like the French, was one of cost and access rather than absolute quantity. The accessible forests of eastern Spain had largely disappeared in the eighth to the eleventh centuries, but large and suitable stands remained in the north into the eighteenth. The Spanish declined to exploit their forest resources, however, and bought timber, naval stores, and occasionally entire ships from abroad before 1720.[83] The Spanish navy purchased oak from Italy at the same time that the French were buying excellent Spanish oak, made hard and fine-grained by dry weather, from Guipúzcoa.[84]

With the renascence of the Spanish navy under Patiño came a renewed assault on the forests of northern Spain. Most of the cutting took place in the oak and beech forests behind Santander, close to the shipyard of Guarnizo. According to Merino Navarro, the Spanish navy consumed 3 million trees in the eighteenth century, equivalent to about 2 million cubic meters of timber and perhaps 65,000 hectares of forest. This flurry of activity produced bare hillsides and eventually a Spanish timber shortage. By 1750 the Spanish navy found good stout oak trunks hard to come by in the vicinity of Santander and once again had recourse to timber from further afield. The Ebro delta was one source, but more important were forests in Tuscany and Calabria, and even poplar stands in Albania.[85] Ensenada tried to rationalize an intricate forest policy hampered by "absurd" legislation. In a single year he planted more than 2 million oaks, enough to replace what had been cut for seventy ships of the line and twenty-four frigates, an initiative which showed unusual long-range thinking. In the 1760s the Spanish began to exploit timber in Navarre and even to import trunks for ship construction all the way from Cuba.[86] With these expedients, the Spanish navy managed to keep an adequate supply of good oak for its shipbuilding program, at least up to the 1740s.

Sufficient good oak allowed the Spanish navy to build hulls, but ships required masts too. The traditional source of mast timber for the Spanish navy was Tortosa in Catalonia. Uztáriz, writing in 1724, opined that the forests of northern Spain could provide suitable trunks. But by 1749 the Spanish recognized that their pine and fir did not match that of the Baltic. Ensenada complained that Spanish masts lacked the durability and safety of Russian ones: coarse grain and low resin made them brittle,[87] and the dearth of tall trunks forced the Spanish to use made masts (*arboladura ensamblage* or *ensamblado*). After 1750 the navy sought to regularize its purchases of Baltic timber, accepting the risk of wartime interdiction in order to enjoy the benefits of higher quality.[88] The Spanish also turned to their American empire for pines and shipbuilding timber in general. The French had resorted to Canadian pine, when faced with similar problems, but never found the quality acceptable. The Spanish, as we shall see in chapter 6, had better luck, especially in the forests of Cuba.

Timber problems may have forced the Spanish navy to sail with poor masts and yards, but the shortage of sailors threatened to keep the navy from going to sea at all. The Spanish population, about 9 million early in the seventeenth century, had declined to 7.5 million in the 1720s. It recovered to 9 million by 1768.[89] Although predominantly peasant, (perhaps 80 percent) the Spanish populace included large numbers of seafarers from Andalucia, Galicia, and the Basque region. Like every European navy, however, the Spanish marine suffered from a manpower shortage. In the eighteenth century, with the demise of the Spanish cod fishery and foreign inroads into Spanish maritime trade, the problem grew more acute.[90] The navy resorted to the press gang in wartime, but even so could rarely man all its vessels.[91] Ensenada wrote that without sufficient numbers of mariners, efforts to expand the navy were pointless.[92] A registry of seamen (modeled on the French *inscription maritime*), proposed in the 1720s and inaugurated in 1737, hardly improved matters. Basques, the most seafaring of Spanish subjects, hesitated to register for what they saw as a Castilian navy.[93] Initial calculations in 1736 found only 6,523 able seamen (this survey, however, included only the Mediterranean coast and Balearic Islands), scarcely enough to man ten fighting ships. By 1735 zealous officials had found about 24,000 sailors, and by 1759 the registry included some 50,000 names, of which about

26,000 were actually available—still inadequate for the navy's needs.[94] The 1737 royal *ordenanza* initiating the registry of seamen exempted all who matriculated from service in the army and promised pensions to those who actually served. Ensenada hoped that higher and more regular pay would attract Spaniards to the navy.[95] None of these enticements sufficed; seagoing Spaniards proved too few and desertion ran too high, so the Spanish navy had to attract foreigners through high wages. Many Irish and French sailors did join the ranks, but the Spanish still emptied prisons at times to help man the navy in Cuba. Prisoners were all the navy could get in Cuba, since the governor resisted the navy's attempt to extend the *matrícula del mar* to Havana (presumably in order to protect Cuban commerce).[96] It was the unavailability of skilled labor rather than lack of funds which effectively limited the size, and thus the power, of the Spanish navy.

In addition to shortages of sailors and good mast timber, the Spanish navy suffered from excessive devolution in administration, low morale among the officer corps, obsolete accounting methods, a general lack of specialization and professionalism, poor maintenance, and consequently short-lived ships. This at least was the opinion of an informed observer in 1755.[97] He might have added a lack of experience to his list: as in the French navy, officers were educated on land, and sea training was kept to a minimum because of the expense.[98] Putting a ship to sea in Spain cost even more than in France because the naval ports (Cadiz, Cartagena, El Ferrol) served as commercial ports too, forcing Spanish naval vessels to compete with merchant ships for men and supplies. In the French naval ports of Brest, Toulon, and Rochefort the navy had little competition from the private sector to drive up the price of sailors, supplies, and services.

To float a ship of the line cost the Spanish navy roughly four times what it cost to stay in port, the difference consisting in the wages and sustenance of sailors.[99] Operating costs varied in direct proportion to the number of men aboard; no economies of scale existed.[100] Spanish costs amounted to about one-quarter more than French: a Spanish sixty-gun ship spent 693,430 *reales* (equals c. 66,000 pesos) to cruise for six months; a French sixty-four cost 191,000 livres (equals c. 51,000 pesos) for an equally long cruise.[101] Costs, however, mattered less to the Spanish than to the French, so perhaps their navy saw more sea duty. In wartime, however, the power of the British navy made the French and Spanish equally hesitant to go to sea.

The wartime enemy and peacetime rival of both Bourbon navies, the British Royal Navy, formed the standard against which they invariably measured their fleets. [102] Since the Dutch wars of the seventeenth century, English security had by conventional wisdom resided in her fleet. In consequence, Parliament did not stint in appropriations, nor did the Bank of England balk at sudden loans. The British did not question their faith in a strong navy, and as a result the Royal Navy eventually outnumbered its nearest rival by more than 100 ships of the line. [103] Furthermore, the British felt able to devote the entirety of naval expense to the ocean fleet, whereas the French and Spanish maintained galleys and other small craft suitable only for action against seafarers of the Barbary Coast. At any given time the British could maintain in American waters alone a fleet the size of the entire French navy. [104]

The sums expended on the Royal Navy show how the British managed to float such a force. The Royal Navy ordinarily spent more than any other government department: "[a]ny study of the administration of public expenditure in the eighteenth century would necessarily have the navy as its centerpiece." [105] In the 1730s and 1740s, according to the leading student of Royal Navy administration, Parliament authorized expenditures of between 2 and 4 million pounds sterling, which at the prevailing rates of exchange amounted to between two and four times the French naval budget. [106] Other figures, appearing in Table 3.6, indicate more modest British naval expenditure, but still normally between two to four times French levels. [107] The larger British naval expenditure went not only into ships, accounting for British numerical superiority, but also into cruises, accounting for the superiority of British personnel. Although beset by manpower problems at least as severe as the French or Spanish, the British had no real timber shortages between 1707 and 1764. [108] The Royal Navy remained ascendant until the war of the American Revolution. A large budget made the difference. [109]

The willingness and ability of the eighteenth-century British Parliament to maintain a large navy allowed new departures in naval strategy. The French and Spanish navies, unable to match the British in size, could not deviate from traditional naval ideas. For centuries European navies

Table 3.6

British Naval Expenditure, 1700–1764 (in 000 sterling)

Year	Amount	Year	Amount	Year	Amount
1700	819	1725	601	1750	1,365
1701	1,046	1726	695	1751	895
1702	2,094	1727	833	1752	1,854
1703	1,724	1728	1,539	1753	849
1704	1,630	1729	925	1754	944
1705	1,772	1730	1,033	1755	1,814
1706	1,949	1731	815	1756	2,714
1707	2,297	1732	700	1757	3,595
1708	1,909	1733	555	1758	3,893
1709	2,117	1734	2,079	1759	4,971
1710	2,422	1735	1,545	1760	4,539
1711	1,237	1736	1,390	1761	5,256
1712	1,776	1737	933	1762	4,892
1713	1,457	1738	819	1763	3,980
1714	1,043	1739	988	1764	2,150
1715	1,205	1740	1,607		
1716	972	1741	2,419		
1717	443	1742	2,795		
1718	1,350	1743	2,736		
1719	1,293	1744	2,709		
1720	1,181	1745	2,688		
1721	705	1746	2,396		
1722	1,666	1747	3,176		
1723	827	1748	3,361		
1724	630	1749	2,764		

Source: Brian R. Mitchell and Phyllis Deane, *Abstract of British Historical Statistics*, pp. 389–90.

had pursued limited objectives: commerce protection, commerce raiding, defense of home waters, and support of land forces. Notions such as command of the sea did not figure, and for good reason. Given eighteenth-century conditions, command of the sea was impossible except in a local sense, in narrow seas or port approaches.

Before the War of the Spanish Succession, fortified bases constituted the strength of overseas empires. With the possible exception of the seventeenth century Dutch, no one had considered navies as primary agents of colonial enterprise. Navies of imperial states consisted of the comparatively small number of ships necessary to ensure that profitable colonial trade took place; they existed to provide "protection rent."[110] By minimizing the hazards to shipping, a navy bestowed upon merchants a savings (from losses or high insurance) that they might invest in any number of wealth-producing ways. Without that savings—protection rent—merchants make less profit, and may well choose not to trade at all. The application of force to produce protection rent took place in two ways: plundering one's rivals, which tended to create diminishing returns since rivals might abandon the trade; or protecting one's own, which tended to create increasing returns. By the eighteenth century, European navies began to specialize in warring among themselves, leaving plunder to privateers.[111]

Out of the War of the Spanish Succession emerged a British navy organized to perform other services besides ferrying armies, protecting trade, and guarding home waters. This may be called the imperial navy: it concerned itself with safeguarding colonies as well as colonial trade. It sought control of specific narrow stretches of water such as the Windward Passage, Straits of Florida, or mouth of the Gulf of St. Lawrence. An imperial navy had to be large, but size alone did not distinguish it—the huge French navy of Colbert and Louis XIV was not an imperial navy. Its main purpose had been to carry the French army to Britain by seizing momentary control of the English Channel. The distinguishing characteristic of the imperial navy lay in its conception of its purpose: it sought to control certain passages, straits, bays, etc., in order to defend trade and colonies from maritime attack. The tremendous expansion of British colonial trade since the late seventeenth century rendered it impractical to escort ships. Now it became, for the first time in the Atlantic world, economic to defend the space through which merchant vessels sailed. The growing complexity and scale of commerce protection provoked a new departure in naval practice, eventually leading to the notion of command of the sea.

In the eighteenth century, the British Admiralty deployed permanent squadrons in American waters, a practice consistent with the aims of an imperial navy. The French on the other hand sent out squadrons annually. The Spanish maintained a small permanent squadron in the Caribbean except when fiscal impoverishment prevented it. The Armada de Barlovento, however, did not fulfill the functions of an imperial navy; it helped defend colonial commerce but not colonies. The Spanish relied on fortification for that purpose.

In the last hundred years, naval writers have roundly castigated continental navies for failing to challenge the British at sea.[112] The French and Spanish navies, they say, neglected their duty when they did not seek to win command of the sea. If that is the sole purpose of a navy, then French and Spanish policy indeed squandered their navies. If, however, navies in the eighteenth century could perform useful services without command of the sea, Bourbon naval strategy may have represented a superior wisdom.

Admiral Mahan's famous doctrine of command of the sea derived from the practice of the Royal Navy and suited only the navy with the greatest resources. His counsel did not address the situation of a state that cannot match the naval expenditure of a rival. Whatever increases the Bourbons might choose to make in the size of their navies, they could not hope to equal the British. Inevitably the British would outspend them. In consequence the French and Spanish navies operated from a different set of premises and followed methods of war appropriate to those with meager resources: a guerilla approach to sea warfare, executed from secure land bases like Louisbourg or Havana.

The inferiority of their resources determined the strategy and tactics of French and Spanish navies. Both navies avoided battle as studiously as the British sought it.[113] Battle, even if victorious, implied the loss of ships, which the French and Spanish navies viewed as more precious, by reason of their scarcity, than did the British. A naval war of attrition, while acceptable to the British, loomed as disastrous to either Bourbon navy. To maintain a navy involved a struggle for the French and Spanish; to risk large portions of a fleet in a single engagement, whatever the possible rewards, struck them as foolhardy. Thus neither the French nor Spanish had a battle fleet, despite having many ships designed to do battle. The French especially hesitated to concentrate their naval forces for fear of large losses, preferring to deploy their ships in twos, threes, and fours throughout their empire. Even when they did assemble large squadrons they equipped them with strictly defensive orders.[114] No shortage of courage prevented French and Spanish officers from emulating the daring successes of their British counterparts; rather, institutionalized caution, quite logical in the face of numerical inferiority, ruled the French navy after La Hogue (1692) and Toulon (1704), and the Spanish navy after Cape Passaro (1718).[115]

Occasionally the French and Spanish failed to avoid combat. Battle tactics also reflected the Bourbon navies' fears. Once in battle, commanders hoped to get out as quickly as possible with minimal losses. While British gunners tried to sink the enemy by firing at planking, the French and Spanish fired on the uproll at masts and rigging in an effort to prevent pursuit and facilitate flight. The French generally accepted battle only with the leeward gauge (downwind of the enemy) to permit an easier escape.[116]

By their defensive posture, the Bourbon navies conceded to the British the aims of an imperial navy: control of key stretches of water. However, they did manage to prevent a "decisive military encounter between equal forces," (i.e., a major naval defeat) at least until 1756.[117] They chose not to gamble for command of the sea against long odds, but rather to preserve their fleets for more traditional purposes. Their policy, unimaginative though it was, suited their resources. The new approach to naval policy exhibited by the British remained beyond the means of the Bourbon powers.

Traditional mercantilist ideas and traditional navies formed the limits within which Louisbourg and Havana played their imperial roles. Despite the teachings of classical economists and Admiral Mahan, neither mercantilism nor traditional naval policy was misguided. Free trade suits only the producers and traders with the lowest costs and the doctrine of sea power suits only the state with the largest navy. France and Spain in the eighteenth century had to accept imperial strategies appropriate to their resources.

Navies in the eighteenth century constituted the sinews of overseas empire. Only a navy could protect a nation's shipping and imperil that of a rival. Expanded colonial trade required the British to develop a new approach to commerce protection, the imperial navy. Only a navy which construed its duty as imperial would control routes of communication and trade, rather than merely protecting or harassing ships. The characteristics and capabilities of ships, sailors, and bureaucracies varied only slightly between Britain, France, and Spain, so the critical ingredient in sea power became the number of ships in each navy. The number of ships in each navy depended on the size of the naval budget and the availability of credit. Budgets, in turn, hinged on political decisions made at the centers of power and, of course, on the sum of resources available to a government. Although France had the greatest resources, Spain and Britain made political decisions more favorable to their navies. Britain's budget decisions favored the navy even more than Spain's, a reflection of domestic political conditions as well as geography. Britain thus enjoyed the fruits of a large, imperial navy, by virtue of her willingness and ability to pay the price. The French were perhaps able but unwilling to compete with Britain in a naval race; the Spanish were willing but unable. The resulting Bourbon navies wisely confined themselves to guerrilla methods and traditional ambitions.

Against this background of naval inferiority, the French and Spanish systems of imperial defense appear less ill-conceived than their modern critics admit. The Bourbons understood that the maintenance of an imperial navy was beyond their financial means, and would require a successful major naval war against Britain—for the British would not placidly admit a rival. Traditional methods, with a strong emphasis on the role of fortified ports, offered the only feasible strategy of resistance to British expansion. Imperial policy demanded colonial strongholds; geographic, ecological, and demographic conditions in Havana and Louisbourg seemed to suit the requirements admirably. It is the roles of these ports within the Bourbon systems of imperial defense to which we turn in the next chapter.

4 American Ports and Imperial Defense

International frictions in the eighteenth century regularly led to war. To all those in a position to influence affairs of state, war seemed a perfectly acceptable arbiter of disputes. France, Spain, and Britain fought for roughly half of the first sixty years of the eighteenth century, and even in peacetime, mercantilist competition kept war a constant possibility. Every war, whether of American or European origin, featured an American theater. Every peace left room for discreet and extra governmental violence at sea and on coasts. Colonial holdings thus required defense at all times.

At least some colonies had offensive potential as well as defensive requirements. War in the American theater stretched the capacities of forces based in Europe; American bases could supply additional resources closer to the points of deployment, contributing men, ships, food, water, and convenient locations to war efforts. Those colonies that could fulfill many of these functions became indispensable for the continued survival of an empire; they required impregnable defense at all times.

With its hinterland, Havana could provide men, ships, food, and a convenient location for offensive actions against the British in North America or the Caribbean. Louisbourg had less to offer the French: fewer men, no surplus food, less shipbuilding capacity, and a less convenient location. Its shortcomings as an imperial base, however, did not prevent French statesmen from entertaining exalted expectations of Louisbourg's military potential. Louisbourg and Havana suffered equally from Bourbon inferiority at sea. On the whole, the Spanish understood the limits of Havana's military usefulness. The French, however, found their island port a bitter disappointment, for they came to expect more than Louisbourg could provide.

Louisbourg's foundation in 1713 resulted from conscious deliberation. This makes it fairly easy to understand what the French had in mind for Louisbourg, at least initially, and to compare this projected role with Louisbourg's actual role in military affairs. In contrast, the Spanish founded Havana early in the sixteenth century when colonial competition had just begun; what the Spanish intended in 1519 cannot serve as a guide to what they expected two hundred and more years later. Thus, illuminating the theoretical military role of eighteenth-century Havana proves a more difficult task, and the comparison with the actual role carries less confidence.

The terms of the Treaty of Utrecht (1713) transferred sovereignty of Plaisance (in Newfoundland) from France to Britain. Although the permanent population of Placentia (as it was now called) numbered less than a thousand, the French accorded it great importance in their Atlantic empire because the dry cod fishery centered there.[1] Now the British could develop a competitive dry fishery of their own, and the French stood to lose their share of the world cod trade. To protect their dry fishery, the French undertook to create a colony on Ile Royale. With the establishment of the British at Placentia, competition in the fishery had intensified, and the French now required military protection of their operations.

An Intendant of French Canada, Jacques Raudot, had first suggested the establishment of a colony at Ile Royale. Raudot had in mind above all a commercial city which would serve as a relay between Quebec and France. His correspondence with Jérôme Phélypaux, comte de Pontchartrain,[2] the French Minister of Marine, shows that Pontchartrain approved of the idea in general but postponed its execution until after the War of the Spanish Succession.[3] By the time Pontchartrain could turn his attention to the foundation of a new colony, the French needed a new base for the fishery. Raudot's vision of an entrepôt port to spur Canadian development became Pontchartrain's "place to conduct the fishery in safety."[4]

At the time, neither Raudot nor Pontchartrain envisioned a colony that would defend Canada from attack; neither imagined a settlement on Ile Royale could serve as the "clef de l'Amérique." The characteristics they sought for the prospective settlement showed much more modest ambitions. Pontchartrain wanted an easily defended port that held a large number of ships,[5] while the Conseil de la Marine—one of a series of councils established following the death of Louis XIV and abolished upon the majority of Louis XV—wanted, in addition, a port invulnerable to blockade.[6] Rocks, fogs, and shifting winds made Louisbourg as difficult to blockade as any North American port.

These characteristics were hardly those of a bulwark of America.[7] Rather, they correspond to the requirements of a secure fishing base. Pontchartrain viewed the prospective settlement in this light with good reason—in 1713 the fishery mattered more to the French empire than all of Canada.[8] Cod earned more bullion than the exports of Canada, and the fishery additionally served as a nursery of seamen, an advantage of which the French never lost sight.[9]

Given the continual shortage of trained sailors in the navy, French authorities, and the Ministry of Marine in particular, could ill afford to lose any nursery of seamen. The cod fisheries offered employment for thousands of sailors in demanding seas under healthy conditions.[10] Whereas sailors in the Caribbean took ill and died at exorbitant rates, in the North Atlantic disease claimed very few.[11] The rougher weather created better sailors faster than in the Mediterranean or Caribbean. Importantly, all this training took place at no expense to the French crown.[12] The manpower pool available for sea duty when war broke out would have evaporated without the cod fisheries. The defense of this training ground for sailors constituted one of Louisbourg's principal duties.

French authorities, however, expected more from Louisbourg. Although Raudot, Pontchartrain, and their associates knew full well that Louisbourg could not defend Canada, they did expect it to serve as a base for corsairs and privateers.[13] In this they showed a keen appreciation of Louisbourg's advantages. All ships of American origin and European destination preferred to pass close by Louisbourg in order to take advantage of the Gulf Stream and the westerlies. With proper management, Louisbourg, as a safe port beside a sea lane of the first importance, offered limitless privateering possibilities.

These considerations proved pivotal in the French decision to create Louisbourg. From 1713 until 1718, the center of the French settlement on Cape Breton remained in doubt. Pontchartrain and the Conseil de la Marine solicited information on the island from several sources and received conflicting reports. Some informants suggested Port Toulouse—the modern St. Peter's—because the land there appeared more likely to support a large population.[14] Others favored Port Dauphin—St. Anns today—for its more expansive anchorage, comparatively easy defense, good soil, timber, mines, and quarries.[15] The eventual decision to center the colony around the port of Louisbourg rested on its proximity to the fishing banks and the sea route from America to Europe, and on its unsusceptibility to blockade. The higher cost of fortification, scarcity of timber, poor soil, and harsher climate failed to deter Pontchartrain or the Conseil de la Marine.[16] After a 1717 alliance with Britain seemed to assure a peace long enough in which to build fortifications, the French committed themselves to Louisbourg.[17]

The modest ambitions for Louisbourg entertained by Pontchartrain and inherited by the Conseil de la Marine hardly outlasted their administrations. With the end of the regency, Pontchartrain's son, the comte de Pontchartrain et Maurepas, assumed direction of the Ministry of Marine. Very shortly he began to tout the Ile Royale colony as the key to America and to assign it defense functions that it could not possibly fulfill. In so doing Maurepas created the conception of Louisbourg that has lived on in the English-speaking historical tradition.

Soon after Maurepas assumed his post, French expectations of Louisbourg began to change. In the 1720s Maurepas tried to convince officials in Quebec that Louisbourg protected Canada from seaborne attack.[18] Perhaps he had already convinced himself, or perhaps he merely wished to involve Canada in the expense of feeding the Louisbourg garrison. At any rate, Maurepas had begun to entertain notions of Louisbourg's potential far in excess of his predecessors' ideas, notions which he soon expressed to a more general audience. In his mémoire of 1730, Maurepas refers to Louisbourg as "the mainstay of Canada, and even of Louisiana."[19] This idea apparently became general in France.[20] The Canadians, however, and Intendant Beauharnois in particular, remained unconvinced of Louisbourg's capacity to defend Canada: "The entire English army could come to Québec without Ile Royale knowing of it, and even if it was known, what could they do?"[21] Canadians relied not on Louisbourg but on the perils of the St. Lawrence, British memories of past failures, and financial considerations to deter British designs on Quebec.[22] An unidentified author touched on the crux of the issue, the use of sea power: "As regards Louisbourg, a naval force could enter the St. Lawrence by the normal route to Quebec, because Louisbourg to stop them would have to have a squadron cruising between Newfoundland and Ile Royale."[23] The French navy, however, had never used its ships to patrol strategic stretches of water.

Despite logical objections from Quebec, Maurepas and the marine bureaucracy continued to attribute to Louisbourg characteristics of which Pontchartrain and his generation scarcely dreamed. As early as 1724, the engineer in charge of fortifications had reported to Maurepas that Louisbourg "is the strongest place in all America."[24] Indeed, in 1730 Maurepas arrived at the conclusion that Louisbourg was invulnerable to all but famine, a view reportedly shared by Louis XV.[25] Maurepas also took measures to reduce the danger of starvation at Louisbourg, and by 1739 (when war seemed likely) he blithely asserted that the English could not take Louisbourg should they try.[26]

The French also began to expect Louisbourg to serve as base of operations against the British in Acadia and Newfoundland. This idea, although first mentioned in Raudot's time only became general in the 1730s.[27] A war scare in 1734 prompted the governor at Louisbourg and a clerk in the Ministry of Marine in Paris to write that in case of war, Louisbourg forces could drive the British from Acadia (by which they meant the town of Annapolis Royal) and Placentia.[28] In 1740 Maurepas actually instructed the Louisbourg governor to seize Acadia and, if possible, Placentia, as soon as war broke out with Britain.[29]

These three notions—Louisbourg as bulwark of Canada, as impregnable stronghold, and as base for local offensives—appeared only with the accession of Maurepas in 1723. They became accepted within the bureaucracy of the Marine in the 1730s, only to disappear for good after 1745, when French sea power proved unable to save Louisbourg.

Why did Maurepas and his subordinates come to believe Louisbourg a much more potent and important link in French imperial defense than did the prior generation? Perhaps as the walls of Louisbourg grew taller, and as they successfully stood off the wind and sea, a myth of invincibility grew with them. Perhaps the exaggerated expectations stemmed from frustration: lack of resources prevented Maurepas from doing as he wished—populating French America with millions, linking it to France with a thriving commerce, and defending it with hundreds of warships. Unable to fulfill this dream, Maurepas clung to the notion that a series of fortresses might safeguard French America. Since he could do no more than build forts, he invested them with the entire responsibility for the defense of French America. He had nothing to believe in but Louisbourg.

Or perhaps the mounting expense of Louisbourg's fortifications inspired exalted expectations. Louis XV once opined that the streets of Louisbourg must be paved with gold, since the colony had cost him so dearly.[30] Maurepas may have felt obliged to justify the cost of Louisbourg's walls, especially since expenditure almost doubled when he took office. (Table 4.1 shows the expenditure on Louisbourg's fortifications, 1716–49.) In an era of extremely tight naval budgets, this expense must have required explanation to the king, to the Marine bureaucracy, and perhaps to Maurepas himself. French finances had just suffered the disasters of John Law's management; the naval ministry, particularly since Maurepas was new at the job, had to demonstrate that it deserved its budget. Exaggerated claims for Louisbourg thus might have suited Maurepas's purpose in a moment when he might well have feared further budget cuts.[31] These claims then became doctrine within the naval bureaucracy until events proved them illusions. Indeed only in 1758, after Louisbourg had been reduced with comparative ease by the British for a second time, did the marine bureaucracy fully come to accept the military weaknesses of Louisbourg.[32]

Since its founding in 1519, the Spanish expected Havana to assist in the protection of the treasure fleets en route to Spain. Once beyond the range of the guns of Veracruz, silver fleets sailed under the protection of forces based at Havana, with additional help from Florida, until they neared the Spanish shore. Since the early eighteenth century, the Spanish also expected Havana to serve as a base of operations in the international competition for the southeastern corner of North America. Maintenance and expansion of a Spanish presence in these parts required constant flows of men and supplies, which could only come through Havana, whatever their point of origin. Ever since the English took Jamaica in the middle of

Table 4.1

The Cost of the Fortifications at Louisbourg, 1718–1745 (in livres)

Year	Allotment	Source
1718	60,000	AC, B, 41–4: 197–98
1719	80,000	AC, $C^{11}B$, 5: 177 and AC, $C^{11}B$, 4: 284
1720	80,000	AC, $C^{11}B$, 5: 177
1721	80,000	AC, $C^{11}B$, 5: 349–56; AC, B, 44–2: 560–65
1722	80,000	AC, $C^{11}B$, 6: 191; AC, B, 45–1: 262–64
1723	130,000	AC, $C^{11}B$, 6: 209
1724	150,000	AC, B, 46: 82; AC, $C^{11}B$, 7: 4–9; AC, $C^{11}B$, 16: 20
1725	150,000	
1726	150,000	
1727	150,000	
1728	150,000	AC, B, 51: 51
1729	150,000	AC, $C^{11}B$, 10: 142; AC, B, 53: 607–8
1730	152,700	AC, B, 54–2: 277–78
1731	150,000	AC, $C^{11}B$, 12: 113; AC, B, 55–3: 557–62
1732	150,000	AC, $C^{11}B$, 12: 110; AC, B, 57–2: 766–68; AC, B, 56: 234–35
1733	130,335	AC, B, 59–2: 554–58; AC, $C^{11}B$, 14: 151–55
1734	130,335	AC, $C^{11}B$, 15: 178–79; AC, B, 61–2: 614–15
1735	128,900	AC, B, 62: 163
1736	128,900	AC, B, 64: 139
1737	128,900	AC, B, 65: 180
1738	128,900	AC, B, 66: 300
1739	128,900	AC, B, 68: 377
1740	128,900	AC, B, 70: 399
1741	120,000	AC, $C^{11}B$, 23: 205
1742	128,100	AC, B, 74: 589
1743	128,100	AC, B, 76: 507
1744	120,000	AC, $C^{11}B$, 26: 199
1745	128,000	AC, $C^{11}B$, 26: 162; AC, $C^{11}B$, 27: 45–46

the seventeenth century, the Spanish also expected Havana to function as a base from which to menace the growing trade between the British West Indies and the North Atlantic World. In wartime, Cuban vessels could easily intercept much of Jamaica's trade, and in peacetime, patrols based in Cuba could harass British contrabandists. Each of these three expectations, which together constituted Cuba's intended military role within the empire, presupposed the presence of Spanish naval forces in Cuban waters. The extent to which Cuba fulfilled these hopes hinged on the capacity of the Spanish navy in the Caribbean to perform several duties at once.[33]

Throughout the eighteenth century, desperate royal finances made the safe arrival of the treasure fleets from the New World a matter of the utmost importance and anxiety to Spanish monarchs and ministers. To Havana they assigned the responsibility of preparing these fleets for the transatlantic crossing and protecting the silver against the British and Dutch.[34] Since Veracruz had no natural harbor, the treasure lay at risk once aboard ship. Naturally the Spanish tried to get it to Havana as rapidly as possible,[35] for which purpose Patiño—as one of his first acts—reestablished the Armada de Barlovento, with Havana as its base.[36] He subsequently reinforced it and raised Cuban taxes to help pay for it.[37]

Once safely arrived at Havana, the treasure fleet normally remained at anchor for months, refitting for the transoceanic voyage and waiting for other ships from Tierra Firme (generally from Portobello) to join the *flota*. Havana was expected to provide food, water, sailors, munitions—whatever was needed—for the journey to Spain. The British considered Havana one of two places in the Caribbean where they could not get at Spanish vessels.[38] In wartime the flota's escort normally consisted of a squadron dispatched from Spain for the purpose; in peacetime it might consist only of the warships available in Havana from the Armada de Barlovento. Since the Spanish government considered treasure the raison d'être of the Indies, Havana's role as a safe port and a base for escorts was its principal purpose.

No other port could perform the same function. Veracruz's defenses could safeguard the town but not ships at anchorage; should the treasure spend any time at all at anchor off Veracruz, it would surely be lost. Cartagena, although a safe port like Havana, lay south of Jamaica: British fleets or privateers could easily intercept Cartagena shipping bound either for the Windward Passage or for the Gulf Stream via the straits of Florida. But the British could not so easily intercept the Veracruz-to-Havana route because it meant cruising downwind of Jamaica, and the British left Jamaica vulnerable to attack from the windward only with the greatest reluctance.[39] Only Havana, by virtue of its geographical position and its easily defended natural harbor, could conceivably have played this role in the Spanish Empire.

Havana's location recommended it for another major strategic role. Until 1763 the Spanish and British continually struggled for control over southeastern North America. Both sides expected resolution to come from the usual sources—diplomacy and military actions. Spanish authorities looked to Havana as a base of operations against British encroachment in Apalache (the territory north of Florida and south (roughly) of the latitude of Charleston, South Carolina [32° 30']). Once again, Havana's location in combination with its natural and human resources made it the only suitable base in Spanish dominions.

With Spanish settlements throughout the Caribbean and southeastern North America threatened by the British, Havana's responsibility theoretically extended well beyond Apalache. Instructions to the military authorities in Havana included injunctions to succor the settlements of the West Indies or the Gulf of Mexico when needed.[40] One Cuban governor, blessed with more imagination than most, suggested that an expedition from Cuba could retake Jamaica for Spain with six ships and 3,000 men.[41] This proposition received no serious consideration although the idea reportedly appealed to the King.[42]

The one area where British expansion clearly endangered Spanish claims, and where Havana could realistically help defend Spanish interests, was the borderland in what is now Georgia. Beginning in the 1720s, British efforts to establish a buffer colony between the Spanish settlement at Florida and the British in South Carolina resulted in a border dispute.[43] British land grants and forts appeared on land the Spanish considered theirs. To defend Spanish soil, forts and garrisons required help that only Havana military and civil authorities could provide.[44] In the late 1730s, when diplomatic efforts proved fruitless and war with Britain seemed imminent, the Spanish government expected Havana's militia, regular troops, shipyards, and food stocks to complete preparations for an expedition against Georgia.[45] The governor of Havana showed no enthusiasm for discharging this responsibility, feeling that it dangerously weakened Havana's own defenses.[46]

Although after 1748 the boundary dispute ceased to occupy Spanish and British diplomats, the defense of Florida from British depredations remained a Spanish military concern until 1763. Officials at San Agustín frequently expected the British to attack, and Havana continued as Florida's ostensible protector. The Spanish planned no further expeditions against the British; in the 1750s they emphasized fortifications and immigration instead.[47] In the 1740s and 1750s, the Cuban government and the quasigovernmental Havana Company (the Real Compañía de la Habana) shared the burdens of the defense of Apalache and Florida, whereas prior to 1740 the government had assumed most of the responsibility; only occasionally had it farmed out specific tasks to entrepreneurs. Under any of these various administrative arrangements, the responsibility lay with Havana to maintain and defend the Spanish settlements of southeastern North America.

The defense of Spanish interests in the Caribbean involved a seaborne dimension not confined to the regular navy. Cuba's location favored privateering activity more than any other Spanish possession, but also demanded considerable investment in *guarda costas* or coast guards. British Caribbean trade, legal and illegal, centered around Jamaica, less than 100 kilometers from the south coast of Cuba. Spanish authorities expected Cuba to facilitate legal and illegal harassment of that trade, in both war and peace. The *guarda costas* and privateers shared a common purpose: to raise the costs of Caribbean trade to British merchants, and thereby bestow upon Spanish competitors the advantages of protection rent. Distinctions between *guarda costa* and privateer, between legal and illegal trade, and sometimes between war and peace, often escaped those involved—thus the endless international litigations. The Spanish felt that most British traders dealt in contraband, while the British thought that the Spanish *guarda costas* aimed to seize every vessel they could.[48] Under these circumstances, finer points about legally constituted authority and legitimate search evaporated.

Guarda costas and privateers alike combined a measure of private capital with public management, since the Crown could not afford to maintain *guarda costas* from its own purse. Thus evolved the system that blurred distinctions between coast guard and privateer. Individual recipients of special privileges, such as the right to construct a tobacco mill, often paid for the favor by supporting a proportion of the local *guarda costas*, a practice never tried at Louisbourg.[49] The remaining expense fell to the various *presidios* of the West Indies (Havana, Santiago de Cuba, Santo Domingo, Puerto Rico, Florida, and Apalache) whose share in the late 1750s averaged 17,982 pesos a month.[50] The Spanish government managed privateering in the Caribbean not by putting up a proportion of the starting capital (as the French did in the English Channel and at Louisbourg) but by adjusting the distribution of the proceeds. By lowering the royal share and raising that belonging to the outfitter, and perhaps the local governor as well, authorities in Madrid could expand privateering operations anywhere and anytime they chose.[51] By reserving a larger share for the Crown, Spanish authorities could discourage their own privateers when that seemed wise.

Santiago de Cuba was far better located than Havana for intercepting British trade. Only ships in the trade of Honduras, the dyewood trade of Campeche, and occasional stray vessels from Jamaica used the straits of Florida as an ingress to the Gulf Stream; other ships passing by Havana flew the Spanish flag. So the Spanish expected Santiago de Cuba to harbor the largest share of both privateers and *guarda costas*. Most illicit Cuban trade with Jamaica took place in the keys and bays of the south coast between Trinidad and Bayamo, since the coastline there afforded excellent protection from patrols, and Jamaica lay only twenty-four hours' sail away. This smuggling trade, carried on in war and peace throughout the century, provided constant employment for Spanish interceptors based in Santiago de Cuba.[52] Most of Jamaica's trade passed through the Windward Passage between Cuba and Hispaniola. The sugar fleets of June and September, the slaves en route to Charleston, the coin and bullion Jamaican traders had gotten from the Spanish Main, indeed almost all the exports of the British Caribbean paraded by within a day's sail of Santiago de Cuba on their way to the Gulf Stream. The trade winds made it very difficult for British merchantmen to escape Santiago de Cuba privateers and *guarda costas* cruising the Windward Passage without passing directly by Santiago de Cuba (and more interceptors). Lumber, horses, flour, and other products of the British mainland colonies passed through the same straits from the north en route to Jamaica and thus faced the same menace.[53]

Early in the eighteenth century, Cuban privateering received little encouragement from the Crown. The division of the spoils apparently discouraged even adventurous souls. However, in the War of Jenkins' Ear, 1739–48, Spain took extraordinary steps to embolden privateers. A royal order of 1746 awarded to interceptors the prize shares that had formerly belonged to viceroys, captains-general, and governors. Spoils were also exempted from port and sales taxes.[54] The governor in Santiago de Cuba took care to ensure that plenty of corsairs in his port took aim at British shipping to Jamaica.[55] With these measures, Spanish authorities hoped to make Santiago de Cuba a nest of interceptors (whether technically privateers or *guarda costas*), thereby minimizing the British Caribbean trade. When peace came in 1748, letters of marque became commissions and exprivateers pursued the same quarry with the new title of *guarda costas*.

Cuba could perform other minor services for the Spanish military. The island's location vis-à-vis Jamaica allowed it to serve as a military observation post and information clearinghouse. Particularly during the 1739–48 war, authorities in Madrid expected Havana to provide information on the movements of British fleets.[56] Again, Santiago de Cuba's location suited the requirements of naval monitoring better than Havana's. Captured British sailors might furnish information, as might clandestine traders of any nationality with contacts or recent experience in Jamaica. Madrid also instructed the Armada de Barlovento to monitor the movements of British fleets, even before the outbreak of war; any intelligence gained in this way also passed through Havana.[57]

Spanish military authorities, then, expected Cuba to fulfill four functions, three major and one minor: to safeguard the returning *flota* with its silver, to maintain and defend the frontier in Florida and Apalache, to intercept British West Indies trade, and to gather naval intelligence. Success in all of these missions required sea power, regular and irregular, on a large scale. Each role amounted to a traditional naval task: safeguarding the *flota* meant commerce protection; intercepting British trade meant commerce raiding; defending Florida and Apalache meant supporting the army. Bourbon navies of the eighteenth century assumed precisely these functions as their responsibility. Thus the Spanish expected Havana to ease the task of the Spanish navy in the Caribbean.

The Spanish never expected that Havana might serve as the defender of

Spanish America. Despite references to Havana's importance, centrality, or strategic value to Spanish America, the Spanish never developed a grand illusion comparable to the one Maurepas and his associates created concerning Louisbourg.[58] The French expected Louisbourg to protect commerce (the cod trade), raid British commerce (privateering), and support the army in frontier enterprises (Acadia, Newfoundland), responsibilities equivalent to those of Havana. The French, however, also expected Louisbourg to defend a continent.

"The value of a position," wrote Mahan, "is not in the bare position, but in the use you make of it."[59] To make use of the potential of their ports, both the French and the Spanish needed sea power. In practice, Louisbourg and Havana could not fulfill their roles without naval squadrons and willing privateers. Havana had a squadron and ably fulfilled the expectations of Spanish authorities, as far as those expectations fell within the province of the traditional navy. It failed only in providing for and maintaining Florida and Apalache. Louisbourg, too, fulfilled expectations insofar as they fell within the province of a traditional navy, although it did not have a permanent squadron until 1757. The notion of Louisbourg as the bulwark of Canada and Louisiana, however, was perfectly absurd; it required more than Louisbourg could provide even with a squadron. It required an imperial navy. Louisbourg would not have disappointed Pontchartrain and his generation, for it proved a success in defending a French share in the cod fishery and a moderate success as a base for privateers. It did, however, disappoint Maurepas and his contemporaries, proving less than invulnerable, far from a bulwark of French America, and useless for reconquering Acadia or Newfoundland.

With the exception of the war years, 1744–48 and 1756–58, the French cod fishery continued to flourish after the loss of Newfoundland. Operating from several points in France and Cape Breton, French fishermen harvested the Grand Banks with little interference from their British rivals. Two frigates cruising the area sufficed for protection. Sent out each spring from France, these two vessels used Louisbourg as their local base for refuge, supplies, repairs, or whatever the occasion warranted.[60] The frigates discouraged the piracy on the fishing banks which caused complaints in the early 1720s.[61] After the Canceau incident of 1722—a clash between French and British fishermen—the naval presence at Louisbourg effectively secured the French fishery.[62] Only war could prevent the French from confidently pursuing cod on the Grand Banks.

In protecting the fishery the French protected their nursery of seamen. Estimates on the numbers of sailors employed in the fishery varied, perhaps because of fluctuations in the size of the fishing fleets. English estimates put the total of French fishermen at 27,500 in 1745, and 14,800 just prior to the Seven Years' War.[63] French estimates, probably more accurate, suggest a total of 8,000 to 10,000,[64] of whom 3,000 to 4,000 normally used Ile Royale as their base.[65] The presence of Louisbourg protected them all equally. Some of these men worked on *chaloupes*, small vessels with a crew of three, which hardly prepared a sailor to serve on a warship. Others, however, worked on *goelettes* (schooners) and larger ships, and became versatile seamen who could help fill out navy crews. Louisbourg thus eased the manpower shortage of the French navy, protecting their single largest naval training program.

Although not as successful in privateering as in protecting the fishery, Louisbourg nevertheless raised the costs of British traders engaged in the New England–Great Britain trade, at least in wartime. Louisbourg's foremost historian, J. S. McLennan, says that Louisbourg privateers "seriously interfered" with New England's trade;[66] another author claims that in the summer of 1744 French privateers "almost paralyzed the maritime trade and fishery of Massachusetts."[67] In 1744 thirty-six prizes appear in the records of the Louisbourg Amirauté, the majority of them Massachusetts vessels.[68] Eleven of these averaged more than 10,000 livres apiece in value.[69] For three weeks in May 1744, when the French knew of the declaration of war before the news arrived in Boston, and for the next two weeks as well, the success of Louisbourg's privateers delighted the French. By the fall of that year, however, New England privateers had turned the tables on the French and confined French fishing and trading vessels to the safety of Louisbourg's harbor.[70] By the next summer Louisbourg ceased to function as a privateer base because of the arrival of the British fleet, and for the balance of the war Louisbourg remained in British hands.

Louisbourg lived up to French expectations as a privateer's nest for only the briefest period in 1744 because of two main problems. One was a shortage of gunpowder, most acute in wartime; the other was the competition of the fishery for labor, shipping, and capital, most acute in peacetime. Like all French colonies, Louisbourg always lacked gunpowder. Both land defenses and ships protecting the fishery had priority over privateers, who thus found it difficult to operate. Even when they found powder, its cost cut into profits.[71] In peacetime, privateering suffered from a shortage of ships, capital, and labor, since fishing and commerce yielded higher and more reliable returns for both shipowners and seamen.[72] Unlike the situation in Cuba, no peacetime coast guard existed that could rapidly convert to privateer duty. Only with official encouragement could French privateering attract men and money in sufficient quantities to affect British trade. So when war resumed officially in 1756, crown policy had changed: the new Minister of Marine instructed Louisbourg officials to keep all available men in port, even if it meant an end to French privateering.[73]

How well did Louisbourg perform in its third role as bulwark of America and invincible fortress? It is this image of Louisbourg which has survived, especially in the English-speaking historical tradition. British, Canadian, and American authors have accepted Maurepas's vision of Louisbourg; indeed they have embellished it, for the greater Louisbourg becomes, the greater the glory of the Britons and New Englanders who captured it. Endorsement of this interpretation of Louisbourg's role in the French empire first appears in the writing of William Shirley, the Massachusetts governor who organized the first reduction of Louisbourg. By exaggerating Louisbourg's military importance to France, Shirley not only sold London and the Massachusetts legislature on the 1745 expedition, but also camouflaged his real motives: control of the cod fishery for Massachusetts.[74] Three generations of historians have accepted Shirley's view. From Parkman and Fiske to McLennan and Wrong to Parry and Stanley nothing has changed. Even the most recent work on Louisbourg reproduces the old adages.[75] These authors have ignored two salient truths: first, that the French did not originally intend Louisbourg to serve as the protector of Canada, and, second, that it could not possibly do so without a permanent squadron to control the straits between Cape Breton Island and Newfoundland.[76] Curiously enough, the vast majority of anglophone writers have not recognized the importance of sea power to Louisbourg. In this they follow in the tradition of Parkman rather than of Mahan and contribute the weight of their authority to a misconception.[77]

Louisbourg could not prevent the British from sailing up the St. Lawrence; the fortress could not even defend itself. As long as the French could not prevent a landing in the vicinity, they could not hold Louisbourg against an expedition of any size at all. The Marquis de Montcalm, whose judgment in such matters commands respect, considered Louisbourg indefensible for this reason, regardless of the extent of the fortifications.[78] Without sufficient sea power, the French could neither prevent a landing nor relieve a besieged Louisbourg.

The engineers who designed and executed the fortifications of Louisbourg intended a fortress of the sort Vauban developed for the French frontiers in Europe.[79] Vauban hoped his fortresses could, with four thousand men and adequate provisions, hold out for two months against large numbers of besiegers. Within two months, his theory went, French columns could relieve his frontier fortress.[80] Such logic suited Alsace perfectly, but on the barren and isolated shores of Ile Royale, it made not the slightest sense, for the French army could not swim the Atlantic and the French navy could not carry it across. The French needed much more than two months to fit out an expedition large enough to relieve Louisbourg; given the leisurely pace of communications, authorities in Paris could learn of a siege only shortly before Louisbourg fell. To relieve the fortress, the French command had to anticipate the attack by several months and the French navy had to defeat a British squadron off Louisbourg. Neither event was at all likely; their conjunction was virtually impossible. Even if properly built, provisioned, and defended, Louisbourg could not hold out more than eight weeks. In both 1745 and 1758 it lasted seven.

To add to its profound vulnerability, the fortress was not properly built. Most accounts agree that the French exhibited sufficient valor in its defense, but heroics went for nought because of other weaknesses.[81] The French never finished the fortifications despite spending about four million livres.[82] The works progressed slowly for several reasons. At five *sous* per day labor was scarce,[83] and building supplies and skilled masons had to come from afar.[84] The year included only 93 work days, what with seven months' winter and 22 Sundays, 18 *fêtes*, and about 20 storm days in the remaining five months.[85] Furthermore, when finished, the fortifications tended to crumble: sea sand in combination with high humidity resulted in mortar that did not adhere properly.[86] One engineer maintained that he had designed the walls to withstand musket fire only![87] The number of accusations of graft and embezzlement that drifted back and forth between France and Louisbourg suggests that slipshod workmanship and cheap materials helped line several pockets.

Inaccessible to French armies and ringed by poorly built walls, Louisbourg was also handicapped by the surrounding terrain. One Englishman observed, "There cannot be, for a fortified town, a worse situation than the locale of Louisbourg, it is commanded all round by Heights."[88] Small hills to the east of the walls looked down into the town; while they hardly towered above it, they could serve admirably as cannon emplacements and observation posts. Referring to the hills and to the quality of the fortifications, one French officer wrote that Louisbourg resembled an amphitheatre more than a fort.[89]

Louisbourg was, however, properly provisioned. In both 1745 and 1758 the fortress surrendered with plentiful stocks of food and ammunition. In 1758 the British entered to find 10,000 barrels of flour, 50,000 barrels of beef and pork, 5,000 barrels of powder, 13,000 stands of arms, 4,000 shells, and 14,000 shots.[90] In both sieges, the French gave in well before starvation menaced the defenders, but their commanders felt that with no prospect for relief by sea, resistance only delayed the inevitable and inflicted unnecessary hardship in the meantime.

Given all these flaws, it is hard to conceive of Louisbourg as invulnerable no matter how well provisioned. This idea of the fortress has survived only through the negligence of three generations of historians. Indeed, the original idea of building a Vauban fortress under such conditions suggests greater negligence on the part of the bureaucrats and engineers who hatched and nurtured the scheme. Perhaps they understood the limitations of Louisbourg but preferred to see the fortifications go up anyway, since it benefited the local economy and indubitably enriched local officials. If so, why not let the French treasury spend thousands of livres on Louisbourg, and why not encourage such expenditure by accepting and repeating outlandish claims for the continental value of Louisbourg? The men on the spot may have had compelling reasons to acquiesce in Maurepas's folly. Montcalm, who had no such reasons, thought one hundred men "for the policing of the fishery" could accomplish as much as all the fortification at Louisbourg.[91] While Montcalm's judgment reflects his wish that French resources be diverted from Louisbourg to Quebec, it shows a sensitivity to the problems of Louisbourg's location which officials in Louisbourg and Paris appear either to have lacked or willingly suppressed.

To some extent, perhaps, the myth of Louisbourg's power to defend Canada derives from the sequence of events in 1758–59: the British capture of Louisbourg preceded the fall of Quebec, and therefore, one assumes, the former event brought about the latter. In 1745, however, the British reduced Louisbourg and did not attack Quebec in the three subsequent years of the war. They took Louisbourg because they wanted Louisbourg, not because it opened the way to Quebec. In 1711 the British bypassed French settlements at Plaisance, Louisbourg's predecessor, and mounted a large expedition against Quebec.[92] They might have pursued the same strategy in the Seven Years' War; indeed they considered doing so.[93] With French fleets confined to port, Britain could have attacked Quebec with no danger from French reinforcements. The close-watch system (a cousin to blockade), rather than the fall of Louisbourg, enabled the British to conquer Canada.[94]

Only in one limited sense did Louisbourg protect Canada. With their traditional navy the French did not make much use of Louisbourg, but had the British occupied the position, they might have exploited it more fully. They could more easily cruise the straits between Cape Breton Island and Newfoundland and deny the French the use of the St. Lawrence.[95] In 1746, after the first fall of Louisbourg, the British in fact stationed a squadron there.[96] Since an isolated Canada could not have survived long, an expedition like the British one of 1759 would have become unnecessary. Thus, once the French had gone to the expense of making Louisbourg a fortified port, it became much more important that the British be denied Louisbourg than that the French preserve it. Beyond this dubious service, Louisbourg was no help at all in the defense of French America.

On the whole, the Spanish found that Cuba fulfilled its various military roles fairly well. Havana successfully kept the treasure out of foreign hands (at least until the foreign merchants in Cadiz and Seville got their shares). Together with Santiago de Cuba, it functioned successfully as a base for interceptors of foreign commerce, especially early in the 1739–48 war. It provided accurate information on the movements of

British forces. Only as a base for the frontier struggle in Georgia did Havana disappoint Spanish hopes.

British sea forces did their best to intercept treasure fleets by cruising "off the Havanna," but the Spanish managed to defend their silver nevertheless.[97] To do so they employed the Armada de Barlovento and later the Havana squadron, each of which amounted to two or three *navios* (men-of-war) and two smaller vessels in peacetime, and up to ten or twelve *navios* in war.[98] The cost ran high: up to 58,000 pesos monthly in 1742–44, but protection of the silver carried a high priority. The only naval battle fought between British and Spanish fleets in the Caribbean between 1713 and 1762 concerned the defense of a treasure fleet. In September 1748 the squadrons of Reggio and Knowles dueled indecisively off Havana while the silver slipped away to Spain. Only for a treasure fleet would the Spanish risk a naval battle.[99]

The treasure, while never lost, occasionally stayed ashore in Veracruz rather than venture passage on the seas. The brevity of the campaign season in the eighteenth century made for long wars; states could use six months of the year to replenish fleets and armies. Under these circumstances, wars resembled contests of financial attrition, so the best way to win was to ruin the enemy's finances—precisely what the British hoped to do by harrying the treasure fleets. Havana and its warships, however, protected Spain's most valuable trade from British predation. Three fleets sailed during the war of 1739–48.[100]

As a base for interceptors, Cuba proved a partial success. Naval historian Admiral Sir Herbert Richmond considered that the British, on the whole, effectively defended their Jamaica trade, but interceptors may nonetheless have fulfilled their purpose by raising costs to British traders.[101] Ideally, interceptors swept the enemy's trade from the seas, something the Spanish never hoped to do. Their more modest ambition, consistent with their resources, was to seize as much British trade as possible, thereby impoverishing Britain and enriching Spain.[102] In peacetime, Jamaican traders found reason to complain of Spanish interceptors based at Santiago de Cuba.[103] British attempts to take the Cuban port in both 1741 and 1748 indicate the degree to which Santiago de Cuba succeeded in wartime.[104] Cuban privateers roved as far afield as Cape Hatteras and New York. In slightly more than six months in 1742–43, interceptors based in Santiago de Cuba seized twelve British vessels, most of them en route between Jamaica and New England.[105] Others based in other Cuban ports added several more—the total for 1743–45 reached seventy-seven—but toward the end of the war privateering dwindled.[106] Whereas in 1743 two seizures a week by Santiago de Cuba ships had not been exceptional,[107] by 1746–48 the Havana Company reported that its losses to British interceptors far outstripped the Spanish seizures of British trade.[108] The principal explanation for the decline in seizures toward the end of the war lies in the British practice of cruising off Santiago de Cuba. Rather than deploy warships to protect the various Caribbean trade routes, the Jamaica squadron began to blockade Santiago de Cuba. Not only did Spanish interceptors have greater difficulty slipping out, but when returning with a prize in tow, they had almost no chance of evading the British. In this way the British recovered numerous seizures before the Spanish recorded them.[109] Such a policy, while unpopular with Jamaican merchants, proved highly successful in limiting the impact of Cuban interceptors after 1743. Although seizures of British vessels increased again briefly in the early 1750s, Cuba, like Louisbourg, functioned successfully as a base for interceptors only fleetingly. British forces reacted quickly to minimize the damage these ports could do.

As a base of operations in Florida and Apalache, Havana again proved a partial success. The small settlement at San Augustín remained in Spanish hands with Cuban help, but the British frontier gradually moved southward.[110] Havana's militia and detached regulars saw action at Pensacola in 1718; Havana mounted an ill-fated expedition of 2,000 men to coastal Georgia in 1742–43; and silver and supplies channeled through Havana maintained the officials and garrison of Florida.[111]

Supplying Florida with food, arms, and population was one of Havana's principal duties. Before 1740, Florida's sustenance came in the form of a *situado* (roughly ninety thousand pesos of Mexican silver annually) with which Floridians bought supplies in Havana. After 1740, the burden of supplying Florida fell to the Havana Company, which often neglected this duty.[112] The Crown also entrusted the Havana Company with the task of populating Florida with Canary Islanders, a policy that soon proved a failure.[113]

The Havana Company lacked both the resources and the inclination to maintain, protect, and develop Florida and Apalache for Spain. To colonize the area properly and prevent British expansion, Spain needed population and trade. The Company could provide neither. To retain an undeveloped colony, Spain needed abundant supplies provided as subsidy and sure communications. Cuba could muster supplies, but the *flota* often absorbed the lion's share of the island's surplus. Only sea power could ensure communications between Florida and the rest of the Spanish Empire, but the Spanish fleets in the region had higher priorities than Florida. The Havana Company, which owned armed vessels, never functioned as an auxiliary navy. In recognition of Cuba's limitations, the Spanish relied on a policy of fortification in Florida after 1743.[114] Two decades of tranquility ensued on the frontier, and the Spanish gradually reduced Florida's *situado*.[115] The Havana Company greatly diminished its expenditure on Florida after the mid-1740s as well.[116] Without sure seaborne communication, neither the Havana Company nor the state could defend the northern frontier.

In its role as a monitor of British military activity, Cuba served Spain quite well. Information relayed to Spain could have little practical effect because of the slowness of communications, but Cuba furnished abundant and accurate intelligence on British naval forces. For example, the news that Admiral Vernon's 1740 expedition had chosen Cartagena as its target reached Spain through first Santiago de Cuba and then Havana.[117] Cuban officials also accurately reported to the Crown the size, condition, and route of Admiral Knowles's fleet in 1748.[118] Normally the Spanish had good information on British sailings from England, but relied on Cuba for intelligence on fleets in the Caribbean.[119] With accurate information speedily provided, they might perhaps avoid unfavorable one-sided engagements at sea, distribute reinforcements more wisely, and in general use their limited military resources to greater advantage. Officials in Spain seemed pleased with Cuban efforts.[120]

In order to succeed in any of its military roles, Cuba had to defend itself. Like the French in Ile Royale, the Spanish in Cuba relied on a policy of fortification. In the case of Louisbourg this policy was ill-conceived and poorly executed; in Havana, however, the policy suited conditions admirably. The Spanish understood that their naval strength in the Caribbean could never match British power without endangering home waters.[121] Thus the burden of defending Cuba fell to the army, in the form of colonial garrisons, and to militia forces. The presence of yellow fever in Cuba produced a crucial difference between Louisbourg and Havana which made fortification a wiser policy for the Spanish. In Havana, or anywhere else in the Caribbean, local defenders could generally count on decisive assistance from tropical diseases.

The first fortifications at Havana date from 1544, and all the major links in the port's defenses were begun by the mid-seventeenth century, although many remained unfinished a century later.[122] Beginning in the 1720s, however, the Spanish made an effort to bolster the fortifications at Havana and elsewhere in Cuba by engaging Italian and French engineers to draw up plans for improvements at several points around the island.[123] Stone came from Mexico; labor from prisons and state slaves.[124] Funds came from local taxes, such as the *sisa de muralla*, a tax on wine and brandy imports, which between 1736 and 1753 produced about 350,000 pesos for the walls of Havana—equal to 11 percent of total expenditure on Havana's fortifications prior to 1740.[125] The *villas* of Puerto Príncipe and Bayamo each offered to build their own forts at no expense to the Crown (probably hoping to escape assessment).[126] In Cuba as elsewhere in the Caribbean, the local population paid for a large proportion of the fortifications. That the locals would agree to shoulder some of the burden seemed a compelling argument in favor of fortifications rather than ships, which colonials would never agree to pay for, since they might easily be moved to another part of the empire (indeed several times before 1750 the locally funded Armada de Barlovento was joined to the Spanish ocean fleet).[127] The Governor of Jamaica thought that one ship was worth twenty forts in the Caribbean, but for the Spanish, tax considerations overrode strategic ones.[128] By the 1740s, Spanish investment had created fortifications strong enough to deter the British from attacking Havana by sea.[129] Smaller fortifications protected Santiago de Cuba, Matanzas, Jagua, Nipe, and other coastal inlets.

To man the battlements at Havana the Spanish maintained a garrison of about 1,500 to 2,000 men.[130] Militia units numbering 2,457 men in 1740 and 6,342 men by 1760 supplemented the regular troops.[131] At Santiago de Cuba the garrison consisted of about 320 men and the militia of about ten times that many.[132] Clearly the Spanish relied very heavily on militia units for Cuban defense. They had two excellent reasons: cost and durability. In 1719 it cost 23,000 pesos annually to maintain a regular battalion in Havana, but by 1754 the same battalion cost 122,000 pesos, more than three times the cost of maintaining a battalion in Spain.[133] Total garrison costs increased by a factor of eighteen between 1713 and 1741.[134] In addition, regular troops did not last long in Cuba. Many deserted, and of those who did not, roughly 20 percent could not because of illness or injury.[135] Death rates among regular troops, most of whom came from Spain and lacked requisite disease immunities, must have been much higher than among the militiamen, most of whom were born in Cuba. The Cuban militia units enjoyed reputations as good fighters.[136] Although usually very poorly armed, they proved more cost effective than regular troops. At Louisbourg, since regular troops died no faster than civilians and the population was smaller, the reverse was true.

With these fortifications and soldiers, Cuba managed to defend itself admirably until 1762. Indeed, in the Caribbean a handful of local or seasoned soldiers with adequate provisions and defenses always proved a formidable obstacle to European attackers. If the defenders could hold out for six weeks, yellow fever virtually assured their triumph. With full immunities to local diseases, local troops fought at a great advantage against expeditionary forces from Europe or North America, the reason Cuban militia so often compared favorably to Spanish regulars in Cuba.

British military leaders in the West Indies understood the importance of yellow fever very well. Admiral Edward Vernon wrote that operations in the West Indies could last no longer than six weeks.[137] Admiral Charles Knowles wrote, "whatever is to be effected in the West Indies must be done as expeditiously as possible, or the Climate soon wages a more destructive War, than the Enemy."[138] The British public understood, too, at least Samuel Johnson: "[The Spanish dominions] are defended not by walls mounted with cannons which by cannon may be battered, but by the storms of the deep and the vapours of the land, by the flames of calenture and blasts of pestilence."[139] The British misunderstood the reasons which made disease so important in Caribbean sieges, but they drew the correct conclusion: "But delay should never be made in an *attack*, for the reason that makes the great Fabian maxim '*cunctando*,' a certain defence in hot climates, when the defenders are under cover, and their enemy exposed to the weather, which they must be to guard against alarms and surprises; and if the besiegers can be kept from possessing any town, or extensive buildings, they may be left to climate and the 'Tented field': for sickness will prevent European troops succeeding in any attempt, where the service exceeds six weeks."[140]

In 1741 Sebastian de Eslava defended Cartagena against Admiral Vernon's and General Wentworth's attack with decisive help from disease. "Hostilities were simply extinguished by yellow fever," wrote John Fortescue, the historian of the British army. Eslava wrote that 9,000 British and colonials died, while Fortescue maintained the number of effectives fell by half in four days. In the following year, Vernon's and Wentworth's forces tried to take Santiago de Cuba by land, but again the troops fell ill before achieving their goal. About 2,000 men died on this expedition, almost none in combat. Spanish sources claim 75 percent of the British troops fell ill, while Fortescue wrote that not 1 in 10 of the 13,000 troops in these two attacks returned home.[141] In both cases yellow fever destroyed the besieging army before hunger and thirst or a breach in the walls could undo the besieged. The lesson of Cartagena confirmed Spanish faith in masonry.

In Cuba the arrival of yellow fever was reliable in a way that French reinforcements to a besieged Louisbourg were not. Thus fortifications designed to hold out temporarily against a siege made perfect sense in the Caribbean but very little in Cape Breton, where the most a fortress could achieve was a brief delay in the progress of the enemy. To the Spanish the disease factor amounted to another reason to put money in forts rather than ships.

In only one case did this logic fail: the fall of Havana in 1762.[142] In that campaign (6 June to 11 August) the Spanish surrendered just as yellow fever began to intervene. Not long after the town fell the British commander wrote that his entire army was ill and that they had lost "upward of 3,000 men since the Capitulation."[143] Had the Spanish held out slightly longer—as they might have since bombardment rather than starvation prompted the surrender—the normal pattern would have asserted itself and the British victory would have become another defeat.

The Spanish failure to fortify and hold the heights of La Cabaña, overlooking Havana's Morro castle, suggests that they expected the siege to be a short one. They certainly knew that in possession of La Cabaña lay the key to dominion of Havana.[144] Shortly after landing, the British took

La Cabaña "almost without resistance," good fortune which has mystified historians.[145] Either Spanish leadership displayed gross imcompetence, as most writers believe, or the Spanish relied on yellow fever to come to their aid in the weeks it would take the British to drag cannon up La Cabaña, mount them, and destroy the Morro.[146]

Had yellow fever asserted itself two weeks earlier at Havana in 1762, or had the defenders contested La Cabaña more stoutly, the Spanish reliance on fortification and militia units would need no justification. Still, the failure of 1762 should not obscure the underlying wisdom of Spanish policy. The British lost an army at Havana—5,366 men died, 4,708 of them of disease. The British navy lost 1,300 men, of whom only 68 died in action; another 3,300 sailors fell ill.[147] The excessive toll made the British victory Pyrrhic in the view of Dr. Johnson: "May my country be never cursed with such another conquest!"[148] Indeed the British triumph at Havana was a fluke; defenders had every right to expect the same results as at Cartagena, Santiago de Cuba, and elsewhere. For unknown reasons the Aedes aegypti failed to rescue Havana in time.[149]

On the surface, the military policies and events at Louisbourg and Havana bear a strong resemblance. Fortification and successful British sieges figure prominently in both ports' history. Closer scrutiny, however, betrays important differences. At Louisbourg a policy of fortification was absurdly out of place, whereas at Havana it suited the situation admirably. Yellow fever could relieve the besieged in the Caribbean, but at Louisbourg the imperial navy of Britain could prevent any relief.

The French viewed Louisbourg as the protector of the cod fishery, as a privateering port, and as a base for offensive action against British territory in the vicinity. The Spanish saw Havana and Cuba as protectors of the treasure fleets, as privateering bases, and as staging areas for operations against adjacent British colonies. In these modest roles both Louisbourg and Havana served fairly well, although they proved more adept at protection of the local treasure, whether cod or silver, than at the projection of military force against encroaching British forces. The French, apparently through Maurepas, developed an outlandish notion of the defense capability of Louisbourg and eventually considered it the bulwark of French America. The Spanish never developed a comparable illusion about the potential of Havana. Although Bourbon Spain borrowed many colonial institutions and ideas from Bourbon France, Gallic disregard of the realities of sea power did not penetrate the Pyrenees. Whereas Louisbourg ultimately relied on the unreliable French navy for its security, Havana expected to defend itself. Spanish policy took adequate account of naval inferiority, perhaps the silver lining in a century of naval weakness. Colonial defense policy within the French military of marine, however, did not adjust to British maritime dominance after the 1690s.

The French and Spanish defended Louisbourg and Havana in order to profit from them. While their economic resources helped toward military ends, their military roles by and large consisted of defending economic resources, whether in production or in transit. Accordingly, we turn next to the economic policies of the Bourbon empires toward these island ports.

5 Hinterlands and Ports (Theory)

Among the basic tenets of mercantilism is the responsibility of the state to organize the entire economic life of its empire in its own interest. As we have seen in chapter 3, those charged with shaping policy in eighteenth-century France and Spain accepted this premise and strove to order imperial trade and enterprise accordingly. They often failed, having challenged the incentives of the market and the dictates of geography. When they failed, they sacrificed the economic future of Cape Breton and Cuba not to the metropolis, as intended, but to British neighbors in New England and Jamaica. Nothing could have displeased French and Spanish ministers more than when, as they saw it, their colonies enriched the empire of their greatest rival.

The French assigned Louisbourg a modest role in the organization of its Atlantic economy as both a primary producer and entrepôt port. Spain, in contrast, expected Havana to play a central part as both a primary producer and a funnel through which the entire trade of its New World empire (excepting Buenos Aires) should pass. Louisbourg's advantages suited it to the production of only one important export: codfish. Thus the French faced no dilemma between various crops and could focus their attention on the regulation of commerce. Cuba, however, offered tobacco, sugar, and hides for export, so Spanish mercantilists had to decide how to organize each of these enterprises. In that decision lay the roots of Cuba's modern history as a sugar monoculture.

According to mercantilist logic, one of the purposes of colonies was to lower the state's imports by providing substitutes from within the empire. Thus a colony's products and exports mattered a great deal to metropolitan authorities and could not go unregulated. At Louisbourg the production of codfish, and to lesser degrees, coal, lumber, ships, and food crops, obliged French authorities to create policies to govern these enterprises. Despite adherence to the general principles of mercantilism, the French system allowed a wide margin for particularistic treatment of individuals or industries. Over forty-five years, a complex mosaic of rules and policies grew up to govern the economic life of the colony. Although some instructions contradicted earlier ones and others merited endless reiteration, a certain logic informed French policy toward Louisbourg's export economy.

The central concern of French authorities was the perpetuation of a large fishing industry based at Louisbourg. The fishery, besides maintaining a reserve of skilled sailors for the navy, supplied the state with a reliable export item with which to earn bullion or finance imports, obviated any need to expend wealth for foreign fish, and provided coastal and urban France with animal protein in great quantity. To Maurepas it was "the best of all enterprises."[1] In order to foster the fishing industry, the French founded the colony of Ile Royale, adjusted tax rates on codfish and cod oil, and legislated in favor of employers and against laborers at Louisbourg. They based all economic policy around the humble codfish.

The North Atlantic cod (*Gadus morhua morhua*) prefers cold water, between 0° C and 11° C (32° and 52° F), and depths of about 100 meters.[2] The cod exhibits remarkable sensitivity to fluctuation in temperature, migrating in search of comfort as well as food. In summer it seeks the cooler depths; in winter it heads for shallow water. The adult cod is a gluttonous bottom-feeder preferring mollusks, but content to eat shrimp, crab, lobster, herring, squid, alewife, capelin, and occasionally even young cod. Every winter, cod swim by the millions to the Grand Banks to spawn. Each female releases from 3 to 9 million eggs into the sea, of which fewer than ten normally will float to the surface, hatch, and survive. By July the spawning season ends, and the last remaining cod begin their retreat to cold waters. The young that survive reach a length of 20 centimeters (8 inches) in a year (less in colder water) and eventually grow to roughly 70 centimeters in length and 3 to 5 kilograms (7 to 11 pounds) in weight. The largest attain a size of almost 2 meters (over 6 feet) and a weight of 70 kilograms (154 pounds), but a cod of 40 kilograms is nowadays extremely rare, and one of 10 kilograms is a fine catch. The oldest known cod expired at age twenty-two, but quite possibly some live longer. Eighteenth-century cod apparently grew larger than today's.[3]

Cod is occasionally called the beef of the sea. In fact, dried cod is considerably more nutritious than lean beef. It provides 250 percent more protein per calorie than beef, and seven times as much protein per calorie as wheat flour. Codfish is close to the top of the undersea food chain, five links removed from vegetable proteins such as plankton. It takes 100,000 kilograms of plankton to produce a single kilogram of codfish: it is, in fact, the most highly concentrated animal protein available in quantity on the surface of the earth. In addition, cod is rich in several minerals necessary to human good health.[4] Codfish protein was vital to regions that produced very little in the way of meat and dairy products (e.g., the Mediterranean world). Between its nutritional value and its suitability for curing, codfish rewarded expensive, long-distance fishing like no other fish.

The feeding and breeding habits of the cod defined the rhythm according to which men pursued them. They thronged to the Grand Banks from November to July, but the presence of drift ice brought by the Labrador Current divided the season in two. Thus in the eighteenth century, fishermen spoke of the autumn fishery (from November to early January) and summer fishery (from April to August). Few fish remained by August, but the Banks are large and the cod normally swims only three miles per day when on migration, so some fishermen stayed in search of stragglers. Since the sixteenth century, Europeans have flocked to and dispersed from the Grand Banks according to this seasonal rhythm. Basques first exploited the fishery in a large way, and the Iberian diet has ever since depended on cod as a protein source.[5] In the course of the sixteenth century, West Country Englishmen, Bretons, and Normans joined the Basques. The cod fishery has been an international enterprise ever since, and often a bone of contention.[6]

In the eighteenth century, the summer fishery was conducted in two ways—the wet (or green) fishery, and the dry fishery.[7] The wet fishery involved European ships, European labor, European capital, and European equipment. Every spring fishermen followed the forty-fourth and forty-fifth parallel west until they saw shore birds, or until soundings signaled shallow water. Fishermen aimed to arrive as soon as possible after the drift ice disappeared, usually in early April, because the earliest fishing was the best.[8] Once at the Banks, their ship (between 80 and 120 tons)[9] stood at anchor while the fishermen (of whom there were fifteen or twenty) dangled multihooked lines over the sides of the vessel.[10] They deposited their catch with comrades who beheaded and split the cod before arranging it for the salter.[11] The salter had the most important job: if he was too liberal with the salt the catch became stiff as a board, if too sparing it rotted. A 1743 regulation instructed salters to use six barrels per 100 quintals of cod (a quintal equals 100 pounds).[12] When the boat could hold no more or when cod became too scarce, the fishermen returned to France, usually to Breton or Basque ports.[13]

The dry fishery followed a somewhat different pattern. The shore replaced the ship as the base of operations. The fishermen, either Ile Royale residents or Frenchmen, used *chaloupes*, and never ranged more than 15 kilometers from shore. The fishing *chaloupe* typically carried three men, one mast, no deck, and bulked between six and eight tons.[14] In a day's labor a *chaloupe* might land 500 fish. For each *chaloupe*, two additional men remained ashore to handle the chores associated with drying. These shore hands split and cleaned the fish, then stacked them between layers of salt. After five or six days they rinsed the cod in sea water and then spread them out to dry on wooden *graves*, or flakes, made expressly for that purpose. The cod lay thus for seven to ten days, flesh up during the day to dry, and skin up at night. Then the shore crew piled the fish high, skin up, for about a month, by which time about 80 percent of the moisture had evaporated (live cod are about 80 percent water, more than almost any other edible fish). Fish caught and processed this way weighed only about 20 percent of cod processed in the wet fishery.

Both Frenchmen and Ile Royale residents participated in the dry fishery. The Frenchmen set out in mid-March in ships of about 300 tons, bringing supplies for six months. Each ship carried about 120 men, half of them fishermen, the rest carpenters, salters, and other shore hands. They built cabins, piers, and flakes wherever they settled for the summer and left these monuments behind, perhaps to return the next spring.

Dry fishing from Ile Royale involved an *habitant-pescheur* who rented or owned a strip of beach and a few *chaloupes*. In the early spring he hired as many fishermen as necessary *(compagnon-pescheurs)*, often competing with rivals for seasonal labor from France.[15] He bought the season's supplies from French (or New England) vessels, often paying in cod futures. He paid interest in the form of artificially low prices on the cod he delivered at the season's end. A bad season brought unpayable debts for the small *habitant-pescheur* and the threat of becoming a wage-fisherman. Prosperous *habitant-pescheurs* normally did not work alongside their employees and could absorb a bad season without the risk of becoming *déclassé*. Many eventually became merchants as well and no longer had to borrow at all to procure a season's supplies. The wage-fisherman bought his food and drink from his employer, who subtracted the price from his wage. He typically owned no more than his clothes, fishing gear, and an axe or gun. The wage-fisherman normally received his pay in the form of fish; generally an *habitant-pescheur* kept half the catch and distributed the balance among his fishermen. Cod oil was divided in the same manner. A fisherman could usually expect to clear about thirty quintals of cod a year. Most wage-fishermen were *compagnons-pescheurs*, free to come and go as they chose; a few, however, were indentured laborers obliged to work for three years.[16]

All fishermen headed home, whether to Ile Royale or France, when the summer season closed in August after the last cod had departed for deep water. The autumn fishery began in November, using only *chaloupes* and dry fishery methods. In the autumn fishery a *chaloupe* might land 120 quintals of cod, compared to 300 in the summer fishery (a quintal of dried cod equalled about 60 to 100 fish).[17] Since the weather made it a good deal more dangerous than the summer season, fishermen received slightly higher wages in the autumn, somewhat more than half of the total catch. Even in summer the dry fishery ran major risks with the weather. An extended period of fog often spoiled a catch, and a squall sometimes undid hundreds of men and dozens of *chaloupes*.[18] The summer fogs of Newfoundland rendered its coasts less suitable for the dry fishery than those of Cape Breton Island, despite being closer to the Banks.[19] The perils to life and profit only increased in the autumn fishery.

The only major change in the methods of the cod fishing industry at Louisbourg between 1713 and 1758 came with the introduction from New England of the *goelette*, or schooner, in the 1720s. A *goelette* measured fifteen to twenty-five tons and carried a crew of seven.[20] It stayed at sea for several days at a time, ranging up to 100 kilometers from shore, extending the range of Ile Royale enterprise. Fishermen cured the fish as in the wet fishery until they returned to shore, when they dried it: fish as in the wet fishery until they returned to shore, when they dried it: the *goelette* thus allowed a compromise between the two traditional techniques of the fishery. Poorer quality fish resulted, but the *goelette* could catch 550 to 750 quintals of cod per season, compared to 300 for a *chaloupe*, reducing labor costs to a smaller proportion of the product. *Goelettes*, therefore, normally showed a better profit. Only well-established *habitant-pescheurs* could afford to buy and outfit the larger vessels, so the *goelette* fishery centered at Louisbourg, while the *chaloupe* fishery was dispersed around the island. After 1713, the British operated a dry fishery from Newfoundland, a schooner fishery from New England, and even a small wet fishery from the West Country.[21] The wet fishery depended on salt, of course, preferably solar salt, of which Britain had little and France plenty. Thus only the French produced both salted and dried cod in large quantity, which gave them an advantage in the international marketplace.

Basques had pioneered the dry fishery in the sixteenth century, and by the eighteenth century the Iberian and Mediterranean world had developed a taste for dried cod as opposed to salt cod—that is, the product of the dry fishery as opposed to that of the wet fishery. The French exported larger dry cod to Spain and Portugal, often through the agency of Basques.[22] Since the Spanish Basque cod fishery had disappeared with the peace of 1713, Spain imported almost 500,000 quintals of dried cod annually, or about 16 kilograms per family of four. Dried cod being 92 percent protein (by weight), this trade supplied about half the protein requirements of the Spanish population.[23] With approximately 130 meatless days per year in Spain, this market was fairly reliable, although no major price fluctuations tested its elasticity. According to one estimate, Portugal consumed about 30 percent as much cod as Spain.[24] Smaller salt cod the French exported to Italy and the Ottoman lands, normally through Marseilles merchants. Italy may have consumed as much codfish as Spain; estimates for the Levant are mere guesses, but cod contributed significantly to Marseilles's trade with the eastern Mediterranean.[25]

Salt cod, which kept less well than dried cod, had to be eaten within a year. As a result Louisbourg salt cod had only one market—France, and Paris in particular.[26] The West Indies constituted another major market for salted cod. Planters in both the French and British sugar islands who wanted to feed their slaves as cheaply as possible bought large quantities of refuse cod—mostly the heads and organs discarded before salting. Indeed many slaves had almost no source of animal protein except cod.[27] By the 1750s one half of the season's catch—clearly not just refuse cod— went to the West Indies.[28] (The Spanish colonies imported comparatively little dried cod, though small quantities occasionally appeared in Havana.) Since salt cod kept so well, transoceanic sailors ate it regularly. Cod formed a regular part of the rations of every European navy.[29] The large and reliable markets in the Mediterranean and Caribbean made a share of cod trade a valuable prize.

From the outset, the French considered prosecution of the cod fishery the purpose of Louisbourg. Pontchartrain repeated this refrain incessantly.[30] Several others, including the contemporary historian Père Charlevoix and the Conseil de la Marine, agreed.[31] Others thought Louisbourg might secure the entire cod fishery for France, and even help establish a French whaling industry.[32] Subsequent generations of French ministers never lost sight of this economic role and kept reminding officials in Louisbourg of its primacy in the affairs of the colony.[33]

Normally the state's thirst for revenue inspired taxes on every branch of French commerce, but the Crown made an exception for codfish and cod oil. As early as 1669, Colbert had given tax advantages to Canadian cod upon entry into France.[34] In 1713 Pontchartrain extended the preferential treatment to tax exemption for ten years.[35] Although originally designed as a temporary measure to promote the nascent fishery at Ile Royale, this preferential treatment lasted until the fall of Louisbourg. Every ten years the French renewed the exemption.[36] At the same time, they burdened foreign cod (i.e., British) with a high import duty trying to restrict the French market to fish caught by Frenchmen. French cod also entered St.-Domingue and Martinique duty free after 1718.[37] With all import duties removed, fishermen paid only a local tax of one quintal of fish per *chaloupe* (roughly 0.3 percent), which supported the poorhouse (*hôpital*).[38] All this legislation was aimed simply to encourage both the Louisbourg dry fishery and the French wet fishery. In theory, the bullion earned and the sailors created by the fishery offset the loss of tax revenue.

French authorities tried to favor the cod trade in other ways as well. When a scarcity of labor threatened to discourage *habitants-pescheurs*, the

Crown stepped in to restrict competition for fishermen through regulation. The laborer's freedom to negotiate with more than one *habitant-pescheur* vanished, and a ceiling appeared on wages. At one point laws prohibited employers from paying workers more than the value of the cod oil. Thus fortified, the *habitants-pescheurs* of Louisbourg operated continuously, except during war years, until 1758.[39]

The Crown's efforts to bolster the cod fishery extended even to regulation of the town's architecture. In 1721 the Conseil de la Marine reported that the King had agreed to limit the height of all royal buildings, so as not to interfere with the winds necessary to the drying of the catch. An *ordonnance* obliged those who built houses and stores to observe the same limit.[40] The Conseil de la Marine and the ministers who followed invariably exhorted the officials at Louisbourg to do everything within their power to favor the fishery. Through such appeals and legislation, they hoped Louisbourg would sustain an industry they deemed vital to France.

Although the fishery always remained uppermost in their minds, French authorities never envisioned a colony solely dependent upon a single export. Especially in the early years, the French held high hopes for Ile Royale as a source of minerals and stone. The Conseil de la Marine showed an interest in lime, brick, slate, and marble.[41] The principal mining interest, however, always lay in coal. Pontchartrain hoped that with a steady supply from Ile Royale, France might one day surpass Britain as a coal producer.[42] To encourage coal mining, the French removed all import duties on Ile Royale coal, just as they had done with codfish.[43] This exemption, too, extended for ten years, but it lapsed in 1725, and thereafter Ile Royale coal had to pay a high duty established in 1692. Maurepas lowered the duty again in 1729 to give Ile Royale coal an advantage against English competition.[44] In ensuing decades, the French exhorted Louisbourg officials to encourage coal production but made no reductions in the duty.[45] After the first siege of Louisbourg, the French briefly considered mining coal not for export, but to heat the town and barracks of Louisbourg, as the English had done in their short stay.[46]

The French at Louisbourg preferred wood to coal for fuel. They hoped the forests of Cape Breton could provide both fuel and materials for construction and shipbuilding.[47] They used soldiers to open logging roads (the only roads on the island) and contracted with a certain Comte d'Agrain for 60,000 cubic feet of lumber per year (enough for a large frigate). Apparently no one seriously expected Cape Breton to produce lumber for export, perhaps because freight rates prohibited shipment of bulky goods.

The French did, however, hope that Cape Breton timber could assist in the development of a major shipbuilding industry at Louisbourg, envying the example of British North America, which in the eighteenth century built between a quarter and a third of all British ships.[48] Pontchartrain promised to send out shipwrights to the new colony in 1714. Later the Crown offered a bonus per ton on ships built at Ile Royale, expecting this measure to yield about 720 tons annually.[49] In the 1730s and 1740s, Louisbourg authorities acted to restrict purchases of English ships at Louisbourg, hoping thereby to stimulate the colony to build its own. Maurepas considered banning such sales altogether, but decided against it because the fishery would suffer without an abundant supply of boats.[50] Maintaining a ship-building industry clearly took second priority to the fishery.

The French ministry of marine also hoped to complement Louisbourg's export economy with food production. Hoping the colony might grow enough food to feed itself, Pontchartrain tried to get soldiers to stay and Acadians to immigrate to Ile Royale to take up farming. He and his successors constantly implored local officials to encourage agriculture.[51] Later, Maurepas tried to develop Ile St. Jean into a food-surplus colony, so that Louisbourg could survive on locally produced grain.[52] After the first siege, and particularly under the governorship of the Comte de Raymond, the French once again tried to develop the interior of Ile Royale into farmland.[53] The experience of the 1745 siege had made clear how vulnerable the colony remained to starvation.

French ambitions for each of the products of Louisbourg's economy— fish, coal, lumber, ships, and food—assumed traditional mercantilist form. The French hoped to create a colony that could provide the metropolis (and the French West Indies) with staple goods, which otherwise must come from rival empires, and that could feed itself at no expense to the crown.

Like the French, Spanish colonial trade prospered greatly in the eighteenth century.[54] Cuban trade and production participated in the general upsurge, and so colonial ministers faced new problems in regulating the Cuban economy. They sought to solve these by erecting royal and contracted monopolies to manage the Cuban export economy of tobacco, sugar, hides, timber, and ships. At the outset of the eighteenth century, only shipbuilding and tobacco mattered sufficiently to attract royal attention. By the 1730s, however, the production of sugar and hides had expanded so that they, too, were assigned to an *asentista* (sanctioned monopolist). José Tallapiedra, a Cadiz merchant, signed the first major *asiento* (contract) with the Spanish government in October of 1734. The Marqués Casa-Madrid, another Cadiz merchant, signed essentially the same contract four years later,[55] and in 1740 the Real Compañia de la Habana, or the Havana Company, agreed to much the same terms. Adjusted in a second contract in 1744, these terms obliged the *asentista* to supply the Cuban military establishment in return for monopoly privileges in the Cuban export trade and in some imports as well.[56] The Crown entrusted the Cuban export economy to the Havana Company until 1761, when it revoked its privileges in favor of José Villanueva Pico. Before this last *asentista* could begin his contract, Havana fell to the British. Within this general framework of monopoly, the Spanish government enacted specific policies designed to regulate the quantity and quality of the production of various Cuban goods.[57] Tobacco received the most attention.

Nicotiana tabacum long preceded the Spaniards in Cuba. It became an export crop, Cuba's largest by 1650, when cultivated by the Spanish.[58] Tobacco farmers, called *vegueros*, had to expend the greatest care on their crop. In August and September they broadcast tiny tobacco seeds mixed with cinder to prevent overseeding. One in three seeds germinated. After the plant broke the surface, the *veguero* covered it with brush to shield it from the sun. The precise timing mattered greatly. Five to six weeks after seeding (mid- to late October), the *veguero* transplanted the plant from higher altitudes to the alluvial plain of one of Cuba's short rivers. Since tobacco flavor depended more on soil and climate than on the genus of seed, the grower took great pains with transplanting. He placed healthy plants in rows three feet apart to facilitate weeding, culling the diseased and injured ones. For the next three and a half months, the *veguero* and his family weeded and battled insects around the clock. The meticulous also plucked the buds, suckers, and lower leaves from the plant (chores known as *desbotanar* and *deshijar* in Cuba), leaving only eight to twelve leaves to mature. Three workers could raise 10,000 plants or 4,000 pounds of leaf.

After four to five months in the ground (January), the plant stood as tall as the grower, and its leaves now began to darken and droop. The *veguero* then cut the leaves beginning at the top, working carefully since the leaves broke easily, and left them to dry one day in the sun. At sundown he took them to a shed where they dried for another three to four days, after which they hung by rope from poles to dry for two more weeks. By this time the fermenting leaves were dark brown and pliable enough to travel to market.

Cuban tobacco was an extremely sensitive plant, susceptible to several diseases and attractive to many insects. Like any weed it survived hardship readily enough, but only properly favorable conditions could produce quality leaf. It required much rain in the early stages and at transplanting, but almost none as it neared maturity. In order to produce high-grade tobacco, the *veguero* had to treat his plants with delicate care. Thus, in contrast to the Virginia and Maryland product, Cuban leaf was not suited to slave labor on a large scale. The *vegueros* were small farmers, many of them immigrants from the Canary Islands, which had a tobacco tradition. They worked the fields beside their families, although the more prosperous might own a slave or two. The demands of the tobacco plant itself—or more accurately, of a high quality product—imparted a democratic flavor to the industry.[59] Perhaps 10,000 *vegueros* toiled in Cuba.[60] They generally lacked title to the land they worked and either rented or squatted on large estates. Each grower produced about 60 to 65 *arrobas* of tobacco (one *arroba* equals about 25 pounds), worth between 300 and 350 pesos.[61]

Good Cuban tobacco was the world's finest, much in demand in the courts of France and Spain.[62] In the early eighteenth century, the best tobacco lands lay in Guane, Güines, and Bayamo, but most of the island produced some leaf.[63] Most Cuban tobacco came from the region around Havana. A smaller tobacco growing region centered around the San Juan and San Agustín Rivers, near Matanzas. Settlements around San Juan de los Remedios and Santa Clara, also produced some tobacco, but the jurisdiction of Puerto Príncipe grew very little. In the east, a large tobacco industry flourished at Mayarí, Holguín, Bayamo, Guantánamo, Baracoa, and Santiago de Cuba.

Cuban tobacco normally left the hands of the *vegueros* as leaf. Depending on the variety, the tobacco might then be ground in Cuban mills to produce *polvo* or *rapé* (snuff) or shipped to Spain as leaf for cigars. Smuggled tobacco normally went as leaf. Northern European markets favored snuff and pipe tobacco, but Spain, Portugal, and the Americas preferred cigars. On the whole, snuff takers outnumbered cigar smokers by a considerable margin.[64] Apparently all classes of Spanish society smoked, creating a steady demand for cigars, prompting the Spanish to establish huge *fábricas* in Seville: the *fábrica* finished in 1757 was the second largest building in Spain after the Escorial.[65] Although Maryland and Virginia produced much larger quantities of tobacco in the eighteenth century, the Spanish colonies had no rival in quality leaf tobacco and high-grade snuff.[66] Methods of tobacco growing in Cuba and cigar making in Seville changed very little over the years. What did change, and where the scope for government policy lay, was the way in which tobacco got from Cuba to Spain.

The state first involved itself in Cuban tobacco in 1708, making a major purchase for the Seville *fábricas*.[67] Prior to 1708, private merchants had traded the bulk of Havana tobacco to Spain on their accounts, although the state had made occasional small purchases.[68] From the point of view of the Spanish Crown, this system had two major drawbacks. First, with private traders involved, the enforcement of anticontraband regulations proved impossible. Second, the royal *fábricas* in Seville did not receive a steady supply of leaf tobacco when competing in a free market. The *fábricas* needed about 3 million pounds of leaf annually to meet domestic demand. After the outbreak of the War of Spanish Succession in 1701, the difficulty of supplying the *fábricas* grew acute. Not only did British sea power inhibit merchant shipping, but also the Spanish felt compelled to prohibit the import of all Virginia tobacco, which had hitherto supplemented Cuban shipments.[69] To resolve these two problems the state began to buy large quantities of Cuban tobacco, almost exclusively from the Havana area. By 1710, Mexican silver provided for the purpose allowed the state to purchase the lion's share of each year's tobacco crop. From this point on, the state, or its contracted agents, acted as the major legal market for Havana tobacco.

This system shortly gave way to the state monopoly, or *estanco*, proclaimed in 1717. Officially the reasons behind the *estanco* were identical to those which had provoked state purchases in 1708. The King explained, "Having recognized the grave harm which has resulted from the extraction of Cuban tobacco by foreign kingdoms, leaving the peninsula of Spain without what it needs, obliging it to buy from other kingdoms, in clear prejudice to my finances and vassals. . . ."[70] Other factors entered into this decision as well, however. The example of the French tobacco monopoly, instituted by Colbert in 1674, guided Spanish policy after French ministers appeared in the court of Philip V.[71] In addition, the experience of 1708–12 demonstrated the great potential advantages of Cuban tobacco to Spanish revenue. If properly encouraged and controlled, it seemed, the trade in Havana leaf could provide the Crown with untold wealth. Uztáriz thought the tobacco monopoly might yield 6 to 7 million pesos a year to the fisc.[72] According to the *Real Instrucción* of 11 April 1717, the King hoped Cuba could provide 7.3 million pounds of tobacco, 5 million for Spain, 200,000 for Lima and Buenos Aires, 100,000 for Chile, 500,000 for the Canaries, and 1.5 million for export.[73]

The monopoly had one further aim—the deindustrialization of Cuban tobacco. By the same *Real Instrucción* of 1717, the Crown prohibited the construction of tobacco mills in all of New Spain, including Cuba. Legislation in 1720 assigned an import duty on ground tobacco 40 percent higher than on leaf tobacco.[74] In this way Spanish authorities hoped to reserve all tobacco processing for the peninsula, and to confine Cubans to the production of tobacco in leaf.[75] After all, colonial industries that competed with metropolitan ones hardly coincided with the spirit of mercantilism.

The *estanco* provoked revolts led by *vegueros* who resented the low fixed prices,[76] and by merchants and speculators, who resented monopoly.[77] Troops suppressed the discontented, but in 1720 a *real cédula* (royal decree) allowed the "free use" of tobacco.[78] State purchases continued while the monopoly was not in force (1720–27), but familiar problems of contraband and irregularity of supply to Seville again annoyed the Crown.[79] In 1727, Martín de Loynaz, a high functionary of Spain's *renta de tabacos* (which administered the sale of tobacco in Spain), traveled to Havana to reinstitute the monopoly. This time it went by the name of the Intendencia General del Tabaco.

Through the Intendencia, the Crown hoped to realize the benefits of monopoly—profit, reduced contraband, assured supply for Seville—without alienating the Cuban population. In 1731 new instructions included a prohibition on Crown purchases of *polvo*; once again the Crown wished to reserve all tobacco processing for Spain. An annual sum of 200,000 pesos from Mexico covered the cost of each year's harvest.[80]

By 1734 the Crown decided to farm out the tobacco monopoly, presumably because profits did not match expectations or because the Crown hoped private enterprise would show greater efficiency. Patiño awarded the first contract to José Tallapiedra. The 1734 contract stipulated prices, classes, and quantities of tobacco to be bought in Havana and sold to the Seville *fábricas*.[81] In theory, Tallapiedra did not have a full monopoly, since growers could sell tobacco to others once Tallapiedra had filled his quota. In practice, however, this amounted to monopoly since growers had to sell quickly before their leaf spoiled. Tallapiedra's contract called for 3 million pounds of tobacco annually for ten years and specified the areas from which the tobacco should come, almost all near Havana. Tallapiedra's contract underwent slight revision in 1736 and was revoked in 1738.[82]

No one had contested the state monopoly of 1727–34, but once that monopoly fell to private hands, groups in Cadiz and Havana tried to wrest it away from Tallapiedra. Francisco Sánchez de Madrid y Moreno de Mendoza, marqués de Casa-Madrid, captured the contract in October 1738.[83] His contract was for eight years, but by December 1740, a group of prominent Havana merchants led by Don Martín Aróstegui managed to secure the monopoly for themselves. The contract of the Real Compañía de la Habana differed from those of Tallapiedra and Casa-Madrid in that it required several other services beyond the provision of tobacco. The terms concerning tobacco, however, departed only slightly from those of earlier agreements. The quantity (3 million pounds) and the varieties (2.6 million pounds from Havana area, 400,000 from Santiago de Cuba, Bayamo, Sancti Spiritus, Trinidad, and Güines) remained precisely the same.[84] In 1744 the Crown renewed the Havana Company contract for thirty years.

Up to 1744, the aims of royal tobacco policy remained consistent, but after 1744 the Crown developed a new concern—quality control—and accordingly issued a spate of new regulations. The crown had good reason for concern. Tobacco mills had existed in Cuba well before the eighteenth century, because shipping ground tobacco offered a better profit per unit of bulk than leaf. By 1711 the Havana area featured more than 300 tobacco mills, most of which were *piedras* (two stone wheels powered by hand) or *tahonas* (powered by horse or mule).[85] Some, however, made use of water power (*artificios*), a practice pioneered on the estate of María de Moya in 1688.[86] By 1739 the Almendares River, just west of Havana, powered thirty-three such mills, and nine more existed at either Havana (powered by a canal) or Matanzas.[87] Power cost nothing, so these *artificios* worked twenty-four hours per day and had an insatiable appetite for tobacco. As a result, mill operators accepted tobacco of lower quality than would *piedra* or *tahona* operators. Apparently the *artificios* ground the entire plant, not just the leaves.[88] Thus the quality of Cuban-milled *polvo* declined in the first half of the eighteenth century,[89] and tobacco growers who produced poor quality leaf found a market for their wares. By the late 1730s, *artificios* milled between 300,000 and 400,000 *arrobas* of tobacco annually, about three times the quantity Tallapiedra and Casa-Madrid intended to buy.[90]

The Havana Company inherited this situation in 1740. The Crown seized the opportunity to impose new restrictions on the quality of tobacco remitted to the Seville *fábricas*, presumably because higher quality tobacco yielded higher profits. In 1745 the Crown instructed one Antonio Bayona to oversee the tobacco trade of the Havana Company, and in the 1750s grew adamant about certain rules it had imposed.[91] Beginning in 1749, the Crown insisted that the Havana Company buy and send to Seville only tobacco leaves that grew more than half a foot in length,[92] and only clean leaf, free from impurities and without stalks. Leaves that grew close to the ground carried dust and splattered mud, which when ground together with the leaf produced an inferior *polvo*. With this and other regulations, a large part of each grower's crop became ineligible for Company purchase. One estimate predicted that only one-tenth of the crop in some areas would meet the Crown's quality standards.[93] Throughout the 1750s the Crown reminded the Havana Company not to remit low quality tobacco.[94]

Another major concern of the Crown after 1740 was quantity control: according to metropolitan logic, the source of contraband lay in Cuban overproduction. The Spanish market absorbed only 3.5 million pounds of Cuban tobacco, a limit ordained by the capacity of the Seville *fábricas* rather than inelasticity of Spanish demand.[95] Surplus production could only depart the island in the hands of foreigners, since local consumption and exports to other colonies of the Spanish Empire were small. Therefore the Crown sought to lower Cuban tobacco production to the point where it equalled Spanish demand. Among the stated missions of the Havana Company was "to reduce the tobacco harvests to the precise consumption of His Majesty's dominions, and to limit planting to certain men and places in order by this means to cut out contraband at its root."[96]

The Spanish preoccupation with quality control seems logical—higher quality meant higher profits for the royal monopoly and access to foreign markets—but the concern about quantity control appears illogical from a mercantilist perspective. According to prevailing ideas, the Crown ought to have encouraged Cuban tobacco production as the basis for earning bullion through export trade. The French empire produced little tobacco in the eighteenth century, so the French tobacco monopoly relied on British (Maryland and Virginia) tobacco to satisfy French demand. Indeed, after 1730 France replaced Amsterdam as Britain's leading tobacco customer.[97] Uztáriz recommended that Spain develop its own export trade, but although a virtually inexhaustible market for Cuban tobacco, particularly low-quality leaf, existed just north of the Pyrenees, the Spanish made no effort to exploit it.[98]

In 1720 the French assigned a high duty to Havana leaf in order to favor domestic production,[99] but later in the century, after domestic production proved inadequate, the French looked to Brazil and the Ukraine for tobacco. A market existed (French tobacco consumption increased ten-fold between 1676 and 1776), and indeed the French monopoly did buy some Cuban leaf early in the century before its Louisiana sources began to produce in quantity. The flavor of the Cuban product certainly suited French tastes; only its scarcity and price kept it from the French market, and Spanish state policy had a great deal to do with both.[100]

Had the Spanish felt able to control contraband in Cuban tobacco, they might have developed an export trade to France via Seville with excess Cuban leaf. Sure that they could not control contraband, the Spanish tried to reduce Cuban production instead. In confining tobacco production to "certain men and places," the Crown also hoped to destroy the conditions that gave rise to the tobacco revolts of 1717–23, while maintaining the state's profits by insisting on high quality tobacco. Royal tobacco policy clearly had its political and security motives as well. Lower production costs in Havana[101] and the influence of mill owners prevented the Crown from destroying the Cuban tobacco mills.[102] At one point, heeding Uztáriz, it even conceded privileges to a *rollo* factory at Havana.[103] Spanish power over Cubans was less than absolute, and deviations from the mercantilist ideal resulted.

While the Spanish government intervened consistently in the tobacco industry throughout the eighteenth century, it paid comparatively little attention to Cuban sugar. Crown policy toward sugar manifested itself only in the changing rates of taxation and lukewarm sponsorship of the slave trade. While too mundane to attract any attention from historians of Cuba or of sugar, these interventions proved of the utmost importance in preparing the way for sugar's ascendancy in Cuban agriculture.[104]

In the eighteenth century, Cuba grew only one variety of sugar cane, *saccharum officinarum*, which Cubans called *criolla, caña de la tierra*, or *caña Española*.[105] This plant, which came from Spain with the conquistadores, grew to a height of 2–2.5 meters at maturity. Its roots traversed through topsoil, never penetrating much beneath the surface. The cane had no resistance to cold because of its high juice content, 12 to 16 percent of which was sucrose.[106] *Criolla* flourished only where temperatures never fell to freezing, and where plenty of rainfall fell before the growing season but very little during it. Cane required good soil, preferably a clay loam which retained moisture well and included potash, phosphoric acid, nitrogen, and lime. In proper soil a single planting produced a yield for twenty-five years. After that, replanting took place every three years. Cane exhausted even the best soil within forty to sixty years. A single *caballería* (thirty-three acres in Cuba) produced about 1,500 *arrobas* of sugar annually (1.3 metric tons per hectare).[107]

In Cuba the planting began with the autumn rainy season, usually September through early November.[108] Slaves used pointed sticks or hoes to fashion shallow holes less than a meter square into which other slaves placed short cuttings from the top of the cane. (Occasionally they relied on second-year growth, a practice known as ratooning, but ratoons yielded less sugar.) In two weeks, if enough rain fell, new shoots appeared from the joints in the planted cane; after twelve to fifteen months, during which it required minimal attention, the cane towered above the slaves who cut it. Harvests began in the dry season, perhaps as early as November, but lasted as late as May. Slaves cut the cane low to the ground since the base bore the most sucrose. Others cut the fallen cane into lengths of about one meter and then carried it in bundles to two-wheeled carts pulled by a single yoke of oxen. These carts, laden with eighty *arrobas* each, headed for the grinding mill, no more than two days' away, to avoid fermentation.

Grinding mills (*trapiches* if small and *ingenios* if larger) consisted of three wooden rollers, arranged vertically so that one slave could pass cane between the first and second while another passed it back between the second and third.[109] This design originated in fifteenth-century Sicily and persisted until the steam engine revolutionized the extraction process after 1800. Oxen attached to long sweeps imparted motion to the rollers, which expressed cane juice into copper kettles at the rate of 300 to 350 gallons per hour. Oxen moved more slowly than mules and more regularly than the wind, improving the efficiency of extraction. Where oxen were scarce (as in Barbados) windmills were common. In the larger islands animal power was the rule, especially in Cuba (although a few Cuban mills harnessed local streams).[110] The extraction rate (the weight of the cane juice divided by the weight of the cane) of such a mill approached 60 percent. As each kettle filled with cane juice, slaves carried it to the boiling house.

Boiling houses in the Caribbean, like grinding mills, closely resembled those of sixteenth-century Sicily. A series of kettles was arranged in a line, each kettle smaller and hotter than the last. Woodburning furnaces under the kettles produced the heat that clarified and evaporated the cane juice. Boiling houses in Cuba used a separate furnace under each kettle, allowing more precise temperature control (from 110° C in the first kettle to 190° C in the last), but using much more fuel than the "Jamaica train"—a single furnace for all kettles—preferred in the British and French islands. To produce five *arrobas* of sugar—half an hour's work—required 160 cubic feet of wood under the Cuban system. Cheap wood allowed Cubans to avoid the Jamaica train until the 1820s.[111] Evaporation reduced the volume of the juice to the point where a slave could ladle it into the next kettle. A sugar master empirically determined the proper moment to empty the syrup from the last kettle (striking the sugar) into a cooler.

The resultant mass contained sugar crystals and molasses; separating the two formed the next step, a process known as purging the sugar. Purging the sugar involved pouring the crystalline concentrate into conical clay pots (*hormas*) with single holes at the bottom, toward which the molasses drained. Wooden stoppers prevented the molasses from escaping for two or three days while gravity separated the denser molasses from the sugar crystals. When the stoppers were removed the molasses flowed out, often to be boiled again in search of more sugar crystals. Next a moist mass of clay was placed atop the sugar remaining in the cone, and left there for a month or more, during which water from the clay trickled through the cone, dissolving or carrying with it what molasses still adhered to the sugar. The sugar now formed a solid loaf resembling its container in shape. After drying in the sun it was removed from the cone. At the end to which the clay had been applied, the sugar was white; toward the tip, in which some molasses still lingered, the color darkened. The loaf was cut into sections according to shades—white, yellow (*quebrado*), and brown (*cucurucho*). Some mills stopped the process before applying clay, producing a sugar high in molasses and impurities (*raspadura* or *mascobado*). A planter expected a hundred pounds of cane to produce two or three gallons of juice and two or three pounds of sugar. A full day at the grinding mill (twenty-four hours) yielded three or four tons (240 to 320 *arrobas*) of sugar, although the final product appeared only months later.[112]

Only boiling and striking sugar called for skill or judgment, the province of the sugarmaster. Cutting, grinding, and boiling had to take place in rapid succession, requiring immense quantities of unskilled labor applied in a seasonal burst called the *zafra* in Cuba. The labor demands of the *zafra* kept all processes associated with sugar production labor-intensive. With an adequate number of slaves to cope with the *zafra*, the planter had more than enough slaves on hand for every other stage, an incentive to avoid labor-saving devices such as the plow.[113]

Given these labor requirements and the scarcity of white workers, *ingenios* used mostly slave labor, although wage labor persisted until 1790 in Cuba. Most *ingenios* employed fewer than eighty slaves, although the optimum yield came from a force of three hundred.[114] A typical eighteenth-century *ingenio* produced about 4,000 *arrobas* of sugar annually or 100 *arrobas* of sugar per slave—high productivity by British or French standards of the era. Cuban plantations used fewer slaves per harvested acre than those in neighboring islands, sometimes as few as one slave per three or four acres.[115] In general, intensive use of virgin soil resulted in high labor productivity in Cuban sugar. In the British and French islands, where large-scale sugar cultivation had a longer history, depleted soils required more hands to produce as much sugar.

Small *trapiches* employed as few as eight or ten slaves and ground the cane from a single *caballería*. These mills produced only low quality sugar, not generally suitable for export, and thus differed from *ingenios* in more than mere scale. *Trapiches* represented a traditional approach to sugar cultivation. In the course of the eighteenth century, ever larger *ingenios* producing for the European market largely displaced *trapiches*. Although their cane was identical and their grinding mills looked the same, the *trapiche* and the *ingenio* bore vastly different implications for the social and economic character of the Cuban countryside.

Sugar produced by *ingenios* and *trapiches* alike traveled by mule to Havana in boxes of five or six *arrobas*. Roads did not permit the use of carts, but occasionally sugar went by boat, either to Havana, or to Batabano on the south coast and then overland by mule to Havana. Once in Havana, it sat in large warehouses until packed in wooden *cajas* (boxes of sixteen *arrobas*) for the international market.[116]

Caribbean sugar required refining before it was ready for consumption in Europe. Although it is a technically simple process essentially amounting to reboiling and recrystallizing, metropoles generally reserved sugar refining for themselves. Colbert in the 1680s briefly experimented with local refining in Martinique and Guadeloupe, but reversed himself.[117] Cuban sugar producers in the eighteenth century could sell their wares to Spain, to colonies within the Spanish empire, or to European nations that produced little sugar—principally the countries of eastern and central Europe. Cuban sugar made its entry into the international market in 1684, when about 2,500 *arrobas* appeared on the Amsterdam exchange.[118] As late as 1760, however, Cuban sugar production ranked well behind that of Haiti, Brazil, Jamaica, and six of the lesser Antilles.[119] In the international market, and even in the Spanish market, it played a modest role and faced formidable competition, often illegal. After 1727 the French permitted sugar exports to Spain in French bottoms, anticipating the British by twelve years and securing a large share of the Spanish market for Martinique and Guadeloupe.[120]

Only some regions of Cuba could participate in the sugar export trade. Sugar for export required not only suitable soil, but also a ready supply of wood for boxes, grinding mills, and fuel. In all, each *caja* of sugar consumed about 600 cubic feet of wood; a typical eighteenth century plantation thus used 50,000 to 200,000 cubic feet of timber annually, more than went into a ship of the line.[121] It also required either livestock or a stream to power the mill, and cheap food to feed slaves. An *ingenio* needed tools and machinery, and thus could not be buried in the backlands. A location near the sea helped a great deal in reducing transport costs to markets. *Ingenios* had one other major requirement: capital. In 1749 constructing a modest *ingenio* cost 40,000 pesos, exclusive of the price of thirty slaves (another 7,000 pesos).[122] Operating costs on a larger *ingenio* (forty *caballerías* of land and ninety-eight slaves) amounted to more than 9,000 pesos annually. Since sugar did not yield a crop until its second year, only the wealthy could consider making the investment.

Given all these requirements, sugar flourished most readily in the Havana area. The proximity of the market and availability of capital clearly favored Havana, while soil, lumber, power, and other considerations favored more isolated regions. Puerto Príncipe ranked second to Havana as a sugar-producing area because of an abundance of livestock, lumber, and good soil. The *cabildo* (town council) of Puerto Príncipe claimed 70 *ingenios* in 1729, and 61 two years later.[123] The island's total grew rapidly between 1737 and 1757 (see Table 5.1). The *ingenios* at Santiago de Cuba produced an average of only 800 *arrobas* annually, and very likely the others outside the Havana area yielded equally small amounts.[124] *Ingenios* around Havana, however, grew in size as well as in

Table 5.1

The Rise in the Number of *Ingenios* in Cuba, 1737–1757

Region	Ingenios in 1737	Ingenios in 1757	% Increase
Puerto Príncipe	48	56	+25%
Sancti Spiritus	36	25	−25%
Trinidad	19	25	+32%
Santa Clara	12	26	+117%
Bayamo	—	63	—
Santiago de Cuba	—	70[b]	—
Havana	43[a]	88[c]	+105%

Sources: Matricula de los Hatos, Corrales de Ganados de maior y menor, Ingenios (1737), AGI, SD 384. Relación de la Visita de Obispo Pedro Agustín Morel de Santa Cruz, 1755–57, AGI, SD 534 and 2227. This *visita* comes in nine installments, which are cited individually in chapter 2.

[a] Marrero, *Cuba*, 7 : 11.

[b] This includes the fourteen *ingenios* in El Cobre and Caney, neighboring settlements to Santiago de Cuba. The *ingenios* in question were owned by Santiago de Cuba residents according to Bishop Morel. Saco, *Historia de la esclavitud de la raza africana en el Nuevo Mundo*, 2 : 216 cites an anonymous memoir which credits Santiago de Cuba with fifty-two *ingenios* in 1760.

[c] Proyecto para que se tomen los azucares de cuenta de la Real Hacienda, 1759, BNM, Sección de Manuscritos, MSS 20144, Pt. 1.

number. In 1751 the average Havana *ingenio* produced slightly more than 3,000 *arrobas* per year, but by 1760 that average had increased to 4,000 *arrobas*.[125] Thus although *ingenios* appeared throughout the island, sugar production centered in the Havana area by the 1750s. Sugar cane covered about 320 *caballerías* or 10,000 acres of Cuba by 1762.

Through the insistence of an articulate sugar lobby, also centered in Havana, ambitious Cubans managed to influence Crown policy toward sugar. Sugar planters were wealthier and better educated than tobacco growers, and better able to express their interests to authorities in Spain. Beginning in the 1730s they regularly petitioned the Crown, which other interests in Cuba did only very rarely, and never with equal elegance. By appealing to the Crown's fiscal interest, Cuban planters achieved tax policies that created a demand for all the sugar Cuba could produce.

The first Spanish regulations of the eighteenth century concerning Cuban sugar sacrificed its interest to that of the navy. When the Spanish established a shipbuilding program in Havana in 1713–16, sugar mills acquired a major rival for lumber. In 1719 the Crown forbade woodcutting for *ingenios*, reserving the right for the shipbuilding industry.[126] Since the Cuban forest technically belonged to the Crown, such legislation did not interfere with landowners' privileges. Anyway, the rule proved difficult to enforce.[127]

The first major advantage accorded the sugar industry came in 1730, when in response to several complaints the Crown adjusted tax schedules prescribed in the 1720 *Proyecto para galeones y flotas*.[128] The *Proyecto* had levied an import duty of about 25 percent at current Havana prices (2 *reales* per *arroba*) on sugar from the Indies and assessed sugar another 56 percent (45 *reales* per *arroba*) in sales tax (the *millón*). The *Proyecto* also assigned sugar a high freight rate (8 *reales* per *arroba*) in royal transports. Burdened by all these disadvantages, argued several Havana planters, Cuban sugar could not compete with foreign sugar in the Cadiz market.[129] The planters claimed that these measures had greatly retarded the sugar industry and that in the preceding thirty years (since 1696) Crown taxation had forced thirty *ingenios* to shut down. In a *real decreto* of 30 March 1730[130] the King acquiesced, lowering the import duty to 5 percent, the *millón* to 3 *reales* per *arroba*, and freight rates to 5 *reales* per *arroba*. In theory, under the revised tax schedule, Cuban sugar could compete on equal terms with the product of the French West Indies.[131]

Havana planters did not, however, find the reduction of taxes of 1730 entirely satisfactory. Since 1727 French sugar exports to Spain had intensified competition in the Cadiz market. The French sugar islands produced roughly half *mascobado* and half white (or clayed) sugar, and Martinique clayed sugar was whiter than Cuban and so deemed higher quality. (The British islands produced exclusively *mascobado*, testimony to the power of the English refining interest, putting them at a disadvantage in the Cadiz market.) The quality of French sugar (and the skill of French traders at bribing Cadiz customs officials) prompted concern among Cuban planters. In 1737 they complained to the Crown that French sugar paid no higher taxes than Cuban. Although not quite true, this allegation heightened royal interest in the sugar industry. When the Havana Company assumed direction of the Cuban export economy in

1740, the Crown exhorted it to "augment the production of sugar" in Cuba. Spanish reliance upon French sugar already offended Spanish mercantilist sensibilities; any decrease in Spanish output exacerbated a distasteful trend, making the Crown susceptible to the arguments of the Cuban planters. In addition, the planters managed to convey the impression that taxes and costs threatened to drive land and labor into tobacco, an especially unwelcome prospect since the Crown wished to limit the tobacco harvests.[132]

The Council of the Indies endorsed the alarms sounded by the Havana planters, recommending reduction of tobacco harvests in order to help reestablish the sugar industry.[133] The Crown shared the Council's apprehension, and in the *real cédula* which chartered the Havana Company it relieved Cuban sugar of all import duties upon entry into Spain. Thus, Spanish authorities hoped sugar might prosper and tobacco decline, "with neither violence nor precise and obligatory laws, but through economic and governmental measures."[134]

In theory this measure applied to sugar traded on anyone's account, not merely that of the Havana Company. Apparently, however, things worked out differently in practice, because in 1750 the King again exempted all Cuban sugar from taxation. Whatever the reality, the Crown showed itself determined to assist the planters in capturing the Cadiz market.[135]

By 1760, the Crown considered the industry sufficiently established to reduce the preference accorded Cuban sugar. A new tax, the *ramo de azucares*, appeared in the Havana accounts for the first time. Unlike earlier taxes, assessed either at the point of embarkation or upon arrival in Cadiz, the 1760 tax applied to the sugar harvest. The advantage lay in the fact that by 1760 sugar production throughout Cuba had expanded greatly, and a tax on the harvest rather than on exports would not discriminate against the Havana trade and encourage contraband. By taxing harvests, the authorities also increased the total number of *arrobas* subject to taxation. The levy, fixed at 5 percent, was paid in kind in December of each year.[136]

Royal promotion of the slave trade also favored the development of the sugar industry in Cuba. In the eighteenth century the Crown, and many Cubans, had strong reservations about importing large numbers of slaves, since contraband and security problems (especially after the Maroon rebellions in Jamaica of the 1730s) seemed likely to come with them. Before 1739 the British South Sea Company provided Cuba with only small numbers of slaves, having better markets than Cuba.[137] After war broke out in 1739, the Spanish considered themselves free from the terms of the 1713 *asiento* agreement with the British, and they authorized Cuban entrepreneurs to sell slaves to Cuban planters. The failure of the first such contractor, Martín Ulibarri y Gamboa, to fulfill his quota of 1,000 *piezas de Indias* prompted the Crown to entrust the Havana Company with a monopoly privilege in slave imports.[138] As the 1740 contract did not mention slave importing, the Havana Company agreed to several small slaving contracts beginning in 1741.[139] Naturally the planters found the number of slaves imported too low and their price (300 pesos) too high.[140] The Crown eventually agreed that a labor shortage held the colony back, and in 1761 arranged with another *asentista*, José Villanueba Pico, for the annual importation of 1,000 slaves—and more if demand warranted—at reduced prices.[141] The Havana Company objected, but the Crown, displeased with the Company's performance for many reasons, stood firm.[142] By 1760, clearly, the promotion of sugar had become its first priority in Cuban affairs.

Cuban agriculture produced another export commodity besides tobacco and sugar. Ranching, which used more land than any other industry in Cuba, "provided an infinity of hides."[143] Spain had cattle ranches in the eighteenth century, and other parts of the empire produced hides as well, so the Cuban product faced stiff competition in the Cadiz market. Thus most Cuban hides never crossed the ocean, but found buyers in the foreign Caribbean. Although a breach in mercantilist practice, this illegal trade hardly interested the Crown because hides from other sources fully met Spanish demand, and because with Spanish competition Cuban hides could not carry much duty. Thus, no matter how many advantages the Crown awarded to Cuban ranching in the short run, in the long run it could never—unlike tobacco and sugar—become a major source of state revenue. For these reasons the Crown had virtually no policy toward ranching. Local authorities determined the rules governing Cuba's ranching industry.

Ranching demanded minimal technology, comparatively little labor, but a great deal of land. The initial investment required was less than in sugar but more than in tobacco. Large estates, called *haciendas* or *estan-*

cias, in general, or *hatos* and *corrales* depending on their size, constituted the unit of production.[144] The *cabildo* of Havana (or Santiago de Cuba) granted estates in return for an annual contribution (called the *pesa*) in the form of a small proportion of each herd. In 1751 a *real cédula* fixed this proportion at 14 percent, but in Sancti Spiritus it stayed at 7 percent. Ranchers in western and north central Cuba drove their cattle up to 450 kilometers to Havana, the largest market, sometimes as often as three times yearly. There they sold them at fairs, or, increasingly in the eighteenth century, to middlemen who fattened them after the drive and then sold them to slaughterhouses in Havana. In the sixteenth century cattle were killed for their hides alone, but by the eighteenth century a market for beef developed, serving the burgeoning urban population and the crews of countless ships. By 1747, the two slaughterhouses of Havana killed about 29,000 head of cattle a year, most of which had come from the broad plains of north central Cuba.[145] Cattle raised in Bayamo supplied Santiago de Cuba with much of its animal protein, since Santiago de Cuba had very few *haciendas*.

Another major market for Cuban livestock lay across the water in Jamaica. Jamaicans wanted horses and mules for transport and power more than they wanted beef. The economy of Sancti Spiritus centered around producing for this market, since very low prices attracted Jamaican contrabandists.[146] Puerto Príncipe, although it raised cattle for a local slaughterhouse since 1729[147] and boasted tanneries by 1755,[148] also produced large quantities of horses and "more than a thousand mules" per year, most of which could only have gone to Jamaica.[149] Both the *matrícula* of 1737 and the Bishop's *visita* of 1755–57 show that stock raising figured most prominently inland (the *tierra adentro*). In 1737 Puerto Príncipe, Sancti Spiritus, and Santa Clara had the most *hatos, corrales,* and *sitios*.[150] In 1755–57 Puerto Príncipe and Bayamo far outstripped the rest of the island, each having, according to the Bishop, almost twice as many *haciendas* as their nearest competitor, Sancti Spiritus.[151] The Jamaica market seems to have been larger even than that of Havana. Certainly the development of the economy of Cuba's south coast reflected the nature of Jamaican, not Spanish, markets.[152]

Spanish policy toward Cuban ranching showed some consistency but little concern. The 1720 *Proyecto* assigned an import duty on hides from the New World—2 *reales* on tanned hides (*cueros curtidos*) and 1.5 *reales* on untanned (*cueros al pelo*).[153] This duty amounted to about 8 percent in current Havana prices. In 1740 the Crown removed this impost, according hides the same preference that sugar received in the Havana Company charter. This change appears to have resulted from a suggestion of Martín de Aróstegui, first president of the Havana Company, since the words of the 1740 charter almost precisely reproduce those of Aróstegui's memorandum of 1739 to the King.[154] Aróstegui and the Crown aimed to diversify the Cuban economy by favoring ranching (and sugar) at the expense of tobacco. According to the Havana Company charter (article 35), costs had risen in ranching, and the industry had suffered. A note in the *matrícula* of 1737 supports this contention, saying that most of the *hatos* of Trinidad were "depopulated." When the Havana Company signed a revised contract in 1744, the Crown again formally announced that hides carried by the Company should enter Spain duty free.[155]

Except for these occasional attentions, the Crown displayed a consistent lack of interest in the Cuban hide trade, seldom exhorting officials in Havana to prevent the extensive contraband in hides, in marked contrast to its stance on contraband tobacco. The legislation of both 1720 and 1740 came in larger contexts. The *Proyecto* set duties for all exports of the New World, and the duty assigned to hides can hardly be taken as evidence of policy toward the Cuban ranching industry; the exemption from that duty in 1740 came as part of a royal effort to reduce tobacco harvests in Cuba. Favoring ranching amounted to an indirect method of curtailing the growth of the tobacco industry.

The Cuban forest provided the only other product of interest to Spanish authorities: timber for the navy. Havana had long built merchant ships, perhaps one-half of those employed in the Indies trade in the late seventeenth century.[156] Havana constructed ships for the Armada de Barlovento as early as the 1620s,[157] but naval shipbuilding at Havana stagnated until 1713 when, in response to a suggestion made by Agustín de Arriola, the Crown ordered that a royal shipyard in Havana should build twelve ships of sixty guns each.[158] Pensacola and Mexico were to provide some of the mast timber, but on one occasion officials authorized imports all the way from Russia.[159]

Rivers in Cuba made some of the inland timber resources accessible. Cutting for the shipyards took place in fourteen designated *cortes* (cutting areas), mostly in the mountains behind Havana. From 1719, shipbuilders enjoyed woodcutting privileges in these areas while sugar planters had to compete for special dispensations.[160] Henceforward the destruction of the forest proceeded around Havana under very strict regulation.[161] Cutting occurred only between November and February, when mud presented less of an obstacle, but the rivers still filled their banks with the seasonal rains. Slaves often did the actual cutting, while teams of oxen dragged the fallen timbers to the nearest river.[162] They floated to the river mouth whence boats carried the logs to Havana. This process often took up to a year, which delay damaged the wood, although most of the *cortes* lay within thirty kilometers of Havana.

By exploiting Cuban timber resources, the Crown hoped to save on labor and lumber costs in naval construction and to minimize delays in refitting warships on duty in the Caribbean. The Crown also hoped Havana could build more durable warships than the yards in Spain. Cuban cedar had two advantages over Spanish oak: cedar stood up better to the various organisms in tropical waters which promote rot; and cedar did not splinter much when hit with cannonballs, which greatly improved the chances of crews surviving a broadside. Thus the Crown provided funds (120,000 pesos annually) from Mexico and Cadiz to a private contractor (Juan de Acosta) to finance Havana's naval shipbuilding.[163] It also took several measures to assure the shipyards an adequate supply of timber, especially cedar.[164] In 1741 the Crown entrusted the Havana Company with the responsibility of construction in the royal shipyards.[165] Shortly the Crown agreed to allow the Company to import iron for shipbuilding free of all duties.[166] Despite this and other privileges, the Havana Company found shipbuilding for the navy too expensive, and by 1749 the Company managed to extricate itself from that clause of its contract, forcing the Crown once again to put shipbuilding up for private contract.[167]

Preoccupied with the export economy, Spanish authorities made little effort to ensure the adequacy of Cuba's food supply. Most parts of the island grew enough to sustain themselves, but not Havana and Santiago de Cuba.[168] Both cities relied on imported flour to supplement local food crops, so if for any reason imports failed, starvation threatened. The Havana area produced enough surplus beef and rice to supply the Armada de Barlovento, but flour, beans, and vegetables had to come from Mexico.[169] As early as 1669, the Crown prohibited tobacco *vegas* within four leagues of Havana because they exacerbated the food deficit, but this measure failed to solve the problem.[170]

Cubans offered several suggestions for provisioning Havana and Santiago de Cuba, most of which involved trading with foreigners.[171] To the Council of the Indies nothing justified trade with foreigners, not even the threat of starvation. The Council considered any trade with foreigners an invitation to contraband—quite a reasonable position.[172] On most occasions when the Havana governor permitted trade with French or British colonies in order to provide flour for the city, the Crown and the Council of the Indies vehemently disapproved.[173] In the 1750s when drought ruined the banana and cassava crops at Santiago de Cuba, local civil and religious leaders maintained they had to acquire food "wherever it might be found." The Spanish authorities (including the governor at Santiago de Cuba, Lorenzo de Madariaga) felt the situation did not justify bending the rules and enriching foreigners with Spanish money.[174] They distrusted reports of imminent starvation, and in any case maintained that Old and New Spain would relieve any food supply crises.[175] They hoped that Mexico could play the same role for Cuba that Maurepas thought Quebec could play vis-à-vis Louisbourg. The larger, more populated, more secure colony was to produce a surplus that could go to relieve shortages in the smaller, export-oriented colony. Clearly the viability of this system depended on the reliability of these surpluses and the communication and transport nets between the food surplus and food deficit colonies. The combined effects of six months of ice, the proximity of New England with its surplus gain, and poor crop years in Quebec foiled the French plan. In the Gulf of Mexico, however, transport proceeded more regularly—the hurricane season occupied only two months of the year—and nearby Jamaica produced no excess food to tempt Cuban traders. Only Mexican crop shortfalls could force Havana to seek sustenance in foreign markets.[176]

Spanish economic policy toward Cuba was far more complex than French policy toward Cape Breton, a reflection of the diversity of the Cuban economy. In Louisbourg the French faced few quandaries. Both strategic and economic considerations dictated the primacy of the fishery throughout Louisbourg's half century. Competition among hundreds of independent entrepreneurs in France and scores more in Cape Breton produced enough fish for domestic consumption and for an important export trade. The Crown could thus confine itself to fiscal incentives, leaving self-interested entrepreneurs to accomplish state goals. French policy made the best of a good situation.

In Cuba the prevalence of contraband combined with the state's unquenchable thirst for immediate revenue, especially after the War of the Spanish Succession, induced government monopoly in the important sectors of the economy. The state-run tobacco *fábricas* could not flourish without a steady supply of high-grade leaf, which private enterprise did not provide. Furthermore, when the tobacco growers revolted, they lost the support of metropolitan authorities forever—loyal subjects had become security risks. Thus subsequent legislation systematically obstructed both tobacco growing and milling, aiming to limit harvests to high-quality leaf only.

To reduce tobacco harvests, the Crown lowered taxes on sugar and (cautiously) supported the slave trade. Spanish reliance on foreign sugar for the domestic market also inspired royal promotion of Cuban sugar. Much of the planters' success in achieving favorable legislation resulted from advantages, such as literacy, bestowed on them by wealth and social class. Although perhaps no more united or conscious of their self-interest than the *vegueros*, Cuban planters had clearer access to ministers and royalty.

In addition, the loyalty of planters seemed more assured than that of the *vegueros*, because the planters had more to lose in the way of property and status. Despite the necessity of creating a large slave community, a Cuba dominated by sugar would show greater loyalty to Spain than a Cuba devoted to tobacco. A Cuba divided among several enterprises suited the Crown admirably, because distress caused by weather of disaffection with royal policy could never unite the population against the Crown. Thus the demotion of tobacco and promotion of sugar (and hides) made good sense politically. Beyond that consideration, the tobacco growers showed a propensity to trade with foreigners that planters did not, since other empires produced their own sugar. This difference further prejudiced the Crown against tobacco.

To solve the tobacco problem, the Spanish went so far as to favor ranching, an enterprise that could never produce much revenue for the treasury. They did so not only when the immediate need for revenue had slackened in the 1730s, but also in the 1740s and 1750s when royal finances returned to their familiarly desperate condition.[177] The Crown did its best to reserve access to the Cuban forest for royal shipbuilding. The sugar industry, the great competitor for wood, took second priority to the navy, so important to the security of the treasure fleets. Security considerations also prompted royal equivocation with regard to slave imports, although by 1760 the Crown largely overcame its hesitation on that score.

In general, Spanish authorities showed great attentiveness toward military and mercantilist priorities in regulating the productive sectors of the Cuban economy. Security, state revenues, and the balance of trade mattered most to the Spanish, apparently in that order. They ignored market forces when they involved breaches in mercantilist practice. Indeed, the Spanish occasionally failed to obey market imperatives even when they did coincide with mercantilist prescription, e.g., the case of the tobacco export trade that never was.

Out of this matrix of guiding principles the Spanish created a policy that transformed Cuba into a sugar monoculture in the nineteenth century. When the destruction of the canefields of Haiti raised the market price of sugar in 1790 (by which time Cuban sugar responded to international prices instead of legislation), Cuban sugar producers already had the land, labor, capital, technology, expertise, warehouse facilities, and financial structures necessary to take full advantage of the situation. They could not possibly have done so without half a century of unintentional preparation provided by the beneficence of the metropolitan government. Although obscure at the time, the consequences for subsequent Cuban history are clear and vast.

While the French acquiesced to the imperatives of the marketplace and allowed much illegal trade at Louisbourg, permitting Ile Royale to forge ties with New England (as we shall see), the Spanish showed more energy and determination. If Cubans traded tobacco illegally, Spain would replace tobacco with sugar as Cuba's principal export. French policy allowed the colony of Ile Royale to develop imperial economic links with more than one metropolis. Spanish policy aimed to sever the links between Cuba and Jamaica, forcing Cubans into a colonial relationship with a single metropolis—Spain. In the next chapter we examine how well these policies succeeded.

In some cases French and Spanish economic policies proved successful, in others abject failures. Success or failure hinged on the degree to which the metropole recognized and adjusted to the world market and the geographies of Cape Breton and Cuba. In the short run, apparent success may have hinged on price fluctuations and the vagaries of war and weather. But in the longer run, over a period of fifty years, colonial economies responded to state policy only within limits set by the imperatives of market behavior and colonial geography.

The importance of the cod trade in the eighteenth-century Atlantic world defies measurement. Prior to the late eighteenth-century agricultural revolution, fish comprised a much larger share of the European and American diet than in more recent times. Fish protein in some cases was the only animal protein available, and very often the cheapest. Cod has long figured among the cheapest and most protein rich of edible fish.

One method of assessing the value of the Louisbourg cod fishery to France involves calculating the area of land that would have to be brought into production to provide a quantity of protein equal to the cod catch: "fish area." This technique involves a host of variables such as the intensity of farming, fecundity of soils, and the various crops and animals that might provide alternative protein. Given modern French agricultural efficiency, a metric ton of fish protein represents about 17 hectares or roughly 45 acres of dairy land. Translating this into eighteenth-century terms involves assumptions that render quantification very risky. The entire calculation may be presented as follows:

$$F = \frac{H}{A \times B \times C}$$

where F is fish area in hectares; H is the protein value of the fish harvest in kilograms; A is the average milk yield in kilograms per cow; B is the average stocking ratio in cows per hectare; and C is the protein proportion of milk by weight. According to this formula, the Ile Royale codfish catch carried the protein equivalent of at least 746,000 hectares of French dairy land (7,464 square kilometers), and perhaps as much as 1,855,290 hectares (18,533 square kilometers).[1] The entire French cod catch amounted to about three times the fish area of the Ile Royale catch, on the order of 22,500 square kilometers to 55,500 square kilometers. In other words, as much as one-tenth of the area of the kingdom would have had to be converted to dairy farming to provide the same animal protein as the French codfish catch.

Another way to appraise the French cod fishery involves estimating the fraction of the protein requirements of the French population met by the cod catch. Again quantification rests on a string of debatable assumptions. Taking 7.5 kilograms of protein per year as a minimum requirement, the Louisbourg cod catch in its best years could fill the protein needs of more than 800,000 people, almost a quarter of France's urban population.[2] Animal proteins formed about 2 percent of the average Frenchman's diet in the eighteenth century, a large share of which often came as dried or salted cod.[3]

Both of these attempts at measurement—using fish area and protein requirements—leave a great deal to be desired, so perhaps prudence dictates evaluating the cod fishery in terms the French themselves used. Over Louisbourg's half century, the fishery provided France with a trade worth about 3 million livres per year in French prices, twenty times the budget of Ile Royale and one-third the entire annual budget of the marine. Until the 1750s the value of the Cape Breton fishery exceeded that of the Canadian fur trade. If measured in the prices of the Mediterranean countries to which much of the dried cod went, the value of the trade mounted still higher. Thanks to Louisbourg, the French retained almost half of the cod catch of the North Atlantic and half the world's cod trade despite the loss of Newfoundland in 1713. The French fishery, all told, garnered for France up to 20 million livres per year.[4]

Graph 6A
Laborers and Codfish Catch at Ile Royale, 1715–1754

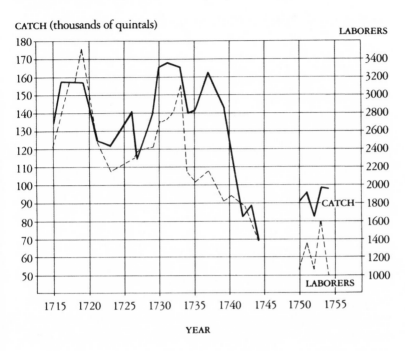

The money value of the cod trade, while always substantial in the eighteenth century, varied significantly from year to year. Price fluctuations had little to do with this—the size of the catch made the difference. Whereas in the twentieth century the catch varied only about 20 percent from the mean, in the early eighteenth century it fluctuated considerably, departing from the mean (128,500 quintals) by as much as 50 percent in either direction.[5] Several factors might have accounted for this variance. One was the number of men and boats involved in the fishery each year, which fluctuated in response to two variables: demand for fish on the one hand, and the relative attractiveness of other employments for men and boats. Another possibility was productivity, or yield—the ratio between the size of the catch and the number of participating boats. Overfishing might temporarily reduce yields, or small changes in water temperature might drive the cod into waters not frequented by fishermen. Table 6.1 and Graph 6A show the fluctuations in the size of the catch at Ile Royale.

Table 6.1

The Catch in the Ile Royale Fishery, 1713–1754

Year	Quintals	Value (in France)[a]	Source
1713			
1714			
1715	135,520	2,981,440 livres	C^{11}B, 1:318
1716	157,500	3,150,000	C^{11}B, 1:488
1717			
1718	156,500	3,443,000	C^{11}B, 3:207
1719	156,520	3,150,000	C^{11}B, 4:223
1720		2,700,000	C^{11}B, 5:149
1721	125,000[b]	2,972,000	C^{11}B, 6:25; C^{11}C, 16:10–15
1722			
1723	121,160	3,212,920[c]	C^{11}B, 6:245
1724			
1725			
1726	140,900	2,958,900	C^{11}B, 3:230
1727	114,680	2,385,280	C^{11}B, 9:259
1728			
1729	140,244[d]	2,945,124	C^{11}B, 10:211
1730	165,630	3,490,200	C^{11}B, 11:69
1731	167,540	3,518,340	C^{11}B, 12:64
1732			
1733	165,365	3,500,185	C^{11}B, 14:232–33
1734	139,810	2,962,080	C^{11}B, 16:257
1735	142,245	3,019,850[e]	C^{11}B, 17:90
1736	151,110	4,391,020	C^{11}B, 18:171
1737	162,200	3,345,340[f]	C^{11}B, 19:281–82
1738	152,470	3,239,040	C^{11}B, 20:220
1739	143,660	3,061,465	C^{11}B, 21:152
1740	123,150	2,629,980	C^{11}B, 22:238
1741		2,585,440	B, 74:588
1742	83,410	1,782,680	B, 76:503–4
1743	69,430	1,458,030	C^{11}B, 26:209

Table 6.1 (continued)

Year	Quintals	Value (in France)[a]	Source
1744	69,430	1,458,030	C[11]B, 26:103
1745			
1746			
1747	no French fishing because of war and occupation		
1748			
1749			
1750	90,560	1,919,860	C[11]B, 29:206–8
1751	95,580	2,026,200	B, 95:282
1752	83,130[b]	1,771,960	B, 97:317
1753	98,450	2,084,450	C[11]B, 33:236
1754	97,729[b]	2,052,309	

[a]The value includes that of cod oil, produced at a rate of one barrel (225 liters) per 100 quintals of cod. When the documents have not provided a value for the catch, I have used a price of twenty livres per quintal and 100 livres per barrel of oil. When the documents do provide a value, it is also an estimate, based on the *commisaire-ordonnateur*'s idea of European prices.

[b]Moore, "Other Louisbourg," p. 80.

[c]C[11]B, 6:223 has 2,357,900—the difference lies in the estimated European price. C[11]B, 6:245 uses 25 livres/quintal and 110 livres/barrel, higher than normal.

[d]This catch is computed from the number of *chaloupes* and *goelettes* in the fishery, using the 1727–31 average for quintals per *chaloupe* and quintals per *goelette*. The value is computed using prices of 20 and 100 livres for a quintal and a barrel.

[e]C[11]B, 18:171 has 4,130,850 livres and 142,495 quintals.

[f]C[11]B, 20:14–15 has 3,172,230 livres.

How can one explain the prosperity of the fishery in 1716–20 and 1730–39, and its minor decline in the 1720s and a major one after 1740? Christopher Moore and Laurier Turgeon, the only writers to express themselves on the subject, suggest that overfishing probably caused the decline after the peak year of 1737.[6] In support of his position, Moore points to falling yields among *chaloupes*. Yields did indeed decline after 1737, but partially recovered in the 1750s, while the catch did not. Furthermore, a large part of the fishery was conducted from *goelettes* after the 1720s, not *chaloupes*, and yields in *goelettes* rose to almost unprecedented levels in the 1750s. The fluctuations in yields appear in Table 6.2.

Table 6.2

Catch per Boat Ratio (in Quintals) in the Ile Royale
Fishery, 1718–1754

Year	Chaloupes	Goelettes
1718	250	—
1719	280	—
1723	280	400
1726	340	400
1727	310	400
1730	340	400
1731	330	400
1733	315	500
1734	—	520
1735	355	520
1736	360	580
1738	370	650
1739	420	850
1740	290	650
1742	—	600
1743	240	600
1744	230	500
1753	275	720
1754	—	760
	Mean: 317.9[a]	Mean: 555.8

Source: AC, C¹¹B, 3:307; AC, C¹¹B, 4:223; AC, C¹¹B, 16:257. Moore,
"Merchant Trade" (thesis), p. 54.
[a] Note: The *chaloupe* figure adds together a figure for the summer fishery
(which averaged 217 quintals per boat) with a figure for the autumn fishery (100
quintals per boat).

Turgeon argues that the introduction of the *goelette* may have been the
cause of overfishing and the reduction of the catch in the 1740s: fishermen
got too efficient for their prey. This has a certain logic to it: if one assumes
that the Ile Royale fishermen operated at levels close to the maximum
sustainable biological yield, the shift in technology would presumably

Graph 6B
The Cyclic Ecology of Fishing

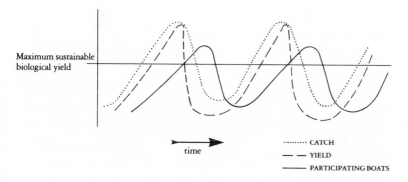

Maximum sustainable
biological yield

time

·········· CATCH
— — YIELD
———— PARTICIPATING BOATS

Note: Adapted from Head, *Newfoundland*, p. 67.

reduce fish populations, lower yields, lower profitability, and thus eventually lower the number of boats participating. Indeed a cycle of periodic
overfishing, declining yields, and recoveries is what one expects in the
ecology of hunting or fishing, as shown in Graph 6B. Turgeon applied his
argument to the fishery at Newfoundland. At Ile Royale (which Turgeon
treats less fully) the data do not clearly support his interpretation. There
the catch and the number of boats participating in the fishery declined
while yields were still climbing (1731–39), and the catch and number of
boats stayed small when yields rose again in the 1750s. While the
ecological explanation of the course of the Ile Royale fishery cannot be
discounted entirely, its usefulness is limited.

The data on yields may well be a red herring in the study of the cod
fishery. The relationship between boats (or fishermen) and the catch
(plotted in Graph 6A) demonstrates a correlation, which, while not
precise, is evident to the eye. (This does not necessarily mean one caused
the other, of course.) Logically enough, if fewer boats participated in the
fishery, a smaller catch resulted. Profitability presumably determined the
number of boats in the fishery—profitability relative to alternative employments for men and boats. It appears that demand for fish in Europe

did not seriously affect the supply from the cod fishery. Turgeon's study of the Marseilles market shows that price declines and the many possible substitutes for cod did not hurt the fishery, perhaps because the market throughout coastal Europe remained fairly steady irrespective of fluctations in one or another town.[7]

If the European market did not strongly influence decisions to fish or not to fish, the burden of explanation lies with the availability of enticing opportunities for men and boats at Ile Royale. The most plausible explanation is that the quantities of men and boats—labor and capital—devoted to the fishery declined after the mid-1730s because commerce provided an attractive alternative employment. Data on the migration of capital do not exist in any useful form, but the ratio between capital and labor in the fishery could scarcely have changed between 1720 and 1760: an employer with two *chaloupes* still needed ten fishermen. The *goelette* may have tipped the balance slightly, making the business more capital intensive, but only marginally so (see Table 6.3). So what accounts for the reduction in the number of boats and men in the fishery? Decisions made by individual seamen may have influenced the trend somewhat, but a more likely explanation lies with choices made by Louisbourg capitalists—owners of boats and hirers of labor. French policy restricted the bargaining power of labor severely, but no legislation inhibited the employment of capital. Capital, then, led a migration into activities other than fishing, and labor followed. *Habitants-pescheurs* became traders, and fishermen became sailors. Perhaps the Molasses Act of 1733, which channeled some newly illegal trade through Louisbourg (see chapter 7) had something to do with this: it was precisely in 1733 that the number of boats and fishermen began falling precipitously.

Or perhaps the trade depression of the 1730s, felt throughout the European-centered world economy, turned law-abiding merchants into smugglers, willing to accept the increased risk of illegal trade. Once they had made their contacts in Louisbourg and learned how to turn a profit there, they, and others like them, traded regularly at Louisbourg. And in response, the population of Louisbourg turned toward entrepôt trade and away from the fishery.

All signs indicate that the local economy, more than European markets or the ecology of the Ile Royale fishing banks, produced the notable trends in the fishery. A check on this conclusion is the rhythm of expansion and contraction in neighboring fisheries: had European cod prices been responsible, or ecological factors (say cooler water temperatures or even overfishing), then one would expect the same trends in the Newfoundland and Labrador fisheries. But at Labrador Malouins recorded increasing catches, and at Newfoundland decline set in only several years after the decline at Ile Royale.[8] Admittedly Moore and Turgeon's view has some validity; nonetheless purely economic factors seem primary. It is hard to make any more precise judgment, especially since other variables affected the catch and yield—war, for instance, which abbreviated the Ile Royale season in 1744, or sated codfish which ignored bait in Newfoundland in 1715.[9]

French policy did nothing to interfere with the trends in the fishery. By allowing a comparatively free market for investment at Louisbourg, the French denied themselves the opportunity to shepherd resources from one enterprise to another and the power to prevent capital from drifting into more lucrative employments. Thus they allowed private entrepreneurs, of whom many flourished at Louisbourg, to conciliate personal interests at the expense of the state's.[10] To the extent that private interests coincided with the state's, such policy saved effort and produced suitable results, as in the fishery before 1740. But as a guide to economic policy in general this restrained mercantilism had drawbacks: it permitted, although it did not cause, the substitution of commerce for fishing at Louisbourg.

Those aspects of French economic policy concerning the soil and minerals of Cape Breton Island proved vastly disappointing to officials of the Marine. Although the cod fishery declined between 1713 and 1758, it never diminished to the point where French officials considered it a failure; whereas mineral and food production increased over the years, but never reached levels where French officials considered them a success. Even the efforts to develop the agricultural capacity of Ile St. Jean went unrewarded.

The experience of Cape Breton in the nineteenth and twentieth centuries clearly demonstrated the island's potential as a coal producer. During the French regime, however, the quantities of coal mined and exported remained minimal. Annual exports to France never surpassed 0.1 percent of the cash value of cod exports.[11] Still smaller amounts of Ile Royale coal found their way to the French West Indies (to fire sugar

Table 6.3

Chaloupes, *Goelettes*, and Laborers in the Ile Royale Fishery,
1713–1754

Year	Chaloupes	Goelettes	Laborers[a]	Source
1713				
1714				
1715	424	45	2,435	AC, C[11]B, 1:318
1716				
1717	626	—	3,130	" C[11]B, 3:207
1718	630	—	3,150[b]	C[11]B, 4:163
1719	559	—	3,441[c]	C[11]B, 4:223
1720				
1721	448	40	2,520	Moore[d]
1722				
1723	352	93	2,161	C[11]B, 6:245
1724				
1725				
1726	365	68	2,301	Moore
1727	385	67	2,394	C[11]B, 9:259
1728				
1729	379	75	2,420	C[11]B, 10:211
1730	406	94	2,688	C[11]B, 11:69
1731	444	74	2,738	Moore
1732	454	79	2,823	Moore
1733	491	95	3,120	C[11]B, 14:232
1734	323	80	2,175	C[11]B, 16:257
1735	305	73	2,036	C[11]B, 17:90
1736	333	62	2,099	C[11]B, 18:171
1737[e]	341	65	2,160	C[11]B, 20:326
1738	314	61	1,997	C[11]B, 20:220
1739	281	60	1,825	C[11]B, 21:152
1740	279	69	1,878	C[11]B, 22:238
1741				
1742	257	67	1,774	Moore
1743	243	52	1,579	C[11]B, 26:200

Table 6.3 (continued)

Year	Chaloupes	Goelettes	Laborers[a]	Source
1744	235	34	1,413	Moore
1745				
1746				
1747				
1748				
1749				
1750	142	45	1,025	B, 95:282
1751	198	54	1,368	B, 95:282
1752	148	46	1,062	C^{11}B, 33:495
1753	250	50	1,600	C^{11}B, 33:236
1754	114	48	1,006	Moore

[a]This refers to both fishermen and shore hands. Where the document cited fails to give a number of *matelots* (sailors), I have multiplied the number of *chaloupes* by five and added it to seven times the number of *goelettes*.

[b]AC, C^{11}B, 4:13 has 3,589.

[c]This figure is unusually high because 255 French *chaloupes* (in the wet fishery) employed between seven and eight men on the average, instead of the normal five. Thus they employed as many as a *goelette*, but they were listed as *chaloupes*.

[d]Moore, "Merchant Trade," p. 53.

[e]AC, C^{11}B, 19:281–82 has 378 *chaloupes* and 61 *goelettes*.

boilers) and to New England.[12] As a survey of the landscape in 1766 showed, the production of a few hundred barrels a year barely scratched the surface.[13] Despite French domestic demand and official encouragement, French mining never amounted to much.

The principal reason for the failure of coal mining was simple. Despite government assistance, coal production remained uneconomic. As long as the state refused to undertake coal production itself, the potential of Ile Royale would go unexploited.[14] Better and more familiar investments in the fishery or in commerce attracted those in a position to operate a coal mine. In the absence of skilled labor, the costs of producing coal proved daunting. Other problems combined to spoil Raudot's and Pontchartrain's plans for Cape Breton coal. Codfish filled almost all the cargo space of ships departing Louisbourg for France because of its higher value in relation to bulk and its greater propensity to spoil, leaving little room for barrels of coal.[15] Furthermore, by the 1740s tests undertaken at Rochefort proved that Ile Royale coal contained too much sulfur for use in furnaces in naval yards. Government enthusiasm dwindled shortly thereafter.[16] Thenceforward the coal of Ile Royale ceased to figure as an export, though growing quantities warmed the barracks and homes of Louisbourg. A fire lit by mutinous soldiers burned in the largest coal pit from 1752 until 1764, effectively curbing the renewed interest in mining that Governor Raymond exhibited in 1750.[17] Faced with these handicaps and assisted only by low tariffs, Ile Royale coal could not develop into a profitable export, leaving France and New England dependent upon British supplies. This the French found regrettable but acceptable.

French efforts at establishing a shipbuilding industry at Ile Royale proved more successful. Shipbuilding was centered in the outports—especially along the northwest coast, around Bras d'Or and near Port Dauphin—far from Louisbourg but near the best stands of timber. Although production never met demand, until 1745 Ile Royale built roughly as many boats as the French at Louisbourg bought from New Englanders. Most of the ships built at Ile Royale bulked at 25 to 100 tons, perhaps slightly smaller on average than boats bought from New England but still suitable for voyages to the West Indies, and even to France.[18] Unlike Cuba, Ile Royale never built ships for the navy, since it lacked skilled shipwrights, giant oak timbers, and cheap labor. Private demand always outstripped the shipbuilding capacity of the colony, so hardly a year went by without numerous purchases of fishing and trading vessels from New Englanders. In 1732, for instance, one-third of the vessels from New England trading at Louisbourg were sold along with their cargoes.[19] Table 6.4 shows the numbers of boats built in Louisbourg and those bought from New England during 1715–54.[20] It appears from these data that the demand for boats at Louisbourg remained fairly constant from 1726 up to the first siege in 1745. What local shipwrights could not produce, merchants and fishermen bought. Very likely a large proportion of the boats purchased were schooners (*goelettes*), in the construction of which Ile Royale craftsmen had no expertise. After the Treaty of Aix-la-Chapelle returned Ile Royale to the French in 1749, the demand for boats clearly intensified. The shipbuilding capacity of Ile Royale did not expand, however, labor being scarce and good timber difficult of access. Instead, purchases from New Englanders grew more common.

Table 6.4

Boats Built and Bought in Ile Royale, 1715–1754

Year	Built	Tons (avg.)	Bought	Tons (avg.)	Source
1715	2	70	—	—	AC, C[11]B, 1:345
1726	8	25–70	7	15–60	C[11]B, 20:14–15
1730	14	—	10	—	B, 57–2:776–81
1732[a]	7	—	13	—	C[11]B, 13:40; C[11]B, 14:39
1733	16	43.1	14	75.8	C[11]B, 14:193–94, 232–33
1734[b]	7	—	9	—	C[11]B, 16:257
1735	4	—	12	—	C[11]B, 17:90
1736	8	—	7	—	C[11]B, 18:172–73
1737[c]	14	50–120	13	25–350	C[11]B, 20:14–15
1738	11	25–120	6	—	B, 68:352–53
1739	12	—	8	—	B, 72:444
1740	7	30–100	12	15–60	C[11]B, 22:238
1741	15	—	5	—	B, 74:588
1742	11	—	9	—	C[11]B, 26:209
1743[d]	5	—	17	—	C[11]B, 25:168
1744[e]	6	—	28	—	C[11]B, 26:103
1749	—	—	14	—	Maude[f]
1750	21	—	30	—	C[11]B, 29:209–10
1753	5	—	35	—	Maude[f]
1754	7	—	24	—	Maude[f]
	180		374		

[a]C[11]B, 13:244 has 6 built and 18 bought.
[b]C[11]B, 16:118 has 3 built and 11 bought.
[c]C[11]B, 20:324 has 10 built and 12 bought.
[d]C[11]B, 26:209 has 4 built and 17 bought.
[e]The figure for boats bought includes several taken by privateers.
[f]These data are taken from Maude, "Settlements," nonpaginated.

In these years, with the fishery in decline, Louisbourg's role as a center of entrepôt trade accounted for the heightened demand for boats.

In addition to stimulating demand for ships, the expansion of Louisbourg's trade intensified competition for labor, which paradoxically stunted the growth of shipbuilding at Louisbourg. Although in 1718 the Conseil de la Marine approved of shipbuilding as a means of employing immigrant Acadians at Port Toulouse, one of the major constraints on the growth of Ile Royale's shipbuilding industry was the scarcity of suitably skilled labor.[21] Those with carpentry skills found employment building flakes and huts for the fishery, or in construction at Louisbourg.

A shortage of suitable timber also hampered shipbuilding. The garrison alone burned 280 cords of wood annually by 1729, and total consumption for heating must have been about a cord per person per year, so timber around Louisbourg disappeared rapidly. This originally affected the outports only slightly since population centered at Louisbourg, but Port Dauphin by the 1750s sent 1,000 cords of fuel wood to Louisbourg annually (equivalent to the consumption of a modest Cuban sugar mill), depleting some of the best and most accessible forest on the Island.[22] In a climate such as Cape Breton's wood disappeared very fast for heating purposes, providing steady and formidable competition for prospective shipbuilders. (In the Caribbean the demands of sugar boiling houses produced the same result.) Furthermore the best shipbuilding timber stood at a distance from the coast, while that more easily accessible proved of poor quality, as did the lumber of Ile St. Jean.[23] Timber and labor costs combined to prevent Ile Royale shipbuilding from developing into a major industry, and thereby contributed to the colony's increasing reliance on New England. Nonetheless, shipbuilding was the most successful segment of the productive economy of Ile Royale after the fishery.

Cape Breton's forest permitted more successful exploitation than its soil. Agriculture persistently disappointed the French. Despite endless official encouragement, cultivation at Ile Royale and Ile St. Jean never approached potential levels. Since the crown permitted only one large *seigneurie*, farming followed a pattern of small family farms. But the anticipated population of peasant cultivators never materialized, and Ile Royale farmers tilled a total of only 600 hectares (c. 1500 acres) before 1758.[24]

French officials explained this modest effort in several ways. The land was bad, they said, the climate too foggy, the farmers unskilled.[25] Each complaint had some truth to it. The soil around Louisbourg indeed lacked the requisite qualities for good farmland. Other parts of Ile Royale, however, were every bit as fertile as Quebec or New England land then under cultivation. The problem lay not so much in the land, but in the crops. The French tried to raise wheat and peas, traditional French staples entirely unsuited to the soils and climate of Ile Royale. Nineteenth-century cultivators succeeded admirably with the potato and hardy grains. Eighteenth-century French farmers, however, considered the potato cattle fodder and neglected to try barley and oats, which would have fared especially well in the western parts of the island, left almost untouched by the French. In addition, Ile Royale boasted "a vast number of beautiful natural meadows with hay above two feet high which rots every year without being cut; and although [there were] scarce sixty head of black cattle in all the island . . . , the product of these meadows in hay is sufficient to nourish thirty thousand of them."[26] Agriculture might easily have prospered at Ile Royale had the French departed from traditional crops and from the island's eastern shore. This instance typifies the failure of metropolitan and local administration to adapt to the dictates of colonial geography and climate.

French officials who complained about the farmers of Ile Royale had good cause. Many had retired from a life of soldiering or sailing, and they lacked the attitude, aptitude, and time for creating a farm out of wilderness. Acadian immigrants, of whom Ile Royale received about 500, rarely farmed, preferring work as fishermen, pilots, or tradesmen. Those who came to farm very often returned to Acadia, after discovering that the soil could not match that of their homeland, and that the degree of independence to which they had grown accustomed did not obtain in Ile Royale.[27] Dissatisfied with the Acadians' failure to transplant themselves to Ile Royale, the French shortly developed the opinion that the Acadians were lazy and dishonest.[28] Maurepas even suggested that slaves from Senegal might be the answer to the problems of agricultural production at Ile Royale.[29] French reliance on the Acadian population as the agricultural backbone of Ile Royale showed little appreciation for the traditions of the Acadians.[30] As in Quebec, so in Ile Royale: the French failure to recruit an adequate farming population insured long-run food deficits.

One further problem, never included among the official explanations, interfered with the progress of agriculture at Ile Royale: greed. As long as the island imported large quantities of provisions, someone made a profit selling them to the population. Clearly the importers and retailers of Louisbourg preferred to see agriculture flounder, and very likely administrators involved themselves in these profits. According to an English memoir: "it would not have been for the interest of the Intendant that the Island should produce the necessary subsistence of its inhabitants as the means of their heaping up Riches proceeds from the immense number of ships sent yearly from France loaded with flower and salt provisions, which they embezzle for their profit, and often pass them twice in their consummation."[31] Under such circumstances merchants and officials at Louisbourg showed lukewarm support for metropolitan sponsorship of Ile Royale agriculture.

Louisbourg officialdom would have been equally lukewarm about the agricultural development of Ile St. Jean, but as it turned out, the fertile island did little to affect the flour trade to Louisbourg. Despite better soil and climate, agriculture at Ile St. Jean fared little better than in Ile Royale. Inadequate population before 1749 kept the total production of the island very low—6,000 quintals of cod, 250 *barriques* of wheat (or 62 tons), and 110 *barriques* of peas in 1732.[32] Then after 1750, a flood of immigrant Acadians generated local demand for whatever surplus the farmers of Ile St. Jean could produce. Indeed, in many years Ile St. Jean could not even feed itself and required succor from Ile Royale—precisely the reverse of the relationship envisioned by Maurepas.

Several other problems afflicted agriculture at Ile St. Jean. As in Ile Royale, the crops raised reflected French tastes and tradition rather than the soil and climate of the island. The populace often found fishing more rewarding than farming and never settled inland at all, again much like Ile Royale.[33] Scarcity of seed and repeated scourges of field mice prevented harvests from providing surplus for export.[34] The French intended Ile St. Jean as a food producer, and when it failed in that role, it failed completely, condemning Louisbourg to decades of flour imports. This necessitated either reliance on the metropolis or trade with foreigners, neither of which suited French policy—but French policy, whether from ignorance or negligence, did not suit local conditions.

In the early years of Ile Royale, grain surpluses in Quebec helped offset agricultural failure. When Quebec harvests failed, Rochefort provided the necessary flour. Statistics on flour imports for the colony as a whole do not exist, but some data concerning the garrison survive. For the garrison alone, flour imports ranged between 1,000 and 2,200 quintals between 1714 and 1728 (see Table 6.5). Since flour cost between 11 and 13 livres per quintal, the bill for flour averaged about 15,000 livres annually.[35] The garrison also imported quantities of biscuit, legumes (usually either 315 or 340 quintals annually), lard, and occasionally salt pork. All this proved expensive to the Crown, the more so since French suppliers did their best to overcharge the government through collusion and cartels.[36] Although after 1718 the garrison never fled to avoid starvation, Louisbourg always remained dependent on imported food.

French economic policy at Louisbourg produced, on the whole, satisfactory if far from ideal results. The production of coal, timber, boats, and especially food never matched the hopes of Pontchartrain and his successors. To a degree their hopes were unrealistic—not because the physical environment could not provide the goods in question, but because French policy concentrated available human and capital resources on the fishery. While helping to make the fishery a great success, this policy handicapped other enterprises at Ile Royale. The population and accumulated wealth of the colony did not suffice to exploit fully the resources of Ile Royale. French policy gave highest priority to the fishery, the ideal mercantilist pursuit, and the market, too, rewarded fishing and commerce. Thus neither profit nor compulsion motivated labor or capital to enter coal, timber, or ship production. Without substantial govern-

Table 6.5

Flour Imports for the Ile Royale Garrison, 1714–1728

Year	Quintals	Pounds per Man	Source
1714	1,100	738	AC, B, 36–3:193–97
1715	1,800	1,208	AC, B, 37–1:238, 375–79
1716	1,196	803	AC, B, 38–1:104–9
1719	1,575	1,057	AC, C^{11}B, 4:4–8
1726	2,100	636	AC, B, 49–1:217–18
1728	2,165	561	AC, B, 52–2:542–43

ment assistance, these enterprises could only flounder while the fishery flourished. Although not equal to the dreams of Raudot and the ambitions of Pontchartrain, the productive economy of Ile Royale, thanks to the fishery, proved satisfactory to metropolitan authorities.

The productive economy of Cuba included more dimensions than that of Ile Royale. Its larger scale and longer tradition made the Cuban economy more difficult to manage, but its diversity allowed greater flexibility. Tobacco, sugar, and hides—like codfish at Louisbourg—formed the base of the export economy justifying the colony's existence. Mineral production in Cuba never caught the fancy of Spanish officials, although copper mines existed from the sixteenth century. Cuban timber, shipbuilding, and food production, however, did interest the Spanish, and state policy, as in Cape Breton, helped determine the success or failure of these enterprises as well as of the export economy.

With its tobacco policy, the Crown aimed to minimize contraband trade in tobacco, to increase the production of high quality tobacco while reducing harvests of low quality leaf, and to bolster the stability and security of the island by thinning the ranks of the *vegueros*. Although Crown policy had no appreciable effect on contraband or on the quality of tobacco produced, it did reduce tobacco production while the rest of the Cuban economy grew rapidly. In so doing, the Crown succeeded in destroying the political importance of the *vegueros*.

Few authors have made estimates of the quantities of tobacco produced and exported in eighteenth-century Cuba. The leading historian of Cuban tobacco, José Rivero Muñiz, confines himself to the statement that exports averaged 200,000 *arrobas* between 1740 and 1760.[37] Conventional wisdom rests on estimates made in the middle of the nineteenth century by a Spanish administrator, Jacobo de la Pezuela. His figures, which appear to be based on the wishes of the Spanish tobacco monopoly, are shown in Table 6.6.

Figures for the period before 1740 are scarce, but scattered documentary evidence suggests major revisions in Pezuela's estimates. Under the Intendencia General de Tabacos (1725–34), exports to Spain probably averaged more than 100,000 *arrobas* annually,[38] while during the years of the Tallapiedra *asiento* (1735–38), exports apparently declined to an average of about 55,000 *arrobas*.[39] Exports always amounted to a good

Table 6.6

Cuban Tobacco Export Figures According to Pezuela
(*arrobas*), 1703–1761

Years	Total Exports	Annual Average
1703–1707	20,000	4,000
1708–1710	360,000	120,000
1711–1716	480,000	80,000
1717	4,000	4,000
1718–1724[a]	720,000	120,000
1725–1734	160,000	16,000
1735–1738	480,000	120,000
1740–1761	3,520,000	160,000

Source: Pezuela, *Diccionario*, 4:571.

[a] Pezuela considers this only a six-year period although elsewhere his dates are inclusive.

deal less than production. Three opinions estimate the total annual harvest at between 330,000 and 400,000 *arrobas* for different years in the 1730s.[40]

The difference between these figures and the export totals comprises Cuban consumption, legitimate exports to Spanish colonies, legal and illegal trade with Britain through the South Sea Company, and other contraband. Between them, these trades therefore accounted for between 200,000 and 350,000 *arrobas* annually. The small Cuban population could not have consumed much tobacco. In the 1730s the Cuban population equalled roughly 1 percent of the Spanish, so even if the average Cuban smoked four times as much as the average Spaniard, Cuba used less than 5,000 *arrobas* of tobacco annually. Legitimate exports to other colonies within the Spanish empire accounted for a somewhat larger share of Cuban production, perhaps 10,000 *arrobas* annually.[41] The vast majority of the difference between production and export totals, however, consisted of tobacco traded to foreigners. The English factor of the South Sea Company bought 160,000 *arrobas* of tobacco annually, according to one Spanish source, while another says the Dutch filled two ships each year with the finest Cuban tobacco.[42] Havana leaf appeared regularly on the Amsterdam market at least as early as 1719.[43] The French and

Portuguese also traded illegally for Cuban tobacco, although on a smaller scale than the British or Dutch. For the period from 1726 to 1740, smuggling accounted for approximately 75 percent of Cuban tobacco production, perhaps more during the Tallapiedra *asiento*.[44]

Well aware of this situation, Spanish authorities considered it a problem of overproduction, while Cubans pointed to a shortage of Spanish shipping. To solve their problem, Cubans created the Havana Company, which the Spanish chartered to solve theirs. Whatever its merits as a tobacco administration, the Havana Company at least inaugurated an era of better statistics. According to Pezuela, the Company remitted 160,000 *arrobas* of tobacco annually; Rivero Muñiz prefers 200,000—which exceeds the amount called for in the Company's contract by 80,000 *arrobas*. Both authorities dramatically overestimated the quantities of tobacco exported by the Company.

Ship manifests drawn up in Havana and certificates of delivery made in Cadiz permit a highly accurate picture of tobacco exports between 1740 and 1760. These, together with half a dozen partial lists drawn up by officials of the Company, show the numbers of ships leaving Havana and arriving in Spain, and the quantities of tobacco carried.[45]

Between 1740 and 1760 a total of 284 ships carrying tobacco sailed from Cuba to Spain. The Havana Company remitted almost all of it (although some went on private or royal account), using ships belonging to the Company, to the Crown, or to private traders, sometimes foreigners.[46] Together these vessels furnished Spain with 1,857,853 *arrobas* of tobacco, an average shipment of 6,541 *arrobas*. Using the departure date from Havana to determine the year to which a shipment belonged, the annual distribution appears in Table 6.7. The annual average for these twenty-two years amounted to 84,448 *arrobas* (about half of the figure reported by Pezuela), an increase from the period of the Tallapiedra *asiento*, but a decrease from the years prior to 1736. The effects of war on shipping probably restrained tobacco exports from 1740 to 1748 and perhaps contributed to the surge following the peace. Royal legislation of 1752 began to influence exports only after a lag of three years.

The proportion of tobacco exported to foreigners may have declined slightly after 1740, since the South Sea Company *asiento* no longer allowed a foothold for surreptitious trade. Several backers of the Havana Company claimed that contraband had declined or disappeared after

Table 6.7

Annual Total Tobacco Remittances to Spain from Cuba,
1740–1761

Year	Arrobas	Quinquennial average	No. of shipments	Avg. Shipment (arrobas)
1740	78,106		6	13,018
1741	80,791		9	8,977
1742	94,004	82,235	11	8,546
1743	86,239		10	8,624
1744	72,034		15	4,802
1745	111,340		13	8,565
1746	40,193		11	3,654
1747	49,564	68,276	17	2,916
1748	42,544		8	5,318
1749	97,720		18	5,429
1750	43,933		6	7,322
1751	151,301		11	13,755
1752	116,519	109,093	13	8,963
1753	106,688		14	7,621
1754	127,026		19	6,686
1755	127,794		18	7,100
1756	44,707		15	2,981
1757	79,312	80,915	17	4,665
1758	89,738		16	5,609
1759	63,023		15	4,202
1760	114,463		19	6,024
1761	40,814	77,639	2	20,407

TOTAL   1,857,853

Source: see note 45.

1740,[47] but royal officials reported that large parts of Cuba traded tobacco solely with foreigners, since the Havana Company refused to buy.[48] Apparently the Havana Company found it profitable to buy and remit the tobacco harvest of the Havana region, but not worthwhile to serve the entire island. Extra transportation costs probably made the difference, although perhaps Company authorities merely preferred to buy from their friends, relations, and neighbors, rather than from strangers at the other end of the island. Whatever the reason, a very large share of the island's tobacco production escaped the Havana Company and the state monopoly. This share probably shrank from the 75 percent of the 1720s and 1730s, but not by much. Certainly the majority of Cuban tobacco continued to find its market through illegal channels.

Despite the preponderance of contraband, the royal tobacco monopoly provided large and steady profits for the Crown. According to the most extensive and authoritative history of Cuba, tenfold profits from the tobacco trade financed the administration of Cuba.[49] Actually the Crown realized profits of between 500 and 600 percent on the tobacco *renta*, producing an annual revenue of between 7 and 10 million pesos from 1740 to 1760. This profit, large enough to finance the entire Spanish navy, easily met the costs of governing and defending Cuba (see Tables 6.8 and 6.9). Even after a dramatic increase in the Havana budget (1740–43), Cuban administrative costs normally came to less than a third of the profit garnered from Cuban tobacco. This profit amounted to about one-fifth the value of the output of Peruvian mines in the same years, or between one-fourth and one-third of the income of the Spanish fisc.[50] The figures in Table 6.8 help explain the attention the crown lavished on Cuban tobacco.

Table 6.8 shows that tobacco consumption in Spain remained fairly static between 1740 and 1760, but that the value of the tobacco sold increased steadily—and more rapidly than administrative costs—producing a gradually rising revenue to the Crown. The cash value of the tobacco trade exceeded by ten times the value of the Cape Breton cod trade. Since the French suffered the cod trade to remain in private hands, no state revenue proceeded from it—although an export trade earned bullion for France. The Spanish, in contrast, managed to extract a revenue of close to 80 percent of the legitimate tobacco trade's value.

Not all of the tobacco sold in Spain came from Cuba, however, so a

Table 6.8
Finances of the Tobacco Administration in Spain, 1740–1764

Year	Total Consumption[a] (arrobas)	Revenue (pesos)	Costs (pesos)	Profit (pesos)	Quinquennial Average Profit (pesos)	Revenue[b] (pesos)
1740	128,012	8,765,933	1,532,733	7,233,200		9,497,999
1741	112,664	8,617,302	1,553,825	7,063,477		9,292,524
1742	101,885	9,091,944	1,489,013	7,602,932	7,502,206	9,706,613
1743	104,798	9,400,344	1,504,939	7,895,405		10,032,440
1744	103,740	9,270,010	1,553,933	7,716,017		9,892,918
1745	103,962	9,347,761	1,568,415	7,779,346		9,997,792
1746	103,498	9,289,127	1,587,904	7,701,223		9,910,647
1747	105,141	9,438,161	1,581,814	7,856,347	7,937,194	10,070,948
1748	103,920	9,324,726	1,612,502	7,712,224		9,950,697
1749	107,208	10,275,213	1,638,385	8,636,828		10,275,213
1750	106,972	10,288,948	1,669,543	8,619,403		10,283,559
1751	110,979	10,655,735	1,707,124	8,948,610		10,283,559
1752	116,410	11,215,626	1,719,241	9,496,389	9,175,709	
1753	117,860	11,348,915	1,787,137	9,561,777		
1754	116,072	11,084,453	1,832,165	9,252,362		
1755	116,690	11,257,862	1,838,729	9,419,132		
1756	121,424	11,719,802	1,856,678	9,863,124		
1757	121,008	11,672,261	1,883,438	9,788,823	9,740,367	
1758	120,344	11,659,926	2,002,711	9,656,815		
1759	123,916	11,974,445	2,000,506	9,973,938		
1760	125,077	12,109,917	1,998,361	10,111,555		
1761	124,885	12,141,201	2,049,438	10,091,763		
1762	130,740	12,655,393	2,152,219	10,503,172	10,194,477	
1763	128,628	12,456,494	2,149,879	10,306,615		
1764	124,244	12,102,687	2,143,406	9,959,282		

Sources: Razon del consumo de Tabacos de todas clases en España; su valor gastos de comun por quinquenios, desde 1740 al de 1798, AMN, Ms. 2186, doc. 19, fol. 66. Very similar figures for every fifth year between 1740 and 1824 appear in Plaza Prieto, *Estructura económica de España*, pp. 818, 820; and Canga Argüelles, *Diccionario de hacienda*, 2:518–19.

[a] To arrive at these figures, I have changed *libras castellanas* into *arrobas* at the rate of 25:1, and *reales de vellón* into *pesos* at the rate of 8:1.

[b] These figures come from Compañía de la Habana, AGI, UM 897. Sobre aumentos de la renta de el Tabaco.

Table 6.9

Havana Budget, 1711–1759

Year(s)	Annual average (pesos)	
1711–1715	166,293	(53 months)
1715–1722	242,595	(78 months)
1722–1728	441,560	(78 months)
1728–1732	481,655	(50 months)
1733	470,117	
1734	527,188	
1735	700,797	
1736	637,747	
1737	822,009	
1738	923,229	
1739	478,936	
1740	707,117	
1741–1742	1,614,389	(24 months)
1743	2,609,906	
1744	2,481,073	
1745	2,583,595	
1746	4,272,736	
1747	2,779,167	
1748	793,359	
1749	2,414,886	
1750	2,436,270	
1751	2,346,286	
1752	2,170,411	
1753	2,674,410	
1754	1,382,039	
1755	1,836,815	
1756	2,084,211	
1757	1,629,961	
1758	—	
1759	1,825,077	

Sources: AGI, Contaduría 1153, 1154, 1163, 1164, 1165A, 1165B.
Note: These figures come from the *data* or debits in the accounts and thus
represent actual expenditure. I have reduced *reales* to pesos by a factor of eight.
Prior to 1733, Cuban accounting observed no regular period, thus the inconvenient form of the data.

slight revision is in order. Comparing the quinquennial averages in Tables 6.7 and 6.8, it appears that between 65 and 95 percent of tobacco consumed in Spain had Cuban origins. The remainder came partly from other sources within the Spanish empire, but largely from Brazil and the Chesapeake.[51] Private contractors handled the import trade from plantations in these foreign colonies, normally in quantities of less than 40,000 *arrobas* of Brazilian tobacco and less than 32,000 *arrobas* of Virginian.[52] Buying in foreign markets allowed the Spanish to match tobacco purchases very closely with domestic demand, without one year refusing Cuban producers they might need the next. What proportion of royal tobacco profits proceeded solely from Cuban leaf? Since the price of Cuban tobacco always greatly exceeded that of Brazilian and Virginian,[53] the value of the revenue the Crown derived from Cuban tobacco amounted to more than the above mentioned 65 to 95 percent of the total profits from the tobacco *renta*. The average may be taken as at least 85 percent. Since total annual profits ranged from 7 to 10 million pesos (Table 6.8), the Cuban tobacco trade from 1740 to 1760 earned the Crown between 6 and 9 million pesos a year, about one-fifth the entire royal income.

It might have been more. Despite the steady growth of tobacco revenues, the potential of the tobacco trade remained but partially fulfilled because the Havana Company never met its contracted yearly quota of 80,000 *arrobas* of high-grade tobacco. During its twenty-two-year contract, the Havana Company had to remit 1,760,000 *arrobas*. Total deliveries exceeded this figure by almost 100,000 *arrobas*, but perhaps 75 percent did not meet the quality stipulations of the Havana Company contract.[54] The spate of royal scoldings provoked by this record was matched only by the excuses offered by the Havana Company. As long as it held its contract, the Company continued to remit large quantities of lower-quality tobacco, either because the requisite grades were unavailable in sufficient quantity, or because the Company preferred to defraud the government. Soil exhaustion certainly inhibited the growth of high-grade leaf around Havana,[55] but the Company could have purchased tobacco from slightly further afield.

Spanish tobacco policy in Cuba produced several unwelcome effects for the *vegueros*. Had the Havana Company obliged the Crown and fulfilled the terms of its contract, the growers' hardships would have intensified, as representatives of the Company often pointed out. Very likely the quality of tobacco declined as the century wore on, prompting metropolitan concern, but nonetheless the growers deeply resented Spanish attempts to confine production to the finest leaf; the *medio pie arriba* ruling of 1752, which excluded about nine-tenths of the harvest, they found particularly distressing.[56] Some *partidos* could not produce tobacco of the stipulated grades, and most growers found that little, if any, of their leaf qualified.[57] In Bayamo and Santiago de Cuba, harvests declined drastically in 1752–53, partly on account of growers' attempts to comply with quality control legislation.[58] After 1752 many *vegueros* also "applied themselves to other products," such as foodstuffs, livestock, or if they could, sugar.[59] Others departed the Havana area in search of virgin soil, which would produce higher grade leaf and perhaps allow the cultivator to evade the authorities as well: new *vegas* appeared in nineteen communities in the western end of the island between 1740 and 1760.[60] Presumably the only reason that royal initiatives of the 1750s did not force more growers into the contraband market was the availability of alternative employments in growing industries, notably sugar. Lands that had produced tobacco prior to the 1750s may not have become canefields, but labor and capital certainly migrated from tobacco into sugar, especially in the Havana area.[61]

In the course of the eighteenth century the Cuban tobacco policy of the Spanish Crown proved a mild success. Like French policy toward the Ile Royale fishery, it allowed extensive exploitation of a bountiful natural resource, although it fell far short of maximizing profits. Spanish policy shrank the tremendous contraband trade of the 1720s and 1730s— though it far from disappeared—and diminished the number of *vegueros* and their power to threaten Cuban security. Nonetheless, legislation could not induce Cubans to produce more high-grade leaf, and Spain never received the quantities the *renta* could sell, leaving the fiscal potential of the tobacco monopoly largely unexploited.

While reducing the importance of tobacco in Cuba, the Spanish hoped to increase sugar production. Sugar required much higher capitalization than tobacco, and its success ensured the rise to prominence of a class that had much to lose through violence and disloyalty and nothing to gain through contraband. Modern scholarship, accepting the judgment of the planter Arango, has characterized Spanish efforts to help sugar as futile and the British capture in 1762 as the dawn of the sugar era in Cuba.[62] Only a few writers have ventured estimates on sugar exports before 1760, and in each case the estimate is identical to Pezuela's—160,000 *arrobas* annually before 1754 and 200,000 *arrobas* annually between 1754 and 1760.[63] As Moreno pointed out, these figures "do not stand up to critical analysis." Moreno, however, has no substitute data on exports for the period prior to 1760, merely production figures for scattered single years. He offers 2,000 metric tons (193,000 *arrobas*) for 1740, 5,484 metric tons (482,592 *arrobas*) for 1758, and 4,639 metric tons (384,472 *arrobas*) for 1760.[64] This latter figure is not new: Rolph in 1917 and Reynolds in 1924 reported the 1760 crop at 4,390 and 4,400 tons, respectively. Among recent authors, Thomas combined arithmetic error with faulty data to get 300 tons (24,000 to 24,400 *arrobas* if his are long tons) as the 1753–59 export average, and 500 tons for 1762. Authors such as Le Riverend and Vicens Vives relied on figures derived from Humboldt (208,000 *arrobas* for 1760) and Raynal (173,800 quintals total, or 115,800 *arrobas* average for 1748–53). In 1927 Guerra offered 21,000 *arrobas* as the average export, 1759–63, a figure which originated with Arango but appeared as recently as 1964 in Rivero Muñiz's work. Deerr's Cuban sugar production statistics for 1760–63 are almost equally inaccurate.[65] No modern writer has seen fit to reproduce Arrate's higher estimate of 200,000 *arrobas* annually for the Havana district alone in the late 1750s.[66]

Cuban sugar statistics for this period clearly leave a great deal to be desired. Only Pezuela's figures have chronological depth. Of the several opinions for 1760, the higher estimates of Rolph, Reynolds, and Moreno are closest to the mark, but they refer to production, not exports. Those relying on Arango, Humboldt, and Raynal vastly underestimate Cuban sugar exports; those who rely on Pezuela underestimate but not so wildly. Ever since Arango, authors have preferred low figures for Cuban sugar exports before 1762 in order to support the view that the Spanish system of monopoly and trade regulation stifled the Cuban economy, and that the British occupation inaugurated a new era of prosperity.

It simply was not so. Documentary evidence reveals that the growth in Cuban sugar exports began before the British capture in 1762. Only scattered data exist for the early eighteenth century, but the Havana

Company included sugar in its ship manifests after 1754, permitting more reliable estimates.

Exports amounted to about 50,000 *arrobas* annually from 1717 to 1724, according to a contemporary estimate, and about 60,000 before 1740. Total production, however, exceeded this figure, reaching 160,000 *arrobas* in the mid-1730s, and perhaps 200,000 later in the decade.[67] This actually may not represent the high point of pre-1740 sugar production, since several sources indicate a depression in Cuban sugar beginning in the late 1720s, which international prices appear to explain.[68] Santiago de Cuba apparently suffered more seriously in the 1730s because its traditional outlet, the Cartagena market, was closed by new vigilance in the collection of taxes, but production levels probably declined in the early 1730s for the whole island.[69]

In the period prior to 1740, Cuban sugar exports and production showed a sensitivity to the international sugar market, since the Crown had not yet assigned the sugar trade to an *asentista*. High prices during and after the War of the Spanish Succession (1701–13) induced several Cubans to put more land into sugar, and to buy slaves from the South Sea Company or private interlopers. Both around Havana and in the interior, the number of *ingenios* climbed (as noted in the previous chapter) and production levels increased accordingly. Prices in most international markets fell, however, beginning in Havana in 1726 and Toledo in 1727, and in Paris and London in 1732. Shipping grew short, and since producers could not wait while their sugar spoiled, they sold at two-thirds cost. They implored Spanish authorities to ease taxation and give Cuban sugar preference in the Spanish market, resulting in the policies discussed in chapter 5.

After 1740, international prices ceased to exert much influence on production, since the Havana Company bought at fixed prices. Sugar now responded to state policy, which discouraged tobacco production and handicapped foreign sugar in the Spanish market. Production and export figures for the period 1740–60 show a very thorough recovery from the depression of the 1730s. While Spain and Britain were at war (1739–48), exports declined to a trickle—12,000 *arrobas* a year on average—but by 1749 a sugar boom had begun in the Havana district.[70] In that year Havana reported sixty-two *ingenios* with twenty-one more under construction, and an export capacity of 93,000 *arrobas*.[71] Puerto

Príncipe with sixty *ingenios* and Santiago de Cuba with fifty produced smaller amounts for export. By 1755, total production reached 35,000 *cajas* or 560,000 *arrobas* for Cuba as a whole, roughly half of which the Havana Company exported to Spain.[72] By 1758, according to one source, the Havana jurisdiction alone produced 25,000 *cajas* (400,000 *arrobas*), while the entire island produced 87,000 *cajas* or 1,392,000 *arrobas*, of which less than half went to Spain.[73] This appears to be an exaggeration, however.[74] The Crown's accountant for the West Indies put Cuba's production at 453,000 *arrobas* in 1759, of which Havana accounted for 75 percent. According to this estimate, 356,000 *arrobas* were available for export to Spain since Cuba retained only 65,000 *arrobas*, and the rest of the Indies took only 33,000 *arrobas*.[75] These contemporary estimates correspond reasonably well with data from ship manifests compiled in Table 6.10, which suggests that Pezuela and his followers ignored a crucial development in Cuban history—perhaps because rapid economic growth under monopoly seemed a contradiction to liberal minds.

The trend so conspicuous in Table 6.10 did not escape the notice of Cuban and Spanish officials. As early as 1748, officers of the Havana Company attributed rapid growth in sugar exports to the "political economy" of the Crown. While the Company pointed to higher official prices and greater slave imports, the governor considered royal tax policy the major factor in the expansion of sugar.[76] Whichever the truth, and

Table 6.10
Cuban Sugar Exports to Spain, 1754–1760
(in *arrobas*)

Year	Annual Total	Average Shipment Size
1754	108,472	5,709
1755	163,754	9,097
1756	173,002	11,533
1757	270,089	15,887
1758	285,232	17,827
1759	286,089	19,072
1760	378,346	19,912

Source: See note 45.

presumably a compromise more nearly represents the reality, all agreed that sugar production had grown tremendously since 1748 and that royal initiatives lay behind this growth.

With this sugar boom came a welcome reduction in Spanish dependence on foreign sources of sugar. Although Granada had canefields dating from the Moors, imports—largely from the French Antilles in the eighteenth century—had long satisfied the vast majority of Spanish sugar needs.[77] By midcentury, however, Cuban sugar began to invade the Cadiz market on an increasing scale; by 1760 Cuba filled about 30 percent of Spanish demand, saving Spain approximately 1,500,000 pesos (in Cadiz prices).

Among the steps taken to promote the expansion of the sugar industry in Cuba was encouragement of the slave trade. Just as the Cape Breton fishery needed a large supply of inexpensive labor, so Cuban agriculture required hands. Conventional wisdom holds that slave imports to Cuba numbered less than 60,000 from 1492 to 1762, 4,986 between 1740 and 1760, and 10,700 during the British occupation of 1760–62. These latter slaves joined an existing population of 31,000 to inaugurate the age of slavery in Cuba.[78]

For the period 1740 to 1762, the accepted figure is certainly too low. The total of 4,986 appears in a document fragment as the number of slaves imported over a twelve-year period, most likely 1741–52.[79] Several other sources indicate that slave imports exceeded this figure, not counting illicit ones. Given the rapid growth of sugar, the gradual growth of other enterprises employing slaves (copper mines, shipbuilding, ranching, construction, etc.), and the high death rate among Cuban slaves (as much as 10 percent annually in the Havana district),[80] it could scarcely have been otherwise.

If the accepted figure is too low, what figure is correct? Data are few and inconclusive, but Spanish and British documents suggest that preconquest totals ran much higher than believed, and that British slave imports in 1762–63 amounted to far less. Before 1739, the South Sea Company enjoyed a legal monopoly on slave imports into Cuba, furnishing the island with a total of 5,321 slaves between 1717 and 1739, according to one source.[81] This corresponds fairly well with the recent tabulations of Colin Palmer, who calculates that the South Sea Company sold 5,784 slaves to Havana in the same years, and 6,387 for the years

1715–38. Havana's imports accounted for one-tenth of the South Sea Company's slave trade to Spanish America, putting Havana fourth among slave importing cities in the Spanish world. In these years Havana's slave imports averaged about 250 to 275 annually, with great fluctuations. During 1730–32, when imperial legislation aiming to bolster the sugar industry inspired hope among Cuban planters, imports averaged 797 per year; but after 1732 the slave trade to Havana dwindled to 83 per year. Santiago de Cuba imported about one-fourth or one-third as many slaves as Havana in this period, putting the island's total at about 8,000.[82] These, of course, are official figures and certainly underestimate the actual total.

After 1740, the slave trade fell to the Havana Company and the occasional private contractor. Projections based on Company accounts suggest that imports averaged about 484 *piezas de Indias* annually between 1743 and 1761, or more than 10,000 for 1740–60.[83] This total corresponds well with a source not related to the Havana Company, which claimed that between 1740 and 1747 Cubans bought more than 4,000 slaves; projected over the period 1740–60, this yields 10,500.[84] Other fragmentary evidence provided by Havana Company records suggests this figure might be high, but not by much.[85] All things considered, the number of slaves legally imported by the Havana Company alone between 1740 and 1760 probably amounted to more than 8,000 and less than 11,000—roughly double the accepted figure. And the total for 1713–60 comes to about 15,000 to 18,000.

During the British occupation of Havana (12 August 1762 to 6 July 1763) the British introduced many fewer than the 10,700 slaves reported by most authors. With only nine weeks left in the occupation, Cubans had officially bought only 1,700 slaves.[86] The total for the entire eleven months may have reached 4,000, but certainly fell far short of 10,700.[87] Aimes probably inadvertently converted 1,700 into 10,700. In the slave trade, as in other respects, the British occupation in 1762–63 affected Cuban society much less than historians have supposed: rather than radically increasing the volume of trade, the occupation merely made legal and visible what had formerly been covert commerce.

Any attempts to pinpoint the number of legally imported slaves cannot give an accurate total, since so many slaves entered Cuba as contraband. The Spanish tax of 33-1/3 pesos on the sale of each imported slave, 11 percent of the official price, induced buyers and sellers to avoid legal channels. Thus Jamaican traders competed with the South Sea Company by exchanging slaves for coin, hides, or tobacco along Cuba's south coast at one-third the official price. These contraband traders, according to the directors of the Company, took a large part of the trade away from the Company. Indeed in 1734 the Company recalled its factor in Santiago because business did not warrant his presence.[88] Estimates put the totals of slaves illegally entering Cuba between 1714 and 1730 at 3,000, and at 6,000 between 1739 and 1743.[89] These figures inspire minimal confidence, however, since their authors had no way to substantiate them and perhaps had reason to exaggerate. An attempt at measurement is warranted.

One way to estimate the illegal slave trade is to calculate the replacement rate for Cuban slave society: how many slaves must have been imported and born to produce the rate of growth in the slave population? This technique is only as valid as its assumptions are accurate, of course, and in this case can at best give only a rough indication of the size of the illegal slave trade.

Let us begin with the following assumptions:

(1) P_2 slave population in 1760 = 35,000
(2) P_1 slave population in 1700 = 10,000
(3) CDR slave crude death rate = 75/1000
(4) CBR slave crude birth rate = 20/1000

The first assumption is based on the proportion of slaves in the total Cuban population. In 1774 that proportion was 26 percent, and the slave population was 40,300, according to what is generally called the first Cuban census (widely suspected of serious underreporting, especially of slaves). P_2 is 12 percent higher than the 31,000 offered by many authors, but their figure comes from subtracting the fictitious 10,700 slaves of 1762–63 from the 1774 slave population.

The second assumption, shakier than the first, is a further backward extrapolation of the proportion of 1774; it implies that the growth in slave numbers matched the growth in the overall population. Very possibly P_1 should be lower.

The third assumption is based on data from various sources. Cuban documents claim a death rate among slaves of 8–10 percent; Moreno Fraginals finds a death rate of 61–63/1000 among slaves during

1835–41 and 1856–60 (and these nineteenth-century slaves were vaccinated against smallpox—which killed more blacks than whites in Cuba). Bourdé finds a death rate of 47.6/1000 among all blacks and mulattoes in Santa María del Rosario in 1775; Knight notes that nineteenth-century observers estimated slave mortality at between 5–10 percent.

The fourth assumption rests on data from Moreno Fraginals, who finds a birth rate of 19/1000 for Cuban slaves during 1835–41; from Higman and Engerman, who each find 23/1000 for Jamaican slaves of the early nineteenth century; and from Craton who finds a birth rate of 20/1000 at Worthy Park, Jamaica, during 1784–1834. This low birth rate ("natural" birth rates range around 40–45/1000) is accounted for in part by sex ratios in slave society, as high as nine males to every female among Africans, and nine to two among creole slaves in Cuba, 1746–90.[90]

Cuban slave society would have disappeared without the slave trade. The net loss to the slave community (births minus deaths) came to perhaps 5.5 percent annually. That the slave population did grow indicates that annual slave imports must have averaged more than 5.5 percent of slave population. Mere maintenance of slave numbers required about 550 slaves annually in 1700, and about 1,920 slaves annually by 1760. Over the course of the period between 1700 and 1760, this means a total of about 75,000 slaves must have entered Cuba. From this total one can subtract the total of legally imported slaves, at most 20,000 and probably only 18,000, which leaves 55,000–57,000 as the number of slaves imported illegally. Thus roughly two-thirds of the slave trade to Cuba during 1700–60 was contraband.[91]

Revising the assumptions, of course, yields different results. If we lower P_1 to 5,000, then only 66,000 slaves must have entered Cuba. If we lower the CDR to 60/1000, we get 54,000 slaves. But there are good arguments for assuming a higher CDR in the eighteenth century than for the better-documented nineteenth, centering on the character of the Cuban disease environment, the provision of medical services to slaves, and the proportion of Africans to creoles within the slave population.

One additional factor suggests that the figures offered above for the clandestine slave trade might be too low rather than too high. In 1774 Cuba's population included 30,847 free blacks. Throughout the 1700–60 period a free black population existed, many of whom must have been manumitted slaves. These were people who, statistically speaking at least, left the slave community: emigrants. They, too, had to be replaced to maintain slave numbers, and so the CDR ought to have added to it a component representing the manumission rate—and the runaway rate too, although that was apparently small in the eighteenth century.

It is arguable that death rates among slaves were lower in the eighteenth century than in the early nineteenth century when the plantation system reached its apogee. Those who believe overwork and mistreatment influenced death rates more profoundly than the disease environment and patterns of immunity may subscribe to this view. Moreno Fraginals's data, however, suggest the period 1746–90 was more lethal to slaves than the nineteenth century. All things considered, a total of 75,000 slaves imported during 1700–1760 might well be low rather than high.

These calculations, if anywhere close to correct, suggest that the slave trade to Cuba before 1762 was much more substantial than anyone has recognized, and that the illegal component of this trade, which has generally been written off as beyond measurement, was primarily responsible for the maintenance and growth of Cuban slave society. Given the expansion of sugar production and the rise in the number of plantations, a flourishing slave trade should come as no surprise (barring, of course, natural increase among the slave population).[92] Given the extent to which contraband dominated the export of Cuban tobacco (see above 154–62), the role of contraband in the slave trade should also come as no surprise. To understand the Cuban economy of the early and mid-eighteenth century, one must bear in mind the extent of exchange outside the legal channels, and the extent to which production depended on illegal markets.

The Cuban ranching industry prospered in the eighteenth century despite comparatively insignificant support from the Crown. Statistics on hide production and exports are almost as plentiful as those on sugar and tobacco. Cuban hides formed an important source of leather for Spain—especially early in the eighteenth century before the rise of Argentine ranching—and for Britain and Holland as well.[93] Still, ranching never approached the importance to the Cuban economy it had enjoyed in prior centuries.[94]

Unlike sugar, tobacco, or codfish, hides served many purposes within the colonies which produced them, so that total production exceeded exports by a large margin. The high bulk per value ratio in shipping hides also contributed to the localization of consumption. At midcentury, total annual production probably ranged between 60,000 and 90,000 hides, with Havana leading the island, because slaughterhouses centered there.[95] Ranching had grown only slowly from the early part of the century.[96] Exports, however, expanded significantly over time, probably a result of greater traffic and cheaper cargo space between Cuba and Europe. The available information on hide exports to Spain is summarized in Table 6.11. These figures do not substantiate those provided by Raynal, who wrote that between 1748 and 1753 Cuba exported a total of only 1,569 hides.[97] However, Raynal's figures for sugar and tobacco exports during 1748–1753 fail to inspire confidence. Raynal's contemporaries mention large numbers of cattle slaughtered for their hides alone and in two instances a figure of 10,000–12,000 hides is given as the average annual export.[98]

The trends evident in Table 6.11 probably resulted from the expansion of transport that accompanied the rise of sugar in Cuba. The lowest figures correspond to those years when British sea power endangered Spanish shipping, while the highest accompany the sugar export boom of 1754–60. Coastal shipping between various small ports and Havana presumably increased, as did transatlantic crossings. Although planters always felt cargo space inadequate, a cargo of hides often found its way on a Havana Company, royal, or private ship. Indeed, ship manifests show that hides almost invariably crossed the ocean as minor freight on ships carrying larger and more valuable cargoes of tobacco and sugar. Neither crown policy nor international prices can account for the increased hide exports—West Indian hides traded on the Amsterdam exchange varied in price only marginally between 1742 and 1765.[99] Only the increased availability of shipping could have prompted such a trend.

As with tobacco exports and slave imports, the illegal market formed a major component of the Cuban hide trade. Early in the century, the Dutch provided the principal outlet and perhaps continued to do so,[100] but by the 1750s Britain took one-third as many Cuban hides as did Spain. These hides appeared in Britain as Jamaican products, but since Jamaica supported little ranching in the mid-eighteenth century, they

Table 6.11

Cuban Hide Exports to Spain, 1735–1760

Year	Number of Hides	Year	Number of Hides
1735	7,989	1748	—
1736	7,989	1749	—
1737	7,989	1750	—
1738	7,989	1751	4,351
1739	7,989	1752	—
1740	7,989	1753	—
1741	2,419	1754	6,104
1742	5,769	1755	5,705
1743	3,918	1756	10,471
1744	—	1757	7,378
1745	—	1758	12,807
1746	1,200	1759	18,762
1747	2,305	1760	20,327

Sources: Consejo de Hacienda, 1 junio 1743, AGI, SD 2004; Consejo de Hacienda, 14 enero 1744, AGI, SD 2004. For the years after 1743, I have consulted the ship manifests cited in note 45.

presumably entered Jamaica from Cuba. British statistics arranged in Table 6.12 lend credence to this suspicion. Except for 1763, Jamaica always ranked second to Ireland as a source of hides to England. Before Havana became open to British traders, England imported several thousand hides annually from Jamaica, but during the British occupation, when Havana traded freely with British ships, England imported very few from Jamaica. Under normal conditions, Jamaican smugglers operated on the Cuban south coast where both ranches and smugglers' coves abounded, bringing back several thousand hides yearly; but in 1763 British traders dealt with the Cuban ranchers through middlemen in Havana, undercutting the more traditional illegal trade route. Very possibly the same Jamaican merchants operated both trades. At any rate, Cuba apparently provided Britain with between 3,000 and 10,000 hides annually before 1762. The annual average derived from the total imports during 1758–67 was 5,985, which equalled almost 30 percent of the

Table 6.12

British Hide Imports from Jamaica and Havana,
1758–1767

Year	Jamaican Hides	Havana Hides
1758	3,168	0
1759	7,150	0
1760	9,199	0
1761	4,964	0
1762	1,416	0
1763	938	14,802
1764	3,441	3,205
1765	1,135	0
1766	4,690	336
1767	5,410	0

Sources: An Account of the Quantities of Raw Hides and Raw Calf-skins Imported into England for the Last Ten Years ending at Christmas 1767 distinguishing each Year and the Quantity Imported from each foreign Country in every Year, PRO, T. 64/276A, #227. Imports from Havannah in the Underwritten Years, 1763–64, PRO, T. 38/363, fol. 190.

Spanish import average for 1758–60. Since hides in Havana sold for three pesos each, the total value of Cuban hide exports (legal and illegal) amounted to less than 75,000 pesos in most years, much less than the value of Cuban sugar or tobacco, or Cape Breton codfish. Spanish, and later Argentine, competition prevented ranching from becoming a major export trade in the eighteenth-century Cuban economy.[101]

When the French considered a shipbuilding industry at Louisbourg, one inspiration was the royal shipyard (*astillero*) in Havana. Beginning in the 1720s, Havana built more durable ships more cheaply than any port in Spain. Indeed, the revival of the Spanish navy in the early eighteenth century owed much to the success of the Havana *astillero*.

After a decade of negotiation, the royal shipyard began work in 1723. Before the English capture of Havana in 1762, the *astillero* built forty-six ships for the Spanish navy. Thirty-two of them carried fifty or more guns and fourteen mounted twenty-four or fewer; the largest ship had eighty guns, and smallest fourteen. The average ship of the line built in Havana carried sixty guns; the average among the smaller ships had seventeen guns.[102] This flurry of shipbuilding accounted for nearly two-fifths of Spanish naval construction in these years. The Spanish navy built two or three ships of the line per year to maintain itself; Havana built thirty-two such vessels in thirty-nine years and became the single most important shipyard of the Spanish empire in the eighteenth century.[103]

Havana not only built more ships than any port in Spain, it also built larger and more durable ones. Since accessible large timbers had become scarce in Spain, Havana built a disproportionate number of large ships. Of nine vessels of more than eighty guns in the Spanish navy of 1778, six had been built in Havana, all before 1770.[104] In 1771 six of the eight largest ships in the Spanish navy were Havana built.[105] According to Uztáriz, ships made of European timber lasted only twelve to fifteen years in tropical waters, while those built of Cuban cedar and oak lasted thirty.[106] Indeed many ships built in Havana in the 1740s continued to serve in the Spanish navy in the 1770s and 1780s.[107] The thirty ships built for the Spanish navy between 1744 and 1762 lasted an average of 12.25 years before their first careening. Those built in Europe averaged only 10.6 years, while the Havana-built ships lasted an average of 19.33 years. The European ship with the greatest longevity lasted nineteen years, whereas *El Dragon*, launched in Havana in 1774, endured thirty-two years of service before its first careening.[108] Better timber certainly accounted for a good deal of the durability of the Havana ships, but since vessels built by the Havana Company (between 1743 and 1749) had by far the best endurance records, it may be that the shipwrights and craftsmen employed by the Company excelled their Spanish counterparts. Certainly they excelled those who built ships in Havana between 1724 and 1740.[109]

Vessels built in Havana lasted longer than European ones and cost less as well. For twelve ships of the line built by the Havana Company, the Crown paid 889,893 pesos, or slightly less than 74,000 per ship, about the price paid Juan de Acosta during his shipbuilding contract in the 1730s.[110] The Havana Company claimed to have lost 643,725 pesos building these twelve ships, meaning actual construction costs amounted to slightly less than 128,000 pesos per vessel, including administrative overhead. An eighty-gun vessel in Havana (*El Rayo*) cost 143,640 pesos.

The seventy-gun *Invencible*, built in Havana, cost 126,841 pesos, whereas a sixty-eight built in Cartagena, Spain (*El Atlante*), cost 289,148 pesos, a difference which Havana Company officials considered representative. Although the Company expected seventy-gun ships to cost only 75,000 pesos—which is what the Crown paid for them—actual Havana costs still amounted to only 44 percent of Spanish costs.[111] Elsewhere the Havana Company claimed larger losses, but even using these figures (which the Company supplied in hopes of escaping shipbuilding obligations in its contract) Havana construction costs for seventy-gun ships averaged only 152,300 pesos, less than 53 percent of Spanish costs for sixty-eights. Costs for the two sixty-six-gun ships and the two eighty-gun vessels built by the Havana Company overran anticipated costs by the same margins of about 100 percent, but still presumably amounted to much less than Spanish costs (or costs in other American shipyards) for like vessels.[112] Havana shipbuilding costs, low but still higher than expected, prompted the Company to seek exemption from its shipbuilding obligations, but since the Crown found the contract extremely advantageous it resisted until 1749.[113] Shipbuilding continued from 1749 to 1762 under the direction of L. Montalvo, a navy official, but contractors generally eschewed ships of the line, preferring less costly frigates and brigantines. Never again would the navy build so many large ships in Havana as in 1723–49, and never again would it enjoy such bargains as during its contract with the Havana Company.

The availability of cheap lumber and labor accounted for the low shipbuilding costs of Havana. Together these costs amounted to 68 percent of the total construction costs of two seventy-gun ships, the same proportion on two sixty-gun ships, and 69 percent on an eighty-gun ship.[114] Fitting out (sails, cordage, pitch, etc.) came to no more than 30 or 32 percent of the total cost of building these warships in Havana, less than in Europe. Labor and lumber costs on these three vessels were almost equal but this accounting included only wages paid to craftsmen and not the cost and maintenance of slaves—of whom the arsenal employed 230.[115] Including all the lumber used in docks, buildings, and other structures, lumber costs for ten years of shipbuilding amounted to 46 percent of all costs, counting salaries, insurance, interest on debts, and other overhead items. Skilled labor amounted to only 22 percent of the total, whereas ironwork, nails, and slaves (a single category in the accounts) accounted for 27 percent of total costs. The absence of competition for resources from private shipyards—prohibited in 1713—helped limit costs, and slave labor certainly helped depress the wage bill in the *astillero*. But the greatest savings over Spanish costs must have come from the reduced cost of timber.[116]

Low shipbuilding costs accelerated timber exploitation. In one season the Havana Company employed 383 cutters and laborers, 322 oxen drivers, and 1,449 teams of oxen in thirteen *cortes*, felling 21,766 cedar trunks and 4,565 hardwoods.[117] All told, one month's operation in all fourteen *cortes* cost the Company 41,830 pesos.[118] By the 1740s good cedar had grown scarce around Havana—sugar planters needed it for their boxes since it retarded spoilage and imparted no flavor to the enclosed sugar—so shipbuilders began to use pine from the hills southeast of Havana in decks as well as in masts and spars. Tall pines for masts and large cedars for keels grew particularly rare,[119] so that by 1749 the Crown took steps to conserve and replant cedar in Cuba. The competition for wood between shipbuilders and planters extended beyond cedar and pine. All timber costs gradually increased as lumbering penetrated into increasingly remote parts of the forests. By 1760 sugar boiling alone consumed 15 million cubic feet of wood annually, the quantity cut for twelve or thirteen ships of the line.[120] Sugar's assault on the forest centered on the hills behind Havana, but it also extended to parts of central and eastern Cuba, where shipbuilding had no effect. Although sugar boxes required cedar, sugar boilers could use wood of almost any kind and often burned *bagasse*, the dried out stalks of pressed cane. Perhaps planters preferred hardwoods because they provided more energy per unit of bulk than softwoods, but sugar's appetite for timber lacked the discriminating standards of the navy's. Shipbuilding required compass timbers with which to fashion knees, and tall, straight, and stout trunks for keels, beams, planking, and masts. Thus while sugar devastated the forests it used, shipbuilding culled suitably aged and well-formed cedars, oaks, and pines, leaving the rest. Despite sugar's competition, Cuban timber costs in shipbuilding remained well below Spanish ones up to 1763.

Acquiring adequate amounts of iron for the Havana shipyard proved more difficult. A ship of seventy guns required approximately 75 tons of iron and an eighty-gun ship needed about 85 tons. All this had to come from the Basque provinces, which (despite an expanding iron industry) provided the necessary quantities only irregularly.[121] Iron—at least anchors and armament—lasted much longer than wood, however, and could be recycled. Thus although the difficulty of supplying iron held back ship construction in Havana somewhat, the comparatively abundant timber supply—especially of good cedar—made the shipbuilding program a brilliant success. The Crown occasionally voiced dissatisfaction at the pace of naval construction, but especially during the contract of the Havana Company, the royal *astillero* served Spanish interests exceedingly well.[122]

The absence of any royal policy governing the production of food crops in Cuba allowed occasional food shortages in both Havana and Santiago de Cuba. When adequate supplies of flour failed to arrive from New Spain, Havana authorities invariably sought succor in foreign colonies, accepting the inevitable reproach from Spain. The most severe food shortages in Havana occurred in 1718, 1737, 1745, and 1753, when the connection with Veracruz failed and no local surpluses met the shortfall.[123] Santiago de Cuba's leanest years came in the mid-1750s, when drought destroyed local production and vigorous enforcement of the law complicated traditional trade with Jamaica and Haiti.[124] Crown sponsorship of export crops helped diminish the prospects of feeding Havana and Santiago de Cuba with locally grown food. Cubans with land and labor at their disposal generally preferred to raise tobacco or sugar rather than cassava and bananas. This did not distress Spanish authorities, who expected that the trade between Havana and Veracruz (and between Santiago de Cuba and Cartagena) would benefit, expanding royal revenues. Before 1739, however, the South Sea Company traded flour to Cubans whenever shortages raised the price. Between 1740 and 1748 Haiti and Martinique sold flour to Havana (presumably of French or even Quebec origin). After 1748 flour shipments from Philadelphia, New York, and Providence became more common.[125]

Recourse to foreign markets offended the Spanish in general, but they might have accepted the flour trade had it not also invited other contraband imports. Spanish authorities saw the flour trade with foreign colonies as a dangerous precedent, more than as an evil in itself. Thus they remained rigidly opposed to the arrangements which Cubans so often made to feed themselves, whereas the French eventually came to countenance the flour trade between Louisbourg and New England which also contradicted both the spirit and the letter of imperial legislation. The Spanish refused to encourage food production in Cuba on any scale, since it could only attract labor away from enterprises that contributed directly toward royal revenues. Full adherence to mercantilist prescriptions mattered more to the Spanish than to the French.

In the mid-eighteenth century, both Cape Breton and Cuba remained frontier societies with bounteous land, limited population, and all the advantages of a virtually unscathed landscape. As yet largely undepleted forests, soils, and mineral resources aided the growth of both colonies— Cuba more so than Cape Breton, but the teeming fishing banks compensated Cape Breton for the relative poverty of its hinterland. Resource exploitation responded to both the carrot and the stick: to profit motive and compulsion, to international market and imperial command. In Cape Breton, legislation hardly interfered with the incentives of the market, which doomed coal and timber to local importance, and eventually allowed the fishery to decline while labor and capital migrated to commerce. In Cuba, vigorous royal intervention, often through the agency of *asentistas*, profoundly affected the development of the economy. Efforts at diversification provoked an upsurge in sugar production while tobacco stagnated, just as the Crown wished. Only through the refusal to confine production to high-grade leaf and to abate contraband trade did the Cuban tobacco economy fail to respond satisfactorily to royal policy.

The French failed to combat actively the natural tendency of Louisbourg to tailor its economy to the large and accessible New England market. Ritual exhortation alone could not prevail against the temptations of the marketplace. Thus the export economy stagnated while the entrepôt economy grew.[126] The French lacked either the will or the power to develop the Ile Royale economy along purely mercantilist lines. The link with New England solidified, satisfying the local merchants but upsetting metropolitan plans. No doubt the French could not have avoided the eventual rise of a local bourgeoisie, given the burgeoning of Atlantic trade in general, but their policy did nothing to inhibit it. The Spanish, on the other hand, did their best to counteract the influence of Jamaica on Cuban economic development. They recognized the rivalry between Spain and Jamaica for the leading role in Cuban trade, and the importance thereof.[127] Thus the encouragement of sugar and the de-emphasis on tobacco—indeed the entire initiative associated with the Havana Company—represents a Spanish effort to direct the Cuban economy into a subservient relationship with Spain rather than with Jamaica. Jamaica would never trade for Cuban sugar, and if tobacco harvests shrank sufficiently, it could no longer trade for Cuban tobacco. Thus the Spanish tried to break the Jamaican link by consuming a much larger share of Cuban exports than they had in 1713. In so doing they largely broke the power of the tobacco growers, encouraging the emergence of the sugar elite which in the nineteenth century showed enduring loyalty to the Spanish empire.

Production alone could not justify the maintenance and defense costs of an overseas colony. Without trade binding the colony to the mother country, imperialism had no logic. Thus the French and the Spanish sought to control colonial commerce, not merely production, and here again Louisbourg and Havana seemed well suited to the task. We turn to their commercial roles within the Bourbon empires in the next chapter.

7 American Ports and Imperial Trade

A new era in colonial trade began with the Peace of Utrecht in 1713. Demographic and economic growth in both Europe and the American colonies contributed to an intensification of the exchange across the Atlantic. The volume of French colonial trade expanded sixfold to 140 million livres by 1744, and Spanish colonial trade grew to more than twice that in the same period.[1] Governments of the time well understood the connection between maritime trade and prosperity, and so encouraged trade in every way. In France, Maurepas wrote that the kingdom owed its wealth to seaborne commerce, of which colonial trade formed the largest and most reliable component.[2] In Spain, the state tried to undermine the nobility's traditional distaste for commercial activity, particularly by involving the Crown's prestige in overseas trading ventures such as the Havana Company.[3]

The general expansion of colonial trade required new state policies for its protection and promotion. Britain's development of an imperial navy reflected this trend, but the French and Spanish continued to designate certain safe ports as guardians of colonial trade. If well fortified and garrisoned, and if well situated astride natural arteries of communication, such ports could devote themselves chiefly to commerce and relying on trading partners for provisions.[4] The colonial authorities of France and Spain expected that Louisbourg and Havana, in addition to contributing to the enrichment of the metropolis through their export economies, could further imperial interests by serving as safe entrepôts for colonial commerce. The French consciously assigned this role to Louisbourg in the eighteenth century. In the Spanish empire, Havana had fulfilled this purpose since the sixteenth century, but in the eighteenth century ministers found reason to articulate this commercial policy again and again.

In the early years of Louisbourg, Pontchartrain and the Conseil de la Marine hoped and expected that the island colony would greatly increase the trade between Quebec and France—indeed the Conseil included this among the motives for founding Louisbourg.[5] Ice restricted the activity of traders at Quebec to half the year, whereas Louisbourg enjoyed a longer ice-free season. More importantly, the perils of navigation along the St. Lawrence encouraged the use of fairly small boats, unsuited to transatlantic crossings. With the foundation of Ile Royale, smaller craft might ply the route between Quebec and Louisbourg while larger ships traversed the ocean. The existence of a safe port near the mouth of the St. Lawrence permitted greater specialization, and presumably efficiency (reflected in costs) on the Quebec-France route. By reducing the length of sea voyages, Louisbourg as an entrepôt might also lower the rate of sickness among sailors.[6]

A second major commercial role assigned to Louisbourg involved trade between Quebec and the French West Indies. In the seventeenth century population growth in the French Antilles had created strong demand for livestock, flour, and lumber, which Europe could not meet.[7] French authorities envisioned a regular trade among their Atlantic colonies, with these goods going from Quebec to the French Antilles, sugar and rum from the West Indies to both Quebec and Ile Royale, codfish and timber from Ile Royale to the West Indies, and flour from Quebec to Ile Royale. This vision consisted of a network of reciprocal trades rather than a triangular trade; the involvement of Louisbourg as an entrepôt on the Quebec-Antilles route merely complicated the pattern. This trade, indeed all French commercial policies for Louisbourg—and to a lesser degree Canada—aimed to promote the welfare of metropolitan merchants and the French sugar islands, always the highest priorities of French colonial administrators.

From the outset, French officials encouraged this three-cornered trade, but only after 1726 did they take direct steps to foment it. Shortly after his accession to office, Maurepas tried to reconcile the practice of French colonial trade to mercantilist ideals. He wished to sever the growing commercial ties between New England and the French West Indies, as well as less galling ties between New England and Louisbourg.[8] Rather than merely exhort administrators to forbid trade with New England, Maurepas tried to make it less attractive by lowering taxes on trade between the French West Indies and other French colonies. This included a royal decree erasing tariffs on sugar traded to Quebec and Ile Royale and on building materials going to the French Antilles.[9] These exemptions were renewed after ten years and complemented by others designed to involve St.-Domingue in trade with the North Atlantic.[10] After the war of 1744–48, the French made renewed efforts to expand trade between Quebec, Ile Royale, and the Caribbean,[11] but French sugar planters continued to trade with New England, and managed to force legislation allowing them to buy wood and livestock there.[12]

The linchpin to this entire trading system was the food-producing capacity of Quebec. Maurepas considered Quebec a source of beaver pelts for France and of food for the French West Indies.[13] Like Pontchartrain and the Conseil de la Marine, he also expected and encouraged Quebec to feed Louisbourg.[14] Should Quebec for any reason fail to fulfill its responsibility, both Louisbourg and the French Antilles would quickly turn to New England, first for food, then inevitably for timber and livestock, too.

In defining the ideal pattern of colonial trade, metropolitan authorities took care to preserve mercantilist forms. The Conseil de la Marine announced in 1717 that henceforth French colonies could only trade within the empire, except for the import of salt beef from Ireland and Denmark and the export of sugar to Spanish colonies—exceptions designed to favor the sugar islands.[15] Several further exceptions followed in the letters patent of 1727, which allowed Louisbourg, for example, to import livestock and building materials from New England.[16] The youth of the colony justified such measures, according to Maurepas,[17] but doubtless he liberalized regulations because he could not enforce them. Regulations still forbade the import of foreign food, except when "indispensible."[18] The letter patent of 1727 remained the basis for French colonial commerce until after the fall of Louisbourg. Maurepas reminded successive administrators of the letters' prohibitions and exceptions, and his successors always based instructions on them.[19] Through legislation and tax incentives the French hoped to minimize Louisbourg's trade with New England, while at the same time maximizing trade with Quebec and the French Antilles. French officials never seriously questioned the efficacy of these traditional methods to confine burgeoning trade to their imperial system.[20]

Like the French, the Spanish resorted to traditional solutions in their effort to organize and secure imperial trade in the eighteenth century. Between 1702 and 1713 the French had carried a significant share of the Indies trade, so the Spanish revived the *flota* system in hopes of recovering it. After 1713 they tried to reaffirm Havana's role as the rendezvous point for the *flota*.[21] Since the *flota* and *avisos* (dispatch ships carrying only 70–100 tons) only appeared at Havana on their return voyage after having sold their cargoes of European goods on the mainland, individual Spanish merchants could fit out *registros* (individual, specially licensed ships) to trade with Cuba.[22] After 1713, Cubans could also trade for European goods through the South Sea Company factors in Havana and Santiago de Cuba.[23] In addition to slaves, the South Sea Company traded English manufactured goods to the Caribbean in an "annual ship," legally restricted to 300 tons, but often a means to extensive contraband.

After 1734 a Spanish *asentista* also served the Cuban market, trading European goods for agricultural exports. Spanish authorities hoped that with monopoly privileges an *asentista* could eliminate Cuban contraband by supplying the entire island. Both the private *asentistas* and the Havana Company employed factors in Cadiz to whom they annually remitted Cuban products together with a shopping list reflecting Cuban demand for European goods. The factor tried to buy what Cubans wanted and send it to Havana each spring. By employing a monopolist to carry the trade of Cuba, the Crown aimed to expand legitimate Cuban trade and lower contraband. In theory, the monopoly depressed commodity prices and raised retail prices, leaving a large revenue from which the monopolist paid the heavy costs of transatlantic trade. Without the monopoly, far less trade could take place because lower profits would not justify the costs.[24] The danger of this system was the complete reliance on a single business organization to conduct colonial trade. Should the Havana Company fail to carry on trade energetically, or fail to survive the losses of war, hurricanes, and price fluctuations, Cubans would turn to contraband in the absence of other legitimate channels. After 1728 the Spanish drew inspiration from the performance of the Caracas Company and chartered several monopoly companies, whereas by the eighteenth century the French found that competitive business organizations could muster adequate capital to undertake enterprises like the wet fishery or Ile Royale-France commerce; they no longer relied on monopoly companies.

Illicit trade worried Spanish authorities a great deal more than it did the French. Spanish law distinguished between three types of illegal trade, of which only trade between foreigners and Spaniards concerned Cuba.[25] All three offenses often went by the generic name of contraband. The Spanish solution to the prevalence of contraband in Cuba always featured vigorous police actions. Constant exhortations to stop contraband by whatever means translated into the constant application of force, either by *guarda costas* or the army. Whenever officials considered the volume of contraband intolerable, they commissioned more troops or *guarda costas* in the area. A propensity for contraband earned Trinidad, Puerto Príncipe, and Bayamo the regular attention of increasing numbers of Spanish soldiers.[26] Neither soldiers nor the death penalty, however, had any effect on the Cuban predilection for trade with foreigners.[27]

The Spanish allowed far fewer exceptions to the prohibition on trading with foreigners than did the French. Whereas Maurepas excused breaches in mercantilist theory for the import of planks to Louisbourg, the Spanish permitted foreign goods at Havana only to forestall starvation.[28] Frequently local officials in Havana or Santiago de Cuba permitted foreign trade on the grounds that starvation loomed, prompting rebukes from Cadiz and Madrid. Metropolitan authorities rarely trusted the men on the spot to invigilate anticontraband legislation.

The metropole had good reason not to trust colonial administrators in Cuba because many involved themselves in illicit commerce, either directly or through bribes. In fact virtually every prominent official in Cuba in the early eighteenth century was accused of complicity in illicit trade, and at least one spent years in prison in Santiago de Cuba for his activities. Assuming such graft was commonplace, commercial reform became very difficult. The bureaucracy charged with administering trade had a vested interest in retaining strict anticontraband legislation since it engendered endless bribes. Spanish ministers may have wished to liberalize the regulations governing commerce in Cuba; but as long as traders found breaking the law sufficiently inexpensive and officials found it adequately remunerative, few would support reform.

On the whole, French and Spanish commercial policies were very similar. Traditional mercantilist beliefs informed both policies, although the French showed less concern than the Spanish about imperial autarky. The Spanish aimed to link Cuba to Spain in an effort to foster the economic development of the mother country, while the French hoped to integrate Louisbourg into a colonial framework designed to further the interests of metropolitan merchants and the sugar planters of the French Antilles. Neither design worked out according to plan.

Trade at Ile Royale grew remarkably in the fifty years of the colony, but its pattern always disappointed the French. Trade with Quebec developed only slowly, while that with New England grew rapidly, especially after 1749, so New England eventually filled the role in French colonial trade which Maurepas had reserved for Quebec.

Louisbourg traded with only five regions: France, Quebec, the French West Indies, Acadia, and New England.[29] On the whole, French merchants—predominantly from St. Mâlo and St. Jean de Luz—controlled the trade between Louisbourg and France, but Ile Royale merchants often undertook the trade with Quebec, Acadia, and the Antilles. Traders like the Faneuil family from Boston, and later others from Newbury and Piscatequa, dominated the New England-Louisbourg route.[30]

Until 1749 Louisbourg traded in greater volume with France than with any other region. French food, clothing, building materials, and even luxuries filled between twenty and sixty ships a year, generally amounting to between 2,000 and 6,000 tons.[31] Quebec traded flour, biscuit, peas, and wood products to Ile Royale in exchange for cod, occupying between four and seventeen ships, between 500 and 1,200 tons in all.[32] Trade with the French Antilles consisted very largely of the exchange of cod for rum and molasses, ordinarily from Martinique or St.-Domingue, using up to fifty-seven ships totaling as much as 4,364 tons.[33] Trade with Acadia never amounted to more than 300 tons, usually of Acadian surplus food exchanged for French goods. New England traded flour, planks, barrels, nails, and sundry other items for rum and molasses originating in the French West Indies. After 1749 this trade occupied up to 116 vessels totaling 4,685 tons, but before 1744 thirty ships had usually sufficed. The volume of Louisbourg's trade during 1719–52 appears in Table 7.1. Considering all sources, food (54 per-

Table 7.1
Trading Vessels Arriving at Louisbourg, 1719–1752

Year	France Ships	France Tons	Quebec Ships	Quebec Tons	New England Ships	New England Tons	Antilles Ships	Antilles Tons	Acadia Ships	Acadia Tons	Other Ships	Other Tons	Total Ships	Total Tons
1719	22	1,838	10	530	1	50	3	120	2	90	1	20	39	2,648
	56%	69%	26%	20%	3%	2%	8%	5%	5%	3%	3%	1%		
1721	59	6,130	7	290	9	265	9	425	3	48	2	89	89	7,247
	66%	85%	8%	4%	10%	4%	10%	6%	3%	1%	2%	1%		
1726	18	—	15	—	33	—	9	—	0	0	0	0	75	—
	24%	—	20%	—	44%	—	12%	—	0%	0%	0%	0%		
1730	23	—	23	—	35	—	17	—	0	0	0	0	98	—
	23%	—	23%	—	36%	—	17%	—	0%	0%	0%	0%		
1733	54	4,600	13	722	20	745	18	1,006	0	0	0	0	105	7,073
	51%	65%	12%	10%	19%	11%	17%	15%	0%	0%	0%	0%		
1737	56	—	10	—	35	—	19	—	11	—	0	0	131	—
	43%	—	8%	—	27%	—	15%	—	8%	—	0%	0%		
1742	34	2,065	9	689	38	1,563	19	1,251	18	242	7	910	125	6,720
	27%	44%	7%	10%	30%	23%	15%	19%	14%	4%	6%	14%		
1743	45	4,429	5	420	31	1,290	18	1,252	21	269	0	0	120	7,660
	38%	58%	4%	5%	25%	17%	15%	16%	18%	4%	0%	0%		
1752	36	4,342	4	465	116	4,685	57	4,364	0	0	0	0	213	13,856
	17%	31%	2%	5%	54%	34%	27%	31%	0%	0%	0%	0%		

Sources: AN Outre-Mer G¹, vol. 466, #59. AC, C¹¹C, 9:10–20; AC, C¹¹B, 14:276–92; AC, C¹¹B, 9:50–95. AN, F2B, 9:12–18, 2023. Archives départmentales de la Charente-Maritime, Série B, Régistre 272. Data for 1726 and 1730 from Mathieu, "Quelques aspects du rôle de Louisbourg dans le commerce Nouvelle-France—Antilles."

Note: Similar tables appear in Moore, "Merchant Trade" (thesis), p. 20; and Moore, "Commodity Imports," p. 26. Somewhat different tables appear in McLennan, *Louisbourg: Foundation to Fall*, p. 222; and Chard, "Impact of Ile Royale" (thesis), p. 43A.

cent), building materials (33 percent), and clothing (18 percent) made up 95 percent of Louisbourg's imports.[34] Imports usually exceeded exports in value, but a great deal of trade between Port Toulouse in Ile Royale and Canso in Nova Scotia went unregistered, which throws the overall balance of trade into doubt. The official value of imports plus exports climbed from 3 million livres before 1744 to almost 6 million livres by 1753. These figures, drawn up by Louisbourg officials, usually vastly underreported trade with New England—or so Maurepas believed.[35] French ships carried the largest and most valuable cargoes, as shown in Table 7.2. Along most routes the average tonnages of trading vessels varied little,[36] but the size of ships trading between Louisbourg and the Antilles increased from about 50 tons early in the century to more than 100 by 1752. This probably reflects the rise of the rum and molasses trade after 1749.

By the 1750s, the tonnage in the Louisbourg-Antilles trade outstripped the Louisbourg-France trade. Louisbourg imported molasses and rum from Martinique and St.-Domingue in great quantity, almost all of which found its way to New England. By the eighteenth century, thirsty New Englanders wanted more rum and molasses than the British West Indies could supply,[37] while at the same time the French and Danish West Indies produced more than they could market,[38] because France did not buy Antilles rum in deference to the French brandy interest.[39] French planters solved this problem by trading with New England, a practice decried alike by Maurepas and British colonial administrators. Then, in 1733, the British planters forced the passage of the Molasses Act, which placed a 100 percent duty on foreign molasses entering British colonies. The Act's ostensible purpose was to protect the British sugar industry from French competition, but since the British planters could sell as much as they produced, a more likely intention was to destroy the growing New England rum-distilling industry in the interest of British and West Indian distillers.[40] This legislation forced New Englanders and French planters to resort to smuggling, which they eventually found convenient to do through Louisbourg and Canso, since they were only a few days' sail from Boston and because metropolitan administrators tolerated this roundabout breach in mercantilist practice but protested at more direct routes.[41] In return for their rum and molasses, French planters accepted livestock, building materials, and low-grade cod from New

Table 7.2

Average Tonnages and Cargo Values in Louisbourg Trade,
1740–1742

Origin	Average Tonnage	Average Cargo (livres)	Average Value per ton (livres)
France	87	15,102	173
Antilles	66	12,559	190
Quebec	77	7,126	92
Acadia	13	2,351	180
New England	41	1,625	39

Sources: See Table 7.1, and Maurepas à Bigot, 13 mai 1740, AC, B, 70:400, for cargo values.

England via Louisbourg. The volume of this trade impressed both French and British officials, most of whom objected to it, although Maurepas did not.[42] The planters of the French Antilles preferred to trade directly with New England (although the 1727 letters patent forbade this) and complained that Louisbourg should not be granted special dispensations. Maurepas, however, preferred to see Louisbourg serve as a conduit for the trade he could not prevent and would not sanction.[43] As the population and distilleries of New England increased faster than the molasses production of the British West Indies, this trade could only accelerate.

The failure of Quebec as a food producer also contributed to the rise of New England trade at Louisbourg. Demand for flour intensified with population growth in Quebec, Louisbourg, and the French Antilles; Canadian harvests could not keep pace. Quebec suffered food deficits in 1715–22, 1724–25, and 1737–39, halting food exports.[44] Louisbourg received no food from Quebec in 1714–18, 1723, and 1736–37. In these years the colony turned to New England for sustenance, and the French Antilles also sought other sources of flour. In the 1740s Quebec shortfalls grew worse—leading the Intendant in 1743 to ask officials in Louisbourg to buy flour in New England for Quebec. The flour trade between Quebec and Louisbourg, which had averaged 26,000 quintals (1,300 tons) between 1727 and 1739, never recovered. Ile Royale became dependent upon New England supplies, buying no food at all from

Quebec in 1742–48 and 1752–58. The Canadian harvests of the middle 1750s failed completely, so New England entirely usurped Quebec's role in Louisbourg's trade.[45] The figures in Table 7.1 clearly reflect this trend. Even when Quebec had surplus food to trade, New England competition often prevailed. The navigational perils and higher turnaround time (a function of distance, currents, and winds) of the Quebec-Louisbourg route lowered profits. New England also enjoyed the advantages of lower production costs.[46] Furthermore, shipping was always scarce at Quebec. These factors jeopardized the Quebec-Louisbourg route more than the Quebec-French Antilles route, so Canadian ships often passed by Louisbourg, heading directly to the stronger markets in the French Caribbean.[47] New Englanders eagerly supplanted Quebecois in Louisbourg's trade.

The seasonal rhythms of Louisbourg's trade also handicapped Quebec. New England ships could arrive at almost any time of year, although they preferred July and August, and French ships began to appear each April. No Quebec ships could sail before May, when prices at Louisbourg had dropped in response to fresh supplies from New England or France. The knowledge that Quebec flour could not arrive until late spring encouraged Louisbourg traders to sail to New England in March or April when food was especially short at Ile Royale.[48]

Authorities at Louisbourg normally considered trade with New England perfectly legal, despite the spirit of French legislation. If the slightest doubt arose concerning the arrival of flour from France or Quebec, the *commissaire-ordonnateur* authorized merchants to trade with New England. Sometimes they did so as early as October, well before food shortages could have menaced the colony.[49] French merchants never failed to protest this practice, but it continued nonetheless. Since local officials did not wish to discourage New Englanders, seizures of British vessels took place only rarely at Louisbourg and apparently decreased over time.[50] With regulations so relaxed, Louisbourg and New England merchants did not have to engage in smuggling, although some did take place, especially in the outports. Whenever Louisbourg officials threatened the legitimized New England trade at Louisbourg, smuggling increased. In the absence of government obstruction, the New England-Louisbourg trade grew so rapidly, especially after 1749, that New England outstripped all Louisbourg's other trading partners. Indeed, as many ships plied the sea between Boston and Louisbourg in the 1750s as between Boston and the Caribbean.[51]

The trade between Acadia and Louisbourg consisted of sheep, cattle, and grain, in exchange for French manufactures.[52] British authorities did their best to stop what they considered illegal and disadvantageous, and because the trade route passed by British settlements at Annapolis Royal and, after 1748, at Halifax, the British could harry vessels on this route. Surely, however, the Acadians' tradition of self-reliance and subsistence farming had more to do with their low volume of trade with Louisbourg than did British interference.[53]

The total annual value of Louisbourg's trade amounted to more than 5 million livres by 1752, an increase of 40 percent over 1737.[54] Trade with France held steady in value, while commerce with both the French West Indies and New England quadrupled. Although the tonnages involved were roughly equal in 1752, the cash value of the French and Caribbean trades each greatly exceeded the worth of commerce with New England. Nonetheless the distinguishing trend in Louisbourg's commerce remains the rise of both New England and the French Antilles as trading partners, owing largely to the suitability of Louisbourg as a conduit for commerce between these two expanding economies.

Conventional wisdom holds that Cuban trade languished before the British occupation of 1762–63. Taking their cue once again from Arango, generations of Cuban writers have maintained that before 1762 Havana's trade occupied only two or three vessels a year.[55] Anglophone historians have dispensed with the numbers but accepted the conclusion: that monopoly prevented Havana from engaging in widespread trade until the British, with more liberal views about trade with British possessions, resurrected Havana's commerce.[56] This thesis appears in almost every work which considers eighteenth-century Cuban trade. Like Cuban sugar cultivation, however, Cuban commerce did not need a British stimulus to embark upon significant expansion. Figures published by Pezuela, a liberal eager to accept Arango's views, suggest that the value of Havana's legitimate trade in 1740–60 had increased by 34 percent over 1714–34 levels. The effect of the 1739–48 war with Britain no doubt retarded and diminished this expansion. Nonetheless the dramatic growth apparent from several sources clearly contradicts the prevailing published opinion.[57]

Havana traded regularly with almost a dozen ports in the Spanish Caribbean as well as with Spain and the Canary Islands. Less frequent trade took place with colonies of the foreign Caribbean and North American mainland. Santiago de Cuba carried on a lively trade with the northern littoral of South America, especially Cartagena, usually in small ships. Havana's legitimate trade amounted to roughly ten times that of Santiago de Cuba (by tonnage), and included the bulk of Cuban commerce.

Havana's chief trading partner in the Caribbean was Veracruz. Havana relied on Mexican flour, most of it from the Puebla region, to feed the growing urban population.[58] The volume of Havana imports from Veracruz gradually increased except for a major setback during the 1739–48 war. Havana traded little besides tobacco to Mexico—and not much of that—so trade between the two ports was almost always very unbalanced (see Tables 7.3 and 7.4).[59] After 1725, Havana developed a trade with Campeche involving maize and wheat flour for tobacco.[60] Many ships, especially after 1748, undertook a triangular trade sailing

Table 7.3
Total Ship Traffic to and from Havana, 1715–1759

Year	Veracruz	Campeche	Cartagena	Portobello	Canaries	Britain & Br. Colonies	Spain
1715	15	0	7	1	6	0	1
1720	12	0	2	3	5	0	2
1725	26	5	9	3	0	1	5
1730	26	2	5	3	2	3	2
1735	30	4	5	4	5	2	4
1740	12	4	0	2	4	0	17
1745	32	16	8	0	7	0	19
1750	12	13	7	2	3	0	10
1755	13	9	5	7	0	0	21
1759	16	9	4	7	3	0	19

Sources: AGI, Contaduría 1153, 1154, 1163, 1164, 1165A, 1165B, *almojarifazgo* accounts; AGI, Contratación 1460–1471, 2471–81.

Table 7.4

The Routes and Value of Havana's Nonpeninsular Trade, 1715–1759 (in pesos)

Year	Veracruz		Campeche		S. America[a]		Portobello[b]		Canaries		Britain & British Cols.		Total[c]	
	Imports	Exports	Imp.	Exp.	Imp.	Exp.	Imp.	Exp.	Imp.	Exp.	Imp.	Exp.	Imp.	Exp.
1715	54,487	7,436	—	—	—	1,440	—	1,300	58,583	8,225	—	—	113,070	18,501
1720	47,768	13,820	—	—	—	600	—	5,625	6,623	36,385	—	—	54,391	56,430
1725	84,464	11,480	1,288	2,155	2,638	12,876	3,775	—	—	—	—	2,225	91,895	28,736
1730	65,949	18,360	4,840	—	333	12,770	—	4,550	8,821	—	1,073	26,185	81,016	61,865
1735	163,320	38,550	10,998	1,205	5,788	600	8,600	7,575	12,951	21,230	—	15,530	201,657	85,480
1740	89,856	3,635	2,740	1,810	—	—	19,250	—	10,574	3,165	—	—	122,420	8,610
1745	73,706	76,850	6,521	2,650	10,000	3,880	—	—	9,328	6,870	—	—	99,555	90,250
1750	66,906	—	3,330	8,770	2,267	3,795	8,732	860	2,024	4,945	—	—	83,259	18,370
1755	134,578	2,765	9,581	8,995	8,631	3,415	77,566	5,180	—	—	—	—	230,624	20,355
1759	123,950	7,690	950	9,075	100	10,820	46,458	1,275	2,459	1,670	—	—	173,917	30,530

Sources: AGI, Contaduría 1153, 1154, 1163, 1164, 1165A, 1165B. Values are obtained by multiplying the *almojarifazgo* paid by the rate of taxation.

[a] Includes Cartagena, Santa Marta, La Guayra, Maracaibo, Cumaná, Isla de Trinidad, Caracas.

[b] Includes Río Chagre.

[c] This table ignores the minuscule trade between Havana and other islands of the Caribbean, and the large trade with Spain.

clockwise between Havana, Campeche, and Veracruz, a route which took better advantage of the winds.

Havana's trade with Cartagena, Santa Marta, La Guayra, Maracaibo, and other ports on the northern shore of South America remained fairly stable after 1725 except for wartime disruptions. Neither the number of ships involved nor the value of their cargoes increased significantly. Havana occasionally imported maize from Cartagena, but more often bought goods of European origin, particularly textiles, brought there by the *flota*.[61] Havana's exports to these ports normally consisted of tobacco. Havana exported more to La Guayra and Caracas than it imported, unique in Havana's American trade. Santiago de Cuba's exports to Cartagena were primarily tobacco and sugar.

The trade with Portobello (and neighboring Rio Chagre) was a trade between two entrepôts. Havana normally imported a great deal more than it exported in this trade, generally taking cacao from Guayaquil (in today's Ecuador). The smaller traffic going the other way presumably consisted of tobacco, since Portobello and Lima each bought more Cuban tobacco than any other port in the Indies besides Cartagena.[62] Portobello served the communities of the Spanish Pacific in much the same way Havana served those of the Spanish Caribbean: as the funnel through which traffic went to Europe. The Portobello trade increased tremendously in the 1750s, approaching half the value of the Veracruz trade, perhaps a reflection of the spectacular expansion in the cacao trade.[63]

Havana traded very little with other islands of the Spanish Caribbean, presumably because they produced largely the same products and lay between Havana and Spain on returning voyages. Trade with the Canaries, however, figured prominently in Havana commerce.[64] Much of this was actually trade with Spain, since ships routinely stopped in Tenerife on the transatlantic journey, especially outbound from Spain, but Havana and the Canaries traded on their own account, too. For example, between 1755 and 1760 the Canaries imported large quantities of sugar and hides, probably from Havana,[65] and occasionally Cuban tobacco contributed to cargoes going to Tenerife.[66] Havana imported *aguardiente de caña* (cane liquor), wine, vinegar, and dried fruits from the Canaries,[67] serving as the Islands' principal market in the Indies: 68 of 167 vessels sailing from the Canaries to the Indies went to Havana.[68]

Although Havana's trade with both Veracruz and Portobello grew significantly between 1715 and 1759, by far the greatest expansion occurred in trade with Spain. The *flota* carried very little of this trade since it sailed only rarely—none sailed between 1739 and 1757[69]—and since it served several larger markets before it reached Havana.[70] Instead, independent ships (*registros*) shuttled between Havana and Cadiz with greater frequency (see Table 7.5). Other parts of the Spanish empire came to rely on *registros*, too, despite the efforts to revitalize the *flota*,[71] but Havana's location encouraged Spanish merchants to trade there: the turnaround time—and thus cost—was lower at Havana than any other major port in the Indies. Spanish merchants found it more convenient to sell their wares and purchase return cargoes in Havana than to travel to the mainland. Indeed the breakdown of the *flota* system after 1737 probably accounted for the rise in Havana's trade as much as the growth of the Cuban economy. The unsteady but significant expansion of Havana's exports to Veracruz, Cartagena, and Portobello after 1735 probably also reflects the transition from the *flota* to the *registro* system in the Indies trade: although the *flota* used Havana as the base for return voyages to Spain, its decline signaled an even larger commercial role for Havana as the clearinghouse for the Indies trade.

Havana traded tobacco, sugar, and hides to Spain for the products of Mediterranean agriculture and northern European manufacturing. Havana bought large quantities of wine and olive oil produced in Spain, and innumerable varieties of cloth and clothing from France, Germany, and the Netherlands.[72] Havana imported very little flour from Spain, in contrast to Louisbourg's large imports from France: Mexico succeeded where Quebec failed.

The total volume of Havana's imports from Spain is difficult to measure. Some goods brought by the Havana Company, for instance, did not pay port duties, so these cargoes do not appear fully in the accounts. In 1749, a Havana university professor estimated that Havana needed a million pesos to pay for Spanish imports,[73] but actual sales of Spanish imports in twelve months, 1760–61, amounted to only 264,175 pesos.[74] According to Havana Company documents, the volume of Spanish imports to Cuba averaged 536 tons per year during 1741–51, years in which war with Britain inhibited shipping.[75] This amounted to only 14

Table 7.5

Registro Traffic between Havana and Spain, 1713–1762
(total numbers of ships)

Years	Havana-Spain	Spain-Havana
1713–1717	5	6
1718–1722	6	6
1723–1727	5	3
1728–1732	3	6
1733–1737	8	12
1738–1742	36	13
1743–1747	21	13
1748–1752	27	11
1753–1757	14	10
1758–1762	30	29

Sources: AGI, Contratación, 1460–71, 2471–81.

percent (by tonnage) of French imports to Louisbourg in the same years, indicative of the independence of Cuba from Spanish supplies. Other figures provided by the Company indicate that the value of Spanish imports to Havana actually declined in the 1750s (see Table 7.6). This document had a polemical purpose (to discredit the new directors of the Company who took office in 1752) and probably greatly exaggerated a minor decline in traffic from Spain to Cuba. *Registro* traffic declined only slightly in the 1750s (Table 7.5) so unless prices or ship tonnages declined (and there is no evidence for either event), the alleged drop was negligible.[76] Whatever the trend of the 1750s, Cuban imports from Spain certainly increased greatly after 1740, a result of the curtailment of the *flota* system and the growth of Cuban population and exports to Spain.

Spanish imports to Havana generally stayed within the city walls. The Havana Company maintained retail stores in six centers around the island, but Havana invariably proved the best market. The distribution of Spanish imports for twelve months in 1760–61 appears in Table 7.7. The geographical distribution of Spanish imports within Cuba hardly

Table 7.6

Value of Spanish Imports to Cuba, 1740–1757 (pesos)

Years	Value of Imports	Annual Average
1740–1744	1,875,252	375,060
1745–1749	1,147,432	229,486
1753–1757	541,651	108,330

Source: Instrucción para los Interesados de la Real Compañía, n.d. (c. 1758), AGI, UM 255.

Table 7.7

Distribution of Spanish Imports in Cuba, 1760–1761

Region	Quantity of Imports Purchased (pesos)	Population (1755–1757)
Havana	209,209	35,000
Santiago de Cuba	39,430	15,471
Bayamo	5,786	12,653
Puerto Príncipe	2,589	12,000
Trinidad	803	5,840
Sancti Spiritus	359	5,492
San Juan de los Remedios	1,463	2,527
Matanzas	4,531	2,041

Sources: Cuenta en Resumen de todo lo vendido desde 1 de Abril de 1760 hasta fin de Marzo de 1761, 31 marzo 1761, AGI, SD 2026. The same document appears in AGI, UM 942. For population: Table 2.8.

corresponded with the geographical distribution of population. Certainly Habañeros led the island in purchasing power and had more Europeanized tastes, but this pattern presumably indicates that most of Cuba relied on illegal trade for European goods.

Contraband had existed from the sixteenth century, but in Cuba it increased when the English acquired Jamaica in 1655. Then, during the War of the Spanish Succession, Cubans came to rely on contraband trade, particularly French, since Spanish shipping grew scarce. The *flota* sailed but once during the war, because the French sought to forestall it—it cut into their trade with the Indies—and the British hoped to seize it.[77] French traders began sailing around Cape Horn to Spanish colonies in the Pacific, bypassing the traditional Caribbean route altogether,[78] which reduced the amount of Spanish shipping stopping at Cuba. Cubans responded by developing ties with Jamaica which continued after the war, since shipping remained short.[79] As long as (contraband) European goods glutted the markets of Peru and Mexico, Spanish traders refused to go to the Indies. Andalusian merchants had grown used to high profits and restricted competition; competing in a more open market did not fit their conception of business. With inadequate Spanish shipping, Cubans resorted to contraband, both to sell their products and to purchase European goods.

Contraband trade in Cuba took place in one of two ways: either foreigners met Cubans clandestinely on deserted keys or bays, or they traded in ports after bribing the appropriate officials. By the Treaty of Madrid of 1667, foreign ships could enter Spanish ports if in need of repair, and, once in port, they easily found ways to trade. The Dutch and English apparently preferred bribery to the hazards of desolate shores. In wartime, British traders used flags of truce to gain entry to Spanish ports.[80] The South Sea Company used its access to Spanish ports to indulge in extensive illicit trade with Cuba—indeed the British sought the slave *asiento* at the peace negotiations in 1712–13 in part to expand contraband trade to the Spanish colonies.[81] South Sea Company employees regarded Cuba as one of their best markets for slaves and presumably for contraband as well.[82] But the South Sea Company's participation in contraband, which the directors acknowledged in 1725, declined in the 1730s with more vigorous Spanish prosecution of contraband and new Company management.[83]

Several merchants in Jamaica besides the South Sea Company dealt in contraband with Cuba. Indeed, in the 1720s they complained that the South Sea Company had ruined them by undercutting their Cuban trade.[84] These traders, with less easy access to Cuban ports, traded on the beaches and in river mouths from small boats. In 1760 a Cuban patrol encountered twelve boats at Santa Cruz in the Puerto Príncipe district alone. Several mounted up to ten cannon, more than the *guarda costa* vessel, and four carried deserters from the Spanish army.[85] After 1739 these traders no longer had the South Sea Company as competition, and their share of the Cuban contraband trade presumably increased.

Although Havana attracted its share of illicit trade,[86] the preponderances of Cuban contraband always entered through the south coast. The *cabildo* of Santiago de Cuba pointed out that in areas such as Puerto Príncipe only illicit trade could provide clothing or a market for hides. Virtually the entire commerce of the south coast consisted of contraband since the Havana Company and its predecessors generally confined operations almost exclusively to the Havana area. When legal European goods did appear on the south coast via Havana their comparatively high prices prevented any decrease in contraband. British traders could sell slaves and European goods at about one-third of official prices.[87] When Havana authorities appointed officials to combat contraband they provoked rebellion. Puerto Príncipe in 1729 and 1735–37, and Bayamo in 1749, refused to recognize the authority of the *visitadores, tenientes de justicias*, and *juezes de comisos* sent from Havana. Eight hundred men participated in the smaller of the two revolts in Puerto Príncipe.[88] War (1739–48) in no way diminished the Cuban or British appetite for contraband—indeed, it had the reverse effect since legitimate Spanish shipping decreased— and in the years following the war, tobacco legislation forced more and more Cubans to seek illegal markets for their leaf.[89] If the value and quantity of cargoes seized by Cuban authorities is any indication, contraband continued unabated into the 1740s and 1750s (see Table 7.8). Of course, the number of seizures (*decomisos*) reflects the intensity of official vigilance as well as the actual volume of contraband; the apparent contraband boom of the 1740s may represent a wartime crackdown rather than an expansion of illegal trade.

Estimating the total volume of contraband is particularly difficult since those involved kept no records, and *decomiso* accounts cannot help determine the amount of goods which escaped the attention of *guarda costas*. Nonetheless a few clues exist. A Spanish prisoner at Port Royal, Jamaica, recorded 143 vessels trading with Cuba's south coast in just nine months in 1719. One of these, he claimed, sold 40,000 pesos worth of goods, suggesting that the value of this trade exceeded the total value of Havana's legitimate trade in 1720.[90] If contraband accounted for 75 percent of Cuba's tobacco production in the 1720s and 1730s, the value of

Table 7.8

Contraband Seizures in Cuba, 1711–1759

Year	Seizures	Value^a (*reales*)	Year	Seizures	Value
1711–1713	5	259,486	1741	2	630,075
1713–1715	7	141,757	1742	7	69,765
1715–1717	1	151,932	1743	18	1,227,172
1717–1718	12	115,038	1744	12	1,409,574
1719	2	1,551	1745	4	20,019
1720–1722	9	36,092	1746	6	303,918
1722–1725	16	140,070	1747	9	378,316
1725–1727	12	146,834	1748	12	774,152
1727–1728	2	79,621	1749	6	123,191
1728–1731	9	302,151	1750	11	151,400
1731–1732	3	69,502	1751	10	99,040
1733	4	25,067	1752	11	321,327
1734	10	55,023	1753	6	106,089
1735	7	440,251	1754	4	267,795
1736	3	7,867	1755	2	2,691
1737	3	29,166	1756	6	281,746
1738	1	19,626	1757	6	12,466
1739	2	36,185	1758	—	—
1740	2	380,642	1759	5	15,957

Sources: Decomiso accounts, AGI, Contaduría 1153, 1154, 1163, 1164, 1165A, 1165B.

^aThis refers to the value owed the Crown, usually 5 percent of the value of the goods seized. A seizure might well include more than one boat, or it might be a shipment already landed and perhaps inland. Thus the wild disproportion between values and seizures from year to year. Prior to 1733, random intervals suited Cuban accountants, thus the inconvenient form of the early data.

illegal exports probably approached 600,000 pesos annually in Havana prices. This estimate matches fairly well with one made in 1768, which claimed that illicit trade amounted to 1.4 million pesos annually: 700,000 each in imports and exports.[91] Probably the total value of contraband grew slowly before 1740, perhaps even slumping after the *asientos* of Tallapiedra and Casa-Madrid, then rose sharply in the war years, only to decline again in the 1750s; meanwhile the volume of legitimate trade with Spain grew more steadily and, after 1740, far more dramatically. By 1758, according to a Havana governor, legitimate shipping carried 57 to 62 percent of Cuba's produce, leaving only 38 to 43 percent to go as contraband. While confining illegal trade to two-fifths of total commerce may appear no great feat, it did amount to a significant improvement from early in the century. Spanish attempts to limit contraband and link Cuba more closely to Spain proved a modest success.[92]

The principal contraband import items were slaves and European cloth and clothing. Cuban contraband exports included tobacco, hides, mules, horses, and even timber.[93] Jamaican traders also came away with large amounts of silver, creating a perpetual money shortage in Santiago de Cuba and prompting continual interest in the possibility of a local copper mint.[94] Cubans engaged in contraband with the French in St.-Domingue, trading tobacco from Mayarí and Baracoa for clothing and rum.[95] After 1722, when the Crown prohibited direct imports of Cuban tobacco into the Spanish Basque provinces, a trade grew up between French and Spanish Basque ports—Bayonne and St. Jean de Luz on the French side and Bilbao and San Sebastian on the Spanish. Cuban tobacco thus entered northern Spain via St.-Domingue and southern France. This double smuggle (to the Spanish, not the French since Bayonne was a free port) apparently provided tobacco more cheaply than the Spanish state monopoly. In 1746–50 Bayonne alone exported an annual average of about 80,000 pesos worth of Cuban tobacco to Spain.[96]

The quantities of various goods in contraband probably changed somewhat over the years. The share of export contraband accounted for by livestock increased, while the proportion consisting in tobacco declined. By 1768 St.-Domingue and Jamaica imported about 7,000 horses, mules, and oxen annually, worth about 350,000 pesos in 1765 Havana prices.[97] Since Havana prices exceeded those of the areas in which this trade took place, perhaps the value of contraband livestock was somewhat less, but in any event it amounted to a major share of illegal trade, much more than it had earlier in the century.

Whatever the quantity of contraband, it was large enough to shape the economic development of Puerto Príncipe and Bayamo. The growth of Puerto Príncipe from a backwater of 2,766 persons in 1701 to a bustling commercial center of more than 12,000 in 1729 suggests inmigration explicable only by unusual opportunity.[98] Considering the paucity of trade with Havana and the character of the landscape in these areas, only large-scale livestock production for the Jamaican market could have accounted for this growth. Cuban officials, in fact, considered Puerto

Príncipe and Bayamo "dependent" on Jamaica. The bond between Cuba's south coast and Jamaica, although weakened, survived all efforts to destroy it.[99]

The French and Spanish envisioned similar commercial relationships within their American empires. They thought colonies such as Ile Royale and Cuba could rely on food-surplus colonies (Quebec and Mexico) for sustenance, while serving in export and entrepôt roles. In both cases the weakness in this vision lay in the proximity of large, trade-oriented British settlements—New England and Jamaica. Neither the French nor the Spanish could prevent illicit trade from transoceanic distances—even within Europe, states could not effectively restrict the market impulse to that extent. The unreliability of New France as a food-surplus colony forced the metropolis to condone trade with New England at Louisbourg, but the success of the Veracruz flour trade to Havana justified strict observation of the law in Cuba. With tacit approval the Louisbourg-New England trade ballooned after 1749—especially since Louisbourg served admirably as a conduit for the New England-French West Indies commerce—allowing population growth even as the fishery declined. Cuban trade with Jamaica, on the other hand, expanded but slowly and irregularly, never enjoying official approval, although local bureaucrats frequently connived at it.

While the French allowed Louisbourg to violate basic tenets of mercantilism to benefit West Indian planters, the Spanish tried their best to bring all of Cuba within their commercial system. They failed, but nevertheless managed to secure for the peninsula most of the trade of the expanding Cuban economy, so the expansion of legitimate commerce greatly outstripped the growth of contraband—in part because of the successful promotion of the sugar economy. The French, in contrast, watched New England's share of Louisbourg's trade expand while that of the mother country stagnated; the growth of the Ile Royale economy featured sectors unwelcome to, if countenanced by, the French. The divergence between commercial theory and practice—the proportion of total trade conducted with foreigners—was greater in Cuba than in Cape Breton, but Spanish policy diminished this divergence while French policy permitted it to grow. Spanish efforts improved a bad situation, while French indifference allowed a better one to worsen. Had Quebec produced grain, livestock, and lumber as cheaply as New England, or had the French wrought changes in Ile Royale's economy comparable in magnitude to the substitution of sugar for tobacco (e.g., the development of an agricultural surplus), the French Atlantic system would have proved more satisfactory to the metropolis. Even with the assistance of Ile Royale as an entrepôt between Quebec and the French Antilles, however, Maurepas did not succeed where Colbert had failed.

Conclusion

In the decades between 1700 and 1763, the French and Spanish saw their nemesis, the British, emerge as the dominant economic and naval power of the Atlantic world. Perhaps the very success of Spain and France in earlier centuries hindered them in the changing world of the eighteenth century. Imperial systems and strategies dating from golden ages gone by could not easily be adapted to the new circumstances that rapid demographic, economic, and commercial growth ushered in after 1713. The British, who had lesser past glories with which to justify traditional policies, proved more adaptable and emerged from this period with an expanded empire and a navy that almost always kept Britain's rivals on the defensive. The conservative, traditional, and defensive strategies of empire employed by the Bourbon kingdoms served well enough in routine matters; they were well suited to extracting profit from the staple exports of Cuba and Cape Breton Island. And they were consistent with the limited financial resources which the Bourbons felt able to expend on their empires. But these methods could not prevent the eclipse of the Bourbon empires. The French and Spanish could achieve much toward the twin mercantilist goals of wealth and power in time of peace, but very little in time of war. The experience of Havana and Louisbourg illustrates the limited degree to which the Bourbons could profit from their Atlantic empires.

The conventional images of both Louisbourg and Havana emphasize island fortresses defending the approaches to large American empires, their historical significance commensurate with their military might. Eighteenth-century observers, however, appreciated the cities' economic importance to the French and Spanish empires above all else. The real contributions of Louisbourg and Havana lay not in their value as overseas bases for military use, but in their capacity to organize and channel the production of their hinterlands, and to serve as entrepôts lowering costs and expanding volume in colonial trade. Especially in the English-speaking historical tradition, the drama surrounding the events of 1745, 1758, and 1762 has obscured the important, if prosaic and unobtrusive, economic contributions made by Louisbourg and Havana.[1]

The natural resources and geographical positions of Louisbourg and Havana potentially allowed them to play important roles both strategically and economically. Each port overlooked an important sea route between America and Europe, and each stood beside one of the two entrances to the interior of North America. Thus situated, each port might have played important military and commercial roles. Each port also overlooked a productive hinterland—the fishing banks off Cape Breton and the soils of Cuba—endowing them with the potential to export staples, in accordance with accepted mercantilist ideas. In order to reap full advantage of the multiple blessings of Louisbourg and Havana, however, the Bourbon empires required the constant application of sea power.

By the eighteenth century, French and Spanish ministers understood the importance of sea power in imperial matters, but neither empire could afford sufficient resources to create an imperial navy. Shortages of money, men, and specialized timbers plagued both Bourbon navies so that neither could create a fleet even half the size of the British navy. Important contributions from Cape Breton and Cuba—the training of sailors and the provision of timber—only slightly reduced the difficulties facing the French and Spanish navies. Conscious of their inferiority, both navies followed defensive tactics and strategy when confronting the British, severely reducing the strategic values of Louisbourg and Havana. In the absence of naval power adequate to match the British, neither empire could exploit the strategic significance of the geographical situations of Louisbourg and Havana. Given greater sea forces, the French and Spanish could have used their island ports as naval bases from which to project their power into North America and the North Atlantic. Without such forces, neither empire could prevent the expansion of British territory and power in North America. Neither Louisbourg nor Havana could serve as the key to a continent.

The restrictions on the strategic value of Louisbourg and Havana influenced expectations in Paris and Madrid. The roles assigned to these ports in the eighteenth century were chiefly economic; the ministers understood what Louisbourg and Havana could not do—the only exception being Maurepas's illusion concerning Louisbourg's might. The administration of both colonies reflected the primacy of economic concerns in the roles expected of them. At Louisbourg the *commissaire-ordonnateur* eclipsed the governor—unlike New France where military overshadowed civil authority.[2] In Cuba the Crown invested the Havana Company with quasigovernmental responsibilities at the expense of the imperial bureaucracy, amounting to the partial substitution of civil for military authority.

The French and Spanish expected Louisbourg and Havana to play military roles of local, not continental importance. Louisbourg was to protect French trade while menacing British commerce, and perhaps serve as a base for local conquests in Acadia or Newfoundland. Havana, similarly, was to protect Spanish traders, while serving as a base for commerce raiding and frontier actions in Florida and Georgia. The balance of sea power in the North Atlantic and the Caribbean prevented the French and Spanish from charging their island ports with greater responsibilities.

While the military roles assigned to Louisbourg and Havana—excepting Maurepas's illusion—were local and almost purely defensive, the metropoles expected major economic functions of the two ports. The French expected Louisbourg to ensure and expedite the prosecution of the cod fishery, the basis of an important export trade to the Mediterranean world. The Spanish expected Havana to do the same for Cuban export crops, particularly tobacco and sugar, since tobacco earned the Crown a large revenue through the state monopoly and sugar exports from Cuba reduced costly Spanish imports from foreign sources. In addition, the French intended Louisbourg to foster colonial trade between the major regions of the French Atlantic empire, while the Spanish expected Havana to facilitate commerce between the mainland empire and Spain.

Whereas the lack of imperial navies prevented Louisbourg and Havana from playing pivotal strategic roles for the Bourbon empires, nothing comparable impeded realization of their economic potentials. By the eighteenth century, colonials responded readily to market forces, so to the degree that French and Spanish authorities could influence market forces, they could manipulate the economic behavior of Louisbourg and Havana. British rivalry inhibited fulfillment of economic possibilities much less than military ones. Whereas neither the French nor the Spanish could afford a navy able to defend an empire, both could direct enough private capital into imperial trade to secure a growing proportion of their expanding colonial commerce.

Louisbourg provided the French with a share of the cod fishery for four decades, and thus successfully carried out its most important mission. Its rise as an entrepôt port, however, came in part at the expense of the fishery, since local labor was insufficient to support both activities. The success of the entrepôt trade at Louisbourg gratified French authorities considerably, although the emergence of New England in the role assigned to Quebec certainly vexed them. On the whole, despite the gradual decline of the fishery and the existence of trade with foreigners, the French found Louisbourg satisfactory. The real problem in the French system lay with Quebec, whose failure largely caused the discrepancies between theory and practice in economic affairs at Louisbourg.

Havana provided Spain with a steady supply of excellent tobacco with which the state earned annual profits of up to 10 million pesos, several times greater than the sums spent on the colony. By 1760 it also provided Spain with almost a million pesos worth of sugar annually, far more than anywhere else in the Spanish empire. Cuba's contribution of hides significantly supplemented that of Buenos Aires. Although export production in Cuba never reached potential levels under existing technology—which the Ile Royale fishery probably did in the early 1730s—the steady expansion proved a source of constant satisfaction to the Spanish. Even the radical decision to replace one staple crop with another proved a success in most of the island.

The rise of Havana as an entrepôt after 1740 did not reduce the volume of Cuban exports to Spain. Unlike the Ile Royale fishery, Cuban agricultural production grew even as boats, men, and money went into the Caribbean carrying trade. Apparently the capacity of the Seville tobacco factories, the size of the Spanish home market, and scarcity of transatlantic shipping limited exports as much as the availability of Cuban land, labor, and capital.[3] The rate of population growth and capital formation in Cuba supported the rapid expansion of both sugar production and

entrepôt trade, perhaps with the help of resources withdrawn from tobacco production.

Excepting the south coast, the Spanish by and large managed to
confine the growth of the Cuban export and carrying trades to their
empire. The western and northern shores of Cuba produced for the
Spanish market via Havana. The south coast, on the other hand,
produced very largely for the illegal market in Jamaica, much as Ile
Royale's carrying trade by the 1750s was conducted very largely for the
New England market. Distances, currents, and winds created this dual
economy in Cuba: the natural market for the south coast lay twenty-four
hours away in Jamaica, while the natural market for the north coast lay
downwind at Havana. Thus, by and large, only north-central and western Cuba participated in the accelerating transition to sugar between
1740 and 1760, while the south coast persisted in the production of
tobacco and livestock. Topographical characteristics and soil exhaustion
played a role in the development of this pattern, too, but as late as 1760
the factors determining transportation costs probably exercised greater
influence. Metropolitan authorities were powerless to counteract these
geographical facts—indeed there is much to suggest they did not understand them—and so contraband continued to flourish on the south coast.

In the eighteenth century imperial governments had to permit a
measure of flexibility in administration, a gap between theory and practice. The French on the whole allowed greater deviation than did the
Spanish, especially after 1740. Whereas the French lent tacit approval to
the trade between Louisbourg and New England, the Spanish never
relented in their condemnation of trade between Cuba and Jamaica.
Whereas the French recognized and tolerated the complicity of a Louisbourg governor in illegal trade, a Santiago de Cuba governor languished
in prison in consequence of similar activity.[4]

It is possible that the clearest example of policy differences between the
French and Spanish lies in their responses to the worldwide trade depression of the 1730s. When Cuban sugar planters voiced their grievances,
the Crown reacted vigorously. When the Ile Royale fishery slumped, the
French Crown did nothing at all. While it is true that planters could
express themselves to metropolitan authorities more easily than humble
fishermen, some great French merchants were involved in the cod trade,
and the French marine officials were certainly aware of and concerned

about the decline in the fishery. This apparent lassitude on the part of the French perhaps derives, in the final analysis, from the fact that imperial matters, whether triumphs or disasters, mattered less to France than to Spain.

In general, Spanish policy toward Cuba was more forceful and energetic than that of the French toward Ile Royale. Whereas the French allowed resources to drift from the fishery into commerce, the Spanish actively shepherded land, labor, and capital from tobacco into sugar and ranching.[5] Their failure to prevent contraband should not obscure their commitment to shaping the Cuban economy to suit metropolitan priorities. On balance, this vigorous effort (a manifestation of Bourbon prereformism)[6] produced the intended effects in the short run: higher revenues for the state and a more diversified and disunited Cuba. By the nineteenth century, however, what had begun as an attempt to diversify gave rise to an economy more thoroughly devoted to sugar culture than it had ever been to tobacco. Of course, other factors contributed to this transformation—most notably the collapse of Haitian exports in 1790 and the steady growth in European demand for sugar—but Cuban planters could exploit these developments only because of the processes that state policy had set in motion. It has proved an enduring irony in Cuban history that in undoing what they saw as a tobacco monoculture the Spanish created a sugar monoculture instead. This policy lies at the root of all subsequent Cuban history.

The history of Louisbourg and Havana in the eighteenth century represents the interplay of imperial policy—conservative policy based on undue ignorance and an unexamined trust in traditional methods—with colonial conditions. The population, geography, and natural resources of Cape Breton and Cuba, together with financial and naval limitations, defined the boundaries within which imperial policy could determine colonial history. Historians who have ignored these local factors in favor of imperial policy alone have misunderstood the importance of these island colonies, seeing their military roles as paramount. Other historians who have ignored imperial policy in order to concentrate on social and economic patterns in the colonies (and precious few among this newer generation of historians have turned their attention to Cape Breton or Cuba) have failed to see the critical impact—often unintended—of imperial policies in shaping colonial destinies.

Appendix A.
French and Spanish Terms

almojarifazgo	a port tax in the Spanish empire
aguardiente de caña	liquor distilled from cane juice; rum
arboladura ensamblado	masts made of fitted timbers bound together
artificio	water-powered mill for grinding tobacco
asentista	trader who holds an *asiento*
asiento	contract, usually a monopoly
astillero	shipyard
aviso	dispatch ship, usually 70 to 100 tons
bagasse	dried, squeezed sugar cane, used for fuel in sugar mills
cabildo	town council
chaloupe	shallop, a three- to five-man open boat
commissaire-ordonnateur	highest-ranking civilian authority at Louisbourg
compagnon-pescheur	wage-earning fisherman
conucos	plots on which Cuban slaves grew their own food
corral	small livestock estate
cortes	timber cutting areas
cueros curtidos	tanned hides
cueros al pelo	untanned hides
decomiso	seizure of contraband
estanco	government sales monopoly
fábrica	factory
flota	Spanish convoy of merchant ships to and from Spain

goelette	schooner, a five- to seven-man one-masted vessel
graves	wooden racks for drying fish
guarda costa	coast guard charged with preventing smuggling and protecting Spanish shores
Habanero	native of Havana
habitant-pescheur	fisherman or merchant who employs fishermen
hato	small ranch
indulto de negro	a tax on imported slaves in the Spanish empire
ingenio	sugar mill or sugar plantation
inscription maritime	French registry of able-bodied seamen
legajo	a bundle of documents in Spanish archives
mascobado or muscovado	unrefined, dark sugar
matrícula del mar	Spanish registry of able-bodied seamen
mâts d'assemblage	masts made of fitted timbers bound together
navio or *navires*	ship of the line or any ocean-going vessel
ordenanza	ordinance
ordonnance	ordinance
partido	rural district
pieza de Indias	a unit of account equal to one healthy, adult male slave
polvo	tobacco in powder
presidios	administrative unit of the Spanish empire
proyecto	a scheme, plan or regulation in Spanish empire
ramo de construcción de vageles	shipbuilding accounts
rapé	snuff
real orden	royal order
registro	officially sanctioned merchant vessel outside the *flota*
renta de tabacos	state tobacco administration
rollo	rolled tobacco
seigneurie	seignory, manor
situado	military subsidy

trapiche	small sugar mill
vega	tobacco field
veguero	tobacco farmer
visita	visit, inspection, census

Appendix B.
Weights, Measures, and Money

1 *arroba* = 25 *libras castellanas* = 25 pounds = 11.36 kilograms

1 quintal = 100 livres = 100 pounds = 45.45 kilograms

1 *caballería* = 33 acres = 14 hectares (the Cuban *caballería* is different from that of the rest of Spanish America)

1 *caja* = 16 *arrobas* of sugar (see note 116, Chapter 5)

1 *barrique* = 1 barrel = 110 kilograms of wheat flour

On tons, *tonneaux*, and *toneladas* see note 33, Chapter 3

1 livre = 20 *sous*

1 peso = 8 *reales de vellón* = 32 *maravedís*

After 1727, as a rule, 25 livres = 1 £ sterling = 6 or 7 pesos. For greater precision, see McCusker, *Money and Exchange*, pp. 95, 105.

Notes

The following archival abbreviations are used in the notes.

AA   Albemarle Archives (Ipswich and East Suffolk Record Office)
AC   Archives Nationales, Fonds des Colonies (Paris)
AGI   Archivo General de Indias (Seville)
AGI SD AGI, Gobierno, Audiencia de Santo Domingo
AGI UM AGI, Ultramar
AGI IG AGI, Indiferente General
AGS   Archivo General de Simancas (Simancas)
AHN   Archivo Histórico Nacional (Madrid)
AMN   Archivo del Museo Naval (Madrid)
AN   Archives Nationales (Paris)
BNM   Biblioteca Nacional (Madrid)
BNP   Bibliothèque Nationale (Paris)
BPR   Biblioteca del Palacio Real (Madrid)
BL   British Library (London)
BL AM   BL Additional Manuscripts
MPCU   Maurepas Papers, Cornell University (Ithaca, N.Y.)
MP OSU Maurepas Papers, Ohio State University (Columbus, Ohio)
NLSC   Newberry Library, Special Collections (Chicago)
PAC   Public Archives of Canada (Ottawa)
PLMP   Montemar Papers, Perkins Library, Duke University (Durham, N.C.)
PRO   Public Record Office (London)
PRO CO PRO, Colonial Office Papers
PRO T   PRO, Treasury Papers
RAH   Real Academia de la Historia (Madrid)

In the eighteenth century, French and Spanish clerks were sparing in their use of accent and punctuation marks and inconsistent in their spelling. I have done my best to preserve original forms in quotations and citations.

Chapter 1

1. This proposition is hard to prove but still a defensible assumption. The relationship between power and wealth is unclear: one may be the means to the other, but the identity of ends and means remains obscure. On this head see: Viner, "Power vs. Plenty," pp. 1–29; and Chapter 3 of this volume.
2. The most convenient survey is Eccles, *France in America*.
3. The leading study is Innis, *Fur Trade in Canada*.
4. Convenient surveys include: Gibson, *Spain in America*; Parry, *Spanish Seaborne Empire*; Haring, *Spanish Empire in America*.
5. See Haring, *Trade and Navigation*. Haring treats only the sixteenth and seventeenth centuries. A work that covers the eighteenth century is Walker, *Spanish Politics and Imperial Trade*.
6. Pares, *War and Trade*, pp. 311–15.
7. This concept is best expressed in Mahan, *Sea Power*. The idea is applied to empires in Reynolds, *Command of the Sea*.
8. Both phrases mean the key to America (or the New World). One of Cuba's first historians appropriated Havana's nickname, bestowed by a Real Cédula of 1634: Arrate, *Llave del Nuevo Mundo*. See also Savary, *Dictionnaire universel de commerce*, p. 908. Both cities were occasionally referred to as the Gibraltar of America as well.

Chapter 2

1. Technically the soil is of the humo-ferric podzol group; in the southwest of Cape Breton this is mixed with gray luvisol soils. See Canada, Department of Agriculture, *System of Soil Classification*. For an eighteenth-century description of the geography of Cape Breton see Pichon, *Genuine Letters and Memoirs*, pp. 10–53. The first systematic appraisal of Cape Breton's geography is a memoir of 1706, normally attributed to the Intendant of New France Jacques Raudot, *Archives Nationales, Fond des Colonies* C¹¹B, 1:270 passim (hereafter AC, C¹¹B, vol., page). It is partially reprinted in McLennan, *Louisbourg: Foundation to Fall*, pp. 23–31.
2. Storms could and did, however, do damage. Sabatier au Ministre, 4 décembre 1726, AC, C¹¹B, 8:130–31.
3. See Thibault, "Shipwrecks."
4. The climate of North America changes but slowly. See Bryson, "Ancient Climes," pp. 64–73.
5. Pichon, *Genuine Letters and Memoirs*, p. 6. Another, a Scot, called the climate "wretched," Johnstone, *Memoires*, 2:180. The data that follow on the climate of Cape Breton are drawn from two sources: Canada, Surveys and

Mapping Branch, Geographic Division, *National Atlas*; Walters, *1980 Canadian Almanac*. Some of the data are for Sydney, N.S., 20 miles away from Louisbourg, and all of the data are recent. Thus they can only serve as an approximation to the actual climate of eighteenth-century Louisbourg. Discussion of the Cape Breton climate and geography appears in Taylor, *Canada*, passim.

6. *Collection de manuscrits*, 3 : 469.

7. One French visitor thought the cold was unnatural, a fact he attributed to the large number of trees: "jusqu'au mois de mai des froidures ne sont pas naturelles, d'ou, on doit concluire qu'à mesure qu'on détruira les bois, et qu'on découvrira les terres il n'y aura plus tant de neges, et que par conséquent les hyvers . . . ne seront si rudes ni si longs." Mémoire à Pontchartrain (n.d., c. 1706). AC, C^{11}B, 1 : 273.

8. Measuring the practical effect of sea distances by referring to record and average crossing times is a very difficult business. See the attempt and the disclaimers of Braudel, *Mediterranean*, 1 : 358–62.

9. The first sextants and octants appeared in the 1730s, some of which were accurate to $0° 2'$ of longitude, but these were not widely employed, and the problem of fixing one's longitude disappeared only with the introduction of the chronometer in the 1760s, Taylor, *Haven-Finding Art*, 1 : 254–63. A detailed account of French struggles with navigation in these waters is: Chabert, *Voyage fait par ordre du Roi*.

10. For descriptions of the fishing banks, see Loture, *Histoire de la grand pêche*, p. 15; La Morandrière, *Histoire de la pêche française de la morue*, 1 : 27–32.

11. See the survey based on French travelers' accounts: Bentley and Smith, "Forests of Cape Breton," pp. 1–15. Besides the published accounts mentioned by Bentley and Smith, see Minutes de la Conseil de la Marine, 1717, in which quantities of maple are mentioned, AC, C^{11}B, 2 : 28–29.

12. See Lower, *Great Britain's Woodyard*, p. 30, for the distribution of the *pinus strobus*.

13. By 1606 they had learned to sail shallops, according to Lescarbot, *Nova Francia*, p. 84; see also Wallis and Wallis, *Micmac Indians*, pp. 14–49.

14. Upton, *Micmacs*, pp. 32–33. Precontact population estimates traditionally hover around 3,500, but one student has put it at 35,000, Williams, "Aboriginal Micmac Population," pp. 117, 125. French population estimates varied widely. According to Upton, *Micmacs*, pp. 32–33, the French noted 260 families in 1716, 838 persons in 1722, 600 warriors in 1739. Recensement general fait au mois de Novembre 1708 de tous les sauvages de l'Acadie, Newberry Library, Special Collections, Ayer Manuscripts 751 (hereafter NLSC, ms./number), records only 196 Micmacs in Cape Breton Island. Estimates appearing in the documents which Upton did not include are 289 warriors in 1721, 635 *hommes* in 1732, and 670 warriors in 1757,

St.-Ovide au Conseil, 15 septembre 1721, AC, C¹¹B, 5:359; Rapport de M. St.-Ovide, 4 novembre 1732, *Collection de manuscrits*, 3:164; Mémoire sur l'Isle Royalle, décembre, 1757, AC, C¹¹C, 15:280.

15. The names Ile Royale and Louisbourg were assigned by the Minister of Marine, Pontchartrain à L'Hermitte, 26 janvier 1714, AC, B, 36:419. Henceforward Cape Breton Island will refer to the island and Ile Royale to the colony.

16. *Archives Nationales*, Outre-Mer, G¹, CDLXVI, pièce 50 (hereafter AN). McLennan, *Louisbourg: Foundation to Fall*, p. 12.

17. The most convenient treatments of the Acadians are the works of Griffiths, *Acadians: Creation of a People* and *Acadian Deportation*.

18. Pontchartrain à St.-Ovide, 20 mars 1713, AC, B, 35–3:110–15; Pontchartrain à Desmarets, décembre 1713, AC, B, 35–2:692–95; Instructions à Soubras, 10 avril 1714, AC, B, 36–7:89–104; Conseil à St.-Ovide, 15 juillet 1722, AC, B, 45–2:1150; Maurepas à St.-Ovide, 25 juin 1724, AC, B, 45:276–91. In 1731 Ile St. Jean joined Ile Royale as an acceptable destination for Acadian immigration, Maurepas à St.-Ovide, 10 juillet 1731, AC, B, 35–3:566–72.

19. Ordre du Roi, 26 juin 1725, AC, C¹¹B, 1:196–98. (Also in AC, F³, 50:161–62.)

20. Conseil de la Marine à Soubras, 22 avril 1716, AC, B, 38–2:555–56.

21. Trading ships paid a fine of 600 livres if they neglected to bring out with them to Louisbourg *engagés* (indentured servants), who, it was hoped, would develop ties and stay on after their three-year term expired, Circulaire aux Intendants, 9 avril 1722, AC, B, 45-1:280–281. Many of the *engagés* were apparently convicts, Conseil à Rostan, 11 juin 1722, AC, B, 45–1:101. 45–1:101.

22. Pontchartrain à St.-Ovide, 20 mars 1713, AC, B, 35–3:114; Pontchartrain à Vaudreuil, 29 mars 1713, AC, B, 35–3:158–69.

23. The same regions of France which sent fishermen to Ile Royale also supplied the majority of merchants. Of 80 French merchants, 26 were from Gascony, 12 from Normandy, 11 from Guyenne (Bordeaux), and 10 from Brittany, see Moore, "Merchant Trade" (thesis), pp. 41–42.

24. Only ten Acadians lived anywhere other than these places. These comments are all based on the 1752 census as it appears in Public Archives of Canada, *Report, 1905*, 2:4–76. In its original form it is in AN, Outre-Mer, G¹, 466, pièce 81.

25. See McLennan, *Louisbourg: Foundation to Fall*, Appendix C.

26. Those that survive are in AN, Outre-Mer, G¹, 466.

27. For Louisbourg: Durand, "Etude de la population de Louisbourg"; for the outports, see McLennan, *Louisbourg: Foundation to Fall*, Appendix 3; for the island as a whole, see Clark, *Acadia*, pp. 274–296. Clark's is the most

detailed discussion available, but it has arithmetical and other errors, particularly a propensity to omit the entire garrison population.

28. The Ile Royale population by the 1750s exceeded that of Newfoundland, Nova Scotia, and Georgia among British colonies, Wells, *Population of the British Colonies*, pp. 47, 160, 170.

29. The history of the French at Ile St. Jean is ably presented in Harvey, *French Regime*, and in Clark, *Three Centuries*.

30. Etat des troupes de l'Isle Royale, 1722, AC, C ^{11}C, 6:68.

31. In 1733 the first nine months saw a 43-man turnover; in 1735, 31 men had to be replaced; in 1736 the figure was 59. See St.-Ovide à Maurepas, octobre 1733, AC, C ^{11}B, 14:217; St.-Ovide à Maurepas, 10 octobre 1735, AC, C ^{11}B, 17:27; AC, C ^{11}B, 18:53–54.

32. A steady diet of fish, peas, butter, and molasses was the best a soldier could look forward to at Louisbourg, and very often food was scarce. Wages were often appropriated by officers, and if they were not, there was precious little to spend them on. Soldiers could marry, but brides were hard to find, Minutes de Conseil de la Marine, 25 mars 1719, AC, C ^{11}B, 4:4–8 (diet); Minutes de la Conseil 1718, AC, C ^{11}B, 3:7 (marriage); see also, McLennan, *Louisbourg*, p. 47; Johnstone, *Memoires*, 2:172.

33. One was in 1732–1733 and the other in 1755. See Schmeisser, "Health and Medicine at Louisbourg," unpaginated.

34. Donovan, "Rearing Children in Louisbourg." Donovan defined a child as anyone under the age of twelve. This paper was shown to me through the courtesy of the author. For the Anjou figure, see Lebrun, *Les Hommes et la mort en Anjou*, p. 182.

35. Reports include AC, C ^{11}B, 12:170–71; AC, C ^{11}B, 13:107, 111, 122–23; AC, C ^{11}B, 14:208–209; AC, C ^{11}B, 16:103–105; AC, C ^{11}B, 16:109–110; AC, C ^{11}B, 16:113–14; AC, C ^{11}B, 18:255–58; AC, C ^{11}B, 18:262–66; AC, C ^{11}B, 20:88–92; AC, C ^{11}B, 23:168; AC, C ^{11}B, 30, 230–31. These cover 1731–37, 1741, 1751–52.

36. St.-Ovide et Le Norman de Mezy à Maurepas, 23 janvier 1734, AC, C ^{11}B, 15:52–59.

37. Pouyez, "La population de l'Isle Royale," p. 169.

38. A Louisbourg census was taken in 1749–50 but only a rough version remains in the archives, AN, Outre-Mer, G ^{1}, 466, pièce 65. This census gives 2,454 as the civil population.

39. As a guide to the gradations of French society I have used Goubert, *Ancien Régime*.

40. Mémoire du Roi, 12 mai 1722, AC, C ^{11}B, 6:26. In 1722 Louisbourg supported only a single cleric, who cost 500 livres annually to maintain.

41. Pouyez, "La population de l'Isle Royale," p. 169.

42. Moore, "Merchant Trade" (thesis), pp. 41–42.

43. Fenning, *New System of Geography*, 2:724: "a thousand sail of ships may commodiously ride in it in the utmost safety, without anchor or cable, no wind being able to hurt them." Jefferys, *Spanish Islands*, p. 78: "the best port in the West Indies." See also, "General Description of the American Coasts and Seas," by pilot Captain Domingo Gonzalez Carranza, 1718, British Library, Additional Manuscripts 28140, fols. 35–64. (Hereafter BL, AM nos.)

44. The following description is based on maps in Archivo General de Indias, Mapas y Planos, Santo Domingo, 160, 176, and 204; and on *Urbanismo español en America*, pp. 26–41; Humboldt, *Cuba*, pp. 105–10; Roberts, *Havana*, p. 41; Campbell, *Spanish America*, pp. 160–64.

45. Testimonio de los Autos formados a fin de establecer un Asiento . . . para la limpieza de las calles y plazas, 1749, Archivo General de Indias, Santo Domingo 1219. (Hereafter: AGI, SD no.)

46. There was only one road worthy of the name, from Havana to Santiago de Cuba, Santovenia, "Politica colonial," p. 33.

47. Chaunu and Chaunu, *Séville et l'Atlantique*, 8:555, 568–69.

48. Climatic data for 1800–1810 appear in Humboldt, *Cuba*, pp. 152–54; for 1854–56 in Pezuela, *Diccionario*, 3:19–20.

49. "Dictamen del Sr. D. Tomas Ugarte sobre la derrota y precauciones con que navegará con más seguridad, una fregata," Archivo del Museo Naval (AMN), Manuscrito 469, fol. 230. To avoid bucking the trade wind, captains sailed north from Vera Cruz almost to the shore of Texas, where the trades were weaker and shore winds could be exploited. At this latitude they sailed eastward toward the western shore of Florida, from which a southward descent to Havana was fairly easy, especially in winter. Also: An Account of the Havannah, 19 April 1740, BL AM 32694, fol. 77.

50. Horsfall, "British Relations with the Spanish Colonies," (thesis), pp. 3–16. Horsfall probably drew her information from the introduction by Newton, *European Nations in the West Indies*. Captains often preferred to exit the Caribbean by doubling Cape San Antonio and passing through the Florida Straits, sailing out into the Atlantic and then returning to the Windward Islands from the east, with the help of the northeast trades. This amounted to a journey of perhaps six times as many miles as a direct route from Jamaica to Barbados, but was often quicker.

51. Data on the climate and winds of Cuba come from Humboldt, *Cuba*, 152–72 (figures here differ only slightly from modern ones suggesting that the climate is little changed by the passage of 180 years); and from Marrero, *Geografía de Cuba*.

52. A translation of a 1718 survey of Caribbean waters made by the *flota* pilot Domingo Gonzalez Carranza is instructive on currents: "General Description of the Spanish West Indies," Public Record Office (PRO), Colonial

Office (CO), 319, 2 (hereafter PRO, group, paper no.); also in BL, AM 28140, ff. 35–64.

53. Pirie, *Oceanography*, p. 103.

54. To an extent winds create ocean currents. The other major factors are, first, the rotation of the earth, which creates Coriolis forces inclining bodies of water in the northern hemisphere to harbor clockwise currents (vice versa in the southern hemisphere), and second, the relief of the ocean's floor, which directs heavy cold water en route from the Arctic and Antarctic to the tropics. Compensation for these bottom water currents is necessarily made by surface currents, Neumann, *Ocean Currents*, pp. 127–226.

55. Varias derrotas entre Cádiz, La Habana y Méjico, AMN, Ms. 582, Doc. 4.

56. Humboldt, *Cuba*, p. 149.

57. Marrero, *Geografía de Cuba*, p. 104.

58. Idea geográfica, histórica, y política de la Isla de Cuba y Ciudad de la Habana (n.d.), BL, AM 17629, fols. 28–33; Humboldt, *Cuba*, pp. 159–60; Jefferys, *Spanish Islands*, p. 73; Marrero, *Geografía de Cuba*, pp. 109–12.

59. In Cuban Spanish there are words for a savanna surrounded by woods (*ciego*); for woods surrounded by savanna (*sao*); and for savanna encircled by woods and a river bank (*ceja*). *Ciego* ordinarily means blind; *ceja* more generally means eyebrow.

60. Iron, chrome, and magnesium exist in quantity too. The Spanish knew of iron deposits near Baracoa from early in the sixteenth century, but no mining took place until the 1880s.

61. Idea geográfica, histórica, y política de la Isla de Cuba y la Ciudad de la Habana, BL, AM 17629, fols. 28–33.

62. See Inglis, "Demography of Cuba" (dissertation).

63. Cassava is the Taino word for yucca (Carib) and manioc (Guaraní).

64. For Cuba's prehistory, consult Guerra, *Manual de la historia de Cuba*, pp. 3–17; Ortiz, *Historia de la arqueología indocubana*; and Harrington, *Cuba before Columbus*. Indian settlements did survive into the eighteenth century at Guanabacoa and Jiguani, Arango, *Obras*, 2:433.

65. González, "Population of Cuba," p. 75.

66. These figures are based on Ortiz, *Hampa afro-cubana*, pp. 21–22.

67. Dictamen sobre los ventajas que pueden sacarse para el mejor fomento de la Isla de Cuba (n.d.), AGI, SD 1156.

68. This figure appears in at least a dozen works, most recently in González, "Population of Cuba," p. 75. It originated, I believe, with Pezuela, *Diccionario*, 4:238; see, e.g., Grellier, *Cuba*, p. 103.

69. Guerra, *Manual de la historia de Cuba*, p. 130.

70. These are approximations made from the graphs in Bourdé, "Sources et méthodes," pp. 408–9.

71. Bourdé, "Sources et méthodes," p. 407, admits that his parish is not typical,

though he offers as the reason that it is close to Havana; he, of course, was discussing its entire history, not just that of its early years.

72. Guerra et al., *Historia de la nación cubana*, 2:109, has 140,000 for 1759. Grellier, *Cuba*, p. 103, has 150,000 for 1760. Maryland in 1755 had 153,505 people, 70.5 percent white and 29.5 percent black, Wells, *Population of the British Colonies*, p. 146.

73. The bishop's *visita* survives in nine documents. Relación de la visita de Obispo Pedro Agustín de Morel y Santa Cruz, 2 julio 1755, Havana, AGI, SD 2227. Also in SD 2227 : 28 julio 1756, Bayamo, and 28 octubre 1757, Havana. In AGI, SD 534 : 14 septiembre 1756, Santiago de Cuba; 17 agosto 1756, Bayamo; 2 septiembre 1756, Santiago del Prado; 8 diciembre 1756, Santiago de Cuba; 16 diciembre 1756, Santiago de Cuba; 4 abril 1756, Havana. The *visita* is also in the Archivo Episcopal de la Habana, legajo 18. The *visita* appears in part in Marrero, *Cuba*, 6:44–45, 66–70. Unfortunately Marrero has sixteen copying or typesetting errors and some arbitrary extrapolations and deletions.

74. Humboldt, *Cuba*, p. 194. Marrero comes up with 50,000, achieved by multiplying an incorrect 10,000 households by an arbitrarily chosen multiplier of five persons per household. The same figure appears (for 1762) in Pérez de la Riva's introduction to *Documentos inéditos sobre la Toma de la Habana*, p. 17.

75. Razon de la gente que Contiene esta Ciudad de la Havana sacada por los Padrones del año proximo pasado de 1728, AGI, SD 2104. A 1691 *padrón* ("count") counted 11,940 *Habañeros*, Inglis, "Demography of Cuba," p. 73. A Spanish writer, however, estimated 26,000 for 1700, Campbell, *Spanish America*, p. 162. Campbell may draw his information from Coreal, *Voyages de François Coreal*, 2:147, which has 25,000 for 1697.

76. An Account of the Havannah, 14 November 1740, BL, AM 32694, fol. 74, "there may be 40,000 people in the town."

77. Table 2.9 calls for some lengthy explanation. The number of people that the bishop actually reported is only 121,083. This excludes the population of five settlements—Regla, Macuriges, Matanzas (town), Camarones, and Ciego de Avila—which the bishop acknowledged, but for one reason or another he neglected to include a head count for them. For Regla and Matanzas (town) a projection may be made on the basis of the number of households in the settlement, using as a multiplier the average household size in the area. For the other three a less reliable estimate must be made, but because none of these communities exceeded more than a few hundred persons, the error involved will be small. The city of Havana is the only other settlement for which an adjustment in the bishop's reported figure is required (see pp. 37–38). A further refinement is called for, however: an addition made to compensate for the bishop's underreporting. Here an

additional 20 percent is added for all communities whose totals have not already undergone adjustment. This 20 percent comes to 24,103 across the whole island. It is not entirely arbitrary, although it is certain to be wrong. It is derived from two cases in which civil counts can be compared with bishops' counts. In one such case, that of Guanabacoa in 1756, the bishop's figure is 84 percent of that reported by civil authorities; in the other such case, that of Santiago de las Vegas in 1766, the bishop's figure is only 76 percent of the civil count. Put together, these two cases (the only ones of which I know) suggest that ecclesiastical counts, for whatever reasons, are in this time and place about 20 percent low. One might, of course, prefer to conclude that civil counts tend to be inaccurately high; in some cases, depending on the purpose for which the count was made, they certainly were. In the two cases above, however, no motive behind the counts can be expected to produce overreporting. In general it may well be that civil counts tend to underreport as well; Humboldt certainly felt this way with regard to the 1774 and 1791 censuses: "Everyone is aware that both these were made with great negligence, and a large part of the population was omitted," (Humboldt, *Cuba*, p. 193). If Humboldt is correct and the 1774 figure is indeed much higher than the 172,620 officially reported, then the 1755–57 figure offered here fits fairly well with a steady trend of growth from 1700 to 1791. Since what little property taxation existed went to the church and not the civil government, the populace had stronger motives to mislead an ecclesiastical counter than a civil one. For this reason civil counts are more reliable than ecclesiastical ones, and the discrepancies between them are more likely to represent underreporting on the part of the bishop, than overreporting on the part of the civil authority.

78. According to the bishop's *visita*, Guanajay had 33 households and 32 ranches. Pinar del Rio counted 76 households and 80 tobacco farms. Guane had 98 households and 98 tobacco farms plus ranches. These Marrero counts as urban, Marrero, *Cuba*, 6:44–45. While it is unclear what makes a city (in Europe it was walls), surely a stricter definition than Marrero's is more helpful.

79. The *visita* divides only one community into town and country, Matanzas, in which about one-third of the total reported population lived in town and two-thirds in the surrounding *partido*. Should the same ratio hold for towns such as Puerto Príncipe, Bayamo, and Santiago de Cuba, as seems plausible, then the urban population of Cuba amounted to only 30 percent.

80. See Carter, *Yellow Fever*, pp. 3–23; Burnet and White, *Infectious Disease*, pp. 242–49.

81. Carter, *Yellow Fever*, pp. 187–90; Blake, "Yellow Fever in Eighteenth-Century America," pp. 673–86.

82. Parkinson, *Trade Winds*, pp. 121–40. The Royal Navy must not have taken

into account the West African coast. Martínez Fortún, *Epidemiología*, p. 29. Many medical historians believe (wrongly, I think) that yellow fever spared Cuba between 1648 and 1761.

83. Hamshere, *British in the Caribbean*, p. 186.

84. For eighteenth-century ideas on the cure of yellow fever, see Tytler, *Plague and Yellow Fever*, for the wisdom of a Cuban medico, see the treatise of Dr. Tomás Romay, 27 junio 1804, Bibliotica Nacional (Madrid) MS 18698 [10] (hereafter BNM). This document was brought to my attention by Dr. William Coker.

85. Each *flota*, for example, brought about 5,000 sailors to Havana, who stayed an average of 44 days in the sixteenth and seventeenth centuries, and at times as long as 198 days, Chaunu and Chaunu, *Séville et l'Atlantique*, 6:280. Other ship traffic brought another 5,000 or 10,000 sailors to Havana for short stays.

86. No data exist on the age and sex of the Cuban population until 1774. Since net migration hardly mattered (except for the growing slave trade), we may assume "natural" proportions for preindustrial populations. See Wrigley, *Population and History*, pp. 23–28, 108–43.

87. Humboldt, *Cuba*, p. 217, says in 1763 Cuba had less than 32,000 slaves. According to Moreno Fraginals, *El ingenio*, 1:35, the Havana area had only 4,000 slaves before 1762. Klein, *Slavery in the Americas*, p. 147, used 40,000 for the total "colored" population in 1700, a figure from Guerra, *Sugar and Society in the Caribbean*, p. 46.

88. Moreno Fraginals, *El ingenio*, 2:86, says that 88 percent of the slaves on sugar plantations in the Havana area between 1740 and 1790 were born in Africa.

89. Barrett, "Caribbean Sugar Production," p. 166, shows that throughout the British Caribbean a slave's value averaged about 4,000 pounds in low-grade sugar. In Cuba slaves brought a price almost twice as high: the equivalent of 300 *arrobas*, or 7,500 pounds of sugar.

90. Houston, *Memoirs*, p. 224.

91. The mortality rate among slaves on the middle passage in French slavers in the eighteenth century was 12–14 percent. See Stein, "Mortality," pp. 35–42; also, Dionisio Martinez de la Vega al Marques de la Paz, 15 enero 1732, Archivo Histórico Nacional (Madrid), Sección de Estado, *legajo* 2333 (hereafter AHN, Sección, no.).

92. Arango, *Obras*, 2:161: "el negro que nace en casa ha costado más, cuando puede trabajar, que el de igual edad se compra en pública feria."

93. Moreno Fraginals, *El ingenio*, 2:86. The same demographic data on slaves also appear in Moreno Fraginals, "Africa in Cuba," pp. 191–93.

94. These are in fact related to some degree. Many bacteria and viruses can survive in warm and humid climes but not in colder, drier ones. Cape

Breton's cool summer and long winter made it invulnerable to several infections that troubled Cuba. Cape Breton may be no less humid than Cuba on average but is always cooler.

95. Using the 1752–53 count for Cape Breton and the 1755–57 count for Cuba, population densities were in Cuba, 1.39 per square kilometer and in Cape Breton, 1.09.

Chapter 3

1. On mercantilism in general, see Deyon, *Mercantilisme*; Coleman, *Revisions in Mercantilism*; Morini-Comby, *Mercantilisme et protectionnisme*; Cossa, *L'Interpretazione scientifica del mercantilismo*; Blitz, "Mercantilist Policies," pp. 39–55; and Buck, *Politics of Mercantilism*.

2. Smith, *Wealth of Nations*, book 4, chapters 7–8. Heckscher, *Mercantilism*.

3. Keynes, *General Theory*, p. 339.

4. Schmöller, *Mercantile System*, especially pp. 49–51; Cunningham, *English Industry*. On the history of the term mercantilism and the idea, see Herlitz, "Concept of Mercantilism," pp. 101–20; Coleman, "Eli Heckscher," pp. 3–25; and Wilson, "Mercantilism," pp. 181–88.

5. Parry, "Transport and Trade Routes," p. 210.

6. Wilson, "Decline of the Netherlands," p. 23.

7. Howard, *War in European History*, pp. 54–74.

8. The question of bullionism and bills of exchange has largely been fought out in the pages of the *Economic History Review*. Charles Wilson has argued the logic of bullionism against all comers, see Wilson, "Treasure and Trade Balances: The Mercantilist Problem," pp. 152–61; Wilson, "Treasure and Trade Balances: Further Evidence," pp. 231–42; Wilson, "Trade, Society and the State," pp. 509–15; Heckscher, "Multilateralism, Baltic Trade and the Mercantilists," pp. 219–28; Price, "Multilateralism and/or Bilateralism," pp. 254–71; Sperling, "International Payments Mechanism," pp. 446–68. Recently Wallerstein has upheld bullionism in his *Modern World-System*, 2:105–10; while Braudel has outlined the wide use of bills of exchange in *Civilization and Capitalism*, 2:142–48, 214–16. On France, Carrière et al., *Banque et capitalisme commercial*; De Roover, *L'évolution de la lettre de change*; and Lévy-Bruhl, *Histoire de la lettre de change en France*. A sophisticated but anachronistic defense of bullionism involving the relationship between money supply, interest rates, investment, and employment appears in Keynes, *General Theory*, chapter 23.

9. Viner, "Power vs. Plenty," pp. 1–29; Mazzei, "Potenza mezzo di ricchezza e ricchezza mezzo di potenza," pp. 3–18.

10. Silberner, *Guerre dans la pensée économique*, pp. 33–54, 146–50, 171–75;

Deyon, *Mercantilisme*, pp. 50, 62–63; Cole, *French Mercantilism*, pp. 229–72; Fleury, *François Véron de Forbonnais*; Forbonnais, *Principles et observations économiques*.

11. Hamilton, "Spanish Mercantilism," pp. 214–39; Larraz López, *La época del mercantilismo en Castilla*, pp. 109–33; Ainsworth, "Commerce and Reform" (dissertation), pp. 29–30, 39–40. Smith, in "Spanish Mercantilism," pp. 1–11; and "Spanish Antimercantilism," pp. 401–11, discusses the two exceptions which prove the rule.

12. See chapters 21–27 of Uztáriz, *Theorica y práctica de commercio y marina*. John Kippax translated it: *The Theory and Practice of Commerce and Maritime Affairs* (hereafter *Theory*). On Uztáriz's life and work, see Castillo, *Spanish Mercantilism*; Mounier, *Les faits et doctrines économiques en Espagne sous Philippe V*; Wirminghaus, *Zwei Spanische Merkantilisten*; Hamilton, "Mercantilism of Gerónimo de Uztáriz," pp. 111–29; Kochert, *Gerónimo de Uztáriz und Gaspar Melchior de Jovellanos*; Franco's introduction to the Aguilar edition of Uztáriz, *Theorica*, pp. xii–lxxvi; Bitar Letayf, *Economístas*, pp. 75–89; Reeder, "Uztáriz y Colbert," pp. 105–17. On Spanish receptivity to foreign economic ideas see Reeder, "Bibliografía de traducciones," pp. 57–77; and Reeder, "Economia e ilustración en España," pp. 47–70.

13. On Campillo's life and work: Rodríguez Villa, *Patiño y Campillo*, pp. 131–50; Bitar Letayf, *Economistas*, pp. 114–18; Colmeiro, *Biblioteca de los economistas españoles*, pp. 94–95; Ainsworth, "Commerce and Reform" (dissertation), pp. 80–128. See also Campillo, *Nuevo sistema de gobierno*; *Lo que hay en España*; and *España despierta*.

14. See Ulloa, *Restablecimiento de las fábricas y comercio español*; Zavala y Auñon, *Representación al Rey Nuestro Señor Don Felipe V*. On Zavala and Ulloa: Bitar Letayf, *Economistas*, pp. 91–109; Muñoz Pérez, "Ideas sobre el comercio en el siglo XVIII español," pp. 58–60; and Colmeiro, *Historia de la economia política*, 2:945–1062, passim.

15. Wilson, "Other Face of Mercantilism," pp. 82–84.

16. On his life, see Filion, *Maurepas*; Lacour-Gayet, *Marine militaire*, chapter 6; Tramond, *Manuel d'histoire maritime*, pp. 377–78; Rule, "Jean-Frédéric Phélypaux," pp. 365–67; Rule, "Maurepas Papers," pp. 103–7. See also the eulogy by Condorcet, "Maurepas," pp. 79–102 (reprinted in Lamontagne, *L'Atlantique jusqu'au temps de Maurepas*). Maurepas's own *Mémoires* are disappointing.

17. Maurepas, *Mémoires*, 1:164–67. Two long memoranda offer the best insight into his ideas about colonies, trade, and the navy: Situation du commerce exterieure, 1730, Bibliothèque Nationale (Paris), Mss. françaises, 11332, fol. 663–701 (hereafter BNP); Mémoire . . . sur la Marine et le commerce, 1745, Archives de la Guerre, Fonds de la Marine, Vol. 3127, fol. 1–65. The 1730 memoir is in Maurepas's *Mémoires*, 3:19–123, the

1745 memoir in 3 : 196–245. These memoranda will be referred to hereafter as Maurepas's 1730 mémoire and Maurepas's 1745 mémoire.

18. Maurepas, *Mémoires*, 3 : 195. "Le commerce est la source de la félicité, de la force et de la richesse d' un état. . . . La richesse et la puissance sont les vrais intérêts d'une nation, et il n'y a que le commerce qui puisse procurer l' une et l'autre."

19. Antoine-Louis Rouillé, 1749–54; Jean-Baptiste Machault, 1754–57; François-Marie Feirenc de Moras, 1757–58; Claude-Louis, Marquis de Massiac, 1758; Nicolas-René Berryer, 1758–61; Etienne-François, Duc de Choiseul, 1761–66.

20. Jenkins, *French Navy*, p. 107.

21. Rodríguez Villa, *Patiño y Campillo*, pp. 1–130; Béthencourt Massieu, *Patiño en la política internacional de Felipe V*; Coxe, *España*, 1 : 121–29; McLachlan, *Old Spain*, Appendix; Fernández Almagro, *Política naval*, pp. 75–84. Patiño's birth is variously reported between 1666 and 1670.

22. Rodríguez Villa, *Don Cenon de Somodevilla*; Fernández Almagro, *Política naval*, pp. 85–104; Coxe, *Memoirs*, 3 : 82–84.

23. Bitar Letayf, *Economistas*, p. 116.

24. Phelan, "Authority and Flexibility," p. 69.

25. Campillo, *Nuevo sistema de gobierno*, pp. 70–74.

26. Phelan, "Authority and Flexibility," p. 64.

27. Uztáriz, *Theory*, p. 226. Compare Ward forty years later: "Sin marina no puede haber un comercio extendido, y sin un comercio extendido no haber marina en Espana," Ward, *Proyecto económico*, 1 : chapter 14; cited in Colmeiro, *Historia de la economia política*, 2 : 1058.

28. Bernard, "La Casa de Contratación," pp. 253–86.

29. On Spanish international ambitions, see Hargreaves-Mawdsley, *Eighteenth-Century Spain*; Altamira, *History of Spain*, pp. 423–509.

30. Alberoni (1664–1752) negotiated the marriage of Felipe V and Elizabeth Farnese and served as prime minister, 1715–19, see Harcourt-Smith, *Cardinal of Spain*.

31. "The seventeenth century had seen the chief fighting-ship, the 'ship-of-the-line' or 'line-of-battle ship' reach the form in which she remained, save for a few minor improvements, until steam did away with sailing warships altogether," Anderson and Anderson, *Sailing Ship*, p. 163. See also Naish, "Ships and Shipbuilding," pp. 495–99; Albion, *Forests and Sea Power*, p. 5; Unger, *Dutch Shipbuilding*, chapter 3; and Merino Navarro, *Armada española*, pp. 18–24.

32. See Baugh, *British Naval Administration*, p. 249.

33. Bouguer, *Traité du navire*, chapter 1; Murray, *Shipbuilding and Navigation*; Duhamel du Monceau, *Elémens*, chapter 2. Late seventeenth century data appear in Mémain, *Marine de guerre*, pp. 580–81. For 1780: Boudriot, *Le*

vaisseau, 1:156. The French foot equalled .3248 meters, about 6 percent longer than the English foot (.3047 meters). Tonnage is a very imprecise business, as tons may refer to weight or volume and always vary between times and places. See Lane, "Tonnages, Medieval and Modern," pp. 213–33; Gille, "Jauge et tonnage des navires," pp. 85–102; Van Driel, *Tonnage Measurement*; and Morineau, *Jauges et méthodes de jauge.* The French *tonneau de mer* equaled 1.44 cubic meters in volume, or 979 kilograms in weight. The normal unit of measure for warships was the number of cannon.

34. Boudriot, *Le vaisseau*, 1:19; Duhamel du Monceau, *Elémens*, pp. 62–63.

35. Merino Navarro, *Armada española*, pp. 347–48, on confused shipbuilding guidelines. Salas, *Marina española*, pp. 161–62, on English shipwrights. By 1759 Englishmen had built about 70 percent of the Spanish line of battle ships according to Charnock, *Naval Architecture*, 3:178. On Spanish shipbuilding treatises, see Fernández Duro, *Armada española*, 6:315–19, on empiricism of Spanish shipwrights; Merino Navarro, *Armada española*, pp. 46–47.

36. See the dimensions in Uztáriz, *Theory*, pp. 243–45; Merriman, *Queen Anne's Navy*, pp. 364–72; San Felipe, *Comentarios de la guerra de España*, p. 601, for comparative data from 1731; and Charnock, *Naval Architecture*, 3:140–58, 245–53.

37. Falconer, *Universal Dictionary*, pp. 236–38; Baugh, *British Naval Administration*, pp. 250–52.

38. Knowles to Anson, 6 January 1745, BL, AM 15956. Anderson and Anderson, *Sailing Ship*, p. 178; and Dorn, *Competition*, pp. 106–7, offer similar claims. See also Charnock, *Naval Architecture*, 3:107, 173.

39. Baugh, *Naval Administration, 1715–1750*, p. 200; Richmond, *Navy*, 2:266–67; MacIntyre and Bathe, *Man-of-War*, pp. 61–62; Baugh, *British Naval Administration*, p. 251.

40. Robertson, *Naval Armament*, p. 41.

41. Gille, "Les écoles des constructeurs," pp. 161–72; Bouguer, *De la mâture des vaisseaux*; Duhamel du Monceau, *Elémens*; Lavery, "Origins of the 74-Gun Ship," pp. 335–37; Tramond, *Manuel d'histoire maritime*, pp. 188–93; Castex, *Idées militaires*, pp. 99–101; Anderson, "Shipbuilding," pp. 218–25. By far the most mathematically sophisticated shipbuilding treatise was the Latin book written by a Swiss German and published in Russia: Euler, *Scientia navalis*.

42. Real orden, 19 diciembre 1742, Archivo del Museo Naval (Madrid), Mss. 439, doc., 1, Arquoes de buques (hereafter: AMN, Mss #, doc. #). Charnock, *Naval Architecture*, 3:173, 187.

43. On the Establishments: Albion, *Forests and Sea Power*, p. 80; Robertson, *Naval Armament*, p. 34; Baugh, *Naval Administration, 1715–1750*, pp. 199–200. Baugh believes that conservatism, not the Establishments,

inhibited progress in British ship design. He does not, however, explain the source of this conservatism.

44. Fernández Duro, *Disquiciones náuticas*, 5 : 216 – 17; Merino Navarro, *Armada española*, pp. 49–53.
45. In 1739, however, Maurepas hired Duhamel du Monceau in hopes of achieving some degree of unity in French naval construction, Lacour-Gayet, *La marine militaire*, p. 99. According to Lambert de Saint-Croix, *Essai sur l'histoire de l'administration de la marine de France*, p. 163, Duhamel was made Inspector-General in 1740.
46. Antonio Sopeña al Marqués Grimaldo, 3 octubre 1742, AHN, Estado 2339; Salas, *Marina española*, p. 165. Merino Navarro, *Armada española*, pp. 351–52, says Spanish costs ran 30 percent higher than French. (Sopeña was a shipbuilder commissioned to investigate the feasibility of buying ships abroad for the Spanish navy.)
47. Fifth-rates had fewer than fifty guns. Vessels with fewer than three masts were not generally called ships (*navires* or *navios*), although in English a frigate is always called a ship. For French small craft see Extrait de la liste gñale des Vaisseaux et autres batiments du Roi (c. 1732), MPCU, Lot 38, Item 5.036.
48. On Spanish ship types: Desdevises du Dezert, "Institutions," p. 513. On the French: Pritchard, "Men, Ships and Commerce" (dissertation), pp. 11–12. For a more general discussion: Creswell, *British Admirals*, chapters 1–2. On frigates: Lewis, *Navy of Britain*, pp. 101–2. A monumental confusion exists concerning ship nomenclature of the eighteenth century within the English language alone. To cope with the French and Spanish, see Falconer, *Universal Dictionary*, which has a French appendix, and Amich, *Diccionario marítimo*.
49. Bromley and Ryan, "Armies and Navies," p. 821.
50. Cole, *French Mercantilism*, pp. 105–11; Symcox, *French Sea Power*; Neuville, *Etat sommaire*, pp. 610–11.
51. Chabaud-Arnault, "Etudes," p. 53; Légohérel, *Les trésoriers généraux de la marine*, facing p. 180. Figures close to Légohérel's are in Extrait des états au vrai fonds reçues du trésor royal (c. 1732), MPCU, Lot 38, Item 5.037.
52. The proportion of ships unfit for duty was usually lower in wartime than in peacetime. Liste générale des vaisseaux du Roy, Novembre 1746, MPCU, Lot 48, Item 9.087; Mémoire d'Ollivier, 1 Octobre 1743, MPCU, Lot 44, Item 8.039. The navy of 1746 included one vessel built in 1697, another from 1714, and nine from the 1720s.
53. Liste générale des vaisseaux du Roy, Novembre 1746, MPCU, Lot 48, Item 9.087.
54. Mahan, *Sea Power*, p. 259.
55. "[I]t was obvious that the decrepitude of the French navy was chiefly caused

by want of money," Pares, "American vs. Continental Warfare," p. 453. Also: Lacour-Gayet, *Marine militaire*, pp. 34, 91–92.

56. Estate des dépenses fixes et ordinaires de la marine pour l'année 1732, MPCU, Lot 38, Item 5.035; Maurepas's 1730 mémoire. Construction costs ranged from 100,000 to 300,000 livres for ships of the line in 1730. In 1680 a fifth-rate cost 96,000 livres and a first-rate 441,000 livres, Mémain, *Marine de guerre*, pp. 580–81.

57. Maurepas's 1745 mémoire.

58. MPCU, Lot 38, Item 5.040. If any ships failed to last twenty years, or if any cost more than expected, France would have fewer than sixty ships. Maurepas thought he needed a budget of 20 million livres to field sixty ships. Nicolas, *Puissance navale*, p. 232. After 20 years the cumulative damage of *teredo navalis* (sea worms) and dry rot destroyed the best of oaken hulls. Maurepas's 1730 mémoire.

59. For 1689–1713 the ratio between army and navy expenditure was eight to one. See Duffy, "British Sea Power," p. 79; and Dickson, "War Finance," p. 299. A single ship cost as much to maintain as 840 footsoldiers or 306 horsemen in the 1720s (see Uztáriz, *Theory*, p. 267), so if these relative costs remained constant the French peacetime army of 160,000 men cost as much as 192 ships. See Corvisier, *L'Armée française*, 1:152; and Leonard, *L'Armée et ses problèmes*, p. 192. The wartime army was twice as large, or the equivalent of 380 ships, roughly eight times the size of the French navy. See Richmond, *Navy in the War*, 1:15. For 1756–61 the ratio shrank to about 5:1; see Kennett, *French Armies*, p. 90. For royal revenues see Marion, *Histoire financière de la France*, 1:64, 88, 120–21, 160n, 171, 191; Guéry, "Finances," pp. 216–39, esp. 239; and Maurepas, *Mémoires*, 4:202–12. Revenues ranged from 165 million livres in 1715 to 190 million in 1749, but jumped to 285 million livres in 1759. Royal expenses generally ran slightly higher than revenues, but the deficit skyrocketed from 30 million livres to 218 million between 1749 and 1759. In general, finances stabilized after 1726 until the Seven Years' War.

60. Neuville, *Etat sommaire*, pp. 615–17. The navy's debt was 6 million livres in 1745, 14 million by 1756, and more than 40 million by 1758.

61. Mémoire sur l'état actuel de la marine, Novembre 1746, MPCU, Lot 48, Item 9.085. This figure is an average for the French fleet. A seventy-four-gun vessel cost 253,000 livres to float for six months; a sixty-four cost 191,000 livres; a forty-six cost 132,000 livres; a thirty-gun frigate cost 100,000. Estat de trente vaisseaux ou fregates qu l'on propose d'armer (c. 1739), MPCU, Lot 40, Item 6.016. By midcentury relative costs had produced a navy of 563 administrators and 940 active officers. Jenkins, *French Navy*, p. 118. Nicolas, *Puissance navale*, p. 243, quotes these figures for 1739.

62. Russo, "L'enseignement des sciences de la navigation," pp. 177–94; Chabaud-Arnault, "Etudes," passim; Lamontagne, *La vie et l'oeuvre de Pierre Bouguer*; Lacour-Gayet, *Marine militaire*, pp. 99–101; Castex, *Idées militaires*, pp. 98–109; Artz, *Technical Education in France*, pp. 102–9.

63. Duffy, "British Naval Power," p. 80.

64. McLennan, *Louisbourg: Foundation to Fall*, pp. 204, 207, 300. The Chevalier de Johnstone wrote that five French warships could have destroyed what remained of the British fleet; de la Motte had 18.

65. The correspondence between Des Gouttes and French officials on shore is in AC, F^3, 50:529–633.

66. Bamford, *Forests and French Sea Power*, p. 11; Bouguer, *Traité du navire*, p. 10; Duffy, "British Naval Power," p. 60; MacIntyre and Bath, *Man-of-War*, p. 74. In Colbert's time, a sixty-gun ship needed 50,000 cubic feet of oak, while a 100-gun vessel required twice that, Mémain, *Marine de guerre*, p. 580; Nicolas, *Puissance navale*, p. 154. A seventy-four-gun vessel used 78,000 cubic feet of oak, or 2,800 trees of 100 to 120 years of age, Boudriot, *Le vaisseau*, 1:54–55. Apparently only half this timber went into the ship; the other half was waste. British ships seem to have used slightly more oak: 160,000 cubic feet for an average ship of the line, and 120,000 (equivalent to 60 acres of Hampshire forest) for a seventy-four-gun vessel. Albion, *Forests and Sea Power*, p. 20; Holland, *Ships of British Oak*, p. 30. Charnock, *Naval Architecture*, 3:140–41, gives 300,000 cubic feet of wood as the total in the Royal George, a first-rate launched in 1756. In the Havana shipyard in 1748, a first-rate consumed 184,000 cubic feet of wood. Pezuela, *Diccionario*, 3:147.

67. Albion, *Forests and Sea Power*, pp. 7–9, 47, 83; Bamford, *Forests and French Sea Power*, pp. 11, 27–29, 70–112, 208; Boureau-Deslandes, *Essay sur la marine et sur le commerce*.

68. Boudriot, *Le vaisseau*, 1:55. In British ships, oak amounted to slightly less of the total, between 70 and 88 percent. Albion, *Forests and Sea Power*, p. 20; Charnock, *Naval Architecture*, 3:140–58.

69. On *mâts d'assemblage*: Bamford, *Forests and French Sea Power*, p. 13. On masting problems in general: Bamford, *Forests and French Sea Power*, pp. 113–34; Mémain, *Marine de guerre*, pp. 617–30. On timber in general: Boudriot, *Le vaisseau*, 1:50–59. On Canadian masts: Fauteux, *Essai sur l'industrie au Canada*, 1:210–11. On Pyreneean masts: Charbonneau, "Documents sur la mâture des Pyrénées," pp. 478–84. On the Baltic market: Lower, *Great Britain's Woodyard*, pp. 22–23.

70. On pitch, copper, iron, coal, and hemp (mostly after 1780), see Merino Navarro, *Armada española*, pp. 267–81; and Alcala-Zamora, "Producción de hierro," pp. 175–77.

71. On population: Goubert, *Ancien Regime*, p. 32; Henry, "Population of

France," pp. 434–56. On the seafaring population: Chassériau, *Précis historique de la marine française*, 1:637; Bromley and Ryan, "Armies and Navies," p. 822.

72. The French carried 9.3 men per gun on a 100-gun vessel while the British and Dutch averaged 8.3, and the Spanish only 8, Uztáriz, *Theory*, p. 240. These averages declined in smaller ships: a Spanish seventy-gun ship carried only 400 men, or 5.8 men per gun. Estado comprehensivo de los vageles de guerra, 1749, AMN, MS 236.

73. Mémoire sur la marine par Antoine Gardane, 21 décembre 1741, MPCU, Lot 43. French merchant marine wages ranged between 32 and 50 livres per month. Pritchard, "Ships, Men and Commerce" (dissertation), p. 20.

74. Nicolas, *Puissance navale*, p. 240. By 1740 merchant ships numbered 1,600; their share in French coastal trade, fisheries, and the slave trade still declined. France had neither enough ships nor sailors to seize the full opportunity of eighteenth-century commercial growth. Mémoire sur la navigation Hollandaise d'un port a l'autre de l'Europe, MP OSU, Lot 22–3.

75. Pares, "Manning of the Navy," p. 48.

76. Mémoire sur les moyens de procurer au Roy tous les matelots nécessaires pour le parfait rétablissement de la marine (1745), MPCU, Lot 46, Item 9.045. Many deserted by early adulthood.

77. Nouveau plan touchant la marine de France, 27 décembre 1740, MPCU, Lot 42, Item 6.063. Some sailors did not set foot on shore for fifteen years because their officers knew they would desert. On morale: Memoire de 1743 MPCU, Lot 44, Item 8.004. Dr. Johnson is quoted in Robson, "Armed Forces," p. 184.

78. Louis de Vendôme al Rey, 19 julio 1711, Archivo General de Simancas (hereafter AGS), Guerra (Moderna), 3616. Accompanying this letter is a "Project pour empecher les Anglais de réussir dans le dessein qu'ils ont formé de faire établissement dans le mer du sud." In European waters Spain depended entirely on France. Kamen, *Succession in Spain*, pp. 58–59, 229–30.

79. During the war, ministers such as Bergeyck and Orry had laid plans for reviving the navy, but little happened until 1717, Kamen, *War of Succession*, pp. 379–80. More specific plans, eventually adopted, emerged from a commission headed by Bernardo de Tinajero, Secretary of the Council of the Indies, Inglis, "Spanish Naval Shipyard at Havana."

80. Mahan wrote: "[T]he Spanish navy was practically annihilated," *Sea Power*, p. 237. See Fernández Duro, *Armada española*, 6:146–62. Twenty-one ships were lost. Some Spaniards felt the British navy consisted inordinately of former Spanish ships: "Es de advertir que la Marina que subsistente la Inglaterra, no es otra que la antigua española," Discurso general sobre la Marina, por Joaquin Aguirre, AGI, Indiferente General, 3167. Aguirre generally exaggerated the plight of the Spanish navy.

81. These data do not bear out Hamilton's contention that public expenditure tripled from 1701 to 1745: see his "National Bank in Spain," p. 316. Spain's gross national product (a rather chimerical statistic at best) was estimated at 2.7 million pesos for midcentury, Plaza Prieto, *Estuctura económica de España*, pp. 25−26.
82. Campillo, *Lo que hay en España*, pp. 25−26.
83. Lombard, "Arsenaux et bois de marine dans la Mediterranée musulmane, pp. 53−99; Kamen, *War of Succession*, pp. 379−80.
84. Bamford, *Forests and French Sea Power*, pp. 99, 108.
85. Merino Navarro, *Armada española*, pp. 186−87, 195−97, 214−15, 263; Vicens Vives, *Economic History*, p. 533.
86. Desdevises du Dezert, "Institutions," p. 518; Uztáriz, *Theory*, p. 292; Fernández Duro, *Armada española*, 6:360−61; Merino Navarro, *Armada española*, pp. 215−20, 251.
87. Ensenada al Embajador de España en Francia, 24 marzo 1749 (printed in Fernández Duro, *Armada española*, 6:377−78); Informe al Rey (por Ensenada), 1751, (printed in Coxe, *España*, 4:561−81, especially 574); Desdevises du Dezert, "Institutions," p. 524; Merino Navarro, *Armada española*, pp. 212, 255.
88. Merino Navarro, *Armada española*, pp. 221, 255−59. Good mast timber had to measure 12 to 26 meters in length and 30 to 90 centimeters in diameter.
89. Using 1712−17 data, Uztáriz, *Theory*, p. 54, arrived at 7.5 million for the total Spanish population. This estimate is accepted by Nadal, *La población española*, pp. 23−24, and by Domínguez Ortiz, *La sociedad española*, p. 57. Vilar, *La Catalogne dans l'Espagne moderne*, pp. 18−19, prefers 5.7 million for 1717, but this is certainly wrong since it requires subsequent population growth rates entirely out of line with European experience. See Livi Bacci, "Fertility and Nuptiality Changes," pp. 84−85. Romero de Solis, *Población*, p. 138, puts the 1717 total at 7.6 million. The administration of the tobacco monopoly estimated population at 7.4 million in 1748 according to [Forbonnais] *Considérations sur les finances d'Espagne*, p. 7. The 1768 census, the first in Spain, counted 9.3 million. See Vicens Vives, *Economic History*, p. 484. Romero de Solis, *Población*, pp. 140−42, says this is too high.
90. Ulloa, *Rétablissement des manufactures et du commerce d'Espagne*, 2:45−47; Brown, "Spanish Claims," p. 81.
91. Desdevises du Dezert, "Institutions," p. 473; Uztáriz, *Theory*, p. 311; Coxe, *España*, p. 4:88.
92. Informe al Rey, 1751, in Coxe, *España*, 4:574.
93. Desdevises du Dezert, "Institutions," pp. 466, 469; O'Dogherty, "La matrícula," pp. 347−48.
94. The *matrícula del mar* originated in 1607; it reappeared in 1625. See Salas, *Marina española*, chapters 6 and 8. Uztáriz in 1724 suggested such a registry,

probably influenced by Colbert's example, *Theory*, p. 305. Patiño began working on it in 1726, but the King's *ordenanza* came a year after Patiño's death (it is printed in Salas, *Marina española*, pp. 144–50). For the numbers: Salas, *Marina española*, p. 156, and Coxe, *España*, 4:89. In 1786 the *matrícula* included 51,381 men; in 1798; 68,741. Salas, *Marina española*, p. 184; Merino Navarro, *Armada española*, p. 85; Desdevises du Dezert, "Institutions," p. 468; O'Dogherty, "La matrícula," p. 358. Curiously, the payroll of the navy in 1760 included about 50,000 men, Coxe, *España*, 4:16; Clarke, *Letters*, p. 219. Patiño's navy included 25,000 men according to the *Enciclopedia universal ilustrada* (Madrid, 1948), 33:170, s.v. "Marina."

95. Ensenada al Embajador de España en Francia, 24 marzo 1749, in Fernández Duro, *Armada española*, 6:378.

96. Only Catholics might serve in the navy, virtually the sole restriction on eligibility. On convict crews: [?] a Cagigal de la Vega, 17 agosto 1751, AGI, SD 1501; and Ogelsby, "Spain's Havana Squadron," p. 486. On wages: a sailor made 70 *reales* per month, a novice only 45, Uztáriz, *Theory*, 278. In 1752 wages ranged from 75 to 150 *reales* per month, see Quenta del costo y gastos del navio nombrado la marques Damu, 4 marzo 1752, AGI, IG 2556. The wages were comparable to those of Havana laborers, Marrero, *Cuba*, 8:80, 93. On the governor versus the navy: O'Dogherty, "La matricula," p. 361.

97. Discurso generale sobre la Marina, AGI, IG 3167.

98. Desdevises du Dezert, "Institutions," p. 482. The first officer school was founded in 1717 in Cadiz. Rodríguez Villa, *Patiño y Campillo*, p. 110; Merino Navarro, *Armada española*, pp. 36–37.

99. Uztáriz, *Theory*, pp. 278–79.

100. Estado del gasto mensual que ttendra un navio armada de ochenta cañones: uno de setentta: otro de sesentta: y otro de cinquentta, comprehendidos sueldos y raziones (1724), AHN, Estado 2329.

101. Spanish figures: Uztáriz, *Theory*, p. 278; Quenta del costo y gastos del navio nombrado la marqués Damu, 4 marzo 1752, AGI, IG 2556. French figures: Estat de trente vaisseaux ou frégates que l'on propose d'armer (c. 1739), MPCU, Lot 40, Item 6.016. Uztáriz's calculations refer to a sixty-gun ship; the Marqués Damu was a sixty-four. In comparing pesos and livres, I use McCusker, *Money and Exchange*, pp. 95, 105.

102. I have consulted here Duffy, "British Naval Power;" Richmond, *Navy*; Michael Lewis, *Navy of Britain*; Baugh, *British Naval Administration*; Albion, *Forests and Sea Power*; Marcus, *Heart of Oak*.

103. According to Mahan, who drew his information from John Campbell, *Lives of the Admirals*, the British Navy's size fluctuated as follows: 1728—84 ships of the line; 1734—70; 1744—90; 1747—126; 1756—130. These figures do not include ships of less than fifty guns, or frigates of whatever size. Mahan, *Sea Power*, pp. 259, 291. If one includes all ships above forty guns, as does one French observer, the 1746 figure mounts to 161. Recapitulation

general des tous les vaisseaux anglois, 1 fevrier 1746, MPCU, Lot 48, Item 9.080. Baugh, *British Naval Administration*, p. 246, has 140 for 1739. Nicolas, *Puissance navale*, p. 243, has 116 for 1749 and 142 for 1756.

104. Vaisseaux de guerre anglois au Amerique . . . (c. 1740), MPCU, Lot 42, Item 6.045 and Pellerin Mémoire, c. 1741, MPCU, Lot 42, Item 7.010: "Les Anglois ont actuellement 52 vaisseaux en Amerique."

105. Baugh, *British Naval Administration*, p. 453.

106. Baugh, *British Naval Administration*, p. 456. Filion, *Maurepas*, p. 74, claims the British budget was six times that of the French. The exchange rate hovered around 24 to 26 livres to the pound sterling after the stabilization of French finances in 1726. See McCusker, *Money and Exchange*, pp. 95–97.

107. Estat de la depense de la marine d'Angleterre depuis l'annee 1736, novembre 1746, MPCU, Lot 48, Item 9.084, has figures suggesting British naval spending ran four times as high as the French, 1736–46.

108. Baugh, *Naval Administration, 1715–1750*, pp. 237–41. The Royal Navy needed up to 50,000 men in wartime. Merriman, *Queen Anne's Navy*, p. 170.

109. Britain's insularity certainly favored large naval expenditure, but the role of centralized credit should not be underestimated. On timber, see Albion, *Forests and Sea Power*. On manpower, see Pares, "Manning of the Navy"; and Baugh, *British Naval Administration*, chapter 4. On naval finance, ibid., chapter 9. The manpower problem might have been solved by paying higher wages, a solution that logically ought to have occurred to the British, because they approached other problems that way (i.e., when timber was scarce they paid the price, when victuals were short, they paid the price). This remedy apparently did not receive serious attention. British ships, like the French, were essentially floating prisons. For British construction and maintenance costs, see Bourne, *Queen Anne's Navy*, Appendixes A and B.

110. This illuminating concept is Lane's, *Profits From Power*, pp. 1–21, 37–49.

111. Andrews, *Elizabethan Privateering*, chapter 1. Vignols, "La course maritime," pp. 196–200, explains the theory and practice of corsair warfare after 1692. Governments of course concerned themselves with plundering and very often bankrolled privateers. Also: Ducéré, *Histoire maritime de Bayonne*; and Bromley, "French Privateering War," pp. 203–31.

112. See Nicolas, *Puissance navale*, pp. 275–76; Lacour-Gayet, *Marine militaire*; Castex, *Idées militaires*; Tramond, *Manual d'histoire maritime*; Chabaud-Arnault, "Etudes"; Richmond, *Navy*; and Graham, *Empire of the North Atlantic*. Jane, *Heresies of Sea Power*, pp. 145–89, considers the dilemma of second-rate naval powers.

113. Graham, "Naval Defense," pp. 95–110. Keene to Newcastle, 14 July 1739, BL, AM 32801: "As to the marine force of Spain . . . they will not expose their ships out of their ports, unless they have intelligence where

they may meet . . . a force infinitely inferior to theirs." Castex, *Idées militaires*, pp. 29–78.

114. For example, De la Motte's orders for eighteen ships of the line at Louisbourg in 1757, Corbett, *England in the Seven Years' War*, 1:173. He was instructed to avoid battle without compromising the honor of the flag.

115. Felipe V al Admiral Rodrigo Torres, 10 julio 1740, AGS, Marina 396.

116. Castex, *Idées militaires*, chapters 1 and 2; Desdevises du Dezert, "Institutions," p. 502.

117. Mahan, *Sea Power*, p. 209. Mahan observes that until 1778 no really decisive actions between equal forces took place. He admits that Hawke's victory at Quiberon Bay or Byng's at Minorca came close, however. The major losses suffered by the French or Spanish came only when their forces were so outnumbered that even defensive methods could not prevent disaster.

Chapter 4

1. Europeans fished for cod in two ways, called the wet and dry fishery. The wet was conducted from European bases, while the dry required local facilities. The details and importance of this distinction are discussed in chapter 6.

2. Pontchartrain (the father of Maurepas) came from a long line of civil servants; his father, Louis, had been Minister of Marine from 1690 to 1699. The family hailed from Blois and had a tradition in law and finance.

3. Raudot à Pontchartrain, 30 novembre 1706, AC, C¹¹G, 3:76; Pontchartrain à Raudot, 30 juin 1707, AC, C¹¹A, 29:87v; Raudot à Pontchartrain, 6 juillet 1708, AC, C¹¹G, 3:183. The 1706 document, often referred to as the Raudot memorandum, is reproduced in part in McLennan, *Louisbourg: Foundation to Fall*, pp. 22–31. Here it is considered anonymous, but its author was certainly Raudot. Crowley discusses its authorship in "Beginnings," p. 71n. The Raudot memorandum is paraphrased in [Bollan] *Advantage of Cape Breton*, pp. 63–74. It also appears in AC, C¹¹C, 8:10–39; and in AC, C¹¹B, 1:269–87.

4. Mémoire de 1714, AC, F³, 50:11. The original: "endroit pour y faire la pesche en sureté." An unsigned memoir of January 1713 says a defensible harbor from which to conduct "la peche de la morue avec sûreté" is the goal, AC, C¹¹B, 1:17–18. The Conseil de la Marine agreed: "L'Etablissement de l'Isle à été jugé absolument nécessaire l'année dernière pour procurer à la France une pêche sedentaire de Morüe," Minutes de Conseil, 25 février 1715, AC, C¹¹B, 1:241. The *pêche sedentaire* is the dry fishery.

5. Mémoire de Pontchartrain, c. 1713, AC, C¹¹B, 1:17.

6. Minutes de Conseil, 26 février 1717, AC, C¹¹B, 2:21–27; Mémoire du

Roi, 18 juillet 1719, AC, B, 41–4, 1193–1200; Mémoire du Roi, juillet 1719, AC, C¹¹B, 4:120.

7. In all the correspondence of Pontchartrain and the Conseil de la Marine I have noted only one reference to Louisbourg as a protector of Canada: AC, B, 45–1:262–64.

8. Mémoire sur le Cap Breton (c. 1759), BL, AM, 38332, fols. 146–49: "La peche de la morue est beaucoup plus essential que [le commerce du castor].

9. Instructions pour St.-Ovide, 20 mars 1713, AC, B, 35–3:116–32; Minutes de Conseil, 1712, AC, C¹¹B, 1:3–5; Beauharnois à Maurepas, 13 octobre 1727, AC, C¹¹E, 10:142; Mémoire, 26 février 1714 (non signé), AC, C¹¹B, 1–2:372–74.

10. Fishing employed four times the number of men per boat that coastal shipping (*cabotage*) did: the average number of sailors per fishing vessel was 20.3; aboard those in *cabotage* it was 5.2. Maurepas 1730 mémoire.

11. Mémoire non signé, 25 février 1715, AC, C¹¹B, 1:2, 372–74. The governor of New France, La Galisonnière, considered the fishery all the more important in the training of French sailors because the trade to the French West Indies killed sailors faster than it trained them. La Galisonnière à Maurepas, 24 août 1747, AC, C¹¹A, 87:204–5.

12. The cod trade is "une branche de commerce plus precieuse pour l'Etat que tout l'or de Pérou puisqu'il ne peut pas former un seul matelot et qu'elle en forme plusieurs milliers par an." La chambre de commerce de Saint-Malo a MM. de Choiseul et Berryer, 8 juillet 1761, Quebec (Province) Archives, *Rapport de l'Archiviste*, p. 202. The whole nursery of seamen argument is put forth very well, albeit from the point of view of the British navy, by Graham, "Fisheries," pp. 24–32. Graham points out that the entire relationship hinges on the kinship of naval vessels to fishing and trading ships. Once specialization in sea craft becomes too great, experience aboard one sort of ship does not qualify as training for another. In the eighteenth century this process of specialization was but little advanced.

13. See the Raudot-Pontchartrain correspondence cited in notes 3 and 4. An anonymous memoir of 1717 envisioned Louisbourg as a base for commerce raiding undertaken by the French navy, citing: "les avantages considerables que la situation de cette ile présente pour inquiéter particulièrement les Anglais et interrompre toutes les branches de leur navigation en temps de guerre. Pour cet effet il ne faudrait qu'une frégate d'environ 36 à 40 canons, avec une équipage de 350 hommes, qui servirait également à protéger le commerce et la pêche des Français et à faire des course sur les Anglais." AC, C¹¹B, 2:313–14. In recounting the advantages of Louisbourg's geographical position, another memoir of 1734 adds: "Ces avantages du Port de Louisbourg attireront vrai Semblement nombre de Corsaires qui feront beaucoup de tort au commerce des Anglois." Mémoire sur l'état actuel des Colonies françaises, avril 1734, MP OSU, Lot 2.

14. It had the great disadvantage of a sandbar across its harbor mouth: ships of more than 150 tons could not pass, and no more than forty ships could fit in at once. Minutes de Conseil, 1713, AC, C[11]B, 1:243; Clark, *Acadia*, p. 270; Crowley, "Beginnings," pp. 56–60; Ministre à Costebelle et Soubras, 17 mars 1715, AC, F[3], 50:28.

15. Soldiers and engineers preferred Port Dauphin. Clark, *Acadia*, p. 270; Crowley, "Beginnings," pp. 56–60; Mémoire de 4 juin 1715, AC, F[3], 50:36–44; Ministre à l'Hermitte, 26 janvier 1714, AC, F[3], 50:11; Mémoire sur l'Establissement de l'isle du Cap Breton, AC, C[11]B, 1:17–18.

16. The decision, taken first in 1714, was reversed in favor of Port Dauphin in 1715, then made finally in favor of Louisbourg in 1718. In addition to material cited in notes 14 and 15, see Pontchartrain à d'Artaguette, 6 mars 1713, AC, F[3], 50:3; Pontchartrain à l'Abbé Goulin, 29 mars 1713, AC, C[11]B, 1:13–21, 68–71, 427–97, 650–70. Another drawback of Port Dauphin was the ridge of hills to the west which blocked the breezes necessary for the drying of fish.

17. The Conseil de la Marine's reservations about extensive fortification lasted only as long as peace remained in doubt. Memoires du Conseil, 13 novembre 1717, AC, C[11]B, 2:163–89.

18. Mémoire du Roy à Vaudreuil et Robert, 30 mai 1724, AC, B, 47:92–117. Maurepas à Beauharnois, 14 mai 1728, AC, B, 52–1, 499–502. Here Maurepas claims Louisbourg is the rampart of Canada, and that Quebec should therefore help supply Ile Royale.

19. This passage appears in Maurepas's *Mémoires*, 3:108. The mémoire seems to have the king as its intended audience.

20. "Monsieur le General m'à dit plusieurs fois qu'on croyait en France que le Port de Louisbourg était le boulevard de ce pays." Mémoire sur le Port de Louisbourg et le moyens pour empêcher les Anglais d'y faire aucune entreprise, et l'expédition qu'ils voulaient faire à Quebec, 1738, AC, C[11]B, 20:300–302.

21. "Toute l'armée d'Angleterre pourroir venir à Quebec qu'on ne scauroit rein à l'Isle Royalle et quand mesme on le scauroit en ce pays que pourroient-ils faire?" Beauharnois à Maurepas, 13 octobre 1727, AC, C[11]E, 10:100.

22. Mémoire sur l'état actuel des Colonies françaises, avril 1734, MP OSU, Lot 2.

23. Mémoire sur le Port de Louisbourg et les moyens pour empêcher les Anglais d'y faire aucune entreprise, 1738, AC, C[11]B, 20:300–324: "A l'égard de Louisbourg, une armée navale peut entrer dans le fleuve St. Laurent pour venir à Québec par l'entrée ordinaire, car Louisbourg pour les empêcher d'entrer dans la fleuve il faudrait tenir une escadre à croiser dans les passages entre l'Ile Terre-Neuve et l'Ile Royale."

24. Verrier à Maurepas 2 août 1724, AC, C ^{11}B, 7 : 135: "la plus forte place de toute l'Amérique." The fortifications were far from finished at this time.

25. Maurepas à St.-Ovide et Le Normant de Mezy, 2 juin 1733, AC, B, 59 : 532.

26. Maurepas à de Forant, 12 août 1739, AC, B, 68 : 381.

27. Mémoire pour mettre les premiers fondments de l'Etablissement proposé dans l'Isle du Cap Breton, 1708, NLSC Ayer Manuscripts, 293. The author here claims that one day a French settlement on Cape Breton could seize Boston.

28. St.-Ovide à [?] octobre 1734. Mémoire sur l'état actuel des colonies françaises, avril 1734, MP OSU, Lot 2: "il sera aisé de reprendre l'Accadie."

29. Maurepas à DuQuesnel, 18 septembre 1740, AC, B, 70 : 429–30.

30. As early as 1722 the King complained of Louisbourg's high cost and scant results, Mémoire du Roi, 1722, AC, C ^{11}B, 6 : 32.

31. In 1733 Maurepas specifically argued that Louisbourg was worth the 1,200,000 livres spent on it so far because the fortifications contributed to the defense of Canada. The King appears to have accepted such reasoning. Mémoire du Roy à Beauharnois et Hocquart, 12 mai 1733, AC, B, 59 – 1 : 470 – 80.

32. Mémoire du Drucourt, 10 novembre 1758, AC, F ^{3}, 60 : 529 – 38. Here readers are instructed that Louisbourg should no longer be considered a stronghold, since its capture owed not to lapses on the part of the defenders but to the inability of the French to relieve the beleaguered fortress. Drucourt, at least, understood that until the French navy could match the British in the North Atlantic, Louisbourg remained highly vulnerable to a British siege.

33. Both the British and Spanish were well aware of British naval superiority in the Caribbean and its consequences. See Instructions to Vice-Admiral Hosier, 29 September 1726, BL, AM 33028, fol. 59–66. Cagigal de la Vega al Rey, 31 agosto 1743, AGI, SD 364. The Spanish navy in the Caribbean could expect little help from the French. The French navy maintained no permanent force in the West Indies, and expeditions from France suffered from such problems as months of unrelieved disease and supply shortages in long crossings. For the French navy in the Caribbean, see Pares, *War and Trade*, pp. 280–81.

34. By the eighteenth century a large proportion of each fleet belonged to French merchants based in Seville or Cadiz, so the French no longer tried to seize on the high seas what would be theirs upon arrival in Spain. This contributed considerably to the Franco-Spanish entente which lasted until the French Revolution. Mémoire pour faire connoitre la situation actuelle de commerce, 1745, MPCU, Lot 21, Item 9.041. According to this document, French traders owned two-thirds of the value of the *flota* and *galeones*. See Boisrouvray, "La nation française de Cadix," pp. 177–84; Sée, "Documents sur le commerce de Cadix."

35. On Veracruz, as well as the other fortified ports in the Caribbean, see An Account of the Havannah and other Principal Places Belonging to the Spaniards in the West Indies, BL, AM 32694, fol. 72–100.

36. Fernández Duro, Armada española, 6:217. Urrutia, Obras, 2:137 says the Armada de Barlovento shifted from Veracruz to Havana in 1737. Also, see note 98.

37. Patiño a Marqués Casafuerte, 8 diciembre 1730, AGS, Marina, 392; Dionisio Martinez de la Vega a Patiño, 25 agosto 1728, AGI, SD 380.

38. Narrative of Intelligence which the Army were furnished with, BL, AM 23678, fol. 7. This was written by Charles Knowles, who had been in Havana in 1756. The second safe port in the Caribbean was Cartagena.

39. Wager to Vernon, 10 June 1730, Vernon-Wager Manuscripts, Library of Congress. For the defensive cast of mind of the British at Jamaica: Pares, War and Trade, pp. 230–38, 302–3. These considerations came to bear only during wartime, and only when the French as well as the Spanish were at war with Britain. Knowles in 1748 felt Jamaica safe enough without the protection of his squadron, and thus he cruised off Havana to intercept the treasure. In 1744, when an earlier treasure fleet successfully made it to Spain, the British, aware of French forces upwind of Jamaica, felt unable to depart far enough downwind of Jamaica to menace the Veracruz-Havana route.

40. Instrucción para el Capitan del Puerto de la Habana, AMN, MS 1219 Colección Guillen, doc. 15, 17 marzo 1756, fol. 45–51.

41. Arcos Moreno a Ensenada, 26 octubre 1747, AGI, SD 1202. Jamaica's population in 1730 was 83,008, but slaves of dubious loyalty outnumbered the militia by about forty to one. Wells, Population of the British Colonies, pp. 196, 207–8.

42. San Lorenzo a Arcos Moreno, 11 mayo 1748, AGI, SD 1202. The retaking of Acadia from Louisbourg held a like appeal for the French king.

43. For this chapter in the history of Anglo-Spanish conflict see Lanning, Diplomatic History of Georgia, esp. pp. 55–65, 75–76, 82–83, 87.

44. Razon de las consultas executadas por la junta, y port el ex^{mo} s^{or} Conde del Montijo sobre dependencias de la Georgia (c. 1739), AGI, IG 1602.

45. Consejo de Indias, AHN Estado 2318 (Papeles varios) (c. 1737 or 1738); Güemes y Horcasitas a Quintana, 12 octubre 1739, AGI, SD 1201.

46. Dionisio Martínez de la Vega a Consejo de Indias, 23 agosto 1737, AHN Estado 2318. Veracruz, and Mexico in general, was charged with assisting in the defense of Havana if necessary, just as Havana was charged with assisting in the defense of Florida and Apalache. [?] a Real Audiencia de Mexico, 9 enero 1742, AGI, SD 2106.

47. Cagigal de la Vega [?], 6 noviembre 1760, AGI, SD 2113; Alfonso Fernández de Heredia a Eslava, 12 junio 1756, AGS Guerra (Moderna) 3616.

48. Nicholas Lawes to Board of Trade, 9 July 1722, PRO CO 137/14.

49. Consulta de Consejo de Indias, 19 avril 1719, AGI, SD 1643. They paid up to sixty pesos a year.

50. Informe de los Officiales Reales de la Habana, 7 octubre 1761, AGI, SD 1643; Informe de los Contadores de las Islas de Barlovento, 24 octubre 1764, AGI, SD 1632. This figure covers the period from 9 September 1756 to 28 December 1761, and represents the cost to all the *presidios*, not just Havana and Santiago de Cuba. The proportion borne by Cuba equals perhaps one-third or one-fourth of this total.

51. Informe de Manuel Martínez Carbajal a Patiño, 31 enero 1732, AGI, SD 2167.

52. For the smuggling activity of the south coast versus the north, Matheo Lopez al Rey, 28 diciembre 1719, AGI, SD 2026.

53. Ships bound for Barbados or Antigua first and Jamaica second would not, however, use the Windward Passage, but would sail out into the Atlantic and approach the Caribbean from the east. They avoided Spanish privateers this way, while taking advantage of the trade wind, but ran the risk of meeting French privateers based at Martinique or Guadeloupe.

54. Real Orden de 22 febrero 1746, AGI, SD 391.

55. Cagigal de la Vega al Rey, 22 enero 1747, AGI, SD 366.

56. Quintana (?) a Cagigal de la Vega, 24 diciembre 1741, AGI, SD 2106; Güemes y Horcasitas a Quintana, 10 octubre 1741, AGI, SD 1201; Güemes y Horcasitas a Marques Torrenueba, 8 agosto 1738, AGI, SD 1201.

57. Somodevilla (the future Marqués de Ensenada) a Pizarro, 19 abril 1738, AGI, IG 2556.

58. Havana's port was "one of the most important in America," AMN, MS 1219, Coleccion Guillén, doc. 15, 17 marzo 1756, fol. 45. It was "el punto zentrico, de adonde deven salir las lineas, que preserven, las otras partes de estas Americas," and it was "el Alma, que a todos los miembros de este Cuerpo Americano debe repartir," Güemes y Horcasitas a Conde del Montijo, 29 febrero 1742, AGI, SD 386. It was the "llave de la América, y antemuro de los dos Reynos," Berezal al Rey, n.d. (c. 1759), AGI, SD 1504. It was "la Voya mas preciosa que tiene le Corona en las Americas," Güemes y Horcasitas a Carvajal, 2 febrero 1747, AHN, Estado 2320. Güemes, a governor at Havana and later Viceroy of New Spain, led all competitors in hyperbolic exaggeration of Havana's potential, but his ideas never gained currency within the Spanish bureaucracy the way Maurepas's did within the French.

59. Mahan, *Mahan on Naval Warfare*, p. 57.

60. Estat des vaisseaux et frégates qui doivent estre armés en 1741, octobre, 1740, MPCU, Lot 42, Item 6.052. This memoir, written by Pellerin, Maurepas's secretary, explains that Louisbourg normally got two vessels, a sixty-four and a forty-two, at a total cost of 408,443 livres annually. The

ships stayed until November when they returned to France. Four ships went to the Leewards, two to the Windwards, two to India, one to the Guinea Coast, two to Constantinople, fifteen to the English Channel, while twenty were reserved for expeditions, which in peacetime meant either staying in French ports or convoy duty.

61. Le Normant de Mezy au Ministre, 7 août 1722, AC, C ^{11}B, 6:52; Bourville au Ministre, 13 novembre 1723, AC, C ^{11}B, 6:283; Minutes de Conseil, mai 1722, AC, C ^{11}B, 6:23; Le Normant de Mezy au Ministre, 23 novembre 1723, AC, C ^{11}B, 6:233.

62. The Canceau incident concerned the use of the shore around present-day Port Hawkesbury, N.S. for drying fish. New Englanders destroyed a tiny French establishment there after a brief skirmish. Minutes de Conseil 1723, AC, C ^{11}B, 6:144.

63. [Bollan], *Advantage of Cape Breton*, p. 84; The State of the Several Fisheries before the present War, n.d. (1763), BL, AM 38366, fol. 84–85.

64. BNP 5399, numéro 2550–51 has 7,500 to 10,500 as the total of French cod fishermen (cited in La Morandrière, *La pêche française de la morue*, p. 42). Maurepas's 1730 mémoire put the total at 7,489, but it grew in later years. Mémoire pour faire connoître la situation actuelle de commerce (1745), MPCU, Lot 21, Item 9.041, has 10,000 fishermen for 1744. O'Heguerty, '*Remarques*, p. 117, says 15,000 to 16,000 French sailors worked in the fishery and attendant trade. Tramond, *Manuel d'histoire maritime*, p. 534, has 50,000 for 1719, certainly wide of the mark.

65. In 1718, 3,589 men; in 1719, 3,441 men: Minutes de Conseil, AC, C ^{11}B, 4:13; St.-Ovide au Conseil, 29 novembre 1719, AC, C ^{11}B, 4:223. Houston, *Memoirs*, p. 371, has 3,400 for 1744; see *ibid.*, pp. 373–76 for Louisbourg's protective services.

66. McLennan, *Louisbourg: Foundation to Fall*, p. 118.

67. Rawlyk, *Nova Scotia's Massachusetts*, p. 138.

68. Amirauté et Conseil des Prises, AN, G ^{5}, 253, Carton 258. Cf. Bigot à Maurepas, 12 octobre 1744, AC, C ^{11}B, 26:103, which records only twenty-eight.

69. AC, C ^{11}B, 27:116. McLennan to the contrary, most were fishing vessels, not traders.

70. This is the opinion of Rawlyk, *Nova Scotia's Massachusetts*, p. 139. For particulars: Chapin, *Rhode Island Privateers*, pp. 42–63.

71. Etat de provisionnement nécessaire pour la défense des colonies françaises, avril 1734, MP OSU, Lot 2–1. France actually had five fewer gunpowder mills in 1745 than in 1713; presumably powder had grown more scarce in France during the peaceful reign of Cardinal Fleury. If scarce in France, it stands to reason that powder was exceedingly short in the colonies. Mémoire sur l'établissement d'un moulin à poudre (c. 1754), MP OSU, Lot 71–2.

72. Privateering during peacetime was officially known as piracy, and govern-

ments had the civility not to encourage it openly, but showed little inclination to discourage it. When merchants pursued restitution through legal channels, the affair normally took years to resolve and frequently provided no satisfaction to the injured party. Eighteenth-century statesmen considered commerce a form of international competition; those who undertook to hinder a state's rival could expect at least tacit approval from their own government.

73. Machault à Drucourt et Prévost, 20 mai 1756, AC, B, 103 : 189–90.

74. "He viewed the capture of Louisbourg in 1756 . . . not in terms of conquest but of codfish," Andrews, "Anglo-French Commercial Rivalry," p. 547. See Lincoln, *Correspondence of William Shirley*, 1 : 162–63, William Shirley to the Duke of Newcastle, 14 January 1745. Admittedly Shirley's motives were not so simple—he had a genuine concern for expanding British power in general at the expense of the French. See Rawlyk, *Nova Scotia's Massachusetts*, chapter 8; McLennan, *Louisbourg: Foundation to Fall*, p. 134; Schutz, *William Shirley*, pp. 80–104. Shirley's close friend, Judge Robert Auchmuty, explained how Massachusetts could take over the cod fishery: The Importance of Cape Breton to the Brittish Nation, 1744, BL, AM, 32702, fol. 320.

75. Parkman, *Old Regime*, p. 467: "Louisbourg, the strongest fort in America." Fiske, *New France and New England*, p. 225: "It blocked the way to any English ascent of the St. Lawrence," and p. 226: "one of the strongest places in the world, scarcely surpassed by Quebec or Gibraltar." McLennan, *Louisbourg: Foundation to Fall*, p. 2: "The value of Cape Breton, as a naval base to protect Canada . . . is so obvious that it need not be more than mentioned." Stanley, *New France*, p. 62: "its military and strategic role as the guardian of the St. Lawrence and the key to New France." Parry, *Trade and Dominion*, p. 101: "a defence for Canada and a threat to New England," and p. 113: "Louisbourg guarded the St. Lawrence, and served also as base for a considerable privateer fleet." Lloyd, *Atlas of Maritime History*, p. 38, calls Louisbourg the "Key to the St. Lawrence." Wilson prefers "the key to Canada," *England's Apprenticeship*, p. 284. Moore, "Maritime Economy," p. 45: "Isle Royale was intended to protect the entrance to the St. Lawrence system." Moore, whose work on the trade of Ile Royale is the best to date, failed to point out that its principal role was not military. Some French authors have exhibited the same uncritical acceptance. See Tramond, *Manuel d'histoire maritime*, p. 369: "Louis XIV ordonnait de fortifier Louisbourg, pour assurer la securité du Canada." Lacour-Gayet, *Marine militaire*, p. 359: "Louisbourg était la clef même du Saint-Laurent et de Québec."

76. To my knowledge only two authors have pointed out that without a squadron Louisbourg had virtually no strategic value: Dorn, *Competition*, p. 166; and Graham, *Empire of the North Atlantic*, p. 120; ibid., p. 154: "Defensively Louisbourg remained of little more than symbolic value."

77. Parkman was insensitive to sea power, according to one who should know.

See Morison's Introduction to Parkman's *Montcalm and Wolfe*, p. 10. Mahan, Parkman's contemporary, never expressed himself in writing on the subject of Louisbourg, but he certainly knew its limitations in the absence of sea power.

78. Montcalm-Gozon, *Journal*, 7:446.
79. See Fortier, "Fortifications at Louisbourg," pp. 17–31.
80. Vauban, *Manual of Siegecraft*, p. 12.
81. Cf. Bougaineville, *Adventure in the Wilderness*, p. 218. According to this soldier-mathematician, Louisbourg surrendered prematurely in 1745 because the Intendant and the merchants wanted to save their property from further bombardment.
82. Raynal, *Trade in the East and West Indies*, 5:190, incorrectly puts the cost at 30 million livres.
83. Minutes de Conseil, 24 janvier 1716, AC, C¹¹B, 4:66; Etat des ouvrages qu'on propose, 1726, AC, C¹¹B, 7:334. Warehouse and home construction distracted labor, largely soldiers, provoking an ordinance to remedy the situation: Ordonnance, 8 avril 1721, AC, B, 44–2:551–52. Some even blamed the proliferation of cabarets for distracting the labor force: Mémoire du Roy a St.-Ovide et Le Normant de Mezy, juin 1721, AC, B, 44–2:557.
84. Pontchartrain à Beauharnois, 15 janvier 1714, AC, B, 36–2:547; 17 mars 1716, AC, B, 38–2:547; Garner au Ministre, 10 novembre 1725, AC, C¹¹B, 7:342; Boucher au Ministre (?), 1 novembre 1723, AC, C¹¹B, 6:320–22.
85. Mémoire 1718 (non signé), AC, C¹¹B, 3:479–85; Minutes du Conseil, 4 janvier 1719, AC, C¹¹B, 4:66–68.
86. Frégault, *Bigot*, 1:79; *Collection des manuscrits*, 3:468 (anonymous mémoire); Loture, "La siège de Louisbourg en 1758," pp. 52–70.
87. Bigot au Ministre, 1 août 1745, AC, F³, 50:368–85.
88. *Collection des manuscrits*, 3:468.
89. Roma au Ministre, 11 mars 1750, AC, C¹¹B, 29:366.
90. On 1745: Richmond, *Navy*, 2:214. On 1758: *Collection des manuscrits*, 3:485, anonymous mémoire.
91. Montcalm-Gozon, *Journal*, 7:446.
92. Fifteen ships and 12,000 men sailed under Admiral Hovenden Walker but were shipwrecked in the St. Lawrence. See Graham, *Walker Expedition*. Sir William Phips had tried in 1690 but retreated from the October cold.
93. Considerations Offered Upon A Scheme for Attacking Louisbourg and Quebec, Minutes, 13 March 1757, Chatham Papers, printed in Pargellis, *Military Affairs*, pp. 294–98. Bower contends that Louisbourg's reputation and eighteenth-century habits prevented the British from bypassing the fortress in 1745, "Louisbourg, The Chimera," pp. 33–34.
94. For a treatment of the close-watch system see Graham, "Naval Defense," pp. 95–110.

95. 4 October 1744, BL, AM, 32702, fol. 320; Mémoire sur le Cap Breton (1759), BL, AM, 38332; *Great Importance of Cape Breton*, p. 70.
96. Gwyn, *Royal Navy and North America: The Warren Papers*, p. vii.
97. Minutes of Council of War held on Board HMS Bredak, 9 March 1726, BL, AM, 33028, fol. 117; Diario que haze el ingeniero Don Antonio de Arredondo durante la guerra (1739), AGI, SD 385.
98. The Armada de Barlovento had up to thirteen *navíos* in the seventeenth century, but in the eighteenth normally had only three. The squadron was created in 1595, disbanded in 1610, but started up again in 1635. In 1648 it joined the ocean fleet, but in 1677 separated again. In 1737, it moved to Havana from Veracruz. For its history, duties, and size: Satisfazion de una orden de Su Majestad, 22 marzo 1718, AGI, IG 2556; Spinola a Patiño, 15 febrero 1731, AGS, Marina 392; Montalvo a Somedevilla, 6 noviembre 1739, AGS, Marina 395; Idea geográfica, histórica, y política de la isla de Cuba, fols. 30–33, BL, AM, 17629; Urrutia, *Obras*, 2:137; Rodríguez Villa, *Patiño y Campillo*, p. 189; and Ogelsby, "Spain's Havana Squadron," pp. 473–88.
99. Ogelsby, "Spain's Havana Squadron," pp. 486–87; Richmond, *Navy*, 3:136–42; Testimonios de autos, 1748 (6 quadernos), AGI, SD 1204; Cagigal de la Vega a Ensenada, 26 octubre 1748, AGI, SD 1204; Urrutia, *Obras*, 2:145.
100. Ogelsby, "Spain's Havana Squadron," p. 479. These fleets are not, however, mentioned in Walker, *Spanish Politics and Imperial Trade*; or García-Baquero, *Cádiz y el Atlántico*.
101. Richmond, *Navy*, 3:147–50.
102. See, for example: Proyecto para impedir a los Ingleses Comerciar sin que sean obligados de tener grandes Comboies (1741), PLMP, Montemar Papers, Group VIII, Sobre Ynglaterra. These papers, not yet fully catalogued, were shown to me through the courtesy of Leyte-Vidal of Perkins Library.
103. The Whole Proceedings of Capt. Dennis' Expedition to the Governor of Havana, 1718, PRO CO 137/13; Lawes to the Board of Trade, 28 December 1718, PRO CO 137/13.
104. In 1741 Vernon and his troops from the Cartagena expedition tried to take Santiago de Cuba by land after landing at Guantánamo. In 1748 Knowles tried to force the harbor at Santiago de Cuba with the express purpose of clearing out a privateers' nest. Richmond, *Navy*, 3:147; Fayle, "Deflection of Strategy," pp. 286–87; Diario de lo occurido en Santiago de Cuba, 1741, AGI, SD 364; Portell Vila, *Historia de Cuba y sus relaciones con Estados Unidos y España*, 1:52–53.
105. Relazion de la Presas hechas a los Enemigos Ingleses por los Corsarios de este Puerto de Santiago de Cuba, AGI, SD 364. Four were sailing to or from Rodeilon (Rhode Island), five more to or from other New England

ports, one from Glasgow, and two from Virginia. On board were horses and food on the southbound ships, Spanish coin, Cuban tobacco, and sugar on the northbound vessels. On the Jamaica-New England trade, see Pares, *Yankees and Creoles*, pp. 37–138. These prizes exclude those made by *guarda costas* in the same months. *Guarda costa* seizures tended to include more European and fewer North American goods. Guerra et al., *Historia de la nación cubana*, 2:250. In this era Cuba floated more than thirty *guarda costas*. See Fernández Duro, *Armada española*, 6:245.

106. Marrero, *Cuba*, 6:111.

107. Cagigal de la Vega al Rey, 31 agosto 1743, AGI, SD 364.

108. Cargo (de la Real Compañía de la Havana) por . . . las presas . . . de la Compañía Armadas en corso, 1754, AGI, Ultramar 894. Los justificantes de las perdidas de embarcaciones . . . en tiempo del segundo quinquennio, AGI, Ultramar 986. In the same period the Spanish lost 211,994 pesos in goods while the British lost 75,875 pesos.

109. Cagigal al Rey, 31 agosto 1743, AGI, SD 364. Admiral Vernon suggested this practice in 1740. Vernon to Captain Windham, January 1740, printed in Ranft, *Vernon Papers*, p. 54.

110. On St. Augustine's military history: TePaske, *Governorship*, pp. 108–58.

111. Few colonial militia units served far from home in the eighteenth century; that Cubans fought in Apalache and Georgia shows the degree to which the Spanish considered Havana responsible for the protection of the northern frontier with the British. Andres de Pes a Grimaldo, 11 junio 1720, AHN, Estado 2331. Junta General de la Real Compañía de la Habana, 11 diciembre 1760, AGI, IG 1745. For the *situado* of Florida and Apalache: AGI, Contaduría 1169. For the 1742 expedition: Ivers, *British Drums*, pp. 151–73; Urrutia, *Obras*, 2:40–42; Béthencourt Massieu, "Felipe V y la Florida," pp. 95–123; and "The Spanish Official Account of the Attack on the Colony of Georgia," *Collections of the Georgia Historical Society*, pp. 1–110.

112. TePaske, *Governorship*, pp. 96–100.

113. Despacho del Rey, 16 diciembre 1741, AGI Contratación 5004.

114. Quenta . . . de . . . la . . . fortificazion de Florida y Apalache, AGI Contaduría 1169; Relacion . . . del caudal destinado a la fabrica del Fuerte de Apalache, AGI Contaduría 1169; and TePaske, *Governorship*, p. 155.

115. The Havana Company managed to free itself from the Florida obligation in its 1740 contract and the *situado* system returned. The *situado* figures run as follows:

1747	184,965 pesos	
1749	193,219	
1749	193,219	
1750	122,525	
1752	126,192	
1753	122,246	

1754	116,652
1755	54,985
1756	64,238
1757	56,996
1759	57,023

Source: AGI, SD 2108–2112. Each *legajo* (bundle of documents) has several *estados* or *notas* concerning the distribution of treasure to the various *presidios* of the West Indies.

116. According to figures provided by the Company, Florida cost about 260,000 pesos annually in the early 1740s. In 1743 alone the Company had to provide 25,000 *arrobas* of flour, 4,000 of beef, 2,000 of pork. By the end of the decade, the Company spent only about 22,000 pesos annually on Florida. Relazion, de 14 octubre 1750, AGI, SD 2010; Aróstegui a Ensenada, 6 octubre 1744, AGI, SD 2004; Instrucción para los Interesados de la Real Compañia de la Habana, marzo 1757, AGI, SD 2014.

117. Cagigal a Su Magestad, 21 avril 1740, AGI, SD 1203. The news of Vernon's arrival at Cartagena left Havana seven months later, Cagigal a S.M., 21 noviembre 1740, AGI, SD 1203.

118. Arcos Moreno al Rey, 14 avril 1748, AGI, SD 366; Cagigal al Rey, 24 avril 1748, AGI, SD 366. In a margin note on this latter letter a clerk noted that the Consejo de Indias was pleased with the prompt notice Cuba gave of British movements. The note is dated 8 agosto 1748.

119. Quintana a Blas de Lezo, 27 agosto 1739, AGI, IG 2556.

120. Despacho de Consejo, 3 julio 1742, AGI, SD 343; Consulta de Consejo, 11 agosto 1728, AGI, SD 340.

121. Mapas y papeles de Barthólome Tendall Cuervo, AGI, SD 2015; Cagigal de la Vega al Rey, 31 agosto 1743, AGI, SD 364; Somodevilla a Pizarro, 19 abril 1738, AGI, IG 2556.

122. Idea geográfica, histórica, y política de la Isla de Cuba, BL, AM 17629, fol. 32; Arrate, *Llave del Nuevo Mundo*, pp. 68–72; Hoffman, *Spanish Crown*, passim; Andrews, *Spanish Caribbean*, passim; Segre, "Significación de Cuba en la evolución de las fortificaciones," pp. 25–37.

123. The inspiration apparently came from an unfavorable French report of 1725 on the state of Havana's defenses. Consulta de Consejo, 5 noviembre 1725, AGI, SD 325. On military engineers: Relacion General de los Ingenieros . . . en actual servicio . . . en . . . America (Abril 1737), AGI, IG 1905. Of twenty-one engineers in Spanish America, four were at Havana, including the highest ranking, a colonel named Bruno Cavallero. Most of the names are French or Italian. These engineers were the best in Spain, Patiño a Marqués Castelan, 30 julio 1730, AGI, IG 1905. See also Marzal Martínez, "Fortificaciones de Cartagena," pp. 29–41; and Pérez Guzmán, "Documentos," pp. 181–200.

124. Testimonio de las diligencias hechas sobre los pregones y Remate de 21,605

cantos (1758), AGI, SD 420. The Whole Proceedings of Capt. Dennis's Expedition to the Governor of the Havana (1718), PRO, CO 137/13.

125. This figure is a total based on the accounts in AGI Contaduría 1167 and 1169. By 1762 it yielded 32,000 pesos annually, see Blanck, *Papeles*, p. 108. Up to 1740 the walls of Havana had cost three million pesos over two hundred years according to Pezuela, *Diccionario*, 3 : 59. In 1741 expenditure proceeded at the rate of almost 3,000 pesos a month, slightly more than the *sisa de muralla* produced. Estado General de los fondos (1741), PLMP, Group III, Ynstruir al Ministerio de Guerra, no. 4.

126. Despacho de Consejo, 14 abril 1725, AGI, SD 339.

127. The British in Jamaica faced the same situation: planters would pay for forts but not for ships. Trelawny to the Board of Trade, 1 June 1743, PRO CO 137/23. See also Pares, *War and Trade*, p. 240. Foisting naval costs on colonies has always proved difficult, as the British discovered anew in the early twentieth century.

128. Trelawny to the Board of Trade, 17 July 1751, PRO CO 137/25. In 1732 the Consejo de Indias had to adjudicate a squabble between engineers who wanted to extend a wall and José Pizarro, the commander of the Barlovento Squadron, who felt the wall would prejudice careening wharfs. The Consejo decided in favor of the engineers. In general they chose to favor fortifications over ships. Minuta de Consejo de Indias, n.d. (1732), AHN, Estado 2333. English historians thought fortifications of little value, too, Pares, *War and Trade*, p. 240.

129. Minutes of a Council of War, 28 October 1741, BL, AM 22680, fol. 9. An Account of the Havana and other Principal Places in the West Indies, 14 April 1740, BL, AM 32694, fol. 75.

130. The Havana garrison grew faster than the Havana population:

Year	Men	Source
1732	733	Extracto de la revista . . . guarnicion de aquella plaza, 6 junio 1732, AGI, SD 2104
1737	1,506	Extracto de revista . . . de infanteria, diciembre, 1737, AGI, SD 2105
1741	1,167	Relazion de los offiz[s], Sarg[s], y Sold[s] que tienen en esta plaza, 6 agosto 1741, AGI, SD 1201
1742	2,087	Relazion de diciembre 1742, AGI, SD 2107
1743	2,113	Relazion de diciembre 1743, AGI, SD 2107
1747	1,470	Extracto de revista que se la paso del Batallon Infanteria, diciembre 1747, AGI, SD 2093
1756	1,663	Estado de la Revista . . . del Reximento de Infanteria de la Havana; Estado de la Revista . . . de dragones de la Havana, 1756, AGI, SD 2111
1759	2,040	Estado . . . de que se compone este reximento, AGI, SD 2112

1763   2,899   Extracto de Revista . . . de Julio 1763, AGI, SD 2093

131. On the militia, Milizias, julio 1740, AGI, SD 1201; Revista de Inspección de la milicias de la Plaza de la Habana, AGI, SD 2112. Arrate, *Llave del Nuevo Mundo*, pp. 68–69, has somewhat higher figures for the Havana militia in 1737.

132. The garrison at Santiago de Cuba:

Year	Men	Source
1738	305	AGI, SD 2105
1748	347	Extracto de la revista, 27 septiembre 1748, AGI, SD 2108
1751	372	Extracto . . . de revista de inspección, AGI, SD 2108
1754	263	Estado de tropa, 31 julio 1751, AGI, SD 2110
1758	260	Resumen general . . . de Santiago de Cuba, AGI, SD 2112

On the militia at Santiago: Estado de tropa de milicias, 16 marzo 1759, AGI, SD 1643; Estado revista que paso a las companias de Milicias, 1754, AGI, SD 2111. These fluctuations represent the number of sick, rather than changes in distribution of forces.

133. Reglamento para la Guarnicion de la Habana, 1719, AGI, SD 2104; Reglamento para la Guarnicion de la Habana, Castillos y Fuertes, 1753, AGI, SD 2110; O'Reilly a Squilace, 8 diciembre 1763, AGS, Hacienda 2342. Soldiers' wages were eleven pesos a month in Havana by 1762. Cuba, Archivo Nacional de Cuba, *Neuvos papeles*, p. 7. For garrison costs see the accounts in AGI Contaduría 1153, 1154, 1163, 1164, 1165A, 1165B.

134. O'Reilly a Squilace, 8 diciembre 1763, AGS, Hacienda 2342.

135. Providencias expedidas . . . para evitar la desercion, 8 mayo 1739, AGI, SD 2106. Relación de los soldados inutiles para poder continuar el real servicio, 29 agosto 1748, AGI, SD 2108. Those incapacitated averaged only twelve years of service.

136. An Account of the Havana, BL, AM 32694, fol. 73–74. Also: Klein, "Colored Militia," pp. 17–27. The militia were divided into white, mulatto, and black units, the majority always being white. See Deschamps Chapeaux, *Los batallones de pardos y morenos libres*, pp. 1–90; and Arrate, *Llave del Nuevo Mundo*, pp. 68–72.

137. Vernon to Newcastle, 23 January 1740, cited in Richmond, *Navy*, 1:44–45. At Cartagena in 1741 Vernon complained to General Wentworth that delay would allow fever to destroy the troops before they achieved their objective, Ranft, *Vernon Papers*, pp. 185–86.

138. BL, AM 23678, fol. 17.

139. Johnson, "Falkland's Islands," pp. 373–74.

140. *On Military Operations.*
141. AHN, Estado 2335 has Eslava's diary, as well as that of the Spanish naval commander Blas de Lezo and Antonio Urrutia. Fortescue, *Empire and the Army*, pp. 72–73; Torres a Villarias, 5 julio 1741, AHN, Estado 2321; Extracto de los particulares noticias, 29 agosto 1741, AHN, Estado 2321; see also Richmond, *Navy*, 1 : 125–30; and Lloyd and Coulter, *Medicine and the Navy*, pp. 101–7.
142. On the campaign see AGI, UM 169, which includes forty-four letters from the Spanish governor Juan de Prado; Prado's siege diary is printed in Pezuela, *Diccionario*, 3 : 27–51; an anonymous Spanish siege journal is in BL, AM 13974; a British engineer's journal is in BL, AM 23678. This and another British siege journal comprise Hale, *Capture of Havana*; documents on Prado's court-martial are printed in Valdés, *Historia*, pp. 166–252; various documents appear in Blanck, *Papeles*. A Spanish journal appears in Martínez Dalmau, *La política colonial y extranjera de los Reyes españoles*, pp. 65–101. Among published accounts I have consulted: Guiteras, *Historia de la conquista de la Habana*; Zapatero, *La guerra del Caribe en el siglo XVIII*, pp. 265–75; Urrutia, *Obras*, 2 : 151–61; Valdés, *Historia*, pp. 113–33; Pezuela, *Historia*, 2 : 428–529; Corbett, *England in the Seven Years' War*, 2 : 246–84; Hart, *Siege of Havana*; Syrett, "British Landing at Havana," pp. 325–31; and Syrett, "Introduction" to *Siege and Capture.*
143. Albemarle to Egremont, 7 October 1762, in Blanck, *Papeles*, pp. 92–93. New Englanders and Britons suffered alike. Of 110 men in Israel Putnam's company, 77 died at Havana. See Connecticut Historical Society, *Two Putnams*, pp. 49–53.
144. Valdés, *Historia*, pp. 117–18. Urrutia, *Obras*, 2 : 153 quotes the engineer Antonelli: "Será dueño de la plaza el que lo fuere de la Cabaña." Juan de Prado stated as much in his diary on 7 June; see Pezuela, *Diccionario*, 3 : 28. The governor was charged derelict in his duty for not properly defending La Cabaña. See the Dictamen Fiscal, Cargo Cuarto, in Valdés, *Historia*, pp. 230–34. This document is a summary of the charges against Prado. See also Syrett's introduction to *Siege and Capture*, pp. xxiii–xxiv. In 1763 the Spanish began a new fort atop La Cabaña.
145. Guerra et al., *Historia de la nación cubana*, 2 : 116.
146. Support for this idea comes from Coxe, *Memoirs*, 3 : 270: "Confiding in the strength of the place, and still more in the baneful nature of the climate, they defied an attack." Admittedly this is an Englishman writing fifty years after the fact. The decision to abandon effectively La Cabaña belonged to the *junta de guerra* (Council of War), not to Prado alone, although he later was made a scapegoat for the loss of Havana.
147. General return of officers, sergeants, drummers, rank and file killed, died by wounds, died by sickness, deserted and missing, 7 June to 18 October 1762, AA, HA 67: 894/B29. Pocock to Cleveland, 9 October 1762, PRO

Admiralty 1/237. Similar figures appear in Southey, *West Indies*, 2:356. According to some (e.g., Marrero, *Cuba*, 6:3), yellow fever killed 3,000 Spanish soldiers in the 1761 epidemic, a number larger than the Havana garrison.

148. Johnson, "Falkland's Islands," p. 374.
149. For instance, the case of Rear Admiral Francis Hosier's fleet of 1726–27, Lloyd and Coulter, *Medicine and the Navy*, pp. 97–100. An unusually large medical establishment may possibly have slowed British mortality at Havana. See Cantlie, *Army Medical Department*, 1:217–18.

Chapter 5

1. Maurepas's 1730 mémoire. Maurepas, *Mémoires*, 3:108: "le meilleur de tous les commerces."
2. For the characteristics of cod: Innis, *Cod Fisheries*, pp. 1–10; Loture, *Histoire de grand pêche*, p. 18; Jensen, *Cod*; and La Morandrière, *Histoire de la pêche française de la morue*, 1:1–3.
3. So says La Morandrière, *Histoire de la pêche française de la morue*, 1:1. This is borne out by Savary, *Dictionnaire universel de commerce*, 2:1414, who says about 132 cod make up a ton, meaning the average fish weighed about 7 kilograms.
4. See Borgstrom, *Fish as Food*, 2:283–84, 325, 341.
5. According to one writer, the Basques fished off American coasts from the fourteenth century. Claveria Arza, *Los vascos en el mar*, p. 264. They were certainly in business by the very early sixteenth century, Sauer, *Northern Mists*, pp. 3–69. Long-distance fishing in the North Atlantic reportedly dates from 1384 when a Dutchman perfected the art of salting herring. Baker, "Fishing Under Sail," pp. 41–43.
6. Innis, *Cod Fisheries*. For the early history see Judah, *North American Fisheries*; and Fernández Duro, *Disquiciones náuticas*, 6:273–427.
7. The following descriptive paragraphs are based on La Morandrière, *La pêche française de la morue*, pp. 13–17; McLennan, *Louisbourg*, pp. 219–20; Jacques Savary, *Dictionnaire universel de commerce*, 2:1411–25; Loture, *Histoire de grand pêche*, pp. 28–39 (this covers the sixteenth and seventeenth centuries only); Charlevoix, *Voyage to North America*, 1:73–79; Denys, *Coasts of North America*, pp. 257–340 (this book was first published in 1672); O'Heguerty, *Remarques*, pp. 95–123. The earliest treatment in English is Anthony Packhurst to Richard Hakluyt, 13 November 1578, in Hakluyt, *Principal Navigations*, Ser. 3, 9–16. The best discussion is La Morandrière, *Histoire de la pêche française de la morue*, 1:145–84. The best eighteenth-century discussion is Duhamel de Monceau, *Traité général des pêches*, vol. 1, chapter 2.

8. Between 1713 and 1758, 77.9 percent of fishing vessels departing French Basque ports left in February, March, and April. Turgeon, *Échanges Franco-Canadiennes"* (thesis), 1:31–32.

9. La Morandrière, *Histoire de la pêche française de la morue*, 1:41–42. O'Heguerty, *Remarques*, p. 95, says 100–150 tons. Jaupart, *Bayonne*, 1:375, says Basque *morutiers* (as codfishing vessels were called) averaged between 80 and 300 tons. This, however, probably includes vessels engaged in the dry fishery, which were often larger, since they had to carry laborers for shore operations. In 1729 the average *morutier* measured 87.8 tons according to Maurepas's 1730 mémoire.

10. A *morutier* carried a captain, a surgeon, and a chaplain, in addition to the crew, one of whom was a *mousse* (novice), along to learn the arts of navigation. All told, crews in 1729 averaged 25.3 men. Maurepas's 1730 mémoire. Nets were very rare until late in the century at Newfoundland and, I believe, unknown at Ile Royale. Turgeon, "Pour une histoire de la pêche," p. 311 n. 64. The best fishermen caught 350 to 400 cod in a day says Savary, *Dictionnaire universel de commerce*, 2:1413. In a fourteen-hour day, that amounts to a fish every two or three minutes.

11. The liver at this stage was placed in a separate barrel of salt water and allowed to disintegrate. The cod oil then rose to the surface, above the salt water, ready for market as "train oil" for lamps or for tanning hides.

12. Règlement, de 20 juin 1743, AC F³, 50:254–60. Today salt cod are at least 14–18 percent salt, usually more. Klaveren and Legendre, "Salted Cod," 3:140.

13. In 1717, 19 of 51 French *morutiers* (37 percent) came from Basque ports. In 1730, 24 of 60 (40 percent) were Basque. Between 20 percent and 27 percent of French fishing vessels were from Breton ports, notably St.-Mâlo. AC C¹¹B, 2:223; AC C¹¹B, 14:232. Arrest du Conseil de l'Etat, 20 juillet 1734, AC F³, 50:209: "la pêche de la morue . . . est le seul commerce de [St. Jean de Luz]." This town of 4,800 normally fit out up to 20 *morutiers*.

14. On colonial and European *chaloupes* (shallop or sloop in English; *sloep* in Dutch), see Baker, *Sloops and Shallops*, especially chapter 5.

15. The average *habitant-pescheur* owned two to three *chaloupes* and employed twelve to eighteen men. Moore, "Merchant Trade" (thesis), p. 106, Table 4.1.

16. Balcom, "Fishing."

17. On the autumn fishery see Mémoire sur les habitants de l'Isle Royale, 7 mars 1739, par Le Normant, AC, C¹¹B, 21:208ff. This is printed in Innis, *Select Documents,* pp. 92–96. This memoir also outlines the wages and profits of the *chaloupe* fishery.

18. Fog and rain destroyed 200,000 livres worth of cod in 1735, St.-Ovide au ministre, 14 août 1735, AC, C¹¹B, 17:25–26.

19. Mémoire [de Raudot] à M. le Comte de Pontchartrain, 30 novembre 1706, AC, C¹¹C, 8:38.

20. *Goelettes* first appear in Louisbourg correspondence in 1723. La Morandière, *Histoire de la pêche française de la morue*, 2:666–67 says *goelettes* weighed forty to sixty tons, and carried ten or eleven men. He suggests the design originated in Bermuda, but Turgeon, "Pour une histoire de la pêche," p. 312, argues for a French origin of the *goelette*.

21. On the wet fishery, Philip to the Board of Trade, 3 January 1719/20, PRO, CO 217/3. On the dry fishery: Lounsbury, *British Fishery*, pp. 245–309. Estimates quoted by Lounsbury, p. 311, suggest that the British dry fishery accounted for about 335,000 quintals of cod per year, the wet fishery about 45,000 in the 1730s, while at the same time the New England fishery brought in about 70,000 or 80,000 quintals. Innis, *Cod Fisheries*, p. 161, says the New England fishery in 1745 had diminished to 230,000 quintals.

22. For Basque involvement: Turgeon, "Echanges Franco-Canadiennes" (thesis), 1:42; Jaupart, *Bayonne*, 1:375. Norman and Breton sailors often took their catch straight to the Mediterranean—to Alicante or Marseilles. O'Heguerty, *Remarques*, p. 115. Many English fishermen did the same: Davis, *English Shipping*, p. 229.

23. These figures come from Uztáriz, *Theory*, pp. 366–67. At prevailing prices (4 pesos per quintal), this trade cost Spain 2,437,000 pesos annually. In Spain cod was commonly fed to the prison population and to sailors on long hauls; the clergy and a large share of the coastal communities also ate cod. McLachlan, *Old Spain*, p. 107; Juan and Ulloa, *Voyage à l'Amérique du Sud*, 2:50–51. In the 1920s, mules carried dried cod to the villages of the Sierra Nevada, a trade that was probably centuries old when reported in Brenan, *South from Granada*. Michell believes Iberian cod consumption grew after 1750: "European Fisheries," 5:183.

24. Reflections Concerning the Island of Cape Breton, 1763, BL AM 38336, fol. 114.

25. Maurepas's 1745 mémoire discusses this trade, as does "Reflections," cited in note 24. Mémoire à Pontchartrain, 30 novembre 1704, AC C¹¹C, 8:38–45; Masson, *Histoire du commerce français dans le Levant*, pp. 424–25; Turgeon, "Pour une histoire de la pêche," passim.

26. Maurepas's 1730 mémoire. O'Heguerty, *Remarques*, pp. 102–4. Parisians paid two livres per quintal, almost twice the Dieppe price.

27. Aykroyd, *Sugar*, p. 49. Debien, "La nourriture des esclaves sur les plantations des Antilles français," pp. 5–9.

28. According to a British estimate, the catch totalled 288,000 quintals: 144,000 went to the sugar islands. Questions and Answers relative to the State of the French and British fisheries at Newfoundland, 1762, PAC Hardwicke Papers, 35913, 48–50. Some say this took place in the context

of a triangle trade (Jensen, *Cod*, pp. 93–102), but the French cod trade was not so arranged.

29. Generally Cuba's cod came from Santo Domingo where there may have been a better market, and also occasionally from Jamaica. Cuban slaves rarely ate imported food in the eighteenth century, but *almojarifazgo* accounts in 1730 and 1743 show small cod imports. AGI, Contaduria 1181, 1183; Marrero, *Cuba*, 8:87; Morineau and Filippini, "Vie matérielle et comportements biologiques," pp. 1150–62.

30. Pontchartrain à Costebelle, 20 mars 1713, AC, B, 35–3:133–42. Pontchartrain à D'Artaguiette, 6 mars 1713, AC, F³, 50:3, in which he writes: "[le roi a] resolu de former un Etablissement à l'Isle de Cap Breton pour y établir une pêche sédentaire de Morue." Pontchartrain à Demaretz, 21 avril 1713, AC, F³, 50:6. Pontchartrain à l'Hermitte, 26 janvier 1714, AC, F³, 50:11: "ce n'est pas un établissement pour la culture des terres que l'on cherche à l'Isle Royalle mais un endroit pour y faire la pesche en sureté."

31. Charlevoix, *Histoire et description générale de la Nouvelle-France*, 3:397. Minutes de Conseil (n.d.) 1714, AC, C¹¹B, 1:99; Mémoire, 25 février 1715, AC, C¹¹B, 1–2:372–74, also printed in Innis, *Select Documents*, pp. 74–75. Crowley, "Beginnings," pp. 54, 60–63.

32. Mémoire à M. le comte Pontchartrain sur l'Etablissement d'une colonie à l'Isle du Cap Breton (n.d.), AC, C¹¹B, 1:269–80, also printed in McLennan, *Louisbourg: Foundation to Fall*, pp. 22–31. Mémoire sur les affaires présentes du Canada (n.d.) 1708(?), NLSC, Ayer 293.

33. Mémoire du Roi à de Foret et Bigot, 22 juin 1739, AC, B, 68:364: "La peche est la base et le fondement de tout le commerce qui se fait à Louisbourg." Mémoire du Roi à Raymond et Prevost, 24 avril 1751, AC, B, 93:223; Mémoire du Roi à Drucourt, 12 mai 1754, AC, B, 99:236.

34. Mémoire du 21 avril 1669, AC, C¹¹A, 125–1:95, also printed in Innis, *Select Documents*, p. 147.

35. Pontchartrain à Desmarets, 21 mai 1713, AC, B, 35–1:250–55; Pontchartrain à duc de Gramont, 19 septembre 1713, AC, B, 35–2:484–86; Pontchartrain à Costebelle, 22 mars 1714, AC, B, 36–7:51–74; Arrets du Conseil, 9 septembre 1713, AC, F³, 50:9.

36. Arrets du Conseil, 3 mai 1723, 17 mars 1733, 26 mars 1743, AC, F³, 50:200, 252; La Morandrière, *La pêche française de la morue*, pp. 56–57.

37. Minutes du Conseil, 27 mars 1718, AC, C¹¹B, 3:54.

38. Minutes de Conseil, 12 mai 1722, AC, C¹¹B, 6:21.

39. Ordonnance, 15 septembre 1721, AC, F³, 50:129; Minutes de Conseil, 5 mai 1722, AC, C¹¹B, 6:14; Ordonnance, 21 septembre 1724, AC, F³, 50:160; Règlement concernant l'exploitation de la pêche de la morue à l'Isle-Royale, 20 juin 1743, AC, F³, 50:254–59.

40. Minutes de Conseil, juillet 1721, AC, C¹¹B, 5:328; Ordonnance, 1 juillet 1721, AC, B, 44–2:555–56.

41. Minutes de Conseil, 10 avril 1717, AC, C¹¹B, 2:147–49; Minutes du Conseil, 1714, AC, C¹¹C, 15:69.

42. Pontchartrain à Demarets, 28 novembre 1714, AC, B, 36–4:170–73.

43. Arret du Roi, 29 janvier 1715, AC, F, 50:27; Pontchartrain à Costebelle, 4 juin 1715, AC, B, 37:382.

44. Ordonnance, 1 mai 1729, AC, F³, 50:187; Maurepas à Peletier, 17 mai 1729, AC, B, 53:40; Maurepas à St.-Ovide et Le Normant du Mezy, 21 juin 1729, AC, B, 53:613–14; Maurepas à Vivean, 21 juin 1729, AC, B, 53:48. The new low duty in 1729 was six livres per ton. The old one was six *sous* per barrel, according to Fauteux, *Essai sur l'industrie au Canada*, 1:23.

45. Maurepas à Le Normant du Mezy, 14 juin 1729, AC, B, 53:611; Rouillé à Desherbiers, 23 mai 1750, AC, B, 91:338.

46. Desherbiers au ministre, 5 novembre 1749, AC, C¹¹B, 28:81–82. Desherbiers wrote that the English had built barracks that could be heated only with coal. The French had in the past used wood. Francis, "Mines and Quarries"; Martell, "Early Coal Mining," pp. 156–72.

47. Le Normant du Mezy au ministre, 27 novembre 1724, AC, C¹¹B, 7:73; Agrain au Conseil, 12 janvier 1721, AC, C¹¹C, 15:162.

48. Davis, *English Shipping*, p. 68. Mémoire (non signé) c. 1743, MPCU, Lot 44, Item 8.004. This memoir suggests Canada and Louisiana as well as Louisbourg as places where the French might emulate the British and Spanish by establishing shipbuilding in the new world. On Quebec shipbuilding: Lunn, "Economic Development" (dissertation), pp. 244–53.

49. Mémoire, 1714, AC, C¹¹B, 1:449–50; see also AC, C¹¹B, 18:16; and AC, C¹¹B, 20:55–56.

50. Maurepas à St.-Ovide et Le Normant du Mezy, 27 juin 1732, AC, B, 57–2:776–81; Maurepas à Bigot, 17 mai 1741, AC, B, 72:444; Maurepas à Bigot, 15 juin 1742, AC, B, 74:588.

51. Pontchartrain à Gaulin, 29 mars 1713, AC, B, 35:33; Maurepas à St.-Ovide et Le Normant du Mezy, 15 mai 1736, AC, B, 64:488; Maurepas à Bigot et de Foret, 22 juin 1739, AC, B, 68:360–61; Rouillé à Raymond, 31 mai 1750, AC, B, 91:343; Rouillé à Raymond, 21 juillet 1752, AC, B, 95:303.

52. Bourville à [?], 30 novembre 1730, AC, C¹¹B, 11:58; also printed in Innis, *Select Documents*, p. 119. Clark, *Three Centuries*, pp. 29–39; Harvey, *French Regime*, chapter 4. In 1749 the French banned cod fishing in Ile St. Jean so as to encourage farming. See Maude, "Settlements"; and Casgrain, *Seconde Acadie*.

53. Maude, "Settlements"; Frégault, *Bigot*, 1:83; Surlaville, *Les derniers jours*, pp. 56–59. See also Rouillé-Raymond correspondence cited in note 51.

54. General treatments include García-Baquero, *Cádiz y el Atlántico*; and Walker, *Spanish Politics and Imperial Trade*.

55. Tallapiedra's *asiento* had been modified in April of 1736; Casa-Madrid inherited the modified contract. Rey al Gobernador de la Habana, 13 agosto 1739, AGI, UM, 999.

56. The terms first appeared in Memorial de D[n] Martin Aróstegui (1739?), AGI, SD 326. A first draft of the contract, Proposiciones, y Reglas para la Compañía de la Isla de la Habana, appears in the same *legajo*. The *real cédula*, which chartered the company, explains the terms in 98 folio pages. Copia de la Real Cedula de Su Magestad, 18 diciembre 1740, AGI, SD 2024. Another lengthy discussion of the terms is in Junta General de los interesados de la R[l] Compañía, 11 diciembre 1760, AGI, IG 1745. An adequate summary appears in Hussey, *Caracas Company*, pp. 206–11. The terms of the 1744 agreement are in *reales cédulas* of 1 mayo 1744 and 15 octubre 1745, AGI, UM 254.

57. Monopoly companies were far from new in 1740. See Hussey, "Spanish Monopolistic Overseas Trading Companies," pp. 1–30. The restrictions governing foreign residence and enterprise in the Indies are discussed in Moreno, "Los extranjeros y el ejercicio de comercio de Indias," 441–54. Also, Antuñez y Acevedo, *Memorias históricas*, pp. 267–330.

58. The following paragraphs are based on Cultura del tavaco en la Isla de Cuba (c. 1800), AGI, SD 2002; Labat, *Nouveau voyage*, 6:272–337; Thomas, *Cuba*, pp. 25–26. Werner, *Tobaccoland*, pp. 222–28, describes the cultivation of Cuban tobacco in more recent times.

59. Klein, *Slavery in the Americas*, p. 149. Klein attributes this flavor to the monopoly instituted in 1717, which, he says, lowered profits, hampered expansion, and somehow prevented slave labor. The democratic flavor existed before 1717, however, and was thus probably a function of the natural requirements of the plant, not state policy. Furthermore, in the French and British Caribbean, tobacco was a poor white's crop. See Pares, *Merchants and Planters*, p. 21; and Davies, *North Atlantic World*, p. 152. See also Ortiz, *Cuban Counterpoint*. Slaves accounted for less than 10 percent of the harvest in 1748 at San Felipe y Santiago, Estado de la cantidad de cujes de tabaco, 8 mayo 1749, AGI, SD 1219.

60. Discurso echo por D[n] Antonio Bayona al Sñr Marqués de la Ensenada sobre el asiento de tavacos (c. 1739), AGI, UM 1001. Moreno Fraginals, *El ingenio*, 1:56.

61. AGI, SD 2006 has many documents on the 1747–48 harvests in Guanabacoa and Güines.

62. Güemes y Horcasitas a Quadra, 12 mayo 1739, AHN Estado 2318; [El Rey?] a Güemes y Horcasitas, 23 junio 1743, AGI, SD 2003; Antonio Fines a [?], 27 agosto 1746, AGI, SD 2005.

63. Discurso echo por D[n] Antonio Bayona, AGI, UM 1001; Hamendaxie y Casanova à Maurepas, 21 juillet 1742, MP OSU, Lot 70–1. Guane

produced the best leaf, Güines the best *verdin*, used for snuff. Rivero Muñiz, *Tabaco*, 1 : 156–58.

64. Rivero Muñiz, *Tabaco*, 1 : 132. Tobacco sent to Spain as leaf might be ground there for snuff. Vanilla was normally added to snuff in Seville. Labat, *Nouveau voyage*, 6 : 320–21. For Spanish tobacco consumption see: Pérez Vidal, *España en la historia del tabaco*, pp. 73–136.

65. "La consommation du tabac est prodigieuse dans toute l'Espagne; le peuple et les paysans sont aussi friands que les hommes de premier ordre." Mémoire de 1741, Archives de la Chambre de Commerce, Bayonne, Sér. G–60, cited in Jaupart, *Bayonne*, 1 : 422. "Il est rare de trouver un Espagnol sans sa provision de cigales," Labat, *Nouveau voyage*, 6 : 322. Pérez Vidal, *La industria tabaquera española*, pp. 5–11; and Pérez Vidal, *España en la historia del tabaco*, pp. 227–36, 249–53, 300–305, 313–18, 319–23.

66. Brooks, *Mighty Leaf*, pp. 150, 156. Between 1721 and 1731, for example, Britain imported 34 million pounds of tobacco, more than ten times Spanish imports. More than two-thirds of this total was reexported, but this still left Britain with three times as much tobacco as Spain. Since the size of the British population was roughly comparable, it appears British per capita consumption was three times higher than that of the heavy-smoking Spaniards. An Account of Tobacco Imported and Exported for Ten Years, 1721–1731, PRO, T, 64/276B. Similar figures for 1703–15 are in Gray and Wyckoff, "International Tobacco Trade," pp. 25–26. According to Hobsbawm, the average Englishman in 1790 consumed one pound of tobacco per year, *Revolution*, p. 18. Price, *France and the Chesapeake*, 1 : 8, says one to two pounds per annum in England was the eighteenth-century average; on p. 377 he says 1–1.5 pounds. Gray and Wyckoff say 1.6 pounds in "Tobacco Trade," p. 25. Davies, *North Atlantic World*, p. 146, has a similar figure for 1700–1710.

67. Where no specific references are offered, what follows is based on García Gallo, *Biografía*; Rivero Muñiz, *Tabaco*, 1 : 67–245; Marrero, *Cuba*, 7 : 41–92; Rodríguez-Ferrer, *El tabac habano*; and Price, *France and the Chesapeake*.

68. Loynaz a Squilace, 29 diciembre 1759, AGS, Hacienda 1836. This letter is a handy history of the administration of tobacco in Spain. It does not mention state purchase of Cuban leaf before 1717, but Rivero Muñiz claims that by 1698 the government had begun to buy, *Tres sediciones*, pp. 10–11. García Gallo, *Biografía*, p. 163, says the first state purchases came in 1708. Prices at Havana in the late seventeenth century were as follows: 12 to 15 *reales* per *arroba* for leaf, 24 *reales* per *arroba* for ground tobacco (*polvo*). The *Real Hacienda* paid slightly higher prices by 1710.

69. Dⁿ Joseph de la Puent [   ] al Conde de Langsseran, 2 Août 1701, BL, AM, 34335, fol. 101. (The manuscript is torn, and the full name of Don Joseph is

unclear.) According to this document, Havana tobacco had always been the most popular in the Asturias, Galicia, and Valencia, but that in Seville, large amounts of Virginia tobacco were bought. Virginia tobacco was blended with Cuban to produce low-grade snuff and pipe tobacco. According to Gray and Wyckoff, "International Tobacco Trade," p. 12, Spain imported 2.5 million pounds of Virginia tobacco annually—more than from Cuba.

70. Real Instrucción de 11 abril 1717, quoted in Rivero Muñiz, *Tres sediciones*, p. 21. The original runs as follows: "Haviendo reconocido los graves daños que resultaban de la saca de los tavacos que produce la Ysla de Cuba para los reynos extrangeros, dejando la Península de España sin el que necessita para su abasto obligando a comprarle en otros reynos, en evidente perjuicio de mi Hacienda y vasallos"; A Consulta de Consejo, 11 agosto 1723, AGI, SD 484, explains that the *estanco* was designed to inhibit contraband trade in tobacco.

71. In *Tabaco*, Rivero Muñiz does not mention the French precedent. In *Tres sediciones*, pp. 12–13, he does, specifically naming Orry as important in involving the state in Cuban tobacco. García Gallo, *Biografía*, p. 163, also mentions Orry as instrumental, as does Marrero, *Cuba*, 7:46. Orry departed in 1715, and Alberoni had become minister by the time the *estanco* became law; the scheme, however, dated from about 1712.

72. Uztáriz, *Theory*, p. 506. Indeed, Uztáriz suggested that, if "well conducted," tobacco revenue could make Philip V the most powerful prince in Europe, *ibid.*, p. 510.

73. Cited in Rivero Muñiz, *Tabaco*, 1:92.

74. Proyecto para galeones, y flotas, 5 abril 1720; *Documentos para la historia argentina*, 5:22–45.

75. There was one exception: the *estanco* provided six-year privileges for a cigar factory at Havana. Uztáriz suggested creating a *rollo* factory at Havana to obviate Spanish purchases of Brazilian rolled tobacco from the Dutch and Portuguese, *Theory*, pp. 509–10.

76. The *estanco* created six classes of tobacco, each with its own price:

verdin o rancio (used for mixing with high quality snuff)	15 *reales/arroba*
somonte o redondo (used for *torcidos* or twists)	11
hoja en manojos ("leaf in handfuls")	11
rollo (used for *picadura* or low-grade pipe tobacco)	11
chupar (for *torcidos*)	?
groso (for mixing with low-grade snuff)	?

These prices are notably lower than those of 1700. See Pérez Vidal, *España en la historia de tabaco*, p. 389, on the classification system.

77. Expediente informando de los dos Ministros Machado y Vequedano sobre los tabacos de la Habana, 13 noviembre 1720, AHN, Estado 2331; Friedlander, *Historia*, p. 71. Rivero Muñiz covers the revolts in *Tabaco*, 1:95–125, and in *Tres sediciones*. Guazo al Rey, 30 junio 1720, AGI, SD 378.

78. *Reales cédulas* of 25 octubre 1720, 17 noviembre 1730, and a *real orden* of 17 junio 1723 dissolved the monopoly. Rivero Muñiz, *Tres sediciones*, pp. 99—100. "Free use" meant that after state purchases had been made, tobacco could legally be traded to other parts of the empire. Machado y Vequedano a Grimaldo, 14 octubre 1720, AHN, Estado 2331.

79. In Spain, tobacco was in such short supply in those years that the *renta* bought it from Bayonne, Gibraltar, and Port Mahon. Proposiciones de el S[r] D[n] Martin de Loynaz en 9 enero de 1755, AGI, UM 882.

80. Martínez de la Vega a Patiño, 5 agosto 1731, AGI, SD 1499.

81. Pliego de Don Joseph Tallapiedra para la provision de Tabacos, AGI, UM 999. The contract was drawn up on 18 August 1734 and approved on 9 October.

82. Tallapiedra's second contract is summarized in several places: [Rey?] a Güemes y Horcasitas, 12 octubre 1738, AGS, Hacienda 1836; Resumen de el Estado Antiguo y Moderno del Asiento . . . del Tabaco (c. 1760), AGI, SD 2014; Rivero Muñiz, *Tabaco*, 1: 167.

83. AGI, UM 999, ramo 1.

84. *Real Cédula*, 18 diciembre 1740, in both AGS, Hacienda 1836 and AGI, SD 2024; Memorial de Ensenada, 16 diciembre 1743, AGI, SD 2026; Resumen de el Estado Antiguo y Moderno del Asiento . . . del Tabaco, AGI, SD 2014; Davalillo a Ensenada, 14 mayo 1745, AGI, SD 2004. Rivero Muñiz, *Tabaco*, 1: 206—24, discusses how the Havana Company got its contract.

85. Rivero Muñiz, *Tabaco*, 1: 85; Marrero, *Cuba*, 7: 45.

86. See the document reprinted from AGI, SD 417 in Marrero, *Cuba*, 7: 43, for Doña de Moya's invention.

87. Discurso echo por D[n] Antonio Bayona al Sñr Mrqs de la Ensenada sobre al asiento de tavacos (n.d., c. 1739), AGI, UM 1001. In article 39 of the Havana Company contract (AGI, SD 2024) it is mentioned that Cuba has more than forty mills, meaning water-driven ones. Jacobo de Flon a Manual Ibañez, 15 marzo 1732, AGI, Hacienda 1836: [In Havana] "ay quarenta artificios de agua." García Gallo, *Biografía*, pp. 53—54, claims that in 1721 there were fifteen mills, in 1718 there were thirty-two, and in 1740 only three or five.

88. Instrucciones para la factoría, 27 junio 1760 (firmada por Esquilache), AGI, UM 233. "Uno de los motivos . . . (de) . . . la inferior calidad del tabaco de polvo de la hoja de los partidos de la Habana, es la novedad introducida en este siglo de molerla en artificios de agua." Manifesto sobre las siembras, beneficio y compra de los tavacos (1782), AGI, SD 2017.

89. It is not entirely clear at what point the *artificios* came to dominate the *polvo* market. The government in 1717, 1731, and 1740 forbade construction of such mills. Marrero, *Cuba*, 7: 43, suggests that a great number of these mills were built between 1701 and 1713. Friedlander opts for 1713—20 in

his *Historia*, pp. 64, 66–67. The Manifesto (see note 88) of 1782 suggests 1720–27. Apparently by 1732 most of the *artificios* had been built, as Flon in 1732 and Bayone in 1739 report roughly the same number. See note 87.

90. Discurso echo por Dⁿ Antonio Bayona, AGI, UM 1001.

91. Manifesto sobre las siembras, 1782, AGI, SD 2017.

92. Representación que . . . hizo el Presidente y los Directores de la Real Compañía de la Habana, 23 mayo 1749, AGI, UM 1001. A *real orden* of 3 marzo 1749 proclaimed: "que su Real Intención es, que no se muelan, ni labren otros tabacos, que los del medio pie arriva de las plantas." AGI, SD 402. A *real orden* of 11 enero 1752 repeated the injunction, according to Cagigal a Arriaga, 28 abril 1759, AGI, SD 2015.

93. Junta general de 19 diciembre 1748, AGI, SD 500.

94. Memorial de Cagigal a los Sñrs Directores, 11 marzo 1758, AGI, UM 986; Documentos remitidos de la via reservada, 12 noviembre 1756, AGI, SD 402.

95. Uztáriz, *Theory*, pp. 506–8. Spanish consumption, according to Patiño, reached 6 million pounds annually by 1737. British imports made up much of the difference. Canga Argüelles, *Diccionario de Hacienda*, 5:165.

96. Instrucción para los Interesados de la Real Compañía de la Habana (n.d., c. 1756), AGI, SD 2014. The original runs as follows: "reducir las cosechas del Tabaco al preciso consumo de los dominios de S. M. y limitar su siembra a ciertos gentes a parajes, a fin de cortar por este medio el contrabando en su raiz." Several other statements of the same aim exist, some of them word for word. Goyeneche a Aróstegui, 18 septiembre 1758 (Aróstegui's reply is in the margin), AGI, SD 402.

97. France had bought Chesapeake tobacco in Amsterdam (the center of the international market) because of low taxes, before resorting to Britain. See Price, "Map of Commerce," 6:851–53.

98. Uztáriz, *Theory*, p. 509; Papeles formado por Secretaria sobre tabaco (n.d., c. 1760), AGI, SD 2016. "The indifference of the Spanish alone is to blame for the small quantity of tobacco which they export," *Verhandeling van den tabak* (Amsterdam, 1770), quoted in Brooks, *Tobacco*, 3:448.

99. The tax applied to British and Portuguese tobacco, too. At 200 livres per quintal, it roughly doubled the price of Havana leaf to French consumers. Price, *France and the Chesapeake*, 1:256; Brooks, *Tobacco*, 3:172.

100. In the years 1701–13 France imported Cuban tobacco. In subsequent years it did so as contraband. Documentos remitidos de la via reservada, 30 marzo 1756, AGI, SD 402. Much of what was licensed to go to Cartagena or Portobello found its way to French colonies. Also: Price, *France and the Chesapeake*, 1:114–15, 405, 451. The Louisiana industry was modeled on Havana. Ibid., 1:303–4, 376–77.

101. The price of tobacco milled in Seville was about 40 *reales/arroba*, while that

of Havana-milled tobacco was only 30 *reales/arroba*. Discurso echo por D[n] Antonio Bayona (n.d., c. 1739), AGI, UM 1001.

102. Rivero Muñiz, *Tabaco*, 1:130. In 1740, at the request of Aróstegui, president of the Havana Company, construction of further mills was outlawed. By this time, however, the existing mills could grind almost all of Cuba's tobacco harvest anyway. Consulta de Consejo, 13 agosto 1740, AGI, SD 1129.

103. Vicens Vives, *Economic History*, p. 548. Apparently this failed, but was considered once again. Bayona a Carbajal, 3 enero 1747, AHN, Estado 2320. Throughout the eighteenth century only a small proportion of Cuban tobacco traveled to Spain as *rollo*, whereas in Brazil and St.-Domingue most tobacco was twisted into rolls by slaves. Labat, *Nouveau voyage*, 6:313−18.

104. Deerr, in his *History of Sugar*, includes a chapter on eighteenth-century policy and legislation, which he considered very consequential (2:408−25). It contains not a mention of Spanish policy. Deerr read Spanish and was interested in Cuban sugar (he lived in Cuba for some years), but he found no published information on which to base an account of Spanish sugar policy. There is no Spanish equivalent to Boizard and Tardieu, *Histoire de la legislation des sucres*.

105. On sugar cane in general, I have consulted the following works: Moreno Fraginals, *El Ingenio*; Reynolds, *Cuban Sugar*; Deerr, *History of Sugar*; Labat, *Nouveau voyage*, 3:321−457. Histories devoted to beet as well as cane sugar include Edmund Oskar von Lippmann, *Geschichte des zuckers seit den ältesten zeiten bis zum beginn der Rubenzucker-fabrikation; ein beitrag zur kulturgeschichte* (Berlin: J. Springer, 1929); and Jacob Baxa and Guntwin Bruhns, *Zucker im leben der völker: eine kultur und wirtschaftegeschichte* (Berlin: Dr. Bartens, 1967). Instructions on planting sugar cane, written in about 1730, can be found in BL, AM 13975, fol. 59−66; and Arango, *Obras*, 1:114−203, "Discurso sobre la agricultura de la Habana."

106. Modern cane is 84 percent to 92 percent juice by weight and up to eighteen percent sucrose. Humboldt, *Cuba*, p. 265, found Cuban cane in 1804 six times as productive by weight as beet sugar.

107. Humboldt, *Cuba*, p. 268. This amounts to 1,981 pounds of sugar per acre, a figure close to those in the British and French sugar colonies. See Barrett, "Caribbean Sugar Production," p. 166. Arango extracted almost 2,500 *arrobas* per *caballería* on his estate: *Obras*, 2:436−37. Humboldt reported that under optimal conditions 4,000 *arrobas* per *caballería* could be achieved. Raynal, *Trade in the East and West Indies*, 4:151, says that 10,000 square meters produced 60 quintals of sugar (or 2.4 acres produced 240 *arrobas*—2,500 pounds per acre), a productivity higher than reported anywhere except Barbados in 1699.

108. Arango, *Obras*, 2:438, says November or December. Barrett, "Caribbean Sugar Production," p. 154, says sixteen months after planting, which he puts in August-November. Thomas, *Cuba*, pp. 40–41, says eighteen months after planting, which he places in "late summer." This, according to Thomas, comes out to "after Christmas." The length of the growing season presumably varied with rainfall and the degree of soil exhaustion.

109. The term *ingenio* also referred to the entire sugar plantation. The following description is based on Belfrage's translation of Moreno Fraginals's, *Sugarmill*, pp. 33–35; and Barrett, "Caribbean Sugar Production," pp. 154–63.

110. Jefferys, *Spanish Islands*, p. 75. In Jamaica in 1768, 57 percent of sugar plantations used animal power, 37 percent used water power, and 6 percent used the wind. Roughly the same proportions obtained on Martinique and Guadeloupe from 1739 to 1769. Deerr, *History of Sugar*, 1:176, 234.

111. Barrett, "Caribbean Sugar Production," p. 161. Barrett cites Leon, *On Sugar Cultivation*. Moreno Fraginals, *Sugarmill*, p. 38, says the Jamaica train arrived in Cuba in the 1780s.

112. Since juice could not be left for more than an hour before boiling, the capacity of the boiling house might considerably slow the possible production rate of the grinding mill. The clever planter, however, equalized the rates of cutting, grinding, and boiling so that no delays could damage the quality of his product.

113. Cf. Deerr, *History of Sugar*, 2:352–54.

114. Moreno Fraginals, *El ingenio*, 1:52. British plantations in the years 1727–55 used about 150 to 500 slaves per plantation. Barrett, "Caribbean Sugar Production," p. 166. The average around Havana was eighty-three slaves according to an estimate in Guerra et al., *Historia de la nación cubana*, 2:213.

115. Barrett, "Caribbean Sugar Production," p. 166, has figures for Barbados, St. Kitts, Jamaica, St. Domingue, and Louisiana. One laborer per acre was the rule of thumb in Brazilian and Caribbean sugar cultivation. Curtin, "Slavery and Empire," p. 8.

116. The *caja* in the early eighteenth century usually weighed close to 20 *arrobas*, but by 1758 it officially weighed 16. From 1754 to 1761 ship manifests scattered through AGI, SD 2004–2024 allow an idea of the evolution of the *caja*, since some manifests list sugar quantities in both *cajas* and *arrobas*. Values obtained are as follows:

1754	22.16	*arrobas* equal one *caja*
1755	20.89	
1756	21.42	
1757	22.29	
1758	15.49	
1759	13.45	

1760   14.25
1761   15.74

When obliged to convert from *cajas* to *arrobas*, I have used the above values when I know the specific years involved. When precise years are uncertain, I have used a value of 20 for years prior to 1758. Most authorities consider one *caja* equal to 16 *arrobas*, but this is inaccurate for those years before 1758.

117. See Deerr, *History of Sugar*, 1 : 231–32, 2 : 464–66; Mims, *Colbert's West India Policy*, pp. 273–79; Davies, *North Atlantic World*, p. 185; Williams, *From Columbus to Castro*, p. 163.

118. Reesse, *De Suikerhandel van Amsterdam*. For the early history of Cuban sugar see: Ulloa, "Sugar Industry," 4 : 75–91.

119. Moreno Fraginals, *El ingenio*, 3 : 40–42. Haiti led with 56,000 metric tons annually, followed by Jamaica with 40,000 and Brazil with 34,000. Cuba, with 5,500, produced only slightly more than the Danish West Indies.

120. French sugar especially sold quickly at Cadiz, Güemes y Horcasitas a [?], 24 julio 1736, AGI, SD 1129. On French sugar policy see Deerr, *History of Sugar*, 2 : 808. One Cuban complained of "el pernicioso estilo de las gracias que los hacen los Administradores de las Aduanas," Expediente sobre la Real Compañía, AGI, SD 488. Bribes opened the Spanish market to all sorts of foreign sugar. In the middle of the eighteenth century, Spain imported 1.25 million *arrobas* of sugar, according to Canga Argüelles, *Diccionario de Hacienda*, 1 : 256.

121. Calculations here are based on the following: (1) 1,000 square feet of lumber made 32 *cajas* (Arango, *Obras*, 2 : 437), (2) 5 *arrobas* sugar used 160 cubic feet of lumber in fuel (Humboldt, *Cuba*, p. 273), (3) 4,000 *arrobas* per *ingenio* (*supra* p. 127)—Moreno Fraginals, *El ingenio*, 1 : 171, says in 1761 the average product was 49 metric tons (on p. 68 he has 43), which equals about 4,300 *arrobas* per *ingenio*.

122. Resumen de los Intereses y posible aumentos de la Isla de Cuba . . . por D[n] Joseph de Irrutia (oidor y catedratico de la Universidad), 1749, f. 19. This manuscript will hereafter be referred to as AGI, SD 1157, Irrutia. Thomas, *Cuba*, p. 30, says slaves accounted for one-third to one-half the initial costs, notably higher than Irrutia. Perhaps scale can explain the discrepancy.

123. Cabildo de Puerto Príncipe al Rey, 3 junio 1729, and 16 marzo 1731, AGI, SD 488. Both claims are probably exaggerated, since the aim of the *cabildo* was to induce the crown to provide more shipping for Puerto Príncipe.

124. Relación de los ingenios en la jurisdicción de Santiago de Cuba, 14 agosto 1758, AGI, SD 2015. This document includes only 38 of Santiago de Cuba's *ingenios*, presumably ignoring the smaller ones, which suggests the average was even lower than 800. The *matrícula* of 1737 (AGI, SD 384)

added: "Se previene que dichos trapiches respecto a los de la Habana son muy cortos en sus labranzas, fábricas, cobres y esclavos, asi como tambien en sus tierras." Saco, *Esclavitud*, 2 : 216, says *ingenios* around Santiago de Cuba often had only three or four slaves, and only rarely as many as twenty or thirty. This suggests 300 or 400 *arrobas* annual production, with 2,000 or 3,000 as the maximum.

125. The 1751 average production per *ingenio* was 3,086 *arrobas*, according to figures derived from Cagigal de la Vega a Ensenada, 19 julio 1751, printed in *Boletín del Archivo Nacional de Cuba*, 14 : 263–67. Cagigal wrote that 81 *ingenios* produced 250,000 *arrobas*. The BNM manuscript (note c. table 5.1) shows 339,000 *arrobas* as the product of 88 Havana *ingenios* in 1759, or an average of 3,852 *arrobas* per *ingenio*. Moreno Fraginals has 43 metric tons as the 1761 average per *ingenio* on one page (*El ingenio*, 1 : 68), and 49 metric tons on another (1 : 171). Moreno's figures come out to either 3,784 or 4,312 *arrobas* per *ingenio*.

126. *Real Cédula*, 7 julio 1719, AGI, SD 326; Despacho de Consejo, 7 julio 1719, AGI, SD 338.

127. Such laws in the Havana area date back to 1641, according to Ulloa, "Sugar Industry," p. 82. Apparently Cubans disobeyed the law, because it appeared again in 1733, *Real Orden*, 19 septiembre 1733, AGI, SD 381. Güemes y Horcasitas al Rey, 24 abril 1734, AGI, SD 381; Juan Pinto al Rey, 29 noviembre 1734, AGI, SD 381.

128. Proyecto para galeones, y flotas del Peru, y Nueva Espana, y para navios de registro, y avisos, que navegaren a ambos reynos, 5 abril 1720, printed in *Documentos para la historia argentina*, 5 : 21–45. These rates continued a trend set in 1713 when the Crown raised taxes on Cuban sugar. Le Riverend, "Desarollo económico," p. 225.

129. Memorial al Rey, septiembre 1726, AGI, SD 380. The governor agreed with the sugar mill owners: Dionisio Martinez de la Vega a Patiño, 25 agosto 1727, AGI, SD 380. The Consejo de Indias approved the planters' recommended reforms: Consulta de Consejo, 22 diciembre 1728, AGI, SD 325; Despacho de Consejo, 5 julio 1727, AGI, SD 339; Despacho de Consejo, 14 junio 1730, AGI, SD 340.

130. In AGI, SD 325.

131. Consulta de Consejo, 16 febrero 1740, AGI, SD 1129.

132. Francisco Vara y Valdéz al Consulado, 13 abril 1737, AGI, SD 433; Idem a idem, 4 noviembre 1737, AGI, SD 433. On taxes: Consulta de Consejo, 15 febrero 1740, AGI, SD 488. On royal exhortation: Consulta de Consejo, 16 febrero 1740, AGI, SD 1129; Junta General celebrada por la Real Compañía, 19 diciembre 1748, AGI, UM 891; Junta General, 11 diciembre 1760, AGI, IG 1656. Memorial de los Dueños de Ingenios de Azúcar de Cuba, 12 mayo 1740, AGI, SD 426.

133. Consulta de Consejo, 16 febrero 1740, AGI, SD 1129, "la idea de reduzir

las cosechas de tabaco al consumo nezessario, considera el Consejo ser muy conveniente para que se restablezca de labor de los azucares." The Consulado of Seville wanted lower taxes for Cuban sugar. Testimonio de Dⁿ Gabriel Cordobez Pintado y Dⁿ Pedro de Olazabal, 30 julio 1739, AGI, SD 488.

134. *Real cédula*, 18 diciembre 1740, articulo 34, AGS, Hacienda 1836; and AGI, SD 2024.

135. Cagigal de la Vega a Ensenada, 28 abril 1751, AGI, SD 1501; Ensenada a Cagigal de la Vega, 20 octubre 1749, AGI, SD 2008; El Rey (?) a Cagigal de la Vega, 12 mayo 1751, AGI, SD 1501; Papel que se ha formado por la secretaria del Estado (n.d.), AGI, SD 1501.

136. Cagigal de la Vega a Arriaga, 23 abril 1759, AGI, SD 1320. Weston to Inkison, 8 December 1763, printed in Blanck, *Papeles*, p. 109.

137. See Scelle, *Traité négrière aux Indes de Castille*, 2:455–680; Aimes, *Slavery in Cuba*, pp. 20–23.

138. A *pieza de Indias* meant a healthy adult male slave. Women, children, and the unhealthy might make up any fraction of a *pieza de Indias*. Normally the term was used as a unit of account; after purchase slaves were called *negros* or *esclabos*.

139. On Ulibarri's contract, see Güemes y Horcasitas al Rey, 28 marzo 1743 and 12 marzo 1744, AGI, SD 387; also, Saco, *Esclavitud*, 2:210; Ensenada a Aróstegui, 12 enero 1741, AGI, SD 2208; Memorial de los Directores de la Real Compañía, 4 agosto 1744, AGI, SD 2208. On the Havana Company contracts: Cagigal de la Vega a Ensenada, 21 marzo 1754, 24 noviembre 1752, 11 enero 1753, AGI, SD 2209; Arriaga a Cagigal de la Vega, 19 marzo 1754, AGI, SD 2209; also Saco, *Esclavitud*, 2:209–13; Aimes, *Slavery in Cuba*, pp. 23–24; Los Directores de la Real Compañía a Ensenada, 20 octubre 1751, AGI, SD 2209.

140. Cagigal de la Vega a Ensenada, 24 diciembre 1752, AGI, SD 2209; Cagigal de la Vega a Ensenada, 3 octubre 1750, AGI, SD 2208. In 1754 a Francisco Xavier Cisneros was awarded a contract to import 500 slaves into the Santiago de Cuba area, Arriaga a Arcos Moreno, 21 marzo 1754, AGI, SD 2209.

141. *Real cédula*, 21 junio 1761, AGI, SD 1135. Saco, *Esclavitud*, 2:214, wrongly says the Havana Company prevented Villanueba from getting his *asiento*. The contract was signed, but war prevented its fulfillment.

142. Villanueba a Esquilace (n.d. but c. 1760), AGI, IG 1745; Junta General de la Real Compañía, 11 diciembre 1760, AGI, IG 1745; Aimes, *Slavery in Cuba*, pp. 302–3.

143. Memorial de Dⁿ Martín Aróstegui, 1739, AGI, SD 326. On ranching in general see Marrero, *Cuba*, 6:191–216; and Le Riverend, "Desarollo económico," pp. 194–99.

144. In Puerto Príncipe in 1737, *hatos* averaged 655 head of cattle apiece, while

21 *corrales* averaged only 269 head. Matrícula de los Hatos, y Corrales, AGI, SD 384.

145. Arrate, *Llave del Nuevo Mundo*, p. 82. Descripción de la Isla de Cuba . . . por Alejandro O'Reilly, 12 abril 1764, AGI, SD 1509. O'Reilly says cattle were not fattened after drives.

146. Martínez Moles, "Sancti Spíritus," 3:577. In 1736, cattle sold for three pesos per head, hogs for two, and horses for eight.

147. Betancourt, "Puerto Príncipe," 3:538, 548.

148. Visita del Obispo Morel de Santa Cruz, AGI, SD 534 (see chapter 2, n. 73, for full citation.)

149. Cabildo de Puerto Príncipe al Rey, 3 junio 1729, AGI, SD 488.

150. Matrícula de los Hatos, Corrales de ganados maior y minor, Ingenios, 1737, AGI, SD 384.

151. AGI, SD 534 and 2227 (see chapter 2, n. 73, for precise citations).

152. El Rey a Cagigal de la Vega, 12 julio 1739, AGI, SD 363; Aróstegui a Carvajal, 3 enero 1747, AHN, Estado 2320.

153. *Documentos para la historia argentina*, 5:42.

154. Memorial de Dⁿ Martín Aróstegui, 1739, AGI, SD 326; *Real cédula*, 18 diciembre 1740, AGI, SD 2024.

155. *Real cédula*, 1 mayo 1744, AGI, Contratación 5004.

156. Clayton, "Ships and Empire," p. 246.

157. Arrate, *Llave del Nuevo Mundo*, p. 88.

158. Instrucción del Rey, 26 agosto 1713, AGI, SD 482.

159. El Rey al Gobernador de Pancacola Dⁿ Gregorio Salinas Varona (n.d.), AGI, SD 428; Béthencourt Massieu, "Arboladuras de Santa María de Chimalapa-Tehuántepec," p. 67; Marrero, *Cuba*, 8:14.

160. Consulta de Consejo, 19 abril 1719, AGI, SD 338. The shipyard was privileged to cut wood on anyone's land. Marrero, *Cuba*, 8:4.

161. Reglamento General de Cortes, Labor y Conduccion de piezas de Madera de Construcción que debe observar la Real Compañía de esta Isla, 14 octubre, 1747, AGS, Marina 645.

162. Of 230 slaves employed in the *ramo de construcción de vageles*, 130 worked seasonally in lumbering. Nota de los efectos que existen de quenta de la Compañía en el astillero de la Habana, 19 diciembre 1748. In 1747 the shipyard employed 800 wage laborers and 238 slaves. Marrero, *Cuba*, 8:18.

163. A copy of Acosta's contract dated 31 abril 1731 is in Documentación referente a construcción de navios en el siglo XVIII, AMN, Colección Guillén, Ms 1209.

164. Fifty thousand pesos were to come from Mexico and 70,000 from Cadiz. Timber legislation: Memorial de Miguel de Recabarren, 22 febrero 1719, AGI, SD 420; *Real orden*, 17 julio 1719, AGI, SD 378; Bacardi, *Crónicas*, 1:306; Despacho de Consejo, 15 diciembre 1735, AGI, SD 341.

165. The Havana Company's contractual obligations are spelled out at length in a printed document in AGI, Contratación 5004; also in AGI, UM 995.

166. *Real orden*, 25 noviembre 1745, AGI, Contratación 5004.

167. On shipbuilding at Havana see Arrate, *Llave del Nuevo Mundo*, pp. 88–92; Guerra, *Historia de la nación cubana*, 2:201–2; Humboldt, *Cuba*, pp. 118–23.

168. Memorial de Aróstegui, 1739, AGI, UM 999.

169. Martínez de la Vega a Patiño, 10 mayo 1731, AGI, SD 1499.

170. Guerra, *Historia de la nación cubana*, 2:170–73. Florida, too, had a food deficit, which it met with imports from British colonies. Consulta de Consejo, 16 febrero 1740, AGI, SD 1129.

171. In 1718 the governor and *ayuntamiento* (municipal government) of Havana proposed a six-year wheat *asiento*, which the Council of the Indies refused to allow. Consulta de Consejo, 21 enero 1719, AGI, SD 325.

172. Consulta de Consejo, 18 mayo 1752, AGI, SD 347.

173. Consulta de Consejo, 5 septiembre 1738, AGI, SD 1129; the same document appears in AGI, SD 342. In this instance all the authorities in Havana had agreed that it was necessary to buy flour from French colonies to avoid starvation, especially among the garrison.

174. Minuta de Consejo, 14 agosto 1756, AGI, SD 371.

175. Consulta de Consejo, 21 enero 1719, AGI, SD 325; Fiscal, 29 Mayo 1756, AGI, SD 371.

176. Santiago de Cuba did not rely on Mexican food imports, but—in theory— on the littoral of what is now Venezuela, Colombia, and Panama.

177. An index of the welfare of the Spanish treasury was the practice of appointing or selling bureaucratic positions. *Audiencia* posts were awarded on merit only when the Crown could afford to do so, such as the years 1720–37. When finances were tight, these positions were sold. Burkholder and Chandler, *From Impotence to Authority*, pp. 18–80.

Chapter 6

1. This idea originated with Borgstrom, see his *Fish as Food*, 2:307–15; and "Fisheries in World Nutrition," pp. 33–38. Borgstrom derives his figures using milk protein, since milk production is the most land-efficient way to produce animal protein.

   I used the following values in my eighteenth-century calculation:

   H = (150,000 quintals cod) × (.92 kilogram protein/kilogram cod)

   A = 700 to 900

   B = .16 to .29

   C = .035

   For eighteenth-century milk yields, see Grigg, *Agricultural Systems*,

193—94; Trow-Smith, *Life From the Land*, p. 112; Slicher van Bath, *Agrarian History*, pp. 284, 335. For stocking ratios, ibid., pp. 291—92, 295 (his figures are in hectares/cow, the inverse of mine). For the protein content of milk, Altschul, *Proteins*, p. 24; United Nations Food and Agriculture Organization, *Milk.*

2. The protein requirement figure comes from Borgstrom, "Protein Feeding," p. 754.

3. Aymard, "History of Nutrition," p. 7.

4. Bertier, Lamontagne, and Vergnault, "Traitement graphique d'une information," p. 992. A quintal of cod in France cost about 18—25 livres, roughly twice the Cape Breton price. In addition each quintal of fish produced oil worth about another livre. According to Uztáriz, *Theory*, pp. 366—67, the Spanish price was five pesos per quintal (c. 1724), equal to about 25 livres. Price data for Portugal and Italy have eluded me, but the price of bread in Portugal rose gradually from 1728 to 1758, which may have moved the poor in coastal regions to buy more cod, thereby raising the price. Precisely this happened in Spain, according to Michell, "European Fisheries." This is sheer speculation for Portugal, however. The price of bread held stable in southern Italy from the 1730s through the 1750s. I have no data whatsoever on prices in the Levant. On Portugal: Godinho, *Prix et monnaies au Portugal*, p. 152. On Italy, or rather Naples: Romano, *Prezzi, salari, e servizi a Napoli*, pp. 69, 125—26. The price of refuse cod sold in Brazil fluctuated wildly between 1688 and 1769, showing no sensitivity to either war or production levels. Dauril Alden, "Commodity Price Movement in Brazil Before, During, and After the Gold Boom, 1670—1769: The Salvador Market," unpublished typescript, Table 10. (This typescript was shown to me through the courtesy of Professor John Tepaske.)

5. For the modern statistics see Sette, "Catch of Cod," pp. 746—47. For eighteenth-century figures see Table 6.1 in this chapter.

6. Moore, "Other Louisbourg," pp. 90—91; Turgeon, "Pour une histoire de la pêche," passim.

7. Turgeon, "Pour une histoire de la pêche," pp. 305—7.

8. Quebec (Province) Archives, *Rapport de l'archiviste de Québec*, pp. 356—404; Lounsbury, *British Fishery*, pp. 310—13; Head, *Newfoundland*, pp. 63—74.

9. Bigot à Maurepas, 1744, AC C¹¹C, 15:250—53. Another letter reported that on account of war (news of which reached Louisbourg in May) fishing would be off by at least 75 percent, DuQuesnel et Bigot à Maurepas, 9 mai 1744, AC C¹¹B, 26:4. Head, *Newfoundland*, p. 63.

10. See Moore, "Other Louisbourg"; "Merchant Trade" (thesis); "Maritime Economy," pp. 33—46; and "Merchants in the Louisbourg Community."

11. In 1721, 272 barrels of coal from Ile Royale arrived at Rochefort, Conseil à Beauharnois, 21 janvier 1722, AC, B, 45—1:10—12. The next year the figure increased to 300, Le Normant du Mezy au Conseil, 1 septembre

1722, AC, C¹¹C, 15:234. In 1740 the total reached 514 barrels, and in 1742 it was 400. Bigot à Maurepas, 1 novembre 1740, AC, C¹¹B, 22:198; Bigot à Maurepas, 24 octobre 1742, AC, C¹¹B, 23:123–24. A barrel was worth about three livres.

12. Fauteux, *Essai sur l'industrie au Canada*, 1:23; *Great Importance of Cape Breton*, p. 33; Bigot au ministre, 3 octobre 1739, AC, C¹¹B, 21:91.

13. Harvey, *Holland's Description* (document), pp. 60–86. The original is in PRO, CO, 5/70. See also Martell, "Early Coal Mining," pp. 156–72.

14. The Crown actually did operate one mine for a while at l'Indienne, but this was to provide coal for the use of the troops, not for an export trade. See Francis, "Mines and Quarries," p. 45; also Pichon, *Lettres et mémoires*, p. 49.

15. Bigot à Maurepas, 6 octobre 1742, AC, C¹¹B, 24:118. This difficulty intensified after 1730 when Maurepas discouraged the use of Crown ships for transporting coal in response to the loss of *Le Profond* in a fire. Maurepas à St.-Ovide et Le Normant du Mezy, 27 juin 1730, AC, B, 54–2:554.

16. Conseil à Costebelle et Soubras, 26 juin 1717, AC, B, 39–5:1021–26; Maurepas à Ricouart, 28 décembre 1742, AC, B, 75:392; Maurepas à Bigot, 12 juin, AC, B, 76:479.

17. Prévost à ministre, 4 décembre 1750, AC, C¹¹B, 29:190–91. On the fire: Francis, "Mines and Quarries," p. 50; Pichon, *Lettres et mémoires*, p. 49.

18. Of 86 vessels returning to Bayonne from Louisbourg between 1713 and 1758, 27 (31 percent) were built in Ile Royale, 55 (64 percent) were built in New England, and 2 came from Quebec and 2 from New York, Turgeon, "Échanges Franco-Canadiennes," 2:172.

19. Minutes de Conseil, 15 mars 1733, AC, C¹¹B, 14:17–20; Bigot au ministre, 7 novembre 1740, AC, C¹¹B, 22:200–202.

20. For slightly different figures on New England ships sold at Louisbourg, see Chard, "Impact of Ile Royale" (thesis), p. 43B.

21. Conseil, 5 avril 1718, AC, C¹¹B, 2:130.

22. Bentley and Smith, "Forests of Cape Breton," p. 10.

23. Conseil à Beauharnois, 1 mars 1722, AC, B, 45–1:28; Conseil à Le Normant du Mezy, 13 mai 1722, AC, B, 45–2:1123–25; Maurepas à Beauharnois, 16 avril 1726, AC, B, 49–1:189–90; Maurepas à De Pensens, 22 mai 1729, AC, B, 53:598–99.

24. Harvey, *Holland's Description*, (document), pp. 60–129; Le Normant du Mezy au ministre, 12 décembre 1725, AC, C¹¹B, 7:278.

25. Le Normant du Mezy au ministre, 28 octobre 1738, AC, C¹¹B, 20:97; DuQuesnel et Bigot au ministre, 17 octobre 1741, AC, C¹¹B, 23:22; Prévost au ministre, 31 octobre 1753, AC, C¹¹B, 33:323–24.

26. *Collection de manuscrits*, 3:469; see also Clark, "New England's Role," pp. 1–12.

27. Pontchartrain à Costebelle, 23 septembre 1713, AC, C¹¹C, 7:226–27.

28. St.-Ovide au Conseil, 30 novembre 1717, AC, C¹¹B, 2:296.

29. Maurepas à St.-Ovide et Le Normant du Mezy, 9 mai 1724, AC, B, 47:254–59. The Compagnie des Indes apparently would provide slaves for 1,000 livres each for this scheme.

30. Pothier, "Les Acadiens à l'Isle Royale," pp. 97–111; "Acadian Settlement" (thesis); "Acadian Emigration," pp. 116–31.

31. Collection de manuscrits, 3:468.

32. St.-Ovide à [Maurepas?], 15 novembre 1732, AC, C¹¹B, 12:263–68. A barrique, or barrel, equaled about 225 liters, or one-quarter of a Bordeaux tonneau.

33. Clark, Three Centuries, pp. 29–34. On Ile St. Jean in general see Bolger, Canada's Smallest Province, pp. 13–32.

34. De Pensens à [Maurepas?], 31 octobre 1728, AC, C¹¹B, 10:157–64. Mice destroyed crops in 1724, 1728, 1738, and 1749. Clark, Three Centuries, p. 39; Harvey, French Regime, p. 62.

35. On prices: Conseil de la Marine à Beauharnois, 24 mars 1716, AC, B, 38–1:152–54; Maurepas à Beauharnois, 5 avril 1729, AC, B, 52:129.

36. Conseil de la Marine à Beauharnois, 2 janvier 1722, AC, B, 45–1:1–2; Conseil à Beauharnois, 14 janvier 1722, AC, B, 45–1:6–7; Maurepas à St. Leon, 13 août 1724, AC, B, 45:108–9.

37. Rivero Muñiz, Tabaco, 1:234.

38. Liquidazion y adjustamiento de los tabacos que remite Dⁿ Martin de Loynaz, AGI, UM 1001. Between 13 August 1726 and 15 June 1730 the factory in Seville received 11,318,120 pounds of tobacco (452,725 arrobas), 83 percent of it polvo. This works out to an annual average of 118,102 arrobas, or approximately seven times the average reported by Pezuela. The average price in these years was slightly higher than two pesos per arroba. If we assume the average price remained the same, then figures for the later years of the Intendencia show an average export of close to 90,000 arrobas annually. Memorial de la Isla de la Habana, 1739, AGI, UM 999, claims that in the years 1733–36 an average of 176,095 pesos of tobacco was exported. Between 1723 and 1737 the average annual purchase was 190,616 pesos, suggesting an annual average of close to 95,000 arrobas. See the accounts of the ramo de tabacos, AGI, Contaduría 1167.

39. Memorial de la Isla de la Habana, 1739, AGI, UM 999.

40. Computo prudenzial de las cosechas (n.d., c. 1738), AGI, SD 488; Discurso echo por Dⁿ Antonio Bayona (1739), AGI, UM 1001; Jacobo de Flon a Manuel Ibáñez, 15 marzo 1732, AGS, Hacienda 1836. A fourth estimate, made sixty years later by Arango (Obras, 1:473) puts total tobacco production at 600,000 arrobas. This is certainly excessive.

41. In 1765–70 and 1766–71, Cuban tobacco exports to the rest of the Indies came to 18,000 arrobas annually. Proyecto sobre tabacos, resumen general, 1 marzo 1765, hasta 15 marzo 1770, AGI, IG 1745; Estado de los tabacos remitidos por la Real Factoría, AGI, SD 2016.

42. Jacobo de Flon a Manuel Ibañez, 15 marzo 1732, AGS, Hacienda 1836. Instrucción para los Interesados de la Real Compañía de la Habana, marzo 1757, AGI, SD 2014: "es notório que los Olandeses cargaban todos los años dos navios grandes de Tabaco introduciendose por el surgidero del Manzanillo que está en el partido del Baiamo." This refers to the period before the Havana Company operated the tobacco trade, that is, before 1740.

43. Posthumus, *Prices in Holland*, pp. 206–7.

44. This estimate, which deserves a measure of skepticism, is based on the following calculations (in *arrobas*):

	80,000	Spanish imports
Legitimate trade, 95,000	5,000	Cuban consumption
	10,000	Spanish colonial imports
	200,000	British share
Illegal trade, 305,000	60,000	Dutch share
	45,000	French and Portuguese share
Total production 400,000	400,000	

The 80,000 figure for Spanish imports is a compromise between the 118,000 of 1726–30, 90,000 of 1733–36, and 55,000 of 1736–39. The distribution of the illegal trade between nations is based on two figures—the 160,000 extracted by the South Sea Company factor (to which has been added another 40,000 for private smugglers operating between Jamaica and the Cuban south coast) and 50,000 for two large Dutch ships, since large Spanish tobacco shipments held about 25,000 *arrobas*. To this 50,000, another 10,000 has been added for small-scale smugglers. This leaves 45,000 for the French, Portuguese, and others.

45. The ship manifests are in AGI, SD 365, 387, 433, 500, 2003–16, 2197; AGI, UM 929, 930, 942, 995, 999, 1000; and AHN, Estado 2320. The *zertificaciones* (certificates) are in AGI, UM 233, 254–57. Partial lists include: Estado de los tavacos que la Real Compañía de la Habana ha embarcado para conducir a los reinos de Castilla, desde octubre 1744 hasta febrero 1749, AGI, SD 2008; Razon de los Tabacos que desde el dia ocho de Junio de 1747 se han remitido la Real Compañia de esta ciudad para los Reynos de Castilla, 18 enero 1749, AGI, SD 2008; Nota de los tavacos que la Real Compañía ha remitido, 15 marzo 1744, AGI, SD 2004; Certificación de los registros, 16 agosto 1745, AGI, SD 2005; Estado de los tabacos que ha remitido la Real Compañía a España desde 28 agosto 1743 hasta 1 junio 1744, AGI, SD 500. Comparing these partial lists with a list compiled from the ship manifests, I found only two ships which appeared on the Havana Company lists for which I did not have a ship manifest. For most ships three manifests were drawn up, and almost always one of them reached the Archive of the Indies. For the period 1752–60 I compared ship manifests with the lists in Quentas del asiento de tavaco . . . de 1752, AGI, UM 999, and with the same account for each of the years up through 1761. Here

two tobacco shipments appear for which I found no manifest, one in 1754 of 7,258 *arrobas* and another in 1755 of 4,718 *arrobas*. These shipments have not been included in the aggregate statistics which follow. Of a total of 293 tobacco shipments, 289 are confirmed, of which 284 sailed between 1740 and 1761. The figures which follow are based on those 284.

46. Of these 284, 9 were French and 4 were Dutch vessels. All the foreign shipments occurred before 1755, most of them during the war of 1739–48.

47. D^n Manuel Alvarez al Rey, n.d. (c. 1760), AGI, UM 1001: "Es notório que desde se estableció la Compañía, no han podido los Estrangeros sacar de la Isla, como antes, los mejores Tabacos." Alvarez worked as an agent of the Havana Company, and his opinion is therefore suspect. Instrucción para los Interesados de la Real Compañía de la Habana, marzo, 1757, AGI, UM 255.

48. Madariaga a Arriaga, 13 septiembre 1756, AGI, SD 1208; Madariaga a Arriaga, 13 septiembre 1756, AGI, SD 1504; Conde Valparaiso a Cagigal de la Vega, 14 mayo 1759, AGI, SD 2015.

49. Santovenia, "Politica colonial," p. 32.

50. These comparisons rest on unpublished data compiled by Professor John TePaske of Duke University; and on Plaza Prieto, *Estructura económica de España*, p. 820.

51. In 1760 14 percent of the tobacco remitted to Spain came from elsewhere than the West Indies, García-Baquero, *Cádiz y el Atlántico*, 1 : 273.

52. Pliego . . . de documentos formales por los quales se prueba, no existir en Dunquerque tabaco alguno de la Habana; sino de Virginia, 1 enero 1759, AGI, UM 1001. Large quantities of British tobacco were smuggled into Spain as well, notably from Gibraltar. Fowkes to the Treasury Board, 6 February 1756, PRO, T. 1/369/5. Discurso echo por D^n Antonio Bayona, 1739, AGI, UM 1001.

53. Posthumus, *Prices in Holland*, pp. 199–208.

54. Figures for 1740–44 suggest that about 24 percent of the tobacco delivered met quality standards. Razon de los tabacos que se han recevido por compra y valuacion a la Compañía, durante su primero asiento, 8 mayo 1745, AGI, SD 2004; Rason de los Tabacos entregados por la Real Compañía de la Habana, 6 mayo 1745, AGI, SD 2004. For the years 1744–47, this figure drops to 12 percent, Ensenada a Cagigal de la Vega, 30 enero 1748, AGI, SD 2007. Over a fifty-two-month period in 1745–49, the percentage rose to almost 20 percent. Estado de los tavacos qua la Real Compañia de la Habana he embarcado para conducir a los Reinos de Castilla, febrero 1749, AGI, SD 2008. In 1754, 26 percent of five separate shipments met the standards, Documentos remitidos de la via reservada, 20 febrero, 1755, AGI, SD 402.

55. Officials in Santa María del Rosario and Guanabacoa (both near Havana)

reported: "la mayor parte de la tierras de sus distritos ya cansadas y por esto ya inhabiles de dar tabacos de selecta calidad." Marrero, *Cuba*, 7 : 64–65. Joseph de San Martin (et al.) a Cagigal de la Vega, 27 junio 1749, AGI, SD 1212.

56. Cagigal de la Vega a Ensenada, 10 junio 1753, AGI, SD 2011; Minuta de 1756, Tabaco extracto substancial sobre Compañía, AGI, UM 899.

57. Cagigal de la Vega a Arriaga, 20 mayo 1760, AGI, SD 2016; Montalvo a Cagigal de la Vega, 14 junio 1749, AGI, SD 1219.

58. AGI, SD 2015. A *manojo* is a handful of tobacco of varying weight. An unidentifiable document reports that in Bayamo the harvest fell from 190,982 *manojos* in 1752 to 16,922 *manojos* in 1753; in Santiago de Cuba production fell from 233,641 *manojos* to 51,977. Drought afflicted Santiago de Cuba in 1753–54, too. Bacardi, *Crónicas*, 1 : 170.

59. Marrero, *Cuba*, 6 : 183; Cagigal de la Vega a Arriaga, 23 noviembre 1760, AGI, SD 2016; Minuta de 1756, AGI, UM 988.

60. Noticia de todas las partidas que tiene la Isla de Cuba donde se siembren y cogen tabaco (n.d.), AGI, SD 2014.

61. Real Academia de la Historia (Madrid), Colección Mata Linares, 75; Minuta de 1756, AGI, UM 988.

62. Suchlicki, *Cuba*, p. 50: "Several factors converged in the late eighteenth century to . . . give the sugar industry the boost it needed. . . . But it was really the English capture and occupation of Havana that shocked Cuban society out of its lethargic sleep." Knight, "Origins of Wealth," p. 243: "The futility of efforts to stimulate Cuban trade between 1740 and 1763 provides an amazing contrast with the rapid growth after the 1760s." Arango, *Obras*, 1 : 117–18; Liss, *Atlantic Empires*, p. 79.

63. Pezuela, *Diccionario*, 1 : 61–62; Friedlander, *Historia*, p. 60; Schmitz, "El desarollo económico de Cuba y las revoluciones burguesas," p. 32. Elsewhere Pezuela says that between 1740 and 1762 combined tobacco and sugar exports averaged 2,000 tons or 160,000 *arrobas* (*Diccionario*, 3 : 343), and that in fifteen years of monopoly under the Havana Company, Cuba exported an average of 5,000 *arrobas* of sugar (*ibid.*, 2 : 28).

64. Moreno, *El ingenio*, 1 : 19, and 3 : 43, 49.

65. Rolph, *Sugar*, p. 203; Reynolds, *Cuban Sugar*, p. 14; Thomas, *Cuba*, pp. 27, 61. Thomas gets 500 tons from 5,841 *cajas* when he should get 1,168 tons, or 87,696 *arrobas*. The 5,841 cajas represent the amount of sugar seized by the British in 1762, not, as Thomas has it, the annual export total. Valdés, *Historia*, p. 175; Le Riverend, "Desarollo económico," p. 191; Vicens Vives, *Economic History*, 545; Humboldt, *Cuba*, p. 252; Raynal, *Trade in the East and West Indies*, 4 : 297; Guerra, *Sugar and Society in the Caribbean*, p. 42 (first published in 1927); Arango, *Obras*, 2 : 18; Deerr, *History of Sugar*, 1 : 129, 131.

66. Arrate, *Llave del nuevo mundo*, p. 85.
67. Irrutia Ms., 1749, AGI, SD 1157; Computo de cosecha, c. 1735, AGI, SD 488; Consejo de Hacienda, 1 junio 1743, AGI, SD 2009.
68. For sugar price series see Hamilton, *War and Prices*, Appendix I, for Toledo prices; Hauser, *Recherches et documents sur l'histoire des prix en France*, p. 142–43, for Paris prices, 1727–1765; ibid., p. 503, for Nantes prices, 1711–60; Pares, *War and Trade*, p. 339, for Bordeaux prices 1740–63; Josa, *Les industries du sucre et rhum à la Martinique*, p. 111, for Nantes prices, 1739–81; Romano, *Prezzi, salari, e servizi a Napoli*, p. 113, for Naples prices, 1734–60; PRO T 64/276B #387 for London prices, 1728–58; Posthumus, *Prices in Holland*, pp. 119–30, 140, for Amsterdam prices of Brazilian, Surinam, and Santo Domingo sugars. Amsterdam prices, 1623–1806, appear in Reesse, *De Suikerhandel van Amsterdam*, 1:cxxxi. The same series in English money is in Deerr, *History of Sugar*, 2:530. Prices from Salvador, Brazil, appear in Alden, "Commodity Price Movements," Table 1.
69. Despacho de Consejo, 2 abril 1737, AGI, SD 342; Francisco Varas y Valdés a Consulado, 13 abril 1737, AGI, SD 433; Consulta sobre la Real Compañía, 16 febrero 1740, AGI, SD 1129; Testimonio de autos, 1728–29, AGI, SD 488; Martínez de la Vega al Rey, 14 junio 1732, AGI, SD 381; Cabildo de la Habana (?) a (?), 25 agosto 1737, AGI, SD 1499; Representación del cavildo, 25 agosto 1737, AGI, SD 488; Testimonio de Juan Agustín Pessio, 8 agosto 1739, AGI, SD 488; Consulta sobre la Real Compañía, 16 febrero 1740, AGI, SD 1129; Moreno Fraginals, *El ingenio*, 1:27; Pitman, *British West Indies*, pp. 83–84; Expediente sobre la Real Compañía, AGI, SD 488; Marrero, *Cuba*, 7:5–10.
70. Junta General de la Real Compañía, 19 diciembre 1748, AGI, SD 500.
71. Irrutia Ms, 1749, AGI, SD 1157. Marrero, *Cuba*, 7:13, mistakenly has 33,000 *arrobas*.
72. Dictamen sobre las ventajas que pueden sacarse para el mejor fomento de la Isla de Cuba, AGI, SD 1156.
73. Joseph de Quinoces a [?], c. 1758, AGI, SD 2015.
74. Abana a Arriaga, 29 noviembre 1758, AGI, SD 2015.
75. Proyecto sobre azucares, por José Antonio Gelabert, BNM, Sección de Manuscritos, Ms 20144, pt. 1. A copy appears in AGI, SD 2015.
76. Joseph Berazal al Rey, c. 1759, AGI, SD 1504; Junta General de la Real Compañía, 19 diciembre 1748, AGI, SD 500; Cagigal de la Vega a Arriaga, 25 octubre 1761, AGI, SD 326; Manifesto de la Real Compañía, 22 marzo 1747, AGI, UM 882.
77. On Spanish sugar: Balaguer y Primo, *Cultivo de la caña de azúcar*. The rest of the Spanish empire produced little cane, Deerr, *History of Sugar*, 1:131–51. Before 1735 British sugar had enjoyed dominance in the Spanish market, but British exports slumped very heavily when the French

permitted direct export in French ships of Caribbean sugar to Spain (1727). French sugar exports through Bayonne to Spain peaked in 1751 at 2,500,000 livres, or 250,000 *arrobas* in Bordeaux prices. Bayonne always outstripped Bordeaux. Jaupart, *Bayonne*, 1:355; Malvezin, *Histoire du commerce de Bordeaux*, 3:212–15. On the British trade: PRO, T.64/276B/359; T. 64/265B/360; T. 64/276B/362; T. 64/276B/368; T. 64/276B/373; and Schumpeter, *English Overseas Trade Statistics*, p. 65.

78. Aimes, *Slavery in Cuba*, pp. 23, 33, 37; Saco, *Esclavitud*, 2:209; Thomas, *Cuba*, pp. 31, 52; Ortiz, *Hampa afro-cubana*, p. 79; Brown, "Illicit Slave Trade" (dissertation), p. 34; Humboldt, *Cuba*, p. 217; Southey, *West Indies*, p. 377; Donnan, *Slave Trade*, 2:xlvi; Deerr, *History of Sugar*, 1:129, 2:280; Williams, *From Columbus to Castro*, p. 145; Corwin, *Abolition of Slavery in Cuba*, pp. 9–11; Franco, "Slave Trade," pp. 88–100; and Knight, *Slave Society*, p. 7.

79. AGI, UM 929. The folio is headed: "Piezas de indias coste y costas." It appears among the papers of the Havana Company's Cadiz factor, Iturrigaray, and probably refers to the twelve years during which Aróstegui headed the Company.

80. Cagigal de la Vega a Ensenada, 21 marzo 1754, AGI, SD 2209. In Santiago de Cuba 2,719 slaves died between 1740 and 1755, or 179 per year. Madariaga a Arriaga, 15 febrero 1756, AGI, SD 2209. In the Havana shipyard, slave mortality averaged about 6.8 per cent yearly. Marrero, *Cuba*, 8:17.

81. Compañía de la Habana. Sobre piezas de negros que ha introducidos, n.d. (c. 1752), AGI UM 897. Le Riverend, "Desarollo económico," p. 208, puts Cuban slave imports at 5,000 to 6,000 during 1713–39.

82. Palmer, *Human Cargoes*, pp. 103–6. See also: Some further Considerations humbly proposed in order to prevent farming out the Factorys upon the Island of Cuba, n.d. (c. 1732), Clements Library, Shelburne MSS, 44, Asiento 2, 913. This document claims the South Sea Company sold 1,549 slaves in Cuba between 10 October 1730 and 11 January 1731. Le Riverend, "Desarollo económico," p. 208, mentions this figure with a slightly different starting date. Several letters appearing in BL, AM 25563 discuss the South Sea Company slave trade in Cuba.

83. This average is derived from a 1759–61 average of 462, a 1752–58 figure of 315, and a 1743–47 average of 675. See Noticias sacadas de la junta general a desde primero Abril de 1758 a 30 marzo 1761, AGI, UM 258; Peñalver a los Reales Oficiales de la Habana, 3 diciembre 1747, AGI, SD 2208. Cuenta General de la Administración de la Real Compañía de la Habana, 1752–58, 28, AGI, UM 898. (This entire *legajo* consists of this single 336-page document.)

84. Manual Alvarez de Toledo Labato, n.d., AGS, Hacienda 1836.

85. Data for the first quinquennium put slave imports at 2,200 or 440 annually,

Resumen General, Primer Quinquennio, AGI, UM 258. Another document suggests that the annual average was only 376 for 1741–51, Cotexo de la Piezas de Negros Introducidos, AGI, UM 986. Another document has 4,320 slaves imported between 1740 and 1752, or 360 annually, Continuación de separados cargos contra la antigua Dirección de la Compañía de la Habana, AGI, UM 883. Should the lowest of these be the truth, total legal imports for 1740–60 still amount to 7,560, 34 percent higher than the figure offered in the published literature.

86. Francisco López de Gamarra a Arriaga, 27 abril 1763, AGI SD 2210.

87. Moreno, *El ingenio*, 1:35; Thomas, *Cuba*, p. 50; Marrero, *Cuba*, 6:130, n. 62.

88. Slaves sold for only 100 pesos in Bayamo, compared to 250–300 in Havana. Informe de 1734, AGI, SD 488. Houston, *Memoirs*, p. 244. Employees of the South Sea Company claimed that Jamaican Jews were prominent in illegal slaving. Company agents could accept only coin—scarce in Cuba— while contraband traders accepted goods. John Meriwether to Peter Burrell, 3 September 1736, Clements Library, Shelburne MSS, 44, 876. Juan de Prado a Arriaga, 13 abril 1761, AGI, SD 2209. Donnan, *Slave Trade*, 2:312n.

89. Consulta de 13 octubre 1730, AGI SD 325; Joseph Antonio Gelabert al Marqués de la Regalia, 22 abril 1744, AGI SD 326.

90. Moreno, "Africa in Cuba," pp. 191–96; Bourdé, "Sources et méthodes," p. 418. Knight himself prefers 4 percent mortality in the nineteenth century, *Slave Society*, p. 82. Engerman, "Slavery," p. 271; Craton, "Hobbesian or Panglossian?" p. 328; Higman, *Slave Population*, p. 115. For Cuban documents on slave mortality see note 80 above. For smallpox discrimination, Marrero, *Cuba*, 6:4–5. For estimates of the slave population from 1755, see Kiple, *Blacks in Colonial Cuba*, p. 4.

91. The mathematics behind these calculations hinges on an exercise in natural logarithms explained in Eblen, "Slave Populations," p. 213. Marrero, the only author who has ventured an opinion on the size of the slave trade during 1701–63, has "more than 800 per year" for the legitimate trade and 9,500 for the entire illegal trade. This works out to at least 59,100, not radically different from my estimate. Marrero posits a high rate of natural increase among slaves—an impossibility given the magnitude of the slave trade. On the later slave trade see Murray, "Slave Trade," pp. 131–50.

92. Curtin, *Atlantic Slave Trade*, p. 32, suggests that prior to 1760 the Cuban slave population increased naturally. Eblen, "Slave Populations," tries to measure that for the period after 1775. Eblen's calculations are vitiated by ahistorical assumptions concerning the vital rates of the Cuban slave population, untenable for either the eighteenth or the nineteenth centuries. He assumes, for instance, birth rates of 52 or 53/1,000 (p. 245), which are very close to the observed historical maximum rates for any society (see Henripin,

La population canadienne, p. 65; Eaton and Mayer, "Fertility Among the Hutterites," pp. 206–64; and Smith, "Cocos-Keeling Islands," pp. 94–130). Eblen's rates are more than double those recorded in Caribbean slave societies and are implausible for reasons summed up in Sheridan, "Mortality," pp. 306–7. Moreover, Eblen assumes death rates ranging from 31 to 39/1,000, derived not from any evidence concerning slave populations, but from mortality schedules derived from the experience of (1) Latin American countries for which statistics existed in about 1900 (probably the healthier ones), (2) Western Europe and North America, and (3) the prehistoric Maghreb. Higher mortality rates than these were routine in preindustrial Western Europe, let alone the Caribbean. For recorded rates in the British Caribbean see Sheridan, "Mortality," pp. 288–89. Eblen's assumptions seem questionable for the nineteenth century and absurd for the eighteenth.

93. The annual hide exports from Buenos Aires amounted to about 150,000 (four times the Cuban contribution) in the 1770s, but before 1735 had been slight. Parry, *Spanish Seaborne Empire*, p. 308; Vicens Vives, *Economic History*, pp. 545–46.

94. In 1568–1615 hides accounted for 88 percent of Cuban exports (by value), Inglis, "Demography of Cuba," p. 87.

95. Irrutia Ms., AGI, SD 1157. According to this treatise, Havana produced 34,000 hides annually, Bayamo, 12,000; Santiago de Cuba, 10,000; Puerto Príncipe, 10,000; and Trinidad, Santa Clara, Sancti Spíritus, and Caio combined to produce 12,000. Altogether this makes 78,000, although Irrutia has 71,000 as the island's total production. Irrutia also says Cuba sold 20,000 pesos worth of beef annually to ships and 30,000 to the population of Havana. Early in the seventeenth century a governor reported that Cuba produced 20,000 cured hides annually, Le Riverend, "Desarollo económico," p. 195.

96. Production figures for Bayamo changed from 10,000 to 12,000 between 1729 and 1749, Cabildo de Bayamo a [?], 8 junio 1729, AGI, SD 488; Consulta de Consejo, 16 febrero 1740, AGI, SD 1129.

97. Raynal, *Trade in the East and West Indies*, 4: 198.

98. Jefferys, *Spanish Islands*, p. 73; Isla de Cuba, su Descripción Geográfica, Política, y Fisica, n.d., BL, AM 17628, fol. 25.

99. Posthumus, *Prices in Holland*, p. 356. The price ranged from 0.40 to 0.45 Dutch *guilders* per pound.

100. An Account of the Severall sea Ports belonging to the Spaniards in America, which John Fengass has been in a Trading with a description of the Fortifications to the best of his knowledge, September 1705, PRO, CO 137/51. Fengass wrote of the Cuban keys Rio Manchate, Bonaventura, Savana de Cruz, Savana de Mer, and Porto María: "The chief trade here is for hides, which Dutch ships from Holland take away in abundance."

101. By Baron von Humboldt's time (1804), Cuban slaves ate Argentine jerked beef, *Cuba*, p. 260.

102. These figures are derived from a list presented in Humboldt's *Cuba*, pp. 119—20; and Valdés, *Historia*, pp. 423—27. Arrate, *Llave del Nuevo Mundo*, p. 91; Pezuela, *Diccionario*, 3 : 147. This list coincides perfectly with partial data in Lista de los Nabios que Su Majestad ha mandado construido . . . desde 1743, 5 marzo 1749, AGI, UM 995; Origen de la Real Compañía . . .; estado de su Asiento de construcción de Navios, 26 abril 1749, AGI, UM 891; Relación . . . del caudal destinado a la construcción y fábrica de Vageles en los Astilleros de este Puerto, 31 julio 1736, AGI Contaduría, 1157 ramo 2; Cuentas del cuadal destinado a Fábrica de Navios, 31 diciembre 1757, AGI, Contaduría 1168; Quentas de Fábrica de navios, 6 enero 1750, AGI, Contaduría, 1168.

103. Merino Navarro, *Armada española*, p. 121. Basque and Galician ports provided the rest. Guarnizo—near Santander—built almost as many ships of the line as Havana, accounting for about 20 percent of Spanish naval building in the eighteenth century. Observations sur la marine d'Espagne . . ., par Antoine d'Albert du Chesne, (c. 1735), MPCU, Lot 64, Item 5.056. Merino Navarro, *Armada española*, p. 343. On Basque shipbuilding: Guiard y Larrauri, *La industria naval vizcaina*, pp. 117—50.

104. Uztáriz, *Theory*, pp. 286—87. Spanish naval vessels grew more durable as the century wore on, Merino Navarro, *Armada española*, p. 353.

105. Relación de los navios perdidos, 1759—1847, AMN, MS 2213, fol. 57—58.

106. Estado de los Navios, Fragatas . . . que se componen la Real Armada de España, 1778, BL, AM 20926, fol. 325. The 114-gun *Santíssima Trinidad* was built in Havana in the late 1760s.

107. Estado que manifiesta las fuerzas maritimas del Rey de España, 1771, BL, AM 15717, fol. 34.

108. Duración media de los navios construidos en la Habana . . ., por Onurato Boujon, 1 enero 1817, AMN, MS 440, doc. 7. Measuring a ship's durability by the time elapsed prior to its first careening gives a better index than the total lifespan of a ship, since many were sunk or captured in battle, dying an early death that was no reflection on the quality of the ship.

109. On timber quality: Cagigal de la Vega a Carvajal, 31 agosto 1747, AHN, Estado 2320. Before 1740 Juan de Acosta had built ships under contract to the Crown, few of which appear to have had long careers, although perhaps the war of 1739—48 had more to do with that than the quality of his work. The Havana Company demonstrated a scientific interest in the art of shipbuilding at the same time as did the French navy under Maurepas. In 1748 a mathematics professor at the Universidad de la Habana, Gabriel de Torres, began work improving ship design for the navy. His hiring appears in the accounts, AGI, Contaduría 1168, ramo 5.

110. Nota de los caudales rezevido de la Real Hazienda . . . , desde 7 mayo 1742 hasta la fecha, 7 mayo 1749, AGI, UM 995; Asiento con el Constructor Dⁿ Juan de Acosta, 21 abril 1731, AMN, Colección Guillén, Ms. 1209, fol. 32−75.

111. Junta General de la Real Compañía, c. 1760, AGI, IG 1745. Instrucción para los Interesados de la Real Compañía de la Habana, marzo 1757, AGI, SD 2014; and AGI, UM 255. Cappa, *Estudios críticos*, 12:347.

112. Compañía de la Habana. Navios Construidos para la Real Armada, n.d., AGI, UM 996 and AGI, UM 897. Fernández Duro, *Armada española*, 6:364−65n, quotes Pezuela saying a first-rate in Havana in 1748 cost 454,898 pesos, much more than indicated by data from Spanish archives. Data compiled by Inglis show a 105 percent cost overrun for seven ships of sixty-four to seventy guns, built at Havana between 1744 and 1748. See his "Spanish Naval Shipyard at Havana," p. 13. On Guayaquil see Cappa, *Estudios críticos*, 12:162. Béthencourt Massieu, "El real astillero de Coatzacoalcos," pp. 371−428.

113. Dos proposiziones, y sus Respuestas sobre el Asiento de Construcción de Vaxeles, n.d. (c. 1749), AGS, Marina, 645; Junta General de la Real Compañía de la Habana, 19 diciembre 1748, AGS, Marina, 645; Aróstegui a Ensenada, 9 enero 1749, AGS, Marina 645; *Real órden*, 23 junio 1749, AGI UM 995; Aróstegui a Ensenada, 25 agosto 1749, AGI, UM 995.

114. Estado del Costo . . . de los navios de 70, n.d. AGI, UM 995; Estado del Costo . . . de los navios de 60, n.d. AGI, UM 995; Estado de los caudales distribuidos en la construcción del Navio de 80 . . . El Fenix, 31 agosto 1749, AGI, UM 995.

115. Nota de los efectos que existen de quenta de la Compañía en el astillero de la Habana, 19 diciembre 1748, AGS, Marina 645.

116. Resumen que manifiesta los cuadales . . . distribuido . . . en [el] ramo de fábrica de vaxeles . . . , desde 1741 hasta 15 agosto 1751, 28 junio 1752, AGI, UM 996. Data por gastos causados en la contrucción de navios, 1759, AGI, UM 894, puts timber costs at about 65 percent of total costs, but this apparently refers to a brief period, about fifteen months, and not the entire ten years of Havana Company shipbuilding. *Real cédula*, 26 agosto 1713, AGI, SD 482. Merino Navarro, *Armada española*, p. 240, cites a document in AGS, Marina 330, which gives 18,000 pesos as the cost of timber for ships of seventy to eighty guns at Havana. This amounts to only 13 to 15 percent of total costs, lower than any other figures I have seen.

117. Estado en que se hacen presentas los operarios, y Juntas de Bueyes que . . . se empleasen . . . en la Labor, y Tiras de Maderas, 8 noviembre 1748, AGS, Marina 645. Another document from one month later puts the number of oxen teams at 1,330, of which 860 were rented, Nota de los efectos que existen de quenta de la Compañía en el astillero de la Habana,

19 diciembre 1748, AGS, Marina 645. Estado en que se ponen presentes los caudales que la Real Compañía . . . ha distribuido, 8 noviembre 1748, AGS, Marina 645; Estado en que se ponen de Manifiesto los Arboles de Cedro y Madera fuerte, 8 noviembre 1748, AGS, Marina 645.

118. Quenta del costo que tiene al mes los catorce cortes de maderas, febrero 1749, AGI, UM 995.

119. Reggio a Ensenada, 15 octubre 1747, AGS, Marina 645; Itinerario de viage de Reggio y Aróstegui, 19 septiembre 1745, AGI, UM 995; Nota de los Palos de Pino que ha conducido la fregata presa de la Compañía, n.d., AGI, UM 995; Testimonio de autos sobre . . . la conserbación de los montes, 1747, AGI, SD 387; Minuto de Consejo, 14 agosto 1756, AGI, SD 371; Pedro de Torres al Gobernador, 24 julio 1747, AGI, SD 387; *Real orden*, 8 abril 1748, AHN, Consejo de Indias 20884.

120. Using Humboldt's 160 cubic feet of wood per five *arrobas* of sugar (*Cuba*, p. 273), and a 1760 harvest of 450,000 *arrobas*. The shipyard, however, used much more wood than went into ships. Assuming the average tree cut for sugar kettles stood 40 feet high and had a 2-foot diameter, the 1760 sugar harvest used only as much wood as the shipyard did in 1747.

121. La Compañía a Ensenada, 14 enero 1746, AGI, UM 995. Estado . . . del Fierro que se necessita para la conclusion de la Fabrica de los tres navios de setenta cañones, 3 abril 1746, AGI, UM 995. Marrero a Ensenada, 3 noviembre 1747, AGS, Marina 645. Estado que expresa el Fierro, Herrages y clavazones necesarios para la construcción . . . de quatro Navios de la porte de setenta Canones, 25 octubre 1748, AGS, Marina 645. AMN, Colección Guillén, Ms. 1209, fol. 32–75. Alcala-Zamora, "Producción de hierro," pp. 117–218.

122. Campillo a Aróstegui, 4 marzo 1743, AGI, SD 2003; Aróstegui a [?], 6 octubre 1743, AGI, SD 400. Havana not only built ships but served as the central refitting port of the Spanish Caribbean, especially after 1746 when a machine for removing and installing masts came into use. A drawing of this machine appears in AGI, Mapas y Planos, SD 218.

123. Consulta de Consejo, 21 enero 1719, AGI, SD 338; Güemes y Horcasitas al Rey, 24 noviembre 1737, AGI, SD 1201; Guazo Calderon a [?], 5 noviembre 1718, AGI, SD 378; Güemes y Horcasitas a [?], 28 septiembre 1743, 31 diciembre 1743, AGI, SD 1194; Cagigal de la Vega a Ensenada, 8 enero 1753, AGI, SD 2011.

124. Expediente de 25 enero 1757, AGI, SD 1133; Madariaga a Ensenada, 15 diciembre 1754, AGI, SD 370; Bacardi, *Crónicas*, 1:170–73.

125. Peñalver a Ensenada, 20 febrero 1750, AGI, SD 1501.

126. Per capita exports fell 9 percent from 1732 to 1754, Moore, "Merchant Trade" (thesis), p. 15.

127. Aróstegui a Carvajal, 3 enero 1747, AHN, Estado 2320: "El fruto principal que los Ingleses an apetizido, y sacado de aqui en su anterior asiento es

el tavaco, que con previas contratas aseguravan de los cosecheros sin detenerse en procurarlo de la mexor calidad, y como es esto lo que apeteze el labrador prezisamente resulta aplicarse a hazerlo como lo piden y no como Su Magestad previene." Cagigal de la Vega al Rey, 10 junio 1738, AGI, SD 363; Rey a Cagigal de la Vega, 12 julio 1739, AGI, SD 363.

Chapter 7

1. Mémoire pour faire connoitre la Situation actuelle de commerce, 1745, MPCU, Lot 21, Item 9.041; Maurepas's 1745 mémoire. Boulle, "French Colonial Trade," p. 50, puts the increase in French colonial trade at only fourfold. Crouzet, "Angleterre et France," p. 263, says French colonial trade grew by a factor of ten during 1716–84.
2. Maurepas's 1745 mémoire: "On ne peut revoquer en doute que ce soit le commerce maritime qui nous a procuré ces richesses." Also: Levasseur, *Histoire du commerce de la France*, 1:487.
3. Callahan, *Honor*, pp. 16–18.
4. O'Reilly a Arriaga, 1 abril 1764, AGS, Hacienda 2342.
5. Mémoire pour servir à l'instruction du Gouverneur, 9 mars 1716, AC, C¹¹B, 1:448–52.
6. Mémoire sur les affaires presentes du Canada, et l'Etablissement du Cap Breton, n.d., NLSC, 293, fol. 1–29.
7. Mims, *Colbert's West India Policy*, pp. vii–viii, passim.
8. Maurepas à St.-Ovide et Le Normant du Mezy, 9 mai 1724, AC, B, 47: 254–59; Mémoire du Roi à Beauharnois, 29 avril 1727, AC, B, 50:500–510; Maurepas à Lalonde-Magon, 12 janvier 1729, AC, B, 53:5–6. Also: Lunn, "Economic Development" (thesis), p. 639; and Gould, "Trade," pp. 473–90.
9. Maurepas à St.-Ovide et Le Normant du Mezy, 10 juin 1727, AC, B, 50–2:576–77. The King's decree was dated 31 December 1726.
10. Maurepas à controleur générale, 19 mars 1737, AC, B, 65:422; Circulaire de 21 juillet 1743, AC, B, 70:127 and AC, F³, 50:261.
11. Mémoire à Desherbiers et Prévost, 25 mars 1750, AC, B, 91:323; Machault à Drucourt et Prévost, 14 juin 1755, AC, B, 101:196–98.
12. Maurepas à Larnage et Maillart, 5 avril 1743, AC, B, 76:213–17.
13. Maurepas's 1730 mémoire.
14. Conseil à Vaudreuil et Begon, 24 mai 1719, AC, B, 41:1081–96; Mémoire du Roi à Beauharnois et Hocquart, 11 avril 1730, AC, B, 54–2:432–33; Maurepas à Beauharnois et Dupuy, 22 avril 1727, 50–2:485–86.
15. Conseil à Ligondais, 7 juin 1717, AC, B, 39–5:1001; Mémoire du Roy aux sieurs de Costebelle et de Soubras, 26 juin 1717, *Collection de man-*

uscrits, 3:25. See Wroth and Annan, *Acts of French Royal Administration*; Dorn, *Competition*, p. 266; McLennan, *Louisbourg: Foundation to Fall*, p. 402; Maggs Brothers, *French Colonisation*, p. 33; Frégault, *Bigot*, 1:87.

16. Lettres patentes, octobre 1727, AC, B, 50–1:333–42; Maurepas à Amirauté, 24 juin 1728, AC, B, 52–2:607. This trade was first sanctioned by a Mémoire du Roi, 12 mai 1722, AC, C¹¹B, 6:25. McLennan, *Louisbourg: Foundation to Fall*, p. 75.

17. Maurepas à St.-Ovide et Le Normant du Mezy, 10 juin 1727, AC, B, 50–2:578.

18. Mémoire du Roy à St.-Ovide et Le Normant du Mezy, 12 mai 1722, AC, C¹¹B, 6:25.

19. Maurepas à Bigot et de Forant, 22 juin 1739, AC, B, 68:358; Rouillé à Raymond et Prévost, 17 juillet 1753, AC, C¹¹B, 33:310; Mémoire du Roy à Raymond et Prévost, 24 avril 1751, AC, C¹¹B, 30:223; Machault à Drucourt et Prévost, 14 juin 1755, AC, B, 101:196–98.

20. Machault in 1756 suggested that Louisbourg be opened to trade with friendly nations, but nothing ever came of this. Machault à Trudaine, 25 mars 1756, AC, B, 104:188–90.

21. See the Proyecto para galeones y flotas of 1720, in *Documentos para la historia argentina*, 5:22–45. Two copies are in AGI, UM 995. AGI, SD 1212 includes about twenty-five letters discussing the revival of the flota system, 1719–20. For eighteenth-century discussion see: Uztáriz, *Theory*, pp. 139–41; Antuñez y Acevedo, *Memorias históricas*, pp. 58–107. See also Walker, *Spanish Politics and Imperial Trade*, pp. 22–27, 107–11.

22. Aprobación de la escritura en que el consulado y comercio de Cádiz se encarga del despacho annual de ocho avisos, 1720, AGI, SD 433.

23. The South Sea Company's contract appears in AGI, SD 2208; AGI, IG 2785; and in French in BL, AM 33032, fol. 19–36. Also: Davenport, *European Treaties*, 2:166–86.

24. See Hamilton, "Role of Monopoly," pp. 33–53.

25. Fraud consisted of unregistered trade in Spanish boats between Spanish ports, essentially tax evasion. Contraband consisted of trade between Spanish ports in proscribed goods. Illicit commerce took place between Spaniards and foreigners. Dictamen dada a Su Majestad por Dⁿ Joseph de Avalos . . . : la descripción que haze de las diferentes clases de contrabandos, 1768, AGI, SD 1156.

26. Consulta de Consejo, 16 abril 1731, AGI, SD 1129; Consulta de Consejo, 25 octubre 1732, AGI, SD 1129; Rey a Cagigal de la Vega, 12 julio 1739, AGI, SD 363; Alonso Arcos Moreno al Rey, 29 marzo 1749, AGI, SD 366; Consulta de Consejo, 6 abril 1750, AGI, SD 1130B; Martín Esteban Aróstegui a Arriaga, 14 febrero 1755, AGI, SD 2110 (Aróstegui, an army lieutenant, was a cousin of the Aróstegui who headed the Havana Company.); Madariaga a Ensenada, 30 septiembre 1754, AGI, SD 2110.

27. Authorities liked to remind one another of the penalty, but rarely imposed it. Güemes y Horcasitas a [?], 1 enero 1745, AGI, SD 1194; Real Cédula, 20 junio 1743, AGI, SD 1207.

28. Cagigal de la Vega a Quintana, 9 enero 1740, AGI, SD 1203; [?] a Güemes y Horcasitas, 28 agosto 1743, AGI, SD 1207; Testimonio de autos . . . sobre el retorno a este Puerto . . . de la Goleta San Francisco Xavier, 1754, AGI, SD 372.

29. The French considered Acadian trade as within the empire and thus legal. Bigot au ministre, décembre, 1740, AC, C^{11}B, 22:207.

30. See Moore, "Merchant Trade" (thesis), p. 66.

31. Flour, lard, legumes, and butter were the usual food items. Clothing included jackets, culottes, hats, smocks, shoes, stockings, and shirts. Minutes de Conseil, 1719, AC, C^{11}B, 4:4; Extrait des Etats . . . des vivres, 18 novembre 1724, AC, C^{11}B, 7:115–16; Moore, "Commodity Imports;" and "Merchant Trade," pp. 21–22.

32. Pritchard, "Ships, Men and Commerce" (dissertation), p. 38; Lunn, "Economic Development" (dissertation), pp. 357–58; Reid, "Intercolonial Trade," pp. 241–42; Labignette, "La farine dans la Nouvelle-France," p. 498.

33. Mémoire de Prévost, 1753, AC, C^{11}B, 33:116; Mémoire de Bigot, 1740, AN, F2B: Cartons 11, 12–18; Balcom, "Commerce"; Moore, "Merchants." Cod amounted to 70 percent of French West Indian imports from Canada and Ile Royale, and 3 percent of all French West Indian imports. Gould, "Trade," pp. 485–86.

34. This is based on data for 1737. Cargaisons apportées dans la colonie, 1737, AC, C^{11}C, 9:50–95. Rum apparently counted as food.

35. See AC, C^{11}B, 23:126–33; Maurepas à Bigot, 17 mai 1742, AC, B, 72:442; Maurepas à Bigot, 15 juin 1742, AC, B, 74:581–83; Maurepas à Bigot, 30 juin 1743, AC, B, 76:510; Maurepas à Bigot, 21 avril 1744, AC, B, 78:405–6; Rouillé à Prévost, 17 juillet 1753, AC, B, 97:317; Rouillé à Prévost, 1 juillet 1754, AC, B 99:260. On Port Toulouse-Canso smuggling: Bigot au ministre, 7 novembre 1740, AC, C^{11}B, 22:200–202.

36. Cf. Boulle, "French Colonial Trade," p. 55, where it says the average tonnage was 60 on the New England-Louisbourg route in 1749.

37. Pitman, *British West Indies*, p. 42.

38. Ostrander, "Molasses Trade," p. 78.

39. Mims, *Colbert's West India Policy*, pp. 221–22. See Deerr, *History of Sugar*, 2:411–13, on laws concerning the rum trade.

40. Ostrander, "Molasses Trade," p. 79. See also Sheridan, "Molasses Act," pp. 62–83.

41. Prévost au ministre, 7 juin 1755, AC, C^{11}B, 35:68. Sheridan, "Molasses Act," pp. 78–79, treats the British colonial market for French Antilles molasses.

42. Minutes de Conseil, 15 mars 1713, AC, C¹¹B, 14:17−20; Rouillé à Vaudreuil, 6 septembre 1753, AC, B, 97:170; Mémoire de Prévost, 1753, AC, C¹¹B, 33:116−21. Robert Young to the Board of Trade, 6 December 1743, Public Archives of Canada, *Canadian Currency*, 1:224−25. Cornwallis to the Lords of Trade, 27 November 1750, in Akins, *Public Documents of Nova Scotia*, p. 630. In 1743 New England imported 6,000 hogsheads of rum from Louisbourg, Public Archives of Nova Scotia, 27:30−33, in Innis, *Select Documents*, p. 132.

43. Maurepas à Clieu et Marin, 8 juillet 1739, AC, B, 68:43−44; Maurepas à Champigny et de la Croix, 28 juillet 1739, AC, B, 68:53−54. Louisbourg officials naturally claimed that the French planters traded illegally with the English in the Caribbean, cutting into Louisbourg's rightful trade. Bigot au ministre, 30 juin 1743, AC, C¹¹B, 25:107; Drucourt et Prévost au ministre, 20 october 1755, AC, C¹¹B, 35:43. See also Innis, "Cape Breton," pp. 76−87.

44. Lunn, "Economic Development" (dissertation), p. 337; Pritchard, "Ships, Men and Commerce" (dissertation), pp. 370−73; see Reid, "Intercolonial Trade," pp. 236−56.

45. On the Quebec harvests and trade see Lunn, "Economic Development" (dissertation), pp. 94−107; Pritchard, "Ships, Men and Commerce" (dissertation), pp. 350−57, 364, 499; Frégault, *Bigot*, 1:145−47; Labignette, "La farine dans la Nouvelle-France," pp. 500−01. Quebec provided the French Antilles with 10 percent to 15 percent of their legally imported flour before 1740, but this trade too disappeared. Gould, "Trade," pp. 486−87.

46. New England horses, for example, cost less to raise and to transport to the French West Indies. Mémoire de Beauharnois et Hocquart au Roi, 26 décembre 1734, *Collection de manuscrits*, 3:170. On the St. Lawrence route: Pritchard, "Ships, Men and Commerce" (dissertation), pp. 32−35. On low profits: Frégault, *Bigot*, 1:100.

47. Bigot au Maurepas, 26 novembre 1742, AC, C¹¹B, 23:134−36; Labignette, "La farine dans la Nouvelle-France," p. 500. For the relative importance of the Ile Royale and French West Indies markets to the Quebec timber trade, see the tables in Lunn, "Economic Development" (dissertation), pp. 468−69.

48. Moore, "Commodity Imports," pp. 24−26; Labignette, "La farine dans la Nouvelle-France," p. 499. For the seasonal rhythm of Louisbourg's trade with French Basque ports, Turgeon, "Échanges Franco-Canadiennes" (thesis), 1:169−70, Graphiques 5A, 5B.

49. In Innis, *Select Documents*, pp. 129−30; and AC, C¹¹B, 14:49. In 1727 a storm threatened to discourage French traders from coming to Louisbourg, so St.-Ovide outfitted an expedition to New England. See Innis, *Select Documents*, pp. 105−7.

50. Admiralty records show only four such cases between 1750 and 1755. Archives Départmentales de la Charente-Maritime, Régistre B–273. In the summer of 1730, however, three seizures were recorded. Minutes de Conseil, 3 janvier 1731, AC, C¹¹B, 12:4.

51. Chard, "Impact of Ile Royale" (dissertation), Table 1, vii. On the commercial relations between Louisbourg and New England: Rawlyk, *Nova Scotia's Massachusetts*, pp. 133–35; Moore, "Merchant Trade" (thesis), pp. 99–100.

52. Philipps to Craggs, July 1720 in Akins, *Public Documents of Nova Scotia*, p. 37. In Innis, *Select Documents*, pp. 124–26.

53. Le Normant du Mezy au ministre, 1724, AC, C¹¹B, 7:51; Armstrong to the Board of Trade, 10 May 1731, PRO, CO 217/6; Beauharnois et Hocquart à Maurepas, 12 septembre 1745, in O'Callaghan, *Documents of New York*, 10:5.

54. This is an estimate based on data presented in Moore, "Merchant Trade" (thesis), p. 25. Filion, *Maurepas*, p. 115, overestimates the value of French trade to Louisbourg alone at 3 million livres.

55. Arango, *Obras*, 1:117: "La Habana había adelantado muy poco en al año de 1760. Victima del monopolio de la Compania exclusiva." Of the 1762 capture: "puede señalarse como la verdadera época de la resurrección de la Habana." And on 1:118: "habian hecho mas en un año los ingleses que nosotros en las sesenta anteriores. . . . para el consumo de la Habana bastaban dos embarcaciones cada año." This latter statistic becomes three ships annually in Sagra, *Historia económico-política y estadística de la Isla de Cuba*, p. 130. Pezuela, *Diccionario*, 1:168, says ten or twelve ships annually used the Havana harbor. Marrero, *Cuba*, 6:121, writes that before 1762 five or six ships sufficed to carry off the fruits of the land. See also Roig de Leuschenring's preface to *La dominación inglesa en la Habana*, pp. xxvi–xxix. Le Riverend, "Desarollo económico," p. 242, cites no numbers in attributing commercial growth to the British occupation. On 2:51, however, he claims fewer than 15 ships traded annually in Havana before 1762, compared to more than 700 during the British stay.

56. Suchlicki, *Cuba*, p. 48: "During the two decades of its existence, the [Havana] company proved a very successful venture for its Spanish stockholders, but Cuba's commercial development was hampered and production lagged." (Actually the company existed well into the nineteenth century, although its monopoly lasted only twenty-one years.) Its stockholders were almost as often Cuban as Spanish, and it did not prove a successful venture for them. See also: Knight, "Origins of Wealth," p. 243; Deerr, *History of Sugar*, 1:129; Thomas, *Cuba*, p. 51; Raynal (admittedly not an anglophone), *Trade in the East and West Indies*, 4:199; Liss, *Atlantic Empires*, pp. 17, 79. Knight, *Slave Society*, p. 10, credits Havana with an annual traffic of six ships prior to 1760.

57. Pezuela, *Diccionario*, 3 : 378. Pezuela presents figures for the intake from port taxes. Since taxation rates changed rarely and price inflation was minimal, these data give a reliable indication of the trends in trade values.

58. Le Riverend, "Desarollo económico," p. 241. Le Riverend, "Relaciones entre Nueva España y Cuba," p. 67, claims this trade expanded sharply in 1737 with the transfer of the Armada de Barlovento to Havana from Veracruz, but this is not borne out by customs data.

59. In five years, 1765–70, Mexico imported only 3,021 *arrobas* of Cuban tobacco, Proyecto sobre tabacos, resumen general, 15 marzo 1770, AGI, IG 1745.

60. Le Riverend, "Desarollo económico," p. 242, suggests the Campeche trade also included jerked beef imports to Havana.

61. These textiles were listed as Spanish, but the majority must have come from northern Europe. See Clarke, *Letters*, p. 257. Le Riverend, "Desarollo económico," p. 242, mentions cacao sent from Caracas to Havana, but this trade was very minor.

62. Proyecto sobre los tabacos, resumen general, 15 marzo 1770, AGI, IG 1745.

63. García-Baquero, *Cádiz y el Atlántico*, 2 : 338–40.

64. On this trade: Morales Padrón, *Comercio*; and Peraza de Ayala, *Régimen*, pp. 101–52.

65. Peraza de Ayala, *Régimen*, p. 149 n. 407.

66. Morales, *Comercio*, p. 243.

67. Morales, *Comercio*, pp. 332–37, has cargo lists for three vessels between Canary Island ports and Havana in the eighteenth century.

68. Morales, *Comercio*, pp. 348–58.

69. See the lists in Antúñez y Acevedo, *Memorias históricas*, Appendix 7; and García-Baquero, *Cádiz y el Atlántico*, 2 : 278–81. The tonnage in the *flota* did not increase significantly between 1715 and 1760. Walker, *Spanish Politics and Imperial Trade*, p. 228.

70. The 1730 *flota* sold goods worth only 9,430 pesos at Havana, AGI, Contaduría 1154.

71. Parry, *Spanish Seaborne Empire*, pp. 286–87; Vásquez de Prada, "Las rutas comerciales entre España y América," pp. 200–208. See Walker, *Spanish Politics and Imperial Trade*, pp. 200–209 on this era in Spanish trade.

72. Nota que manifiesta los frutos y generos . . . de la fregata la Perla, mayo 1761, AGI, SD 2026; Nota que manifiesta los frutos y generos . . . de la fregata Santo Domingo, mayo 1761, AGI, SD 2026; Pliego de examen de differencias de valores de facturas y equibocaciones de sus empaques en las cargazones de los tres vaxeles, 1757, AGI, UM 257; Manifesto de la Real Compañía, los renglones de mas consumo, 22 marzo 1747, AGI, UM 882.

73. AGI, SD 1157, Irrutia Ms. 9–10. Irrutia later says 488,618 pesos were spent yearly on goods imported from Spain.

74. Cuenta en Resumen de todo lo vendido desde 1 de Abril de 1761 hasta fin de Marzo de 1761, 31 marzo 1761, AGI, SD 2026.

75. Compañía de la Habana. Utilidades de la Real Hazienda en el giro de las embarcaciones, n.d., AGI, UM 897.

76. Available evidence suggests neither *registro* tonnage nor prices declined. On the other hand, Company documents have usually proved accurate where corroboratory evidence allows a check.

77. Bourne, *Queen Anne's Navy*, chapter 5; BL, AM 34335, fol. 111.

78. Dahlgren, *Relations*.

79. Cabildo de la Habana, 24 enero, 1720, AHN, Estado 2331: "Havana is in great misery because of the total lack of commerce." Peñalver et al [al Rey], 6 febrero 1735, AGI, SD 1499; Cabildo de la Habana al Consejo, 5 julio 1735, AGI, SD 405; Breve Relación de . . . la Compañia de la Havana, n.d., BPR, Ms. 2818.

80. The Treaty of Madrid appears in Davenport, *European Treaties*, 2:94–109. On contraband methods in the Caribbean see Labat, *Nouveau voyage*, 7:221–28; Campbell, *Spanish America*, pp. 306–18; Uring, *Voyages*; *Real cédula* de 20 julio 1738, AGI, IG 1820; Peñalver a Ensenada, 17 noviembre 1747, AGI, SD 1212. I am indebted to Purificación Medina Encina of the AGI staff for explaining that the mysterious Spanish word *flactruze* means a ship sailing under a flag of truce.

81. Scelle, *Traité négrière aux Index de Castille*, 2:531. See also: Nelson, "Contraband Trade," pp. 55–67; and Izard, "Contrabandistas," pp. 23–86.

82. Directors of the South Sea Company to Cumberlege and Walsh, 31 October 1717, BL, AM 25563, fol. 83. These latter were the Company's factors at Santiago de Cuba. See also: McLachlan, *Old Spain*, p. 127.

83. The acknowledgement: Instructions . . . to Captain John Cleland, 22 July 1725, BL, AM 25567, fol. 184. The directors rather than the shareholders profited from contraband, says Sperling, *South Sea Company*, p. 24. On the decline: ibid., 42–43. Nelson, "Contraband Trade," held the opposite view but without evidence.

84. Horsfall, "British Relations with the Spanish Colonies" (thesis). Her source is an anonymous pamphlet, *The State of the Island of Jamaica* (London, 1726).

85. Alonso a [?], 24 noviembre 1760, AGI, UM 150; Resumen del expediente de la Villa de Puerto Príncipe, n.d. (c. 1734), AGI, SD 381.

86. Jefferys, *Spanish Islands*, p. 80: "A contraband commerce is carried on brisker here than at La Vera Cruz."

87. Houston, *Memoirs*, p. 224.

88. Pedro Rafael Arrate a [?], 30 octubre 1729, AGI, SD 2014; Consulta de Consejo, 24 marzo 1736, AGI, SD 1129; Audiencia de Santo Domingo al Rey (c. 1729), AGI, SD 360; Güemes y Horcasitas al Rey, 11 noviembre 1734, AGI, SD 381; Expediente sobre los motores de la sublevación de

Puerto Príncipe, 1735–37, AGI, SD 496; Arcos Moreno a Ensenada, 21 abril 1749, AGI, SD 1202.

89. Cagigal de la Vega a Campillo, 14 febrero 1743, AGI, SD 1204; Arcos Moreno a Ensenada, 20 marzo 1749, AGI, SD 1130B.

90. Brown, "Contraband Trade," pp. 180–82. See Tables 7.3 and 7.4 for legitimate trade in 1720.

91. Dictamen dada a Su Majestad por D^n Joseph de Avalos, 1768, fol. 15–16, AGI, SD 1156.

92. Cagigal de la Vega a Arriaga, 4 agosto 1758, AGI, SD 2015.

93. Lawes to the Board of Trade, 6 December 1719, PRO, CO 137/13. For a full list of cloth items traded illegally, see Dictamen dada a Su Majestad por D^n Joseph de Avalos, 1768, AGI, SD 1156. Instrucción . . . que paso de . . . Gobernador . . . del Bayamo, 1751, AGI, SD 404.

94. Consulta de Consejo, 7 noviembre 1733, AGI, SD 1129; Expediente sobre fábrica de moneda de Vellon para la Isla de Cuba, 1733, AGI, SD 360.

95. Extracto de la carta del Gobernador de la Habana sobre el frecuente trato ilícito de las colonias francesas, n.d. (c. 1751), AGI, SD 392. Dictamen dada a Su Majestad por D^n Joseph de Avalos, 1768, AGI, SD 1156.

96. Price, *France and the Chesapeake*, 1:480–82; Jaupart, *Bayonne*, 1:414, 421.

97. Mules cost 50 pesos and horses 70. Producto de tres años de un Ingenio, y Gastos, 1765, AGI, SD 1156.

98. See Betancourt, "Puerto Príncipe," 3:543, 548. Cabildo de Puerto Príncipe al Rey, 3 junio 1729, AGI, SD 488.

99. Arcos Moreno a Ensenada, 26 octubre 1747, AGI, SD 1202; Rey a Cagigal de la Vega, 12 julio 1739, AGI, SD 363.

Chapter 8

1. Almost 80 percent of the works in Tennyson, *Cape Breton*, that refer to Louisbourg concern military events or personnel.

2. See Crowley, "Government and Interests" (thesis), pp. 368–81.

3. This was less so of sugar than tobacco, because the Spanish market could easily have absorbed more Cuban sugar by reducing consumption of French, and because the capital requirements of sugar were so much higher than those of tobacco.

4. Crowley, "Government and Interests," pp. 374–75 for St.-Ovide's guilt. The Santiago de Cuba governor was Carlos Sucre.

5. This is a gross simplification, ignoring complex patterns of land use. Often sugar carved fields out of *corrales* (ranches) or virgin land. Tobacco *vegas* often became *estancias* (farms) of one to three *caballerías*. See Marrero, *Cuba*, 6:180, 183.

6. See Domínguez Ortiz, *Sociedad y estado en el siglo XVIII español*, pp. 84–103.

Bibliography

1. Manuscript Sources

Albermarle Archives (Ipswich and East Suffolk Record Office). HA 67/894/
   B29.
Archives Départementales de la Charente-Maritime (La Rochelle) Série B,
   régistres B‒265 to B‒283.
Archives de la Guerre, Fonds de la Marine (Paris), vol. 3127.
Archives Nationales, Fonds des Colonies (Paris).
   Série B, vols. 35‒107
   Série C ^{11}A, vols. 29, 87, 125
   Série C ^{11}B, vols. 1‒38
   Série C ^{11}C, vols. 6‒16
   Série C ^{11}E, vol. 10
   Série C ^{11}G, vol. 3
   Série F ^{2}B, vol. 2
   Série F ^{3}, vols. 50‒51
Archives Nationales, Section de Outre-Mer (Paris).
   Série G ^{1}, vol. 466, 3127
   Série G ^{5}, vol. 253
Archivo General de Indias (Seville).
   Sección de Contaduría, legajos 1153, 1154, 1157, 1163, 1164, 1165A,
   1165B, 1167‒1170, 1173A, 1181‒1184, 1188, 1191, 1192, 1194.
   Sección de Gobierno, Audiencia de Santo Domingo, legajos 325, 326,
   337‒352, 359‒373, 378‒405, 408, 410, 417, 419‒421, 426,
   428‒433, 451, 482, 484, 486‒488, 492, 496, 498, 500, 503, 504,
   534, 1127, 1129, 1130A‒1133, 1135, 1149, 1156‒1158, 1190,
   1191, 1194, 1201‒1209, 1212, 1219, 1220, 1310, 1320, 1343,
   1347, 1499‒1504, 1509, 1632, 1640, 1643, 1812‒1814, 2000,
   2002‒2024, 2026, 2070, 2071, 2093, 2104‒2113, 2143, 2167,
   2197, 2208‒2210, 2227, 2238, 2239.

Sección de Ultramar, legajos 83, 98, 150, 169, 233, 234, 254–258, 882, 883, 885, 891, 893, 894, 896–900, 929, 930, 942, 953, 986, 988, 995, 996, 999–1003.

Sección de Indiferente General, legajos 1602, 1656, 1745, 1820, 1829, 1902, 1905, 2556, 2776, 2785, 2786, 3167.

Sección de Contratación, legajos 1454, 1460–1471, 2462, 2471–2481, 5004.

Sección de Mapas y Planos: Santo Domingo, 141–145, 150, 160, 163, 174, 176, 204, 212, 218, 220, 241, 266, 283, 285, 301, 320, 321.

Archivo General de Simancas (Simancas).

Sección de Guerra (Moderna), legajo 3616.

Sección de Marina, legajos 134–136, 330, 392, 396, 645.

Sección de Hacienda (Siglo XVIII), legajo 1836, 2342.

Archivo Histórico Nacional (Madrid).

Sección de Estado, legajos 2318, 2320, 2321, 2323, 2329–2331, 2333, 2335, 2339.

Sección de Consejos Suprimidos, Consejo de Indias, legajos 20882–20885, 21467, 21468.

Archivo del Museo Naval (Madrid), Manuscritos 236, 436, 439, 440, 469, 582, 1209, 1219, 2186, 2213.

Biblioteca Nacional (Madrid), Sección de Manuscritos, Ms. 18698, 20144.

Biblioteca del Palacio Real (Madrid), Ms. 2818.

Bibliothèque Nationale (Paris), Nouvelles acquisitions françaises, vol. 5399.

Manuscrits françaises, vol. 11332.

British Library (London), Department of Manuscripts.

Additional Manuscripts 9049, 9131, 9940, 13957, 13974–13976, 13985, 13987, 13992, 15717, 15956, 15957, 17628, 17629, 17645, 19034, 19049, 20926, 22680, 23678, 25501, 25510, 25550–25559, 25562–25567, 25581, 28058, 28140, 31357, 32694, 32702, 32776, 32778, 32782, 32800, 32801, 33028, 33032, 34335, 34729, 38332, 38336, 45928.

Stowe Collection, Manuscript 256.

Landsdowne Collection, Manuscripts 846, 885.

Chicago Historical Society (Chicago), Manuscript Division, New France Papers. Beauharnois Collection. Gunther Collection.

Clements Library, University of Michigan (Ann Arbor), Shelburne Manuscripts, vol. 44.

Cornell University Library (Ithaca, N.Y.), Maurepas Papers, Lots 21, 38, 40, 42–48, 60–62, 64.

Duke University, Perkins Library (Durham, N.C.), Montemar Papers, Groups I, III, VIII.

Library of Congress (Washington, D.C.), Vernon-Wager Manuscripts.

Newberry Library (Chicago), Special Collections, Ayer Manuscripts, 293, 299,
    751, 1076A, 1112.
Ohio State University Library (Columbus, Ohio), Maurepas Papers, Lots 2, 16,
    22, 70–71.
Public Archives of Canada (Ottawa), Hardwicke Papers, 35913
Public Record Office (London)
    Colonial Office Papers 137/13, 14, 23, 25, 42, 43, 51, 55; 138/17, 18;
    217/1, 3, 6, 7; 319/2; 326/47, 48.
    Treasury Papers 1/369; 38/363; 64/265B, 276A, 276B.
    Admiralty Papers, 1:237.
Real Academia de la Historia (Madrid), Colección Mata Linares, vol. 75.

2. Published Documents

Akins, T. B. *Selections From the Public Documents of the Province of Nova Scotia.*
    Halifax: C. Annand, 1869.
Baugh, Daniel A., ed. *Naval Administration, 1715–1750.* London: Navy
    Records Society, 1977.
Blanck, Guillermo, ed. *Papeles sobre la toma de la Habana por los ingleses en 1762.*
    Havana: Archivo Nacional de Cuba, 1948.
Boletín del Archivo Nacional de Cuba. Vols. 8, 15, 16, 21, 24, 36, 40, 43.
Collection de manuscrits contenant lettres, mémoires et autres documents historiques
    relatifs à l'histoire de la Nouvelle-France. 4 vols. Quebec: A. Côté, 1883–85.
Collections of the Georgia Historical Society, VIII, Pt. 3 (1913).
Connecticut Historical Society. *The Two Putnams, Israel and Rufus, in the Havana*
    Expedition 1762 and in the Mississippi River Exploration 1772–1773.
    Hartford: Connecticut Historical Society, 1931.
Cuba. Archivo Nacional de Cuba. *Nuevos papeles sobre la toma de la Habana por los*
    ingleses en 1762. Havana: Archivo Nacional, 1951.
Cuba. Biblioteca Nacional José Martí. *Documentos inéditos sobre la Toma de la*
    Habana por los ingleses en 1762. Edited by Juan Pérez de la Riva. Havana:
    Departamiento Colección Cubana de la Biblioteca Nacional, 1963.
Davenport, Frances G., ed. *European Treaties Bearing on the History of the United*
    States and Its Dependencies. 4 vols. Washington, D.C.: Carnegie Institution,
    1917–37.
Documentos para la historia argentina. Tomo V, *Comercio de Indias, 1713–1778.*
    Buenos Aires: Compañía Sud-América de Billetes de Banco, 1915.
Graham, Gerald S., ed. *The Walker Expedition to Quebec, 1711.* London: Navy
    Records Society, 1953.
Gwyn, Julian, ed. *The Royal Navy and North America: The Warren Papers,*
    1736–1752. London: Navy Records Society, 1973.

Hakluyt, Richard. *The Principal Navigations*. New York: Viking, 1965.

Harvey, Daniel C., ed. *Holland's Description of Cape Breton Island and Other Documents*. Halifax: Public Archives of Nova Scotia, 1935.

Havana. Municipio de la Habana. *La dominación inglesa en la Habana*. Havana: Molina, 1929.

Innis, Harold A., ed. *Select Documents in Canadian Economic History, 1497–1783*. Toronto: University of Toronto Press, 1929.

Lincoln, Charles Henry, ed. *The Correspondence of William Shirley, Governor of Massachusetts and Military Commander in America, 1731–1760*. 2 vols. New York: Macmillan, 1912.

Massachusetts Historical Society. *Proceedings*. Vol. 60, *1926–27*. Boston: Massachusetts Historical Society, 1927.

Merriman, R. D. *Queen Anne's Navy. Documents Concerning the Administration of the Navy of Queen Anne, 1702–1714*. London: Navy Records Society, 1961.

O'Callaghan, E. D., ed. *Documents Relating to the Colonial History of the State of New York*. 10 vols. Albany: Weed, Parsons, 1855–58.

Pichardo, Hortensia, ed. *Documentos para la historia de Cuba*. Havana: Consejo Nacional de Universidades, 1965.

Public Archives of Canada. *Report of the Canadian Archives 1905*. Ottawa: F. A. Acland, 1907.

Public Archives of Canada. Board of Historical Publications. *Canadian Currency, Exchange and Finance During the French Period*. 2 vols. Ottawa: F. A. Acland, 1925.

————. *Documents Relating to Currency, Finance and Exchange in Nova Scotia, 1675–1758*. Ottawa: I. O. Patenaude, 1933.

Quebec (Province) Archives. *Rapport de l'Archiviste de la Province de Québec 1923*. Quebec: Archives de la Province de Quebec, 1924.

Ranft, B. McL., ed. *The Vernon Papers*. London: Navy Records Society, 1958.

Syrett, David, Ed. *The Siege and Capture of Havana 1762*. London: Navy Records Society, 1970.

Wroth, Lawrence C., and Annan, Gertrude L., eds. *Acts of French Royal Administration Concerning Canada, Guiana, the West Indies, and Louisiana Prior to 1791*. New York: New York Public Library, 1930.

3. Books and Articles

Aboucaya, Claude. *Les intendants de la marine sous l'ancien régime*. Gap: Imprimerie Louis–Jean, 1958.

Aimes, Hubert H. S. *A History of Slavery in Cuba, 1511–1868*. New York: Putnam's, 1907.

Albion, Robert G. *Forests and Sea Power; the Timber Problem of the Royal Navy, 1652–1862.* Cambridge: Harvard University Press, 1926.

Alcala-Zamora y Quiepo de Llano, José. "Aportación a la historia de la siderurgia española." *Moneda y crédito* 120 (1972): 99–124.

———. "Producción de hierro y altos hornos en la España anterior a 1850." *Moneda y crédito,* 128 (1974): 117–218.

Altamira, Rafael. *A History of Spain.* New York: Van Nostrand, 1949.

Alton, Arthur S. "The Asiento Treaty as Reflected in the Papers of Lord Shelburne," *Hispanic American Historical Review* 8 (1927): 167–77.

Altschul, Aaron M. *Proteins: Their Chemistry and Politics.* New York: Basic Books, 1965.

Amich, Julian. *Diccionario marítimo.* Barcelona: Editorial Juventud, 1956.

Anderson, R., and Anderson, R. C. *The Sailing Ship: Six Thousand Years of History.* London: Harrap, 1947.

Anderson R. C. "Eighteenth-Century Books on Shipbuilding." *Mariner's Mirror* 33 (1947): 218–25.

Andrews, Charles M. "Anglo-French Commercial Rivalry." *American Historical Review* 20 (1914–15): 43–63, 539–56, 761–80.

Andrews, Kenneth R. *The Spanish Caribbean. Trade and Plunder, 1530–1630.* New Haven: Yale University Press, 1978.

———. *Elizabethan Privateering: English Privateering During the Spanish War, 1585–1603.* Cambridge: Cambridge University Press, 1969.

Antuñez y Acevedo, Rafael. *Memorias históricas sobre la legislación y gobierno del comercio de los españoles con sus colonias en las Indias Occidentales.* Madrid: Sancha, 1797.

Arango y Parreño, Francisco. *Obras completas.* Havana: Ministerio de Educación, 1952.

Armas y Céspedes, Francisco de. *De la esclavitud en Cuba.* Madrid: T. Fortanet, 1866.

Arrate y Acosta, José M. F. *Llave del Nuevo Mundo.* Mexico: Fondo de Cultura Económica, 1949.

Arsenault, Bona. *Louisbourg 1713–1758.* Quebec: Le Conseil de la Vie Française en Amérique, 1971.

Artz, Frederick B. *The Development of Technical Education in France, 1500–1850.* Cambridge: MIT Press and The Society for the History of Technology, 1966.

Aykroyd, Wallace R. *The Story of Sugar.* Chicago: Quadrangle Books, 1967.

Aymard, Maurice. "Toward the History of Nutrition: Some Methodological Remarks." In *Food and Drink in History. Selections from the Annales: Economies, Sociétés, Civilisations,* edited by Robert Forster and Orest Ranum. Baltimore: Johns Hopkins University Press, 1979, pp. 1–16.

Bacardi Moreau, Emilio. *Crónicas de Santiago de Cuba.* 10 vols. Barcelona: Tipografía de Carbonell y Esteva, 1906.

Bachiller y Morales, Antonio. *Cuba: monografía histórica que comprende desde la perdida de la Habana hasta la restauración española*. Havana: Miguel de Villa, 1883.

Baker, William A. "Fishing Under Sail in the North Atlantic." In *The Atlantic World of Robert G. Albion*, edited by Benjamin W. Labaree, pp. 41–43. Middletown, Conn.: Wesleyan University Press, 1975.

————. *Sloops and Shallops*. Barre, Mass.: Barre Publishing, 1966.

Balaguer y Primo, Francisco. *Cultivo de la caña de azúcar*. Madrid: Cuenta, 1877.

Balcom, Sandy. "Commerce and the Economy of Ile Royale." Fortress of Louisbourg Library Historical Memorandum #34, 1977.

————. "Fishing and the Economy of Ile Royale." Fortress of Louisbourg Library Historical Memorandum #16, 1977.

Bamford, Paul W. *Forests and French Sea Power, 1660–1789*. Toronto: University of Toronto Press, 1956.

Barrett, Ward. "Caribbean Sugar Production Standards in the Seventeenth and Eighteenth Centuries." In *Merchants and Scholars: Essays in the History of Exploration and Trade*, edited by John Parker, pp. 145–170. Minneapolis: University of Minnesota Press, 1965.

————. *The Sugar Hacienda of the Marqueses del Valle*. Minneapolis: University of Minnesota Press, 1970.

Baudrillart, Alfred. *Philippe V et la cour de France*. 5 vols. Paris: Firmin-Didiot, 1890–91.

Baugh, Daniel A. *British Naval Administration in the Age of Walpole*. Princeton: Princeton University Press, 1965.

————. *Naval Administration, 1715–1750*. London: Navy Records Society, 1977.

Bellet, Adolphe. *La grande pêche de la morue à Terre-Neuve depuis la découverte du Nouveau Monde par les Basques au XIV siècle*. Paris: A. Challanel, 1902.

Beneyto Pérez, Juan. *História de la administración española e hispanoamericana*. Madrid: Aguilar, 1958.

Bentley, P. A., and Smith, E. C. "The Forests of Cape Breton in the Seventeenth and Eighteenth Centuries." *Proceedings of the Nova Scotian Institute of Science* 24 (1956): 1–15.

Bergamini, John. *The Spanish Bourbons: The History of a Tenacious Dynasty*. New York: Putnam's, 1974.

Bernard, Gildas. "La Casa de Contratación de Sevilla, luego de Cádiz, en el siglo XVIII." *Anuario de Estudios Americanos* 12 (1955): 253–86.

Bertier, Jacques; Lamontagne, Roland; Vergnault, Françoise. "Traitement graphiques d'une information: Les marines royales de France et de Grande-Bretagne (1697–1747)." *Annales: E.S.C.* 22 (1967): 991–1004.

Betancourt, Tomás Pío. "Historia de Puerto Príncipe." In vol. 3 of *Las Tres*

Primeros Historiadores de la Isla de Cuba, edited by Rafael Cowley and Andres Pago. 3 : 503–64. Havana: A. Pago, 1876.

Béthencourt Massieu, Antonio de. "Arboladuras de Santa María de Chimalapa-Tehuántepec en las construcciones navales indianas, 1730–1750." *Revista de Indias* 20 (1960): 65–101.

————. "Felipe V y la Florida." *Anuario de Estudios Americanos* 7 (1950): 95–123.

————. *Patiño en la política internacional de Felipe V.* Valladolid: Facultad de Filosofía y Letras de la Universidad de Valladolid, Escuela de Historia Moderna del C.S.I.C., Estudios y Documentos, no. 1, 1954.

————. "El real astillero de Coatzacoalcos (1720–1735)." *Anuario de Estudios Americanos* 15 (1958): 371–428.

Billings, E. R. *Tobacco: Its History, Varieties, Culture, Manufacture, and Commerce.* Hartford: American Publishing, 1875.

Bitar Letayf, Marcelo. *Economístas españoles del siglo XVIII: sus ideas sobre la libertad de comercio con Indias.* Madrid: Ediciones Cultura Hispanica, 1968.

Black, Clinton, *The Story of Jamaica.* London: Collins, 1965.

Blake, John B. "Yellow Fever in Eighteenth-Century America." *Bulletin of the New York Academy of Medicine* 44 (1968): 673–86.

Blitz, Rudolph C. "Mercantilist Policies and the Pattern of World Trade, 1500–1750." *Journal of Economic History* 27 (1967): 39–55.

Boisrouvray, A. "La nation française de Cadix au XVIII siècle." *Revue de Questions Historiques* 125 (1936): 177–83.

Boizard, E., and Tardieu, H. *Histoire de la legislation des sucres, 1664–1891.* Paris: Bureaux de la sucrerie indigène et coloniale, 1891.

Bolger, Francis W. P., ed. *Canada's Smallest Province. A History of P.E.I.* Charlottetown, P.E.I.: P.E.I. 1973 Centennial Commission, 1973.

[Bollan, William]. *The Importance and Advantage of Cape Breton, Truly Stated and Impartially Considered.* London: 1746.

Bonneau, Jacques. *Les législations française sur les tabacs sous l'ancien régime.* Paris: J.-B. Sirey, 1910.

Borgstrom, Georg. "The Ecological Aspects of Protein Feeding—the Case of Peru." In *The Careless Technology: Ecology and International Development*, edited by M. T. Farvar and John P. Milton, pp. 753–74. New York: Natural History Press, 1972.

————, ed. *Fish as Food.* 3 vols. New York: Academic Press, 1962.

————. "New Methods of Appraising the Role of Fisheries in World Nutrition," *Fishing News International* 1 (1961): 33–38.

Boucher, Philip. "French Images of Colonial America and the Evolution of Colonial Theories." *Proceedings of the Annual Meeting of the Western Society for French History* 6 (1978): 220–28.

Boudriot, Jean. *Le vaisseau de 74 canons.* 2 vols. Grenoble: Editions des Quatre Seigneurs, 1973–74.

Bougaineville, Louis Antoine de. *Adventure in the Wilderness, the American Journals of Louis Antoine de Bougaineville, 1756–1760.* Edited and translated by Edward P. Hamilton. Norman: University of Oklahoma Press, 1964.

Bouguer, Pierre. *De la manouevre des vaisseaux.* Paris: Guérin, 1757.

―――. *De la mâture des vaisseaux.* Paris: C. Jombert, 1727.

―――. *Traité du navire, de sa construction et de ses mouvements.* Paris: Jombert, 1756.

Boulle, Pierre. "Patterns of French Colonial Trade and the Seven Years' War." *Histoire Sociale/Social History* 7 (1974): 88–96.

Bourdé, Guy. "Sources et méthodes de l'histoire démographique à Cuba (XVIIIᵉ et XIXᵉ siècles)." *Annales de démographie historique* (1972): 385–424.

―――. "Fuentes y métodos de la historia demográfica en Cuba (siglos XVIII y XIX)." *Revista de la Biblioteca Nacional José Martí,* 3ᵃ época, 16, no. 1 (1974): 21–68.

Boureau-Deslandes, A. F. *Essay sur la marine et sur le commerce.* Paris?: 1743.

Bourinot, John George. *Historical and Descriptive Account of Cape Breton.* Montreal: W. Foster Brown, 1892.

Bourne, Ruth. *Queen Anne's Navy in the West Indies.* New Haven: Yale University Press, 1939.

Bower, Peter J. "Louisbourg, The Chimera, 1745–1748." *Papers and Abstracts for a Symposium on Ile Royale during the French Regime.* Ottawa: National Museum of Man, 1972.

Braudel, Fernand. *The Mediterranean and the Mediterranean World in the Age of Philip II.* New York: Harper and Row, 1972.

―――, and Labrousse, Camille E., eds. *Histoire économique et sociale de la France.* Tome 2. 1660–1789. Paris: Presses Universitaires de France, 1970.

―――. *Civilization and Capitalism, 15th–18th Centuries.* Vol. 2 *The Wheels of Commerce.* New York: Harper and Row, 1983.

Brebner, John B. *New England's Outpost: Acadia before the Conquest of Canada.* New York: Columbia University Press, 1927.

Brenan, Gerald. *South from Granada.* London: Hamilton, 1957.

Brière, Jean-François. "Le trafic terre-neuvier mâlouin dans la première moitié de la XVIIIe siècle, 1715–1755." *Histoire Sociale/Social History* 11 (1978): 356–74.

Bromley, John S. "The French Privateering War, 1701–1713." In *Historical Essays 1600–1750 Presented to David Ogg,* edited by H. E. Bell and R. L. Olland, pp. 203–31. New York: Barnes and Noble, 1963.

―――, and Ryan, A. N. "Armies and Navies: (3) Navies." In *The New Cambridge Modern History.* Vol. 6 *The Rise of Great Britain and Russia,*

1688–1725, edited by J. S. Bromley, pp. 790–833. Cambridge: Cambridge University Press, 1970.

Brooks, Jerome E. *The Mighty Leaf*. Boston: Little, Brown, 1952.

————, ed. *Tobacco: Its History Illustrated by the Books and Manuscripts in the Library of George Arents*. 5 vols. New York: Rosenbach, 1937–42.

Brown, Vera Lee. "Contraband Trade: A Factor in the Decline of Spain's Empire in America." *Hispanic American Historical Review* 8 (1928): 178–89.

————. "Spanish Claims to a Share in the Newfoundland Fisheries in the Eighteenth Century." *Canadian Historical Association Report* (1925): 64–82.

Bryson, Reid A. "Ancient Climes in the Great Plains." *Natural History* 89 (1980): 64–73.

Buck, Philip. *The Politics of Mercantilism*. New York: H. Holt, 1942.

Burkholder, Mark, and Chandler, D. S. *From Impotence to Authority: Spain and the American Audiencias*. Columbia: University of Missouri Press, 1977.

Burnet, MacFarlane, and White, David O. *The Natural History of Infectious Disease*. Cambridge: Cambridge University Press, 1972.

Butel, Paul. *Les négociants bordelais: l'Europe et les Iles au XVIIIe siècle*. Paris: Editions Aubier-Montange, 1974.

Calcagno, Francisco. *Diccionario biográfico cubano*. New York: Imprenta de Ponce de León, 1878.

Callahan, William J. *Honor, Commerce and Industry in Eighteenth-Century Spain*. Boston: Harvard Graduate School of Business Administration, 1972.

Cameron, H. L. "Glacial Geology and the Soils of Nova Scotia." In *Soils in Canada*, edited by Robert F. Leggett, pp. 109–14. Toronto: University of Toronto Press, 1961.

Campbell, John. *A Concise History of Spanish America*. London: John Stagg, 1741. Reprint. Dawson's of Pall Mall, 1972.

————. *Lives of the Admirals*. 8 vols. London: C. J. Barrington, 1812–17.

Campillo y Cosío, José del. *España despierta. Críticas e instructivas reflexiones a varios e importantísimos asuntos para la mejor organización y régimen de la monarquía español*. Edited by Antonio Florza. Madrid: Seminario de Historia Social y Económica de la Facultad de Filosofía y Letras de la Universidad de Madrid, 1969.

————. *Lo que hay de más y de menos en España para sea lo que debe ser y no lo que es*. Madrid: La Ultima Moda, 1898.

————. *Nuevo sistema de gobierno económico para la América*. Madrid: Benito Cano, 1789.

Canada. Department of Agriculture. *The System of Soil Classification for Canada*. Ottawa, 1970.

————. Surveys and Mapping Branch, Geographic Division. *The National Atlas of Canada*. Ottawa: Macmillan, 1974.

Canga Argüelles, José. *Diccionario de hacienda.* 5 vols. London: M. Calero, 1826.

—————. *Memoria presentada a las Cortes generales y extraordinarios sobre las rentas y gastos de la Corona antes y después del movimiento generoso de la nación. . . .* Cadiz: Imprenta Real, 1811.

Cantlie, Sir Neil. *The History of the Army Medical Department.* 2 vols. London: Churchill Livingstone, 1974.

Cappa, Ricardo. *Estudios críticos acerca de la dominación española en la América.* Tomo 12. *Industria naval.* Madrid: Velasco, 1894.

Careri, Gemelli. "La Habana de fines del siglo XVIII vista por un italiano: Gemelli Careri. Presentación por Jean-Pierre Berthe, notas por Juan Pérez de la Riva." *Revista de la Biblioteca Nacional José Martí,* 3ra época, 13 (1971): 63–86.

Carrière, Charles et al. *Banque et capitalisme commercial: la lettre de change au XVIIIe siècle.* Marseilles: Institut historique de Provence, 1976.

Carter, Henry Rose. *Yellow Fever: An Epidemiological and Historical Study of Its Place of Origin.* Baltimore: Williams and Wilkins, 1931.

Casgrain, L'Abbé H.-R. *Une seconde Acadie.* Quebec: Demers et frère, 1894.

Castex, Raoul U. P. *Les idées militaires de la marine de XVIIIe siècle; de Ruyter à Suffren.* Paris: L. Fournier, 1911.

Castillo, Andres V. *Spanish Mercantilism.* New York: Columbia University Press, 1930.

Castro, Adolpho. *Historia de Cádiz y su provincia.* Cádiz: Imprenta de la Revista Médica, 1858.

Chabaud-Arnault, Charles. "Etudes historiques sur la marine militaire de la France: XII: La marine française sous la régence et sous la ministère de Maurepas." *Revue maritime et coloniale* 110 (1891): 49–85.

Chabert, M. de. *Voyage fait par ordre du Roi en 1750 et 1751 dans l'Amérique septentrionale.* Paris: 1753.

Chapin, Howard M. *Rhode Island Privateers in King George's War, 1739–1748.* Providence: E. A. Johnson, 1928.

Charbonneau, Henri. "Documents sur la mâture des Pyrénées au XVIIIe siècle." *Revue historique et archéologique de Béarn et Pays Basque* 44 (1913): 478–84.

Charlevoix, Pierre F. X. *Histoire et description générale de la Nouvelle France.* 6 vols. Paris: Rollin, 1744.

—————. *Journal of a Voyage to North America.* 2 vols. London: R. and J. Dodsley, 1761. Reprint. Chicago: Caxton Club, 1923.

Charliat, P. *Trois siècles d'économie maritime française.* Paris: M. Rivière, 1931.

Charnock, John. *An History of Naval Architecture.* 3 vols. London: R. Faulder, 1800–1802.

Chassériau, F. *Précis historique de la marine française, son organisation et ses lois.* 2 vols. Paris: Imprimerie Royale, 1845.

Chaunu, Pierre. "Notes sur l'espagne de Philippe V (1700–1746)." *Revue d'histoire économique et sociale* 41 (1963): 448–70.

———. "Les routes espagnoles de l'Atlantique." *Anuario de Estudios Americanos* 25 (1968): 95–123.

———, et Huguette Chaunu. *Séville et l'Atlantique.* 8 vols. Paris: Armand Colin, 1955–59.

Clark, Andrew Hill. *Acadia: The Geography of Early Nova Scotia to 1760.* Madison: University of Wisconsin Press, 1968.

———. "New England's Role in the Underdevelopment of Cape Breton Island during the French Regime, 1713–1758." *Canadian Geographer* 9 (1965): 1–12.

———. *Three Centuries and the Island.* Toronto: Toronto University Press, 1959.

Clark, G. N. "War Trade and Trade War, 1701–1713." *Economic History Review* 1 (1928): 262–80.

Clarke, Edward. *Letters Concerning the Spanish Nation.* London: T. Becket and T. A. de Hondt, 1763.

Claveria Arza, Carlos. *Los vascos en el mar.* Pamplona: Aramburg, 1966.

Clayton, Lawrence A. "Ships and Empire: The Case of Spain." *Mariner's Mirror* 62 (1976): 235–48.

Clerk, John. *An Essay on Naval Tactics, Systematic and Historical.* Edinburgh: Archd. Constable, 1782.

Cobban, Alfred. *A History of Modern France.* Vol. 1. *1715–1799.* London: Penguin, 1963.

Cole, Charles W. *Colbert and a Century of French Mercantilism.* 2 vols. New York: Columbia University Press, 1939.

———. *French Mercantilism, 1683–1700.* New York: Columbia University Press, 1943.

Coleman, Donald C. "Eli Heckscher and the Idea of Mercantilism." *Scandinavian Economic History Review* 5 (1957): 3–25.

———, ed. *Revisions in Mercantilism.* London: Methuen, 1969.

Colmeiro, Manuel. *Biblioteca de los economistas españoles de los siglos XVI, XVII, y XVIII.* Mexico City: Universidad Nacional Autónoma de Mexico, Escuela Nacional de Economía, 1942.

———. *Historia de la economía política en España.* 2 vols. Madrid: Taurus, 1965.

Condorcet, Antoine Marquis de. "Eloge de M. le Comte de Maurepas." *Histoire de l'Académie Royale des Sciences* 79 (1781): 79–102.

Corbett, Julian S. *England in the Seven Years' War: A Study in Combined Strategy.* 2 vols. London: Longman's and Green, 1918.

Coreal, Francisco. *Voyages de François Coreal aux Indes Occidentales, contenant ce qu'il y a vu de plus remarquable pendant son séjour depuis 1666 jusqu'en 1697.* 3 vols. Amsterdam: J. F. Bernard, 1722.

Corvisier, André. *L'Armée française de la fin du XVIIe siècle au ministère du Choiseul.* 2 vols. Paris: Presses Universitaires de France, 1964.

Corwin, Arthur F. *Spain and the Abolition of Slavery in Cuba, 1817–1886.* Austin: University of Texas Press, 1967.

Cossa, Emilio. *L'Interpretazione scientifica del mercantilismo.* Messina: F. Nicastro, 1907.

Cowley, Rafael and Andres Pago. *Los tres primeros historiadores de la Isla de Cuba.* 3 vols. Havana: A. Pago, 1876.

Coxe, William. *España bajo el reinado de la casa de Borbón.* 4 vols. Madrid: Mellado, 1846–47.

———. *Memoirs of the Kings of Spain.* London: Longman, Hurst, Rees, Orme and Brown, 1813.

Craton, Michael. "Hobbesian or Panglossian? Two Extremes of Slave Conditions in the British Caribbean, 1783 to 1834." *William and Mary Quarterly*, 3d Ser., 35 (1978): 324–56.

Creswell, John. *British Admirals of the Eighteenth Century.* London: Archon Books, 1972.

Crouse, Nellis. *The French Struggle for the West Indies, 1665–1713.* New York: Columbia University Press, 1943.

Crouzet, François. "Angleterre et France au XVIIIe siècle. Essai d'analyse comparée de deux croissances économiques." *Annales: E.S.C.* 21 (1966): 254–91.

Crowley, Terence Alan. "The Forgotten Soldiers of New France: The Louisbourg Example." *French Colonial History Society. Proceedings of the Third Annual Meeting* (1977): 52–69.

———. "France, Canada and the Beginnings of Louisbourg: In Search of the Great Fortress Myth." *Papers and Abstracts for a Symposium on Ile Royale during the French Regime*, pp. 45–76. Ottawa: National Museum of Man, 1972.

Cunningham, William S. *The Growth of English Industry and Commerce in Modern Times.* Cambridge: Cambridge University Press, 1903.

Curtin, Philip D. *The Atlantic Slave Trade: A Census.* Madison: University of Wisconsin Press, 1969.

———. "Slavery and Empire." *Annals of the New York Academy of Sciences.* Vol. 292. *Comparative Perspectives on Slavery in New World Plantation Societies*, pp. 1–11. 1977.

Cutting, C. L. *Fish Saving. A History of Fish Processing from Ancient to Modern Times.* New York: Philosophical Library, 1956.

Dahlgren, Erik Wilhelm. *Les relations commerciales et maritimes entre la France et les Côtes de l'Océan Pacifique.* Paris: H. Champion, 1909.

Dardel, Pierre. *Commerce, industrie et navigation à Rouen et au Havre au XVIIIe siècle.* Rouen: Société Libre Emulation de la Seine-Maritime, 1966.

————. *Navires et marchandises dans les ports de Rouen et du Havre au XVIIIe siècle*. Paris: S.E.V.P.E.N., 1963.

Davies, K. G. *The North Atlantic World in the Seventeenth Century*. Minneapolis: University of Minnesota Press, 1974.

Davis, Ralph. *The Rise of the English Shipping Industry in the Seventeenth and Eighteenth Centuries*. London: Macmillan, 1962.

Debien, Gabriel. "La nourriture des esclaves sur les plantations des Antilles français aux XVIIe et XVIIIe siècles." *Caribbean Studies* 4, no. 3 (1964): 3–27.

Deerr, Noel. *The History of Sugar*. 2 vols. London: Chapman and Hall, 1949–50.

Delumeau, Jean. *Le mouvement du port de Saint-Mâlo, 1681–1720*. Rennes: Institut des Recherches Historiques de Rennes, 1966.

Denys, Nicholas. *The Description and Natural History of the Coasts of North America*. Edited by W. F. Ganong. Toronto: Champlain Society, 1908.

DeRoover, Raymond. *L'évolution de la lettre de change, XIVᵉ au XVIIIᵉ siècle*. Paris: Armand Colin, 1953.

Deschamps Chapeaux, Pedro. *Los batallones de pardos y morenos libres*. Havana: Editorial Arte y Literatura, 1976.

Desdevises du Dezert, Georges. "Les colonies espagnoles au XVIIIe siècle." *Revue belge de philologie et d'histoire* 3 (1924): 289–98.

————. "Les institutions de l'Espagne au XVIIIe siècle." *Revue hispanique* 70 (1927): 1–556.

————. "La richesse et la civilisation espagnoles au XVIIIe siècle." *Revue hispanique* 73 (1928): 1–485.

————. "La société espagnole." *Revue hispanique* 64 (1925): 225–626.

Deyon, Pierre. *Le mercantilisme*. Paris: Flammarion, 1967.

Dickson, P. G. M. "War Finance, 1689–1714." In *The New Cambridge Modern History*. Vol. 6. *The Rise of Great Britain and Russia, 1688–1725*, edited by J. S. Bromley, pp. 284–315. Cambridge: Cambridge University Press, 1970.

Domínguez Ortiz, Antonio. *La sociedad española en el siglo XVIII*. Madrid: Consejo Superior de Investigaciones Científicas, 1955.

————. *Sociedad y estado en el siglo XVIII español*. Barcelona: Ariel 1976.

Donnan, Elizabeth, ed. *Documents Illustrative of the History of the Slave Trade to America*. Vol. 2. *The Eighteenth Century*. Washington, D.C.: Carnegie Institution, 1931.

————. "The Early Days of the South Sea Company, 1711–1718." *Journal of Economic and Business History* 2 (1930): 419–50.

Donneaud, Alfred. "La marine française et ses arsenaux." *Revue maritime et coloniale* 18 (1870): 682–94.

Donovan, Kenneth. "Family Life in Eighteenth-Century Louisbourg." Manuscript Report, 271. Louisbourg: Parks Canada, 1977.

————. "Rearing Children in Louisbourg, A Colonial Seaport and Garrison Town, 1713–1758." Paper delivered to the Atlantic Society for Eighteenth-Century Studies, Mt. St. Vincent University, Bronx, N.Y., 26 April 1979.

Dorn, Walter L. *Competition for Empire, 1740–1763.* New York: Harper, 1940.

Douglas, W. A. B. "The Sea Militia of Nova Scotia, 1749–1755." *Canadian Historical Review* 47, no. 1, (1966): 22–37.

Douglass, William. *A Summary, Historical, and Political, of the First Planting, Progressive Improvements, and Present State of the British Settlements in North America.* 2 vols. London: R. Baldwin, 1755.

Ducéré. E. *Histoire maritime de Bayonne: Les corsairs sous l'ancien régime.* Bayonne: E. Hourquet, 1895.

Duffy, Michael. "The Foundations of British Naval Power." In *The Military Revolution and the State, 1500–1800,* edited by M. Duffy, pp. 49–85. Exeter: Exeter Studies in History No. 1, 1980.

Duhamel du Monceau, Henri-Louis. *Elémens de l'architecture navale, ou traité pratique de la construction des vaisseaux.* Paris: Jombert, 1758.

————. *Traité générale des pêches.* 3 vols. Paris: Saillant et Nyon, 1767–69.

Durand, Nicole. "Etude sur la population de Louisbourg, 1713–1745." Fortress of Louisbourg Library, Travail inédit no. 49, 1970.

Eaton, J. W., and Mayer, A. J. "The Social Biology of Very High Fertility Among the Hutterites." *Human Biology* 25 (1953): 206–64.

Eblen, Jack Ericson. "On the Natural Increase of Slave Populations: The Example of the Cuban Black Population, 1775–1900." In *Race and Slavery in the Western Hemisphere: Quantitative Studies,* edited by Stanley Engerman and Eugene Genovese, pp. 211–48. Princeton: Princeton University Press, 1975.

Eccles, William J. *France in America.* New York: Harper and Row, 1972.

Edwards, Bryan. *Civil and Commercial History of the British West Indies.* 2 vols. London: J. Parsons, 1794.

Ely, Roland T. *La economía cubana entre los dos Isabeles, 1492–1832.* Bogotá: Aedita, 1962.

Engerman, Stanley. "Some Economic and Demographic Comparisons of Slavery in the United States and the British West Indies." *Economic History Review,* 3d Ser., 29 (1976): 258–75.

Euler, Leonhard. *Scientia navalis.* St. Petersburg: Typis academiae scientarum, 1749.

————. *Théorie complète de la construction de la manouevre des vaisseaux.* St. Petersburg: Académie Imperiale des Sciences, 1773.

Fairnie, D. A. "The Commercial Empire of the Atlantic, 1607–1783." *Economic History Review* 15 (1962): 205–18.

Falconer, William. *An Universal Dictionary of the Marine.* London: T. Cadell, 1780.

Fauteux, Joseph-Noël. *Essai sur l'industrie au Canada sous le régime français.* 2 vols. Quebec: Proulx, 1927.

Fayle, C. E. "The Deflection of Strategy by Commerce in the Eighteenth Century." *Journal of the Royal United Service Institution* 68 (1923): 281–90.

Fenning, Daniel. *A New System of Geography.* 2 vols. London: J. Payne, 1771.

Ferchault de Réamur, R. A. "Réflexions sur l'état des bois du royaume." *Mémoires de l'Académie Royale des Sciences* (1721): 284–300.

Fernández Almagro, M. *Política naval de la españa moderna y contemporánea.* Madrid: Instituto de Estudios Políticos, 1946.

Fernández Duro, Cesáreo. *La Armada española desde la unión de los reinos de Castilla y León.* 9 vols. Madrid: Tipográfico Succesores de Rivadeneyra, 1895–1903.

———. *Disquiciones náuticas.* Tomo 5. *A la mer madera.* Tomo 6. *Arca de Noé.* Madrid: Aribau, 1880–81.

Ferrer de Couto, José. *Historia de la marina española.* 2 vols. Madrid: Ducazal, 1856.

Filion, Maurice. "La crise de la marine française." *Revue d'histoire de l'Amérique française* 21, no. 2, (1967): 230–42.

———. *Maurepas: Ministre de Louis XV.* Montreal: Leméac, 1967.

———. *La pensée et l'action coloniales de Maurepas vis-à-vis du Canada, 1723–1749: l'âge d'or de la colonie.* Montreal: Leméac, 1972.

Fiske, John. *New France and New England.* Boston: Houghton Mifflin, 1902.

Fleury, Gabriel. *François Véron de Forbonnais.* Le Mans: De Saint-Denis, 1915.

Fontana Lázaro, Josep. *Hacienda y estado en las crisis final del antiguo regimen español: 1823–1833.* Madrid: Instituto de Estudios Fiscales, 1973.

[Forbonnais, François Véron Duverger de.] *Mémoires et considérations sur le commerce et les finances de l'Espagne.* 2 vols. Amsterdam: François Changuion, 1761.

———. *Principes et observations économiques.* Amsterdam: M. M. Rey, 1767.

———. *Considérations sur les finances d'Espagne.* Paris: Dresde, 1753.

Forster, Robert, and Ranum, Orest. *Food and Drink in History. Selections From the Annales: Economies, sociétés, civilisations.* Baltimore: Johns Hopkins University Press, 1979.

Fortescue, John W. *The Empire and the Army.* London: Cassel, 1928.

Fortier, Margaret. "The Development of the Fortifications at Louisbourg." *Canada: An Historical Magazine* 1, 4 (1974): 17–31.

Francis, Dilys. "The Mines and Quarries of Cape Breton Island during the French Period, 1713–1760." Fortress of Louisbourg Library, HF–2, 1965.

Franco, Gabriel. Introduction to *Theorica y práctica de commercio y marina,* by Gerónimo de Uztáriz. Madrid: Aguilar, 1968.

Franco, José Luciano. *Armonía y contradicciones cubano-mexicanos, 1554–1830.* Havana: Casa de la Américas, 1975.

————. *Contrabando y la trata negra en el Caribe*. Havana: La Cultura an América Latina, Monograph no. 1, 1973.

————. "The Slave Trade in the Caribbean and Latin America." In *The African Slave Trade from the Fifteenth to the Nineteenth Centuries*, pp. 88–100. Paris: UNESCO, 1979.

Frégault, Guy. *François Bigot: Administrateur français*. 2 vols. Montreal: L'Institut, 1948.

Friedlander, H. E. *Historia económica de Cuba*. Havana: Jesus Montero, 1944.

García-Baquero González, Antonio. *Cádiz y el Atlántico*. 2 vols. Seville: La Escuela de Estudios Hispano-americanos, 1976.

García Gallo, Gaspar Jorge. *Biografía del tabaco habano*. Havana: Comisión Nacional del Tabaco Habano, 1961.

Gibson, Charles. *Spain in America*. New York: Harper and Row, 1966.

Gille, Paul. "Les écoles des constructeurs." In *Le navire et l'économie maritime du Moyen Age au XVIIIe siècle, principalement en Méditerranée*, edited by Michel Mollat, pp. 161–72. Paris: S.E.V.P.E.N., 1958.

————. "Jauge et tonnages des navires." In *Le navire et l'économie maritime du XVe au XVIIIe siècles*", edited by Michel Mollat, pp. 85–102. Paris: S.E.V.P.E.N., 1957.

Godinho, Vitorino Magalhaes. *Prix et monnaies au Portugal, 1750–1850*. Paris: Armand Colin, 1955.

González, Alfonso. "The Population of Cuba." *Caribbean Studies* 11, no. 2 (1971): 74–84.

Goubert, Pierre. *The Ancien Régime*. New York: Harper Torchbooks, 1974.

Gould, Clarence P. "Trade Between the Windward Islands and the Continental Colonies of the French Empire, 1683–1763." *Mississippi Valley Historical Review* 25 (1939): 473–90.

Graham, Gerald S. *Empire of the North Atlantic*. Toronto: University of Toronto Press, 1950.

————. "Fisheries and Sea Power." *Canadian Historical Association. Report of the Annual Meeting* (1941): 24–32.

————. "Maritime Foundations of Imperial History." *Canadian Historical Review* 31 (1950): 113–124.

————. "Naval Defense of British North America." *Royal Historical Society Transactions* 30 (1948): 95–110.

————. *Tides of Empire*. Montreal and London: McGill-Queen's University Press, 1972.

————, ed. *The Walker Expedition to Quebec*. London: Navy Records Society, 1953.

Les Grandes voies maritimes dans le monde. XVe–XIXe siècles. Paris: S.E.V.P.E.N., 1965.

Gray, Stanley, and Wyckoff, V. J. "The International Tobacco Trade in the Seventeenth Century." *Southern Economic Journal* 7 (1940): 1–26.

The Great Importance of Cape Breton, Demonstrated and Exemplified. London: John Brindley, 1746.

Grellier, Joseph. *Cuba, carréfour des Caraibes*. Paris: 1970.

Griffiths, Naomi. *The Acadian Deportation*. Toronto: Copp Clark, 1969.

————. *The Acadians: The Creation of a People*. Toronto: McGraw-Hill Ryerson, 1973.

Grigg, David B. *Agricultural Systems of the World*. London: Cambridge University Press, 1974.

Guerra y Sánchez, Ramiro. *Manuel de la historia de Cuba*. Havana: Cultural S.A., 1938.

————. *Sugar and Society in the Caribbean. An Economic History of Cuban Agriculture*. New Haven: Yale University Press, 1964.

Guerra y Sánchez, Ramiro, José M. Pérez Cabrera, Juan J. Remos, and Emeterio S. Santovenia, eds. *Historia de la nación cubana*, 10 vols. Havana: Editorial Historia de la Nación Cubana, 1952.

Guéry, A. "Les finances de la monarchie française sous l'ancien régime," *Annales: E.S.C.* 33 (1978): 216–39.

Guiard y Larrauri, Teofilo. *La industria naval vizcaina*. Bilbao: 1917.

Guiteras, Pedro José. *Historia de la conquista de la Habana por los ingleses*. Havana: Cultural S.A., 1932.

————. *Historia de la Isla de Cuba*. Havana: Cultural S.A., 1928.

Hale, Edward E., ed. *The Capture of Havana in 1762 by the Forces of George III*. Boston: Lend-A-Hand, 1898.

Hall, Gwendolyn M. *Social Control in Plantation Societies*. Baltimore: Johns Hopkins University Press, 1971.

Hamilton, Earl J. "The Mercantilism of Gerónimo de Uztáriz: A Re-examination." In *Economics, Sociology and the Modern World*, edited by Norman E. Hines, pp. 111–29. Cambridge, Mass.: Harvard University Press, 1935.

————. "Spanish Mercantilism before 1700." In *Facts and Factors in Economic History*, edited by Arthur H. Cole, A. L. Dunham, and N. S. B. Gras, pp. 214–39. Cambridge, Mass.: Harvard University Press, 1932.

————. "Plans for a National Bank in Spain, 1701–1783." *Journal of Political Economy* 57, no. 4 (1949): 315–36.

————. "The Role of Monopoly in the Overseas Expansion and Colonial Trade of Europe before 1800." *American Economic Review. Proceedings* 38, no. 2 (1948): 33–53.

————. *War and Prices in Spain, 1651–1800*. Cambridge, Mass.: Harvard University Press, 1947.

Hamshere, Cyril. *The British in the Caribbean*. Cambridge, Mass.: Harvard University Press, 1972.

Harcourt-Smith, Simon. *Cardinal of Spain: The Life and Strange Career of Alberoni*. New York: Knopf, 1944.

Hargreaves-Mawdsley, William N. *Eighteenth-Century Spain, 1700–1788.* London: Macmillan, 1979.

———, ed. *Spain Under the Bourbons, 1700–1833.* Columbia: University of South Carolina Press, 1973.

Haring, Clarence H. *The Spanish Empire in America.* New York: Oxford University Press, 1947.

———. *Trade and Navigation Between Spain and the Indies.* Cambridge, Mass.: Harvard University Press, 1918.

Harrington, Mark Raymond. *Cuba before Columbus.* New York: Museum of the American Indian, 1921.

Hart, Francis Russell. *The Siege of Havana.* New York: Houghton Mifflin, 1931.

Harvey, Daniel C. *The French Régime in Prince Edward Island.* New Haven: Yale University Press, 1926.

Hauser, Henri. *Recherches et documents sur l'histoire des prix en France de 1500 à 1800.* Paris: Presse Moderne, 1936.

Head, C. Grant. *Eighteenth Century Newfoundland.* Toronto: McClelland and Stewart, Ltd., 1976.

Heckscher, Eli. "Multilateralism, Baltic Trade and the Mercantilists." *Economic History Review,* 2d Ser., 3 (1950): 219–28.

———. *Mercantilism.* 2 vols. London: G. Allen and Unwin, 1935.

Henripin, Jacques. *La population canadienne au debut de la XVIIIe siècle.* Paris: Presses Universitaires de France, 1954.

Henry, Louis. "The Population of France in the Eighteenth Century." In *Population in History,* edited by D. V. Glass and D. E. C. Eversley, pp. 434–56. Chicago: Aldine, 1965.

Herlitz, Lars. "The Concept of Mercantilism." *Scandinavian Economic History Review* 12, no. 2 (1964): 101–20.

Hiemann, Robert K. *Tobacco and Americans.* New York: McGraw-Hill, 1960.

Higman, B. W. *Slave Population and Economy in Jamaica.* Cambridge: Cambridge University Press, 1976.

Hobsbawm, Eric J. *The Age of Revolution, 1789–1848.* New York, New American Library, 1962.

Hoffmann, Paul E. *The Spanish Crown and the Defense of the Caribbean, 1535–1585.* Baton Rouge: Louisiana State University Press, 1980.

Holland, A. J. *Ships of British Oak. The Rise and Decline of Wooden Shipbuilding in Hampshire.* Newton Abbot: David and Charles, 1971.

Horrocks, J. W. *A Short History of Mercantilism.* London: Methuen, 1925.

Houston, J. *Dr. Houston's Memoirs of His Own Life-Time.* London: L. Gilliver, 1747.

Howard, Michael. *War in European History.* Oxford: Oxford University Press, 1976.

Huet, Pierre Daniel. *Comercio de Holanda.* 2 vols. Madrid: Imprenta Real, 1717.

Huetz de Lemps, Christian. *Géographie du commerce de Bordeaux*. Paris: Mouton, 1975.

Humboldt, Alejandro de. *Ensayo política sobre la Isla de Cuba*. Havana: Archivo Nacional de Cuba, 1960.

―――. *The Island of Cuba*. New York: Derby & Jackson, 1856.

Hussey, Roland D. "Antecedents of the Spanish Monopolistic Overseas Trading Companies, 1624–1728." *Hispanic American Historical Review* 9 (1929): 1–30.

―――. *The Caracas Company, 1728–1784*. Cambridge, Mass.: Harvard University Press, 1934.

Ibañez de Ibero, Carlos. *Historia de la marina de guerra española*. Madrid: Espasa-Calpe, 1938.

Inglis, C. Douglas. "The Spanish Naval Shipyard at Havana in the Eighteenth Century." Unpublished paper delivered to the Naval History Symposium, Annapolis, Md., October 1981.

Innis, Harold A. "Cape Breton and the French Regime," *Royal Society of Canada, Proceedings and Transactions*, 3d ser., 29, no. 2 (1935): 51–87.

―――. *The Cod Fisheries: The History of an International Economy*. Toronto: Toronto University Press, 1954.

―――. *The Fur Trade in Canada*. Toronto: Toronto University Press, 1956.

―――. "The Rise and Fall of the Spanish Fishery at Newfoundland." *Royal Society of Canada, Proceedings and Transactions*, 3d ser., 25 (1931): 51–70.

Ivers, Larry E. *British Drums on the Southern Frontier: The Military Colonization of Georgia, 1733–1749*. Chapel Hill: University of North Carolina Press, 1974.

Izard, Miguel. "Contrabandistas, comerciantes e ilustrados," *Boletín Americanista* 28 (1978): 23–86.

Jane, Fred T. *Heresies of Sea Power*. New York: Longman's, Green, 1906.

Jaupart, Fernand. *L'Activité maritime du port de Bayonne au XVIIIe siècle*. 2 vols. Bayonne: Darracq, 1966.

Jefferys, Thomas. *A Description of the Spanish Islands and Settlements on the Coasts of the West Indies*. London: T. Jefferys, 1762.

Jenkins, E. H. *A History of the French Navy*. London: MacDonald's and Jane's, 1973.

Jensen, Albert C. *The Cod*. New York: Crowell, 1972.

Johnson, Samuel. "Thoughts on the Late Transactions Respecting Falkland's Islands." In *The Yale Edition of the Works of Samuel Johnson*. Vol. 10. *Political Writings*, edited by Donald Greene, pp. 346–86. New Haven: Yale University Press, 1977.

Johnson, Willis F. *The History of Cuba*. 5 vols. New York: Buck, 1920.

Johnstone, James Johnston Chevalier de. *Memoirs of the Chevalier de Johnstone*. 3 vols. Aberdeen: D. Wyllie & Son, 1870–71.

Josa, Guy. *Les industries du sucre et rhum à la Martinique (1638–1931)*. Paris: Presses Modernes, 1931.

Juan y Santacilia, Jorge and Ulloa, Antonio de. *Voyage à l' Amérique du Sud*. Paris: 1753.

Judah, Charles B. *The North American Fisheries and British Policy to 1713*. Urbana: University of Illinois Press, 1933.

Kamen, Henry. *The War of Succession in Spain, 1700–1715*. Bloomington: Indiana University Press, 1969.

Kennett, Lee. *The French Armies in the Seven Years' War*. Durham, N.C.: Duke University Press, 1967.

Keynes, John Maynard. *The General Theory of Employment, Interest and Money*. New York: Harcourt, Brace, 1936.

Kiple, Kenneth F. *Blacks in Colonial Cuba, 1774–1899*. Gainesville: University of Florida Press, 1976.

Klaveren, F. W., and Legendre, R. "Salted Cod." In *Fish as Food*. 3 vols., edited by Georg Borgstrom, 3: 133–64. New York: Academic Press, 1962–65.

Klein, Herbert S. "The Colored Militia of Cuba, 1586–1868." *Caribbean Studies* 6 (1966): 17–27.

———. *The Middle Passage. Comparative Studies in the Atlantic Slave Trade*. Princeton: Princeton University Press, 1978.

———. *Slavery in the Americas: A Comparative Study of Cuba and Virginia*. London: Oxford University Press, 1967.

Knight, Franklin. *The Caribbean*. New York: Oxford University Press, 1978.

———. "The Origins of Wealth and the Sugar Revolution in Cuba, 1750–1850." *Hispanic American Historical Review* 57 (1977): 231–54.

———. *Slave Society in Cuba During the Nineteenth Century*. Madison: University of Wisconsin Press, 1970.

Kochert, Rolf-Erich. *Gerónimo de Uztáriz und Gaspar Melchior de Jovellanos*. Zurich, 1940.

Labaree, Benjamin W., ed. *The Atlantic World of Robert G. Albion*. Middletown, Conn.: Wesleyan University Press, 1975.

Labat, Père Jean-Baptiste. *Nouveau voyage aux Isles de l'Amérique*. 8 vols. Paris: Le Gras, 1742.

Labignette, Jean-Eric. "La colonisation de Cap-Breton et le premier siège de Louisbourg, 1745." *Revue historique de l'armée* 13 (1957): 69–80.

———. "La farine dans la Nouvelle-France." *Revue historique de l'Amérique française*. 17 (1964): 490–503.

Lacour-Gayet, G. *La marine militaire de la France sous la règne de Louis XV*. Paris: H. Champion, 1902.

Laevastu, T. "Natural Bases of Fisheries in the Atlantic Ocean: Their Past and Present Characteristics and Possibilities for Future Expansion." In *Atlantic Ocean Fisheries*, edited by Georg Borgstrom and A. J. Heighway, pp. 18–39. London: Fishing News Books, 1961.

Lambert de Saint-Croix, Alexandre. *Essai sur l'histoire de l'administration de la marine de France, 1689–1792.* Paris: Calmann-Levy, 1892.

Lamontagne, Roland. *L'Atlantique jusqu'au temps de Maurepas.* Montreal: Leméac, 1966.

———. *Aperçu structural du Canada au XVIIIe siècle.* Montreal: Leméac, 1967.

———. *Ministère de la marine.* Montreal: Leméac, 1966.

———. *La vie et l'ouevre de Pierre Bouguer.* Paris: Presses Universitaires de France, 1964.

La Morandrière, Charles de. *Histoire de la pêche française de la morue dans l'Amérique septentrionale.* 2 vols. Paris: Maisonneuve et Larose, 1962.

———. *La pêche française de la morue à Terre-Nueve de XVe siècle à nos jours: son importance économique, sociale et politique.* Paris: Ecole Pratique des Hautes Etudes-Sorbonne, 1967.

Lane, Frederic C. *Profits from Power.* Albany, N.Y.: SUNY-Albany University Press, 1979.

———. "Tonnages, Medieval and Modern." *Economic History Review*, 2d ser., 17 (1964): 213–33.

Lang, James. *Conquest and Commerce: Spain and England in the Americas.* New York: Academic Press, 1975.

Lanning, John Tate. *The Diplomatic History of Georgia; A Study of the Epoch of Jenkins' Ear.* Chapel Hill: University of North Carolina Press, 1936.

La Roncière, Charles G. M. B. de. *Histoire de la marine française.* 6 vols. Paris: E. Plon et Nourrit, 1909–32.

La Roque de Roquebrune, R. "La direction de la Nouvelle-France par le ministère de la marine." *Revue d'histoire de l'Amérique française* 6 (1952–53): 470–88.

Larraz López, José. *La época del mercantilismo en Castilla (1500–1700).* Madrid: Atlas, 1943.

[Le Serre, Barbier de.] *Essais historiques et critiques sur la marine de France de 1661 à 1789.* London: Schulze and Dean, 1813.

Lavery, Brian. "The Origins of the 74-Gun Ship." *Mariner's Mirror* 63 (1977): 335–50.

Le Blant, Robert. *Un colonial sous Louis XV, Philippe de Pastour de Costebelle.* Dax: P. Pradeu, 1935.

Lebrun, François. *Les hommes et le mort en Anjou aux XVIIe et XVIIIe siècles.* Paris: Mouton, 1971.

Le Courteois de Surlaville, Michel Balthazar. *Les derniers jours de l'Acadie, 1748–1758. Correspondance et mémoires.* Paris: Lechevalier, 1899.

Légohérel, Henri. *Les trésoriers généraux de la marine (1517–1788).* Paris: Cujas, 1963.

Leon, John A. *On Sugar Cultivation in Louisiana, Cuba . . . and the British Possessions.* London: J. Ollivier, 1848.

Léonard, Emile G. *L'Armée et ses problèmes au XVIIIe siècle.* Paris: Plon, 1958.

Le Riverend, Julio. "Desarollo económico y social." In Ramiro Guerra y
    Sánchez, José M. Pérez Cabrera, Juan J. Remos, and Emeterio S.
    Santovenia, eds. *Historia de la nación cubana*, 2: 137–282. Havana: Edi-
    torial Historia de la Nación Cubana, 1952.
———. *Historia económica de Cuba*. Barcelona: Ariel, 1972.
———. "Relaciones entre Nueva España y Cuba, 1518–1820." *Revista de
    historia de América* 37–38 (1954): 45–108.
Lescarbot, Marc. *Nova Francia: A Description of Acadia*. London: Routledge and
    Sons, 1928.
Levasseur, E. *Histoire du commerce de la France*. Tome 1. *Avant 1789*. Paris:
    Arthur Rousseau, 1911.
Lévy-Bruhl, Henri. *Histoire de la lettre de change en France au XVIIe et XVIIIe
    siècles*. Paris: Recueil Sirey, 1933.
Lewis, Michael A. *The Navy of Britain. An Historical Portrait*. London: G. Allen
    and Unwin, 1948.
Liss, Peggy K. *Atlantic Empires. The Network of Trade and Revolution, 1713–
    1826*. Baltimore: Johns Hopkins University Press, 1983.
Livi Bacci, Massimo. "Fertility and Nuptiality Changes in Spain from the Late
    Eighteenth Century to the Early Twentieth Century." *Population Studies* 22
    (1968): 83–102; 211–34.
Lloyd, Christopher. *Atlas of Maritime History*. New York: Arco, 1975.
———, and Coulter, Jack L. S. *Medicine and the Navy, 1200–1900*. London:
    Livingstone, 1961.
Lombard, Maurice. "Arsenaux et bois de marine dans la Mediterranée
    musulmane (VIIe–XIe siècles)." In *Le navire et l'économie maritime du
    Moyen Age au XVIIIe siècle principalement en Mediterranée*, edited by Michel
    Mollat, pp. 53–99. Paris: S.E.V.P.E.N., 1958.
Loture, Robert de. *Histoire de grand pêche de Terre-Neuve*. Paris: Gallimard, 1949.
———. "La siège de Louisbourg en 1758." *Revue maritime* 175 (1934):
    52–70.
Lounsbury, R. G. *The British Fishery at Newfoundland, 1634–1763*. New
    Haven: Yale University Press, 1934.
Lower, Arthur R. M. *Great Britain's Woodyard: British America and the Timber
    Trade, 1763–1867*. Montreal: McGill-Queen's Press, 1973.
Lugar, Catharine. "The Portuguese Tobacco Trade and the Tobacco Growers of
    Bahia in the Late Colonial Period." In *Essays Concerning the Socioeconomic
    History of Brazil and Portuguese India*, edited by Dauril Alden and Warren
    Dean, pp. 26–70. Gainesville: University Presses of Florida, 1977.
McCusker, John J. *Money and Exchange in Europe and America, 1600–1775, A
    Handbook*. Chapel Hill: University of North Carolina Press, 1978.
Macias Domínguez, Isabelo. *Cuba en la primera mitad del siglo XVII*. Seville:
    Escuela de Estudios Hispanoamericanos, 1978.

MacIntyre, Donald, and Bathe, Basil. *Man-of-War. A History of the Combat Vessel*. New York: McGraw-Hill, 1969.

McLachlan, Jean O. *Trade and Peace with Old Spain, 1667–1750*. Cambridge: Cambridge University Press, 1940.

McLennan, John Stewart, "Louisbourg." *Canadian Geographic Journal* 2 (1931): 249–69.

————. *Louisbourg: From Its Foundation to Its Fall, 1713–1758*. London: Macmillan, 1918.

Maggs Brothers. *The French Colonisation of America as Exemplified in a Remarkable Collection of French Administrative Acts (1581–1791)*. Paris: Maggs Brothers, 1936.

Mahan, Alfred T. *Mahan on Naval Warfare*. Edited by Alan Wescott. Boston: Little, Brown, 1943.

————. *The Influence of Sea Power upon History, 1660–1783*. Boston: Little, Brown, 1890.

Malvezin, Théophile. *Histoire du commerce de Bordeaux*. 4 vols. Bordeaux: Bellier, 1890–99.

Marcus, G. J. *Heart of Oak: A Survey of British Sea Power in the Georgian Era*. London: Oxford University Press, 1975.

Marion, Marcel. *Dictionnaire des institutions de la France aux XVIIe et XVIIIe siècles*. Paris: A. Picard, 1923.

————. *Histoire financière de la France depuis 1715*. Tome 1. *1715–1789*. Paris: Rousseau, 1927.

Marrero y Artiles, Levi. *Cuba: Economía y sociedad*. 8 vols. Madrid: Playor, 1972–81.

————. *Geografía de Cuba*. Havana: 1951.

Martell, J. S. "Early Coal Mining in Nova Scotia." *Dalhousie Review* 25, no. 2, (1945): 156–72.

Martin, Gaston. *Nantes au XVIIIe siècle. L'Ere des négriers, 1714–1774*. Paris: Alcan, 1931.

Martínez Dalmau, Eduardo. *La política colonial y extranjera de los Reyes españoles de la Casa de Austria y de Borbón y la toma de la Habana por los ingleses*. Havana: Siglo XX, 1943.

Martínez Fortún, José. *Epidemiología (Sintesis cronológica)*. Havana: Cuadernos de Historia Sanitaria, 1952.

Martínez Moles, Tadeo. "Historia de Sancti Spíritus." In *Los Tres primeros historiadores de la Isla de Cuba*, 3 vols., edited by Rafael Cowley and Andres Pago, 3: 565–630. Havana: A. Pago, 1876.

Marzal Martínez, Amparo. "Las fortificaciones de Cartagena en el siglo XVIII." *Revista de Historia Militar* 20 (1976): 29–41.

Masson, Paul. *Histoire du commerce français dans le Levant au XVIIIe siècle*. Paris: Hachette, 1911.

Mathieu, Jacques. "La balance commerciale: Nouvelle-France–Antilles au XVIIIe siècle." *Revue de l'histoire de l'Amérique française* 2, no. 4 (1972): 465–97.

———. "Quelques aspects du rôle de Louisbourg dans le commerce Nouvelle-France—Antilles." *Papers and Abstracts for a Symposium on Ile Royale During the French Regime.* Ottawa: National Museum of Man, 1972.

Maude, Mary C. McDougall. "The Settlements of Ile Royale and Ile St.-Jean, 1713–1758," Fortress of Louisbourg Library, HF–9, 1965.

Maurepas, Jean Frédéric Phélypaux, comte de. *Mémoires.* 4 vols. Paris: Buisson, 1792.

Mazzei, Jacopo. "Potenza mezzo di ricchezza e ricchezza mezzo di potenza nel pensiero dei mercantilisti." *Revista internazionale de scienze sociali* 41 (1933): 3–18.

Mémain, René. *La marine de guerre sous Louis XIV: le matériel: Rochefort, arsenale modèle de Colbert.* Paris: Hachette, 1937.

Merino Navarro, José P. *La armada española en el siglo XVIII.* Madrid: Fundación Universitaria Española, 1981.

Meyer, Jean. *L'Armement nantais dans la deuxieme moitié du XVIIIe siècle.* Paris: S.E.V.P.E.N., 1969.

Michell, A. R. "The European Fisheries in Early Modern History." *Cambridge Economic History of Europe.* Vol. 5. *The Economic Organization of Early Modern Europe.* Cambridge: Cambridge University Press, 1976.

Miller, Virginia P. "Aboriginal Micmac Population: A Review of the Evidence." *Ethnohistory* 23, no. 2 (1976): 117–27.

Mims, Stewart L. *Colbert's West India Policy.* New Haven: Yale University Press, 1912.

Mitchell, B. R., and Deane, Phyllis. *Abstract of British Historical Statistics.* Cambridge: Cambridge University Press, 1971.

Montcalm-Gozon, Louis Joseph Marquis de. *Journal du Marquis de Montcalm.* 7 vols. Edited by H.-R. Casgrain. Quebec: Demers et frère, 1895.

Moore, Christopher. "Commodity Imports of Louisbourg." Fortress of Louisbourg, unpublished paper, 1975.

———. "The Maritime Economy of Ile Royale." *Canada: An Historical Magazine* 1, no. 4 (1974): 33–46.

———. "Merchants in the Louisbourg Community." Fortress of Louisbourg Library, HF–33, no date.

———. "The Other Louisbourg: Merchant Enterprise in Ile Royale, 1713–1758." *Histoire sociale/Social History* 12 (1979): 79–96.

Morales Padrón, Francisco. *El comercio canario-americano, siglos XVI, XVII y XVIII.* Seville: Escuela de Estudios Hispano-americanos, 1955.

Moreno, Laudelino. "Los extranjeros y el ejercicio de comercio de Indias." *Anales de la Sociedad de Géografía e Historia de Guatemala.* 14 (1938): 441–54.

Moreno Fraginals, Manuel. "Africa in Cuba: A Quantitative Analysis of the African Population of the Island of Cuba." *Annals of the New York Academy of Sciences*. Vol. 292. *Comparative Perspectives on Slavery in New World Plantation Societies*, pp. 187–201. New York: 1977.

————. *El ingenio. Complejo económico-social cubano del azúcar*. 3 vols. Havana: Editorial de Ciencias Sociales, 1978.

————. *The Sugarmill. The Socioeconomic Complex of Sugar in Cuba*. Translated by Cedric Belfrage. New York: Monthly Review Press, 1976.

Morineau, Michel. *Jauges et méthodes de jauge anciennes et modernes*. Paris: Armand Colin, 1966.

————, and Filippini, J.-P. "Vie matérielle et comportements biologiques," *Annales: E.S.C.* 20, (1965), 1150–1162.

Morini-Comby, J. *Mercantilisme et protectionnisme. Essai sur les doctrines interventionnistes en politique commerciale du XVe au XIXe siècle*. Paris: Alcan, 1930.

Morison, Samuel E. Introduction to *The Parkman Reader*, by Francis Parkman. Boston: Little, Brown, 1965.

Mounier, André. *Les faites et doctrines économiques en Espagne sous Philippe V: Gerónimo de Uztáriz*. Bordeaux: Imprimerie de l'Université, 1919.

Muñoz Pérez, José. "Ideas sobre el comercio en el siglo XVIII español." *Estudios Americanos* 19 (1960): 47–66.

Murray, D. R. "Statistics of the Slave Trade to Cuba, 1790–1867." *Journal of Latin American Studies* 3 (1971): 131–50.

Murray, Mungo. *A Treatise on Shipbuilding and Navigation*. London: A. Millar, 1765.

Nadal, Jorge. *La población espanola. Siglos XVI a XX*. Barcelona: Ariel, 1966.

Naish, G. B. "Ships and Shipbuilding." In *A History of Technology*. Vol. 3. *From the Renaissance to the Industrial Revolution*, edited by Charles Singer, pp. 471–500. Oxford: At the Clarendon Press, 1957.

Nelson, G. H. "Contraband Trade Under the Asiento." *American Historical Review* 51 (1956): 55–67.

Nettels, Curtis. "England and the Spanish American Trade, 1680–1715." *Journal of Modern History* 30, no. 1 (1939): 1–32.

Newmann, G. *Ocean Currents*. Amsterdam: Elsevier, 1968.

Neuville, Didier. *Etat sommaire des archives de la marine antérieures à la revolution*. Paris: Baudoin, 1898.

A New Account of the Inhabitants, Trade and Government of Spain. London: J. Hinxman, 1762.

Newton, A. P. *European Nations in The West Indies*. London: A. and C. Black, 1933.

Nicolas, L. *La puissance navale dans l'histoire*. Paris: Editions Maritimes et d'Outre-Mer, 1963.

O'Dogherty, Angel. "La matrícula del mar en el reinado de Carlos III." *Anvario de Estudos Americanos* 9 (1952): 347–70.

Ogelsby, J. C. M. "Spain's Havana Squadron and the Preservation of the Balance of Power in the Caribbean, 1740–1748." *Hispanic American Historical Review* 49, no. 3 (1969): 473–88.

O'Heguerty, P. A., Comte de Magnières. *Remarques sur plusieurs branches de commerce et de navigation*. Amsterdam: Jean Schreuder and Pierre Mortier, 1758.

On Military Operations in the West Indies. London?: c. 1782?

Ortiz, Fernando. *Cuban Counterpoint: Tobacco and Sugar*. New York: Knopf, 1947.

———. *Hampa afro-cubana. Los negros esclavos*. Havana: Revista Bimestre Cubana, 1916.

———. *Historia de la arqueología indocubana*. Havana: Siglo XX, 1922.

Ortiz de la Tabla, Javier. *Comercio exterior de Veracruz*. Seville: Escuela de Estudios Hispano-Americanos, 1978.

Ostrander, Gilman. "The Colonial Molasses Trade." *Agricultural History* 30 (1956): 77–84.

Palacio Atard, Vicente. "Los Vascogondos y la pesca de Terranova." *Anuario de Estudios Americanos* 1 (1944): 723–39.

Palmer, Colin. *Human Cargoes: The British Slave Trade to Spanish America, 1700–1739*. Urbana: University of Illinois Press, 1981.

Pares, Richard. "American vs. Continental Warfare, 1739–1763." *English Historical Review* 51 (1936): 429–65.

———. "The Economic Factors in the History of Empire." *Economic History Review* 7 (1937): 119–44.

———. "The Manning of the Navy in the West Indies." *Royal Historical Society Transactions*, 4th Ser., 20 (1937): 31–60.

———. *Merchants and Planters*. Cambridge: Cambridge University Press, 1960.

———. *War and Trade in the West Indies, 1739–1763*. Oxford: Oxford University Press, 1936.

———. *Yankees and Creoles*. Cambridge: Harvard University Press, 1956.

Pargellis, Stanley, ed. *Military Affairs in North America, 1748–1765*. New York: Appleton-Century, 1936.

Parkinson, C. Northcote, ed. *Trade Winds*. London: G. Allen and Unwin, 1948.

Parkman, Francis. *A Half-Century of Conflict*. Boston: Little, Brown, 1899.

———. *The Old Regime in Canada*. Boston: Little, Brown, 1934.

Parry, John Horace. *The Spanish Seaborne Empire*. London: Hutchinson, 1966.

———. *Trade and Dominion*. London: Weidenfeld and Nicolson, 1971.

———. "Transport and Trade Routes." In *The Cambridge Economic History of Europe*. Vol. 4. *The Economy of Expanding Europe in the Sixteenth and Seventeenth Centuries*, edited by E. E. Rich and C. H. Wilson, pp. 155–222. Cambridge: Cambridge University Press, 1967.

————, and Sherlock, P. M. *A Short History of the West Indies*. London: Macmillan, 1965.

Peraza de Ayala, José. *El régimen comercial de Canarias con las Indias en los siglos XVI, XVII, y XVIII*. Seville: Universidad de Sevilla, 1977.

Pérez de la Riva, Juan. "Inglaterra y Cuba en la primera mitad del siglo XVIII," *Revista bimestre cubana* 36 (1935): 50–66.

————. "Presentación de un censo ignorado: El Padrón General de 1778," *Revista de la Biblioteca Nacional José Martí*, 3ra época, 19, no. 3 (1977): 5–16.

Pérez Guzmán, Francisco. "Documentos sobre las fortalezas militares de Santiago de Cuba." *Santiago* no. 26–27 (1977): 181–200.

Pérez Vidal, José. *España en la historia del tabaco*. Madrid: Consejo Superior de Investigaciones Cientificas, 1959.

————. *La industria tabaquera española a través de la fábricas de Sevilla*. Madrid: Consejo Superior de Investigaciones Cientificas, 1966.

Pezuela, Jacobo de la. *Diccionario geográfico, estadístico, histórico de la Isla de Cuba*. 4 vols. Madrid: Mellado, 1863.

————. *Historia de la Isla de Cuba*. 4 vols. Madrid: Bailly-Balliere, 1868.

Phelan, John L. "Authority and Flexibility in the Spanish Imperial Bureaucracy." *Administrative Science Quarterly* 5 (1960): 47–65.

Pichon, Thomas. *Genuine Letters and Memoirs Relating to the Natural, Civil, and Commercial History of the Island of Cape Breton. . . .* London: 1760.

————. *Lettres et mémoires pour servir à l'histoire naturelle, civile, et politique de Cap Breton*. The Hague: Pierre Gosse, 1760.

Pirie, R. L. *Oceanography*. New York: Oxford University Press, 1973.

Pitman, Frank. *The Development of the British West Indies*. New Haven: Yale University Press, 1917.

Plaza Prieto, Juan. *Estructura económica de España en el siglo XVIII*. Madrid: Cajas de Ahorro, 1975.

Portell Vila, Herminio. *Historia de Cuba y sus relaciones con Estados Unidos y España*. 4 vols. Havana: Montero, 1938.

Posthumus, Nicolas Wilhelmus. *An Inquiry into the History of Prices in Holland*. Leiden: E. J. Brill, 1945.

Pothier, Bernard. "Acadian Emigration to Ile Royale after the Conquest of Acadia." *Histoire Sociale/Social History* 6 (1970): 116–30.

————. "Les Acadiens à l'Isle Royale, 1713–1734." *La société historique acadienne*, 23e cahier, (1969): 97–111.

Pouyez, Christian. "La population de l'Isle Royale en 1752." *Histoire Sociale/Social History* 6, no. 12 (1973): 147–80.

Price, Jacob M. *France and the Chesapeake: A History of the French Tobacco Monopoly, 1674–1791, and Its Relationship to the British and American Tobacco Trades*. 2 vols. Ann Arbor: University of Michigan Press, 1973.

————. "The Map of Commerce, 1683–1721." In *The New Cambridge*

Modern History. Vol. 6. *The Rise of Great Britain and Russia, 1688–1725,* edited by J. S. Bromley, pp. 834–74. Cambridge: Cambridge University Press, 1970.

———. "Multilateralism and/or Bilateralism: The Settlement of British Trade Balances with 'The North,' c. 1700." *Economic History Review,* 2d ser., 14 (1961): 254–71.

Pullen, John. *Memoirs of the Maritime Affairs of Great-Britain Especially in Relation to Our Concerns in the West-Indies.* London: 1732.

Rawlyk, George. *Nova Scotia's Massachusetts.* Montreal: McGill-Queen's University Press, 1973.

———. *Yankees at Louisbourg.* Orono: University of Maine Press, 1967.

Raynal, Guillaume T. F. *A Philosophical and Political History of the Settlements and Trade of the Europeans in the East and West Indies.* 6 vols. London: Strahan, 1798.

Reeder, John. "Bibliografía de traducciones, al castellano y catalán, durante el siglo XVIII, de obras de pensamiento económico." *Moneda y crédito* 126 (1973): 57–77.

———. "Economía y ilustración en España: traducciones y traductores, 1717–1800." *Moneda y crédito* 147 (1978): 47–70.

———. "Uztáriz y Colbert." *Moneda y crédito* 121 (1972): 105–17.

Reesse, J. J. *De Suikerhandel van Amsterdam; van het begin der 17de eeuw tot 1813.* Haarlem: J. L. E. I. Kleynenburg, 1908.

Reid, Allana G. "Intercolonial Trade During the French Regime." *Canadian Historical Review* 32 (1951): 236–51.

Reynolds, Clark. *Command of the Sea: The History and Strategy of Maritime Empires.* New York: Morrow, 1974.

Reynolds, Philip K. *The Story of Cuban Sugar.* Boston: United Fruit, 1924.

Richmond, Admiral Sir Herbert. *The Navy in the War of 1739–1748.* 3 vols. Cambridge: Cambridge University Press, 1920.

———. *Statesmen and Sea Power.* Oxford: Clarendon Press, 1946.

Ringrose, David. "Perspectives on the Economy of Eighteenth Century Spain." In *Historica Iberica. Economía y sociedad en los siglos XVIII y XIX,* pp. 59–101. New York: 1973.

Rivero Muñiz, José. *Tabaco: su historia en Cuba.* 2 vols. Havana: Instituto de Historia, 1964.

———. *Las tres sediciones de los vegueros en el siglo XVIII.* Havana: Asociación Nacional de Cosecheros de Tabaco de Cuba, 1951.

Roberts, Walter Adolphe. *Havana.* New York: Coward-McCann, 1953.

Robertson, Frederick L. *The Evolution of Naval Armament.* London: Constable, 1921.

Robson, Eric. "The Armed Forces and the Art of War." In *The New Cambridge Modern History.* Vol. 7. *The Old Regime,* edited by J. O. Lindsay, pp. 163–89. Cambridge: Cambridge University Press, 1957.

Rodríguez Casado, Vicente. "La política del reformismo de los primeros
Borbones en la marina de guerra española." *Anuario de Estudios Americanos*
25 (1968): 601–18.

Rodríguez-Ferrer, Miguel. *El tabac habano*. Madrid: Colegio Nacional de
Sordo-Mudos, 1851.

Rodríguez Villa, Antonio. *Don Cenon de Somodevilla; Marqués de la Ensenada*.
Madrid: Murillo, 1878.

―――. *Patiño y Campillo*. Madrid: Rivadeneyra, 1882.

Roig de Leuschenring, Emilio. *Curso de introducción a la historia de Cuba*. Havana: Municipio de la Habana, 1938.

―――. *La Habana: apuntes históricas*. Havana: Municipio de la Habana,
1938.

―――. Preface to *La Dominación inglesa en la Habana*. Havana: Molina, 1929.

Rolph, George M. *Something About Sugar*. San Francisco: Newbegin, 1917.

Romano, Ruggiero. *Prezzi, salari, e servizi a Napoli nel secolo XVIII
(1734–1806)*. Milan: Banca Commerziale Italiana, 1965.

Romero de Solis, Pedro. *La población española en los siglos XVIII y XIX*. Madrid:
Siglo XXI de España, 1973.

Rule, John C. "Jean Frédéric Phélypaux, comte de Ponchartrain et Maurepas:
Reflections on His Life and Papers." *Louisiana Historical Review* 6
(1965): 365–77.

―――. "The Maurepas Papers: Portrait of a Minister." *French Historical Studies*
4 (1965): 103–7.

Russo, R. P. "L'enseignement des sciences de la navigation dans les écoles
d'hydrographie aux XVIIe et XVIIIe siècles." In *Le navire et l'économie
maritime du Moyen Age au XVIIIe siècle principalement en Méditerranee*, edited
by Michel Mollat, pp. 177–94. Paris: S.E.V.P.E.N., 1958.

Saco, José Antonio. *Historia de la esclavitud de la raza africana en el Nuevo Mundo*.
4 vols. Havana: Colección de Libros Cubanos, 1938.

Sagra, Ramón de la. *Historia económico-politica y estadística de la Isla de Cuba*.
Havana: La Viuda de Arazoza y Soler, 1831.

Salas, Javier de. *Marina española*. Madrid: Fortanet, 1865.

San Felipe, Vicente Bacaller y Sanna, Marqués de. *Comentarios de la guerra de
España e historia de su rey Felipe V, el animoso*. Madrid: Biblioteca de Autores
Españoles, 1957.

Santovenia, Emeterio S. "Politica colonial." In Ramiro Guerra y Sánchez,
José M. Pérez Cabrera, Juan J. Remos, and Emeterio S. Santovenia, eds.
Historia de la nación cubana, 2:3–94. Havana: Editorial Historia de la
Nación Cubana, 1952.

Sauer, Carl O. *Northern Mists*. Berkeley: University of California Press, 1968.

Savary, Jacques. *Dictionnaire universel de commerce*. Paris: La Veuve Etienne, 1742.

Scelle, Georges. *La traité négrière aux Indes de Castille*. 2 vols. Paris: Larose et
Tenin, 1906.

Schmeisser, B. "Health and Medicine at Louisbourg." Fortress of Louisbourg Library, HM–4, 1977.

Schmitz, Gerhard. "El desarollo económico de Cuba y las revoluciones burguesas del siglo XVIII." *Islas* 42 (1972): 27–57.

Schmöller, Gustav. *The Mercantile System and Its Historical Significance.* New York: Peter Smith, 1931.

Schroeder, Susan. *Cuba: A Handbook of Historical Statistics.* Boston: G. K. Hall, 1982.

Schumpeter, Elizabeth B. *English Overseas Trade Statistics, 1697–1808.* Oxford: Oxford University Press, 1960.

Schutz, John A. *William Shirley: King's Governor of Massachusetts.* Chapel Hill: University of North Carolina Press, 1961.

Sée, Henri. "Documents sur le commerce de Cadix." *Revue de l'histoire des colonies françaises* 19, no. 4 (1926): 426–520; 20, no. 1 (1927): 33–80; 20, no. 2 (1927): 259–76.

Segre, Roberto. "Significación de Cuba en la evolución de las fortificaciones coloniales de América." *Revista de la Biblioteca Nacional José Martí,* 3ra época, 10, no. 2 (1968): 5–46.

Sette, Oscar Elton. *Statistics of the Catch of Cod Off the East Coast of North America.* Washington D.C.: U.S. Government Printing Office, 1928.

Sheperd, James, and Walton, Gary M. *Shipping, Maritime Trade, and the Economic Development of Colonial North America.* Cambridge: Cambridge University Press, 1972.

Sheridan, R. B. "The Molasses Act and the Market Strategy of the British Sugar Planters." *Journal of Economic History* 17 (1957): 62–83.

―――. "Mortality and the Medical Treatment of Slaves in the British West Indies." In *Race and Slavery in the Western Hemisphere: Quantitative Studies,* edited by Stanley Engerman and Eugene Genovese, pp. 285–310. Princeton: Princeton University Press, 1975.

―――. *Sugar and Slavery.* Baltimore: Johns Hopkins University Press, 1973.

―――. "'Sweet Malefactor': The Social Costs of Slavery and Sugar in Jamaica and Cuba." *Economic History Review,* 3d ser., 29 (1976): 236–57.

Silberner, Edmond. *La guerre dans la pensée économique du XVIe au XVIIIe siècle.* Paris: Sirey, 1939.

Slicher van Bath, B. H. *The Agrarian History of Western Europe, A.D. 500 to 1850.* New York: St. Martin's Press, 1963.

Smith, Adam. *An Inquiry into the Nature and Causes of the Wealth of Nations.* London: Routledge and Sons, 1893.

Smith, Octavio. "Santiago Pita: El Guerrero (La expedición de 1742)." *Revista de la biblioteca Nacional José Martí,* 3ra época, 15 (1973): 159–70.

Smith, Robert S. "Spanish Mercantilism: A Hardy Perennial." *Southern Economic Journal* 38 (1971): 1–11.

―――. "Spanish Antimercantilism of the Seventeenth Century: Alberto

Struzzi and Diego José Dormer." *Journal of Political Economy* 48
(1940):401–11.

———. "Twentieth-Century Cuban Historiography." *Hispanic American Historical Review* 44 (1964):44–73.

Smith, T. E. "The Cocos-Keeling Islands: A Demographic Laboratory." *Population Studies* 14 (1960):94–130.

Southey, Thomas. *Chronological History of the West Indies.* 2 vols. London: Frank Cass, 1968.

Spengler, Joseph J. "Mercantilist and Physiocratic Growth Theory." In *Theories of Economic Growth*, edited by Bert F. Hoselitz, pp. 3–64. Glencoe, Ill.: Free Press of Glencoe, 1960.

Sperling, J. "The International Payments Mechanism in the Seventeenth and Eighteenth Centuries." *Economic History Review*, 2d ser., 14 (1962):446–68.

Sperling, John G. *The South Sea Company.* Boston: Baker Library, Harvard Graduate School of Business Administration, 1962.

Stanley, George F. G. *New France: The Last Phase, 1744–1760.* Toronto: McClelland and Stewart, 1968.

Stein, Robert. "Mortality in the Eighteenth-Century French Slave Trade." *Journal of African History* 21 (1980):35–42.

Suchlicki, Jaime. *Cuba from Columbus to Castro.* New York: Charles Scribner's Sons, 1974.

Surlaville, Michel Balthazar Le Courtois de. *Les Derniers Jours de l'Acadie.* Paris: Lechevalier, 1899.

Symcox, Geoffrey. *The Crisis of French Sea Power, 1688–1697.* The Hague: Martinus Nijhoff, 1974.

Syrett, David. "The British Landing at Havana: An Example of an Eighteenth-Century Combined Operation." *Mariner's Mirror* 55 (1969):325–31.

———, ed. Introduction to *The Siege and Capture of Havana 1762.* London: Navy Records Society, 1970.

Taillemite, Etienne. *Dictionnaire de la marine.* Paris: Collection Seghers, 1962.

Taylor, Eva G. R. *The Haven-Finding Art: A History of Navigation from Odysseus to Captain Cook.* London: Hollis and Carter, 1956.

Taylor, Thomas Griffith. *Canada: A Study of Cool Continental Environments and Their Effect on British and French Settlement.* London: Methuen, 1947.

Tennyson, Brian. *Cape Breton. A Bibliography.* Halifax: Nova Scotia Department of Education, 1978.

TePaske, John J. *The Governorship of Spanish Florida, 1700–1763.* Durham: Duke University Press, 1964.

Thibault, Paul, "Shipwrecks of the Louisbourg Harbour," 1713–58. Fortress of Louisbourg Library, HF–12, (1971).

Thomas, Hugh. *Cuba: The Pursuit of Liberty.* London: Eyre and Spottiswoode, 1971.

Tramond, Joannés. *Manual d'histoire maritime de la France*. Paris: A. Challamel, 1916.

Trow-Smith, Robert. *Life From the Land: The Growth of Farming in Western Europe*. London: Longman's, 1967.

A True and Impartial Account of the Rise and Progress of the South Sea Company. London: T. Cooper, 1743.

Turgeon, Laurier. "Pour une histoire de la pêche: le marché de la morue à Marseilles au XVIIIe siècle." *Histoire sociale/Social History* 14 (1981): 295–322.

Tytler, James. *A Treatise on the Plague and Yellow Fever*. Salem, Mass.: 1799.

Ulloa, Bernardo de. *Restablicimiento de las fábricas y comercio español*, Madrid: A. Marin, 1740.

———. *Rétablissement des manufactures et du commerce d'Espagne*. 2 vols. Amsterdam, 1752.

———. *Voyage historique de l'Amérique Méridionale*. Amsterdam: 1752.

Ulloa, Modesto. "The Sugar Industry in the Havana District (Cuba), 1641–1667." *Beitrage zur Wirtschaftsgeschichte Wirtschaftsfrafte und Wirtschaftwege*. 4. *Ubersee und allegemeine Wirtschaftsgeschichte* (1978): 75–91. (Photocopy in Archivo General de Indias, Seville.)

Unger, Richard W. *Dutch Shipbuilding before 1800*. Amsterdam: Van Gorcum, 1978.

United Nations Food and Agriculture Organization. *Milk and Milk Products in Human Nutrition*. Rome: United Nations Food and Agriculture Organization, 1959.

Upton, Leslie F. S. "Contact and Conflict on the Atlantic and Pacific Coasts of Canada." *Acadiensis* 9, no. 2 (1980): 3–13.

———. *Micmacs and Colonists: Indian-White Relations in the Maritime Provinces, 1713–1867*. Vancouver: University of British Columbia Press, 1979.

Urbanismo español en América. Madrid: Editorial Nacional, 1973.

Uring, Nathaniel. *The Voyages and Travels of Captain Nathaniel Uring*. London: Cassel, 1928.

Urrutia y Montoya, Ignacio José. *Obras*. 2 vols. Havana: Siglo XX, 1941.

Uztáriz, Gerónimo de. *Theorica y práctica de commercio y marino*. Madrid, 1742. Aguilar edition 1968. Translated by John Kippax, under the title *The Theory and Practice of Commerce and Maritime Affairs*. Dublin, 1752.

Valdés, José Antonio. *Historia de la Isla de Cuba y en especial de la Habana*. Havana: Andrés Pago, 1876.

Van Driel, A. *Tonnage Measurement: Historical and Critical Essay*. The Hague: Government Printing Office, 1925.

Vásquez de Prada, Valentín. "Las rutas comerciales entre España y América en el siglo XVIII." *Anuario de Estudios Americanos* 25 (1968): 197–241.

Vauban, Sebastien Le. *A Manual of Siegecraft and Fortification*. Translated by G. A. Rothrock. Ann Arbor: University of Michigan Press, 1968.

Vicens Vives, Jaime. *An Economic History of Spain*. Princeton: Princeton University Press, 1969.

Vignols, Léon. "L'Asiento français (1701–1713) et anglais (1713–1750) et le commerce franco-espagnol vers 1700–1730." *Revue d'histoire économique et sociale* 17 (1929): 403–36.

———. "La course maritime, ses conséquences économiques, sociales et internationales." *Revue d'histoire économique et sociale* 15 (1927): 196–230.

Vilar, Pierre. *La Catalogne dans l'Espagne moderne*. Paris: S.E.V.P.E.N., 1962.

Viner, Jacob. "Power vs. Plenty as Objectives of Foreign Policy in the Seventeenth and Eighteenth Centuries." *World Politics* 1 (1948): 1–29.

Walker, Geoffrey J. *Spanish Politics and Imperial Trade, 1700–1789*. Bloomington: Indiana University Press, 1979.

Wallerstein, Immanuel. *The Modern World-System*. Vol. 2. *Mercantilism and the Consolidation of the European World Economy, 1600–1750*. New York: Academic Press, 1980.

Wallis, Wilson D., and Wallis, Ruth Sawtell. *The Micmac Indians of Eastern Canada*. Minneapolis: University of Minnesota Press, 1955.

Walters, Susan. *1980 Canadian Almanac*. Toronto: Copp Clark Pitman, 1980.

Ward, Bernardo. *Proyecto económico en que se proponen varias providencias dirigadas a promover los intereses de España*. Madrid: Ibarra, 1779.

Wells, Robert V. *The Population of the British Colonies in America before 1776*. Princeton: Princeton University Press, 1975.

Werner, Carl Avery. *Tobaccoland*. New York: The Tobacco Leaf Publishing Company, 1922.

Williams, Eric. *From Columbus to Castro: The History of the Caribbean, 1492–1969*. London: André Deutsch, 1970.

Williams, Virginia P. "Aboriginal Micmac Population: A Review of the Evidence." *Ethnohistory* 23 (1976): 117–27.

Wilson, Arthur M. *French Foreign Policy during the Administration of Cardinal Fleury*. Cambridge: Harvard University Press, 1936.

Wilson, Charles. *Economic History and the Historian. Collected Essays*. London: Weidenfeld and Nicolson, 1969.

———. *England's Apprenticeship, 1603–1763*. London: Longman's, 1965.

———. "The Growth of Overseas Commerce and European Manufacture." In *The New Cambridge Modern History*. Vol. 7. *The Old Regime*, edited by J. O. Lindsay, pp. 27–49. Cambridge: Cambridge University Press, 1957.

———. "Mercantilism: Some Vicissitudes of an Idea." *Economic History Review*, 2d ser., 10 (1957): 181–88.

———. "The Other Face of Mercantilism." *Transactions of the Royal Historical Society*, 5th ser., 9 (1959): 81–101.

———. "Taxation and the Decline of Empires, an Unfashionable Theme." *Bijdragen en Medeelingen Historisch Genootschap Utrecht* 77 (1963): 10–26.

———. "Trade, Society, and the State." In *The Cambridge Economic History*.

Vol. 4. *The Economy of Expanding Europe in the Sixteenth and Seventeenth Centuries*, edited by E. E. Rich and C. H. Wilson, pp. 487–586. Cambridge: Cambridge University Press, 1967.

———. "Treasure and Trade Balances: Further Evidence." *Economic History Review* 2d ser. 4 (1951): 231–42.

———. "Treasure and Trade Balances: The Mercantilist Problem." *Economic History Review*. 2d ser., 2 (1949): 152–61.

Wirminghaus, Alexander. *Zwei Spanische Merkantilisten*. Jena: Gustav Fischer, 1886.

Wright, James L. *Anglo-Spanish Rivalry in North America*. Athens: University of Georgia Press, 1971.

Wrigley, E. A. *Population and History*. London: Weidenfeld and Nicolson, 1969.

Wrong, George M. *The Conquest of New France*. New Haven: Yale University Press, 1918.

———, ed. *Louisbourg in 1745*. Toronto: University of Toronto Studies, 2nd Series, I, 1896.

Zapatero, Juan M. *La guerra del Caribe en el siglo XVIII*. San Juan, P.R.: Instituto de Cultura Puertorriqueña, 1964.

Zavala y Auñon, Miguel. *Representación al Rey Nuestro Señor Don Felipe V*. Madrid: 1732.

Zurburán, Juana. "Biblioteca de la toma de la Habana por los ingleses." *Revista de la Biblioteca Nacional José Martí,* 3ra época, 2 (1960): 44–53.

4. Theses and Dissertations

Ainsworth, Stephen K. "Commerce and Reform in the Spanish Empire during the Eighteenth Century." Ph.D. dissertation, Duke University, Durham, N.C., 1975.

Brown, Genevieve. "The Illicit Slave Trade to Cuba and Other Islands of the Caribbean." Ph.D. dissertation, Ohio State University, 1944.

Chard, Donald F. "The Impact of Ile Royale on New England." Ph.D. dissertation, University of Ottawa, 1976.

Crowley, Terence Alan. "Government and Interests: French Colonial Administration at Louisbourg, 1713–1758." Ph.D. dissertation, Duke University, Durham, N.C., 1975.

Horsfall, Lucy Frances. "British Relations with the Spanish Colonies of the Caribbean, 1713–1739." M.A. thesis, University of London, 1936.

Inglis, G. Douglas. "Historical Demography of Cuba, 1492–1780." Ph.D. dissertation, Texas Christian University, 1979.

Lunn, Alice J. E. "Economic Development in New France." Ph.D. dissertation, McGill University, 1942.

Moore, Christopher. "Merchant Trade in Louisbourg, Ile Royale." M.A. thesis, University of Ottawa, 1977.

Ogelsby, J. C. M. "War at Sea in the West Indies, 1739–1748." Ph.D. dissertation, University of Washington, 1963.

Pothier, Bernard. "Acadian Settlement on Ile Royale." M.A. thesis, University of Ottawa, 1967.

Pritchard, James S. "Ships, Men and Commerce: A Study of Maritime Activity in New France." Ph.D. dissertation, University of Toronto, 1971.

Turgeon, Laurier. "Les échanges Franco-Canadiennes de 1713 à 1758: Bayonne, les ports Basque, et Louisbourg, Ile Royale." 2 vols. Thèse de maitrise, Université de Pau et Pays d l'Adour, 1977.

Index